Classic
Knitting Patterns
from the British Isles

Judy Nelson
1985

Classic
Knitting Patterns
from the British Isles

Men's Hand-Knits from the '20s to the '50s

Jane Waller

with 100 designs, 21 illustrated in color

 Thames and Hudson

This book is dedicated to all those who, by adding their patterns to mine, helped form a far richer collection for future knitters to enjoy

Color photographs by **David Hiscock**

Frontispiece: The Prince of Wales in his Fair Isle, setting the style at Biarritz in 1924

The author and publishers cannot accept responsibility for any error in the original patterns. It is hoped that the authenticity of reproducing direct from the original knitting leaflets will compensate for the unavoidable variations in the printing.

First published in the USA in 1985 by Thames and Hudson Inc., 500 Fifth Avenue, New York, New York 10110

Library of Congress Catalog Card Number 84-51130

Printed and bound in Spain by Artes Graficas Toledo S. A.
D.L.: TO-762-1984

Contents

Introduction

I was reading one of my 1930s magazines the other day when I came across the headline: 'How we have neglected them'. Below this, there was some 'Knitting for the Menfolk'. I realized that this cry of 'neglect' was still justified today. There is not a knitting book that has more than a sprinkling of knitting designs for men, so I decided to compile a book which had enough patterns in it to give a man a lifetime's supply from which to choose.

This book is a record of knitting patterns starting from the end of the First World War, when 'knitting leaflets' as we know them today came into being, and finishing in about 1959, at the time when the fashions become too similar to those that can be bought today.

Every pattern is authentic, as are the models, who range from the homely to the heroic; the effeminate to the fiercely masculine. Examples of these patterns have been knitted up and photographed today to show how well they look.

Readers are encouraged to alter or lengthen any garment to suit individual requirements. In the Thirties and Forties, for example, trousers were held up with braces and were cut high, so that the pullovers were knitted shorter to look right. The modern knitter may want to add length to compensate for this, or alternatively, the man may choose to wear higher trousers with braces! Although there are several patterns for 'unisex' jerseys, nearly all these men's garments would look equally good on a woman.

Wherever possible, pure wool yarn has been recommended in the Index, because, as well as being springier and easy to knit, it makes for a better quality garment. When the patterns are knitted with fine yarns and fine needle-sizes, they result in a close-textured woolly which will last longer whilst retaining its looks.

In ancient times, the women spun flax into linen threads and various animal fibres into woollen yarns, but it was the men who knitted these threads into garments, probably with the help of a wooden frame. In the Middle Ages and Early Renaissance, knitting guilds were set up to supply the courts of England and France with fine hosiery. Before a young man could enter a guild, he had to study the works of a Master Knitter for six years. Then, for his entry examination, he had to complete within thirteen weeks 'a knitted carpet in coloured design containing flowers, foliage, animals and birds, approximately six feet by five feet; to knit and felt a woollen beret, and to knit himself a woollen shirt and a pair of hose with Spanish clocks'.

Male knitters who have hitherto knitted in secret may now knit openly without any fear. After all, the Prince of Wales, the leader of fashion in this book, was reputed to have been able to knit his own sweaters, and every man should follow his example.

the 20s

'A gentleman must never be called one and must not know he is one. The moment he calls himself one, he ceases to be one. He can make a joke at someone else's expense without annoying the subject of it. He can lend money without the borrower feeling a worm. He can suffer without making a fuss. He can die without letting out a secret. In short he is a gentleman.' Lady Troubridge, *Bestway Magazine,* 1920.

The Prince of Wales (later Edward VIII) was considered to be the best-dressed gentleman in the whole world. He set the new trends in fashion one after the other. His innovations and daring ways of breaking with old-fashioned ideas of dress were followed avidly by all the young men. 'The Prince of Wales still leads most of the changes in fashion and popularizes them abroad. He not only puts on several outfits a day but keeps it up week after week' (*The Tailor and Cutter*, 1928). The only person, it seemed, who dissented from this judgment was a Mr Fairchild who wrote in *Menswear Fashions*: 'In my opinion, Prince George is going to be the best dressed man in the Royal Family. He is the tallest and best figure and wears his clothes with that air of nonchalance which conveys the impression that nothing has been thought out and yet everything is perfect.' (1927)

When the Prince of Wales was presented with a Fair Isle sweater by a firm of drapers from Lerwick, and chose to favour this garment by wearing it on the golf course at St Andrews in 1921, he set a trend in fashion that was to last for the following thirty years. A Fair Isle jersey became the most popular woolly to wear. Today it is still as popular, and proudly worn to the office, to a wedding, on sporting occasions; and it is a special favourite with the presenters on television.

In 1921, the Fair Isle came as a blessing upon a British scene of plain sweaters that had been knitted as necessities for the troops, as part of the 1914-18 'war-effort'. Owing to the shortage of wool and dye-stuffs, these wartime jerseys continued to be the only garments available. They were made from fisherman's yarn, double-knitting or 3-ply super wheeling. Warmth came from the thick, often oiled wool, which, with a turtle-neck collar or high-buttoning

shawl collar, provided a trusty garment in all foul weather. Sometimes the welt was worn 'turned up', as were the cuffs.

The cardigan, too, was a 'sensible' garment, worn for function, not fashion. In a grey-green, mottle, brown or plain grey, it was 'the thing' for informal wear after a day at the office, and came with the addition of one or two pockets for tobacco and pipe—those little comforts which a gentleman likes to have about his person.

In 1920, wage-cuts and rising costs had produced a dismal picture for the fashion world. 'One has but to stand a while on any prominent street corner in cities and notice the clothes of the average man to see how much shoddy stuff is worn and how faded and unkempt it soon becomes.' Splashes of colour were added to the plain tweed or homespun jacket by a waistcoat in canary yellow or occasionally in a brick colour. To escape the drab routine of daily life, the former serviceman (who generally arrived in top physical condition from the war) indulged in leisure and sporting activities of every nature, from tennis, football and cycling to motoring and golf. The wartime double-breasted jacket with thick-ribbed collar and hem was suitable for a ride in the open motor, and a high-buttoning cardigan was sensible wear for skating, but many more new garments were needed.

Inspiration came from the women's magazines which sprang up in the early Twenties to help 'cope in the servantless home'. By providing patterns, they persuaded the womenfolk to knit. 'The art of knitting is one of the most useful forms of handiwork that a woman can practise.' Soon she could make a cardigan checked with a large single line; or if she was too inexperienced for this, she could knit a gentleman's waistcoat or 'vest' in two straight pieces, and leave the 'shaping' to the tailor, as the final garment 'must look well'. Neckties were knitted in art-silk, or real silk if this could be afforded. A straight-sided moss-stitch tie in shades of beige or straw was soon part of the well-dressed gentleman's wardrobe. Alternatively, ties in cotton were knitted on fine needles, perhaps with stripes of contrasting colour. Apart from ordinary hose, silk socks for dancing became indispensible items on 'well-shod extremities'.

In America, the heavy shaker cardigan came with a shawl collar buttoned up the front, in maroon, navy and myrtle, with perhaps the cuff and hem in a darker shade of wool. With new interest in hygiene, the magazines recommended a plentiful supply of socks and the necessary 'union' suit. This one-piece under-garment consisted of the vest (under-shirt) and long knitted underpants with buttoning fly-front, excellent to wear under the suit in winter. Let it be remembered that with knitted underwear, 'perspiration is immediately and properly absorbed and danger of colds avoided, but the importance of the daily bath must be emphasized, for the man who bathes daily wants clean underwear each day' (*Menswear*, 1920).

Golf now became available for the middle classes, as new golf courses were opened throughout Britain and America. Sports pullovers and knitted cardigans fought one another for supremacy, replacing the sports jacket for the younger men on the links. The younger set preferred the fashionable Fair Isle, which now came in cheerful greens, reds and blues against a background of fawn. In 1925, Fair Isles reached their zenith with many new experiments in pattern and design.

The women were now adept in knitting 'tubular' garments of every type, and a Fair Isle was no exception. By using circular needles, the knitter could go round and round with no seams at the side and very little shaping. The advantage of this method was that the pattern could always be worked from the front, while the wool-colour held in reserve, carefully woven-in behind, made the weaving soft, supple and warm. Sometimes the welt could be effective in a 'corrugated' two-coloured rib. All was possible if the recipe was followed from the magazine, which reassured the reader that 'Although the pattern looks very elaborate, it's really very simple.' As with a Guernsey or 'Gansey' jumper, the sleeve was knitted as an additional 'tube', causing the armhole seam to hang sideways off the shoulder. Because the sleeve was knitted from the shoulder, decreasing down to the cuff, the bottom end could easily be unpicked and reknitted if it became too worn.

In 1925, men and women had exchanged silhouettes. The women wore shapeless, flat-chested, straight-sided 'tomboy' fashions, and cropped their hair. They enjoyed 'mannish' occupations like motoring, mountaineering and golf. They even tried to fly planes—and they smoked! The men accused women of stealing their identity—not to mention their tailors for feminine suits, and could not understand 'that deplorably masculine fashion of bobbing the hair'. The women accused men of being effeminate. They were smooth-skinned and clean-shaven, and their hair fell below their ears so that it 'shot up' after a drive in the motor. They had taken to wearing skirt-like garments such as plus fours and Oxford bags, in colours of lavender, mauve or a delicate green, with pullovers in pale pastel 'dusted' effects. As for their Fair Isles and their Argyle socks, they were chaotic with colour. HER pullovers remained brown or beige, and had only a calm geometric pattern around the border.

The Fair Isles persisted in an undiminished blaze of scarlet, saxe-blue, green, yellow and rust in Jacquard designs, chevrons, lozenges and bold Argyle checks; and the plus fours were cut even wider, through the undoubted influence of the Oxford bags. 'At their biggest we may smile at them, for youth will have its fling,' said the older men. In Los Angeles that year, Lawrence Grant playing in *The Dark Angel* wore a Fair Isle patterned tie that was at least four inches wide. A new-style Fair Isle jersey had a six-inch rolled neck and was worn with baggy plus fours, as well as with the fashionable grey flannel trousers which had become a craze, sweeping England and the Continent—'and they promise to be an equal success in the United States'. These 'greyers', as they were termed at Eton and Harrow, were part of every kit.

Although the Fair Isle was 'positively *de rigeur*' on the golf links, a few V-necked pullovers in solid colours of blue or yellow were conspicuous on the course at the Hillcrest Country Club in Los Angeles in 1925. 'Von Elm made easily the smartest appearance in his blue shell-stitched sweater. Neville wore a Fair Isle sweater and a one-piece cap and Wilhelm was a study in brown checks from the front of his jacket through his plus fours to his hose.' Never before had men been so 'gay' in their dress.

Golf stockings matched the pullovers in colour, pattern or weave, in all manner of bold geometric lozenges or squares. Plain self-coloured hose with fancy tops or fancy hose with plain tops appeared in jade green, orange, navy, biscuit or fawn. Among the golfers, the Prince of Wales sparkled, wearing his black and white checked cap, a startling jumper and chequered socks.

The Prince of Wales continued to set the fashion. It was he who decided that a sleeveless V-neck pullover was 'right' to wear beneath the casual sports jacket instead of the cloth waistcoat—and it was reputed that he could knit such a pullover himself. Then he had the idea of tucking the pullover into the golf knickers at the waist. Later he made perhaps the most unusual appearance, presenting the prizes at the Boys' Club Boxing Championships in 1929, wearing a grey pullover, soft shirt and a double collar—with dinner jacket!

Only the Prince could successfully decree such innovations. A young gentleman's wear must be 'irreproachable socks' and white kid gloves when dancing the 'Prince of Wales Fox Trot' in the evening; and if he appeared in 'jazzy' designs at the office, his 'mistake' was frowned upon. 'When a man chooses to wear his plus fours to work and introduces a feverish note into a quiet commercial house, he could not be looked upon with favour, for dull of soul and lacking in response is he who is able to harness his attention to a ledger or counter while clad in baggy knickers and a pullover of coloured wools.'

Likewise on the tennis courts, colour should never be worn. An Englishman knows instinctively that cream or white is correct. Yet in 1928, the sweaters worn by the French players at Cannes were highly patterned and figured. Also in that same year, an American player arrived at Wimbledon wearing flannel knickerbockers and jazzy stockings. But it was all 'very bad form'.

A better place for a man to indulge in colour was the seaside. The modern craze for sunbathing lured families down to the sea and gave men a chance to fling aside the navy blue regulation bathing-costume in favour of a striped suit with huge bars of orange, flame-red or bright blue against a background of white. There was a choice between a one-piece suit with shoulder-straps, or the new two-piece suit with the top part striped and the trunks in a plain dark colour. Ramon Navarro wore a horizontal striped shirt with separate blue flannel trunks; but at Biarritz, the men favoured the tight, form-fitting regulation blue rather than the two-piece which was considered 'effeminate'. On the beaches near Manhattan in 1925, diagonal stripes and mortise stripes vied with the horizontal type. 'Bathing suits rival the multi-coloured denizens of the waters under the earth. Fair Isle fantasies are noticed on the sands and the colourful 'tummy stripes' encircle the flat shells of the slightly effeminate beach-comber. It has been noted that the men who bathe the least wear the gayest bathing-suits. Their trunks are short and their torsos hilarious.'

Dismayed by all this femininity, a worried clergyman, the Reverend Hardwick, declared in 1929: 'Man now loves decorative clothes as much as women. Men have stolen women's method of attraction. In due course of time it will perhaps happen that the female will become the dominant sex and openly select its partner.'

With the man giving way on colour and the woman on pattern, the first 'unisex' garment was born. Patterned in shades of brown, a cardigan could now be interchangeable. If it was too troublesome to knit a 'his' *and* a 'hers' version, a single cardigan might be made with two sets of button-holes, one on each edge. The buttons were mounted on a separate sateen band and buttoned through from beneath, on either 'his' or 'her' correct side.

In 1927, the victorious arrival of Lindbergh in Paris after his solo non-stop flight from New York was celebrated with aeroplane motifs appearing on the front of V-necked sweaters. In the same year, while on their tour of Canada, the young English Princes dressed very much alike so as not to outdo one another. All their slipover sweaters were sleeveless.

In America, the best-dressed men at Princeton and Yale chose to wear patternless crew-neck pullovers in solid colours of tan, grey, rust, blue-green and canary yellow; and Walter Hagen, spurning the Fair Isle, wore extremely bright solid-coloured sweaters for his golf. By the end of the decade, Fair Isles had sobered to three or five tones, all in the same hue. Patterns where they did appear were decidely smaller and neater. The shape of pullovers was about to change.

A Three-Colour "Pull-Over"

MATERIALS

USE 12 oz. of Sirdar Coronation Wool No. 832, fawn ; 4 oz. of shade No. 852, biscuit ; 6 oz. of shade No. 84½, dark. A Flexiknit needle No. 7 for working the body in a round, in which case a pair of Stratnoid knitting needles No. 7 will be required for the shoulders. Or a set of four Stratnoid needles with points at both ends will answer for both parts. A set of four No. 9 needles is also required for the neck.

SIZE AND TENSION

Working at a tension to produce 6 stitches to the inch in width when the work is on the needles, the measurement on the diagram will be attained after light pressing, as it should always be remembered that a piece of knitting " gives " when taken off the needles, so there is actually a greater measurement than just the number of stitches to the inch of the knitting. For the next size larger use No. 6 needles, getting 5 stitches to the inch in width.

TO WORK

For working in a round, cast on 240 stitches in the medium shade, and knit 2 medium and 2 dark alternately all round, working into the backs of the stitches for the first round.

Now knit 2 medium and purl 2 dark alternately all round, and repeat this round of ribbing for a depth of 3½ inches.

Now change to the medium shade, and work 2 rounds in this shade, but decreasing twice in the first round thus : K. 118, k. 2 tog., k. 118, k. 2 tog., leaving 238 stitches a multiple of 17, which is right for the two-colour pattern.

These two rows represent the first 2 plain rows on the chart, but in repetition of them there will be no decreasings.

Now the work proceeds from pattern row 3 on the chart to end of row 13, then from row 13 back to row 3, making 22 rounds of colour pattern, and with two plain rounds at the beginning, 24 altogether. These 24

Read This Paragraph Before Working

THE garment illustrated looks a mass of pattern which sometimes strikes awe in the faint heart of the beginner, but after studying the chart of the colour pattern opposite which represents the design for the whole garment, you will realise how easy it is. The whole pattern is in the 17 stitches between the two serrated upright lines, each cross representing one stitch of the colour pattern, and each empty square one stitch in background colour. The colour design is arranged so that only two colours are in action on the same row, the background throughout being in the medium wool, and the pattern alternated light and dark.

In the first pattern the small diamond in the centre is worked in the light shade, and the little triangle and stem pattern above and below this is in the dark shade. After completing a whole pattern of 24 rows, repeat the design with the shades of the pattern work reversed, using the dark wool for the small diamond in the centre and the light wool for the triangle above and below this.

These two methods of working the pattern are alternated throughout the work.

See colour plate on page 136

Adaptable to Various Sizes

rounds are repeated throughout with the reversing of the colours as given above.

Continue until you have completed 4 patterns and 7 rows of the next pattern, or in any other size until the beginning of the V neck is reached.

Here the work is divided for the armholes. First knit the first stitch of the row in the medium wool on the Flexiknit.

THE FRONT

Now, using the straight needle, k. 59 stitches, cast off the centre stitch and knit across 59 more, leaving remaining stitches for back.

Work on the last 59 stitches for half the front. Keep the side edge straight, and k. 2 tog. at the neck edge every fourth row until 17 stitches are decreased away, keeping the pattern correct, as the stitches are taken away.

Complete the pattern on these stitches without further decreasing, then work 8 rows of another pattern. The last row will be a plain medium row. Put these stitches on a spare needle, and work the opposite side of front to match, and put these stitches on a spare needle.

Now work on the 119 stitches of the back quite straight, until you have worked the same depth as the front—less the last plain medium row, as this will be made in the grafting of the shoulder.

Graft the shoulder stitches of front to back with the medium wool, beginning at arm-hole end.

This leaves 35 stitches in centre of back for the neck.

With a No. 9 needle pick up 64 stitches down one side of the neck opening. With another needle pick up the cast-off stitch at centre front, and 64 stitches up the opposite side of the neck opening. Divide evenly on three needles.

On the first row k. 2 medium and 2 brown alternately all round.

Now change to the k. 2 and p. 2 as at lower edge, and work 4 rounds

Now decrease at centre front to get a close fit by knitting 2 tog. on the 3 light ribs at centre front.

On next round k. 2 tog. on each side of the centre decreases. Repeat the decreases again on next row.

On the next row cast off—at the same time k. 2 tog. on each side of centre decreases to further reduce the neck line. The casting off is done with the medium wool all round.

THE SLEEVES

Cast on 102 stitches in medium wool and work one pattern of 24 rows on these stitches. From this point decrease at both ends of every sixth row until only 70 stitches remain. (For any other length these stitches can be continued for length of sleeve required, less about 3 inches for cuff, which does not turn back.) Now work in rib of k. 2 medium and 2 dark alternately in the first row, decreasing 2 stitches in the round. Continue the rib on 68 stitches for about 3 inches.

Cast off with the medium wool.

Press the work well on the right side with a hot iron over a damp cloth, but do not press the ribbing at lower edge and cuffs.

Sew up sleeve seams and sew into armholes, then press all seams.

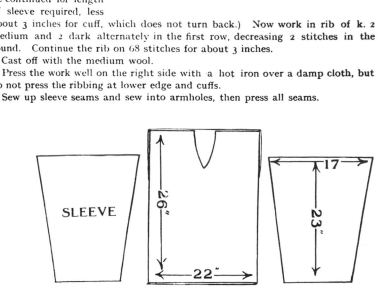

13
12
11
10
9
8
7
6
5
4
3
2
1

2 rows plain.

Follow this simple chart, and you will work the whole pattern easily.

SLEEVE

26"

22"

17

23"

The pullover is made on very simple lines that can easily be adapted for either a man or a girl.

Now is the TIME—

For Golf Or Walking This Pullover Is So Comfortable.

15*th* and 16*th* rounds : K. 2 mottle and 2 dark alternately.

17*th* and 18*th* rounds : K. 2 light and 6 dark alternately. Repeat the first 12 pattern rounds.

Next round : While working the 13th pattern round work as follows : K. 14, slip the next 30 st. on a spare needle for pocket top, and in place work 30 pocket-lining stitches from spare needle, work next 34 st., slip next 30 on spare needle, and in place work 30 pocket-lining stitches, work to end of round.

Work the 14th to 18th rounds in-

THIS pullover is constructed on very simple lines, with straight arm-hole and short V neck, so that it is easily adaptable for either sex. The pattern is so simple (although it looks elaborate) that the beginner will not have any difficulty in following it, even on the short rows at the neck. Up to the armholes it is worked in rounds, and only two colours of wool are in operation at the same time. The colour not actually in use along the row is twisted once over the working thread, so that there are no loose threads at the back of the work.

MATERIALS : Templeton's " Ayr " " F " Fingering, 4-ply, in the following quantities : 6 oz. of mottle, 6 oz. light and 4 oz. dark ; 4 bone knitting needles No. 9, with double points, and four No. 10.

ABBREVIATIONS : K., knit plain ; p., purl ; tog., together ; s.s., stocking-stitch, which is k. on the front of the work and p. on the back.

TENSION AND MEASUREMENTS : Worked at a tension of 6 st. to the inch in width, the following measurements will be obtained after light pressing : From shoulder to hem, 25½ inches ; width all round body at underarm, 38 inches ; underarm-seam of sleeve, 20½ inches.

To Work

BEGIN with pocket linings and, using light wool and No. 9 needles, cast on 30 st. Work 30 rows in s.s., then cut wool and slip these stitches on a spare needle. Work a second lining exactly the same and put both aside for the present.

THE BODY OF PULLOVER : Begin at the lower edge, using mottle wool and No. 9 needles. Cast on 232 st., arranging 72 on the first needle, 88 on the second, and 72 on third needle. Join into a round and work 20 rounds of k. 2 and p. 2 alternately for the ribbed hip-band. It is now ready to begin the multi-colour pattern.

The Colour Pattern

FIRST *and* 2*nd* rounds : K. all light.

3*rd* and 4*th* rounds : K. 2 light and 2 mottle alternately all round.

5*th* and 6*th* rounds : K. 2 mottle and 2 dark alternately.

7*th* and 8*th* rounds : K. 2 dark and 2 mottle alternately.

9*th* and 10*th* rounds : K. 2 mottle and 2 light alternately.

11*th* and 12*th* rounds : K. all light.

13*th* and 14*th* rounds : K. 2 light and 6 dark alternately.

–for the COUNTRY

Made In Shades Of Brown And Fawn, The Perfect Autumn Colouring.

clusive. Repeat the 18 pattern rounds 4 times more, when armhole opening is reached.

Next round : With light wool cast off 2, k. 59 for left front; on a second needle k. 59 for right front; cast off 2, k. remaining 110 all on one needle for back. The work now proceeds in rows, so back or alternate rows will be purled, in pattern.

THE BACK.—Continue with 2nd pattern row, and on every row work items in reverse order to that given, for instance the 3rd and 4th rounds will be "2 mottle and 2 light alternately," which is simply continuing the pattern.

Repeat until the 18th row has been worked for the third time from the

Although the pattern looks elaborate, it is really very simple, and would not present any difficulty to a beginner.

armhole. Work the first 6 pattern rows, then cut threads and leave these stitches until fronts have been worked.

RIGHT FRONT.—Join light wool to beginning of purl row and continue with 2nd pattern row. K. 2 tog. at beginning (neck opening) of two k. rows out of every three (that is, 2 decreasings in every 6 rows) until 40 st. are left for shoulder. Work until 2 rows longer than back. Hold needle with these stitches in front of the matching 40 st. from end of back with the right sides of knitting together. K. tog. 1 from front and 1 from back needles and cast off at the same time.

LEFT FRONT.—Work as described for right front, except that decreasings are at end of k. rows instead of beginning.

THE NECK.—With mottle wool and No. 10 needles pick up 47 st. down left front of neck (taking 3 st. to every 4 rows) for first needle; on second needle pick up 47 st. at right-front neck; on third needle k. 30 back neck stitches. Work 1 round of k. 2 and p. 2 rib, then

work 6 rounds, decreasing at centre front, thus: Sl. 1, k. 1 and pass sl.-stitch over on the last 2 st. of first needle, and k. 2 tog. at beginning of second needle in every round. Cast off rather loosely.

POCKET TOPS.—With mottle wool and No. 10 needles k. 8 rows and cast off.

Sleeves

WITH light wool and No. 9 needles cast on 88 st., 32 on first needle, 24 on second needle, and 32 on third needle. Join in to a round and work in pattern, decreasing on every 4th round. To decrease on first needle, k. 2, k. 2 tog., work to end of needle, work the 2nd needle to within 2 st. of end of 3rd needle, then sl. 1, k. 1, pass the sl.-stitch over. After the 5th decrease round, decrease every 8th round until 56 st. remain. Work for length required, then with No. 10 needles and mottle wool k. 1 round and k. 2 tog. at beginning of first and second needles, also at end of second and third needles (52 st.). Work 22 rounds of k. 2 and p. 2 rib, cast off.

TO MAKE UP.—Sew sleeves to armholes with join of rounds to under-arm. Sew pocket linings to wrong side of pullover, and darn in all ends. Press all, except ribbing, with a damp cloth over knitting.

Man's Cable-Stitch Sleeveless Pullover

Materials required : 8 ozs. "Greenock" Super Fingering, 5-ply.
1 Pair Knitting Needles, No. 8.
1 Set Knitting Needles, No. 10, double pointed.

Measurements.—The Pullover measures from the shoulder to the lower edge 21 inches, width all round underarms (without stretching) 34 inches. It will fit an average size man. The Pullover is worked in a fancy cable pattern and has ribbed bands at the neck, armholes and waist.

The Back.—Commence at the lower edge of the back with two of the No. 10 needles by casting on 104 stitches, knit into the back of the stitches for the first row, then work in ribs of 2 plain and 2 purl for 26 rows.

Now change to the No. 8 needles.

Next row : Knit 3, then *, knit 8, knit into the front and back of the next stitch, repeat from * to end of row, ending with knit 2 (115 stitches).

Now the pattern is commenced.

1st row : Knit 1, then *, purl 8, knit 3, purl 1, knit 3, repeat from * to end of row, ending with purl 8, knit 1.

2nd row : Knit plain.

Repeat these last 2 rows 3 times.

9th row : Same as 1st row.

10th row : Knit 1, *, slip the next 4 stitches on to a No. 10 needle and place behind the work, knit the next 4 stitches, then knit the 4 stitches from the No. 10 needle, knit 7, repeat from * to end of row, ending with knit 1, after the last " twist."

These 10 rows form the pattern which is repeated throughout the Pullover. Please note that when increasing or decreasing is done the continuity of the pattern should be kept as well as possible.

When you have worked 7 patterns and 7 rows of the next pattern start the armholes.

Next row : Cast off 6, knit to the end of the row.
Next row : Cast off 6, work in pattern to the end of the row.
Next row : Cast off 1, work in pattern to the end of the row.
Next row : Cast off 1, work in pattern to the end of the row.

Repeat the last 2 rows, keeping the continuity of the pattern until 85 stitches remain.

Continue working without decreasing until there are 13 whole patterns from the top of the waist ribbing.

*, Work the 1st row of the next pattern, then knit until 9 stitches remain, turn, work in pattern until 9 stitches remain, turn, and knit back. Complete this pattern by working the 5th, 6th, 7th, *, 8th, 9th and 10th rows, repeat from * once.

8th row of 15th pattern : Knit 25, cast off 35, knit 25.

Continue working on the 25 stitches to which the wool is now attached, leaving the other 25 stitches on a spare needle for the time being.

The Left Side of Neck.—Complete the 15th pattern you are now doing. * Work the 1st row of the next pattern, then knit until 9 stitches remain, turn, and work in pattern to the neck. Complete this pattern, working the 4th row next, repeat from * once and work the next pattern (18th). In the next 5 patterns increase 1 stitch at the neck edge in every 4th row and this brings you to the armhole increasings. Whilst working the next pattern and 9 rows of another pattern, increase 1 stitch at the armhole edge in every alternate row, not forgetting to continue the increasings at the neck in every 4th row. The stitches should number 52, leave these stitches on a spare needle while the other side of the neck is worked.

The Right Side of Neck.—Join on the wool at the neck edge and complete the 15th pattern. Now * work the first row of the next pattern until 9 stitches remain, turn, and knit back. Complete this pattern, working the 3rd row next,*. Repeat from * to * once, then work another pattern (18th).

In the next 5 patterns increase one stitch at the neck edge in every 4th row, and work 2 more complete patterns, increasing 1 stitch at the armhole edge in every alternate row, still increasing at the neck (52 stitches on the needle). Now cast on 1 stitch and work in pattern across the other 52 stitches at the other side of the neck.

1st row of next pattern : Cast on 8, work in pattern to end.
2nd row of next pattern : Cast on 8, knit to the end.
3rd row : Knit 4, then *, purl 8, knit 3, purl 1, knit 3, repeat from * to end of row. ending with purl 8, knit 4.

Complete this pattern and work 7 more complete patterns, noting that instead of knitting 1 stitch at the beginning and end of the 2nd, 4th, 6th, 8th and 10th rows as for the back, you knit 4 stitches.

Change to the No. 10 needles and work 26 rows in ribs of 2 plain and 2 purl, then cast off.

Very lightly press the knitting on the wrong side with a warm iron, then join the side seams. Using the set of No. 10 needles pick up and knit 160 stitches round each armhole, work in ribbing of 1 plain and 1 purl for 7 rows, then cast off. Pick up and knit 230 stitches round the neck, work 7 rows in ribbing to match the armholes, but knit 3 stitches together at the front point of the V in every row, then cast off.

Bachelor's Tea Cosy.

This is a charmingly contrived tea cosy; is simple and easily made; and is intended to be kept on the teapot when pouring out the tea. The handle passes through an opening on one side, and the spout has a similar opening on the other side. 3 ozs. of Greenock Double Fleecy Wool will be required; three shades of any preferred colour; either green, crimson, blue or gold will work prettily; about double the quanty of the second shade will be required of the others. With a large crochet hook make a chain of 40 stitches and join. Now take a medium-sized hook for the work; it is done in tufts thus :—1st round—3 chain for the first stitch *, 4 treble into the next loop; take out the hook and place it in the first of these trebles, and then draw through the loop of the fourth; (the tufts are all made in this manner); 1 treble in the next loop; repeat from *, making 20 tufts in the round, joining the round with a single, between the three chains, which began the round and the first tuft. 2nd round—Again 3 chains, *, make a tuft in the stitch, between the tuft and the single treble, 1 treble between the single treble and the next tuft, repeat from * all round, and join with a single as last row. 3rd round—Cut off the wool and join the next shade. Repeat the 2nd round, but at the end do not join, but cut off the wool again, as now an opening is to be left for the handle. 4th round—Join the same shade and work as before for 10 tufts, break off the wool, and now begin the opening for the spout. Join the wool and make 10 more tufts, and again break off the wool. Next work two divided rounds with the lightest shade, then join the second shade, and work a row for ribbon by making 1 treble in each space before and after each tuft. For the edge *, work 5 double crochets very loosely in the top of 1 treble, miss 2 trebles, 1 double crochet in the next, miss 2, and repeat from *, continue all round, and join with a single. Run in the ribbon; which ties above the handle of the teapot, and fasten the ends of the wool.

INSTRUCTIONS
FOR KNITTING

SERIES F, No. 53
GIVEN FREE

Man's Cable-Stitch Sleeveless Pullover

as featured in "MABS WEEKLY"

SCOTCH WOOL & HOSIERY STORES

PROPRIETORS:

FLEMING, REID & CO., LTD., *THE WORSTED MILLS*, GREENOCK

OVER 400 BRANCHES

FOR THE MENFOLK

A KNITTED TIE

THIS tie is worked in a flat piece on two needles, and is afterwards sewn up the long edge to form a circular tie.

MATERIALS : 1 ball (50 grammes) of Clark's Anchor Stranded Cotton and a pair of No. 14 steel knitting needles make a double tie 2 inches wide.

ABBREVIATIONS : K., knit; p., purl; tog., together; m., make.

TO WORK

CAST on 43 stitches and do 3 rows of plain knitting, working into the back of stitches on first row.

4TH Row : K. 3, p. 4, * k. 2, p. 4, repeat from * to end.

5TH Row : K. 3, * m. 1 (by bringing the thread to the front of the needle for an open stitch), k. 2 tog., k. 4, repeat from * until 4 remain, m. 1, k. 2 tog., k. 2.

Repeat the 4TH and 5TH Rows 3 times more, then work the 4TH Row.

13TH, 14TH and 15TH Rows : All plain knitting.

16TH Row : P. 4, * k. 2, p. 4, repeat from * until 3 remain, k. 3.

17TH Row : K. 6, * m. 1, k. 2 tog., k. 4, repeat from *, finishing with k. 1.

Repeat the 16TH and 17TH Rows 3 times more, then work the 16TH Row. This completes one pattern.

Repeat the pattern 7 times more for the long end. Work the first 12 rows of next pattern.

NEXT Row : (K. 3, k. 2 tog.) 3 times, k. 13, (k. 2 tog., k. 3) 3 times (37 stitches).

Work the 2ND Row, and continue pattern up to and including the 12TH Row.

NEXT Row : (K. 4, k. 2 tog.) 6 times, k. 1. You have 31 stitches.

K. 2 rows and p. 1 row.

NEXT Row : (K. 2 tog., k. 2) 7 times, k. 2 tog., k. 1.

There are now 23 stitches, on which p. 1 row and k. 1 row alternately for 13½ inches, finishing with a purl row.

NEXT Row : (K. 1 into front and 1 into back of same stitch, k. 2) 7 times, k. 1 into front and 1 into back, k. 1 (31 stitches).

P. 1 row and k. 2 rows.

NEXT Row : (K. 4, k. 1 into front, and 1 into back of next stitch) 6 times, k. 1, giving 37 stitches in the row.

Begin pattern with 4TH Row and work up to and including 14TH Row.

NEXT Row : (K. 3, k. 1 into front, and 1 into back of next stitch) 3 times, k. 13, (k. 1 into front, and 1 into back of next stitch, k. 3) 3 times.

Continue pattern from 4TH Row then work 4 repeats of pattern and one more repeat to the end of 15TH Row.

K. one plain row and cast off.

Press well on wrong side and sew together the long edges for back of tie with sewing silk of the same shade. Press seam to flatten.

Gent.'s Golf Stockings

Materials Required.
6 ozs. Greenock Super Fingering, 5-ply.
1 oz. Greenock Super Fingering, 5-ply, in contrasting colour.
A set of Knitting Needles, size 12 or 13.

Measurements.

Turn-over Top	... ...	3½ inches.
Leg	... ...	18 inches.
Foot	... ...	10½ inches.

Top—Cast on 84 stitches. Knit 6 rounds in 1 plain, 1 purl, and 3 rounds plain, in ground shade. 2 rounds in contrasting shade. 3 rounds in ground shade.

15th round—Knit 2 in ground shade, * 1 in contrasting shade, 5 in ground shade. Repeat from *.

16th round — Knit 1 ground shade, * 3 contrasting, 3 ground. Repeat from *

17th round—* Knit 5 in contrasting shade, 1 in ground shade. Repeat from*

18th round—As 16th.

19th round—As 15th.

20th round—3 in ground shade, * 1 contrasting, 3 ground. Repeat from *

21st round—1 in contrasting shade, * 3 ground, 1 contrasting, 1 ground, 1 contrasting, 3 ground, 3 contrasting. Repeat from *

22nd round—2 in contrasting shade, * 3 ground, 1 contrasting, 3 ground, 5 contrasting. Repeat from *. This 22nd row is centre of pattern. Now knit from 21st back to 7th round, decreasing the stitches to 80 on last plain round. Turn the top inside out and knit about 3 inches of 1 plain, 1 purl. Then change the Rib to 7 plain, 3 purl. Knit 3 inches. Now commence the shaping for Leg by decreasing one stitch on first and last plain ribs of round. Knit 7 rounds without decreasing, then decrease again on the second plain rib at beginning and second last plain rib from end of round—7 rounds. Decrease again on third from beginning and end. Knit 7 rounds. Continue in this manner until all the plain ribs are reduced to 6 stitches. Knit 5 rows. Decrease the purl ribs to 2 stitches in the same order, always having 5 rows between each decreasing. The rib should now be 6 plain, 2 purl—64 stitches left for Ankle; on these knit about 3 inches, then divide for Heel—32 stitches on Heel needle and 16 stitches on each of the two front needles.

Heel.—Knit plain on right side and slip 1, purl 1, on wrong side. Repeat these two rows for 3 inches.

To Turn Heel.—Begin on right side. Slip 1, knit 21, knit 2 together, turn. Slip 1, purl 1, for 13 stitches, purl 2 together, turn. Slip 1, knit 13, knit 2 together, turn. Slip 1, purl 1 for 15 stitches, purl 2 together, turn. Slip 1, knit 16, knit 2 together, turn. Slip 1, purl 1, for 17 stitches, purl 2 together, turn. Continue in this way until all the stitches are knitted in. Pick up and knit the stitches down left side of Heel. Knit the stitches which were left on the two needles for Top of Foot on to one needle. Pick up and knit the stitches on right side of Heel, and on to this needle knit the half of the stitches left from the turning of Heel. The stitches are on three needles again. Knit the next needle. Knit the top of Foot needle, continuing the ribbing.

Gusset.—On next needle knit 2, knit 2 together, knit to within 4 stitches at end of next needle, knit 2 together, knit 2.

Next round—Plain.

Repeat these two rounds until there are 16 stitches on each of the side needles. Knit without further decreasing until the Foot measures 8 inches, measuring from outer edge of heel.

Toe.—The ribbing on top of Foot is now discontinued. On top of foot needle decrease at beginning and end, at beginning of first and end of second instep needle.

Next round—Plain.

Repeat these last two rounds until 20 stitches remain. Place on two needles (10 stitches on each); knit one from each needle and cast off.

Motoring Mittens

Materials Required.

To obtain the best results use 3 oz. of "Viyella" Yarn, 4-ply, in fawn, and 1 oz. in brown; also a set of No. 14 knitting needles.

The mittens should fit over gloves up to size 6¾. For a smaller size shorten the straight part after working the thumb.

The work is done at a tension of 10 sts. to 1 in.

Begin at the top of the gauntlet by casting on 112 sts. with brown wool, 36 sts. on each of the first 2 needles, and 40 on the third.

Work in a rib of K. 3, P. 1, for a depth of 12 rounds, working into the backs of the sts. on the first round.

Change to the fawn wool and work

10 rounds, then work
8 „ in brown,
6 „ „ fawn,
4 „ „ brown,
4 „ „ fawn.

Should a longer gauntlet be desired work .

2 rounds in brown,
2 „ „ fawn,
1 „ „ brown,
4 „ „ fawn.

From here complete the mitten in fawn wool.

On the next round decrease in every knit rib by knitting the 2nd and 3rd sts. together all round—84 sts. remain.

The rib is now K. 2, P. 1. Continue without further alteration for a depth of 12 rounds.

On the next round again decrease by knitting together the 2 K. sts. in every knit rib. 56 sts. remain on the needle.

The rib is now K. 1, P. 1. Continue in this rib for a depth of 2 in.

Change to stocking st. and on the first round work 2 sts. into every 4th st. all round.

There are now 22, 22, 26 sts. on the needles.

Work a depth of 1 in. without alteration.

On the next round commence the thumb increases.

On the first needle K. 2 sts. into the first st., K. 1, then K. 2 sts. into the next st., then complete the round.

These would make an opportune Gift for your Motoring Friend.

Work 1 round without alteration.

On the next round K. 2 sts. into the first st., K. 3, then K. 2 sts. into the next st. and complete the round.

Work the next round without alteration.

Continue increasing on every alternate round with 2 sts. extra between the increases each time till there are 42 sts. on the needle

Now knit the first 23 sts. on the first needle of the round, and pass these sts. to a piece of wool.

There are now 19, 22, 26 sts. on the needles

Complete the round and cast on 5 sts. at the end of the third needle.

Continue across the 19 sts. of the first needle, then pass the 5 cast on sts. on the previous needle to the beginning of the first needle of the round.

There are now 24, 22, 26 sts. on the needles.

Pass 2 sts. of the needle holding 26 sts. to the one with 22 only, making 24 sts. on each needle.

Continue quite straight for a depth of 3 in.—or more or less as required—then shape for the tip.

On the next round K. 2 tog., K. 34 K. 2 tog., K. 34.

Work 3 rounds without alteration.

On the next round K. 2 tog., K. 33, K. 2 tog., K. 33.

Work 3 rounds without alteration.

On the next round K. 2 tog., K. 32, K. 2 tog., K. 32.

Work 3 rounds without alteration.

On the next round K. 2 tog., K. 31, K. 2 tog., K. 31.

Work 3 rounds without alteration.

On the next round * K. 2 tog., K. 14, and repeat from * all round.

Repeat the decreases on every round always with 1 st. less between the decreases on every round till 28 sts. remain.

On the next round K. 2 tog. all round.

Arrange the remaining sts. on 2 needles and graft together.

The Thumb.

Pass the sts. of the thumb to 2 needles, then pick up and knit through the 5 cast on sts. on the hand, and also 1 on each side—the edge of the row on both sides—making 30 sts. on the needles.

Work over all sts. for a depth of 1¼ in.

The top shaping takes about ¾ of an in. in depth, so try on the thumb to be sure of the right length.

To shape the top :

1st round.—Knit tog. every 9th and 10th sts., then work 2 rounds without alteration.

4th round.—Knit tog. every 8th and 9th sts., then work 2 rounds without alteration.

7th round.—Knit tog. every 7th and 8th sts., then work 2 rounds without alteration.

10th round.—Knit tog. every 6th and 7th sts., then work 2 rounds without alteration.

13th round.—Knit tog. every 5th and 6th sts., then work 2 rounds without alteration.

On the next round K. tog. 2 sts. all round.

Draw the wool through the remaining sts. and fasten off firmly.

The second mitten is made in the same way.

Press out carefully on the right side with a hot iron over a damp cloth, without opening the ribbing at all.

MATERIALS

The original "pull-over" took 4 oz. of Baldwin & Walker's Ladyship Shetland Floss (stone) and, of the same make of wool, 4 oz. in scarlet, 3 oz. in white, 1 oz. in jade green, and 1 oz. in yellow, a circular needle No. 8, and a set of No. 10 needles.

MEASUREMENTS

The "pull-over" measures from the shoulder to the lower edge 27 inches, the sleeves 23 inches including the cuff, while the width round the lower edge is 41 inches.

TENSION

The stocking-stitch is worked at a tension to produce about 14½ stitches to 2 inches in width and about 17 rows to 2 inches in depth.

Commence with the No. 10 needles and the stone wool by casting on 288 stitches, and work in rounds of ribbing of 2 plain and 2 purl for 2 inches. Change the needles for the circular one, and the "Fair Isle" pattern will be started; it is worked all the time in plain knitting, except when the stitches are divided for the armhole, then it is worked in stocking-stitch to produce the same effect.

1st round: All stone.

2nd round: All stone.

3rd round: 2 stone, 2 red; repeat all round.

4th round: Same as the 3rd round.

5th round: 2 red, 2 green; repeat all round.

6th round: Same as the 5th round.

7th round: Same as the 3rd round.

8th round: Same as the 3rd round.

9th round: All stone.

10th round: All stone.

11th round: 3 white, 10 red, 3 white; repeat all round, ending with 3 white.

12th round: 2 white, 2 red, 3 white, 2 red, 3 white, 2 red, 2 white; repeat all round, ending with 2 white.

13th round: 1 white, 2 red, 10 white, 2 red, 1 white; repeat all round, ending with 1 white.

14th round: 2 red, 3 white, 2 red, 2 white, 2 red, 3 white, 2 red; repeat all round, ending with 2 red.

15th round: 1 red, 4 yellow, 6 red, 4 yellow, 1 red; repeat all round, ending with 1 red.

16th round: 1 red, 1 yellow, 2 red, 2 yellow, 4 red, 2 yellow, 2 red, 1 yellow, 1 red; repeat all round, ending with 1 red.

17th round: Same as the 16th round.

18th round: Same as the 15th round.

19th round: Same as the 14th round.

20th round: Same as the 13th round.

21st round: Same as the 12th round.

22nd round: Same as the 11th round.

23rd to the 32nd rounds: Same as the 1st to the 10th rounds.

33rd round: 4 white, 1 red, 6 white, 1 red, 4 white; repeat all round, ending with 4 white.

A New Fair Isle Pull Over

• = YELLOW.   / = GREEN.

X = GRAY.   ■ = RED.   □ = WHITE.

34th round: 3 white, 3 red, 4 white, 3 red, 3 white; repeat all round, ending with 3 white.

35th round: 2 white, 2 red, 1 white, 2 red, 2 white, 2 red, 1 white, 2 red, 2 white; repeat all round, ending with 2 white.

36th round: 3 white, 1 red, 2 white, 4 red, 2 white, 1 red, 3 white; repeat all round, ending with 3 white.

37th round: 4 white, 1 red, 2 white, 2 red, 2 white, 1 red, 4 white; repeat all round, ending with 4 white.

38th round: 1 red, 5 yellow, 4 red, 5 yellow, 1 red; repeat all round, ending with 1 red.

39th round: 2 red, 3 yellow, 6 red, 3 yellow, 2 red; repeat all round, ending with 2 red.

40th round: Same as the 39th round.

41st round: Same as the 38th round.

42nd round: Same as the 37th round.

43rd round: Same as the 36th round.

44th round: Same as the 35th round.

45th round: Same as the 34th round.

46th round: Same as the 33rd round.

Repeat this set of patterns twice more, and then repeat from the 1st to the 9th rounds. On the 10th round cast off for underarm 8 stitches, knit in pattern for next 128, then cast off 16, knit the next 128, cast off the last 8. Continue working backwards and forwards in stocking-stitch on one set of 128 stitches to complete the back. Make the patterns fall exactly over the previous ones and repeat from the 11th to the 46th rounds, and then from the 1st to the 8th rounds. On the 9th round knit the first 52 stitches, cast off the following 24 for the back of the neck, work the remaining 52 to the end of the row, then cast off, or, if preferred, graft them to the front when that is completed.

Join the wool, for completing the front, to the other 128 stitches, and work, as for back, up to the 46th row, but take care to make the patterns come exactly over the previous patterns.

Then work 1 row in stone, and on the second row of stone work 52 stitches, cast off the following 24, and work the remaining 52 to the end of the row. Continue working in pattern over the shoulder, but at the inside edge shape for the neck by casting off 3 stitches; then at the neck edge of every other row cast off 1 stitch twice, work another 6 rows; then at the neck edge of the work increase in the same manner as you decreased; then cast off or graft to the back shoulder. Work the other side of the neck and shoulder to correspond.

THE SLEEVES

Commence at the top of the sleeve, with the circular needle or a pair of No. 8 needles, and work in pattern, decreasing 1 stitch both ends of the work every sixth row; repeat the 46 rounds twice, then, from the 1st to the 32nd round (122 rounds in all), work the last 8 rounds without decreasing; there should now be 74 stitches on the needle. Change the needles to No. 10 and work in the stone colour wool only, knit 1, take 2 tog., purl 2 fourteen times, then knit 2, purl 2.

Continue working in ribs of 2 plain and 2 purl for 5½ inches cast off loosely. The other sleeve is worked in the same manner.

THE COLLAR

With the No. 10 needles and the stone-coloured wool cast on 112 stitches, and work in rounds of ribbing in 2 plain and 2 purl for 6½ inches; cast off loosely.

TO MAKE UP

Sew the sleeve seams together, then set into the armhole, sew the collar to the neck. Then finish by pressing the whole of the knitting on the wrong side with a hot iron.

Isn't it trim and tailored enough to please any man? And think how jolly to borrow it when occasion arises. You only have to fasten the buttons t'other way over.

A SLEEVELESS CARDIGAN

IT BUTTONS

It's just a matter of the buttons! Buttonholes are made in the knitting on both bands; the buttons are on a sateen strip which is attached to left front for a lady's wear, and to the right front for a man's wear, as he buttons over from left to right.

MATERIALS—Eight and a half ounces of 4-ply Second Quality Fingering in dark grey, and 2½ ounces in light grey, a pair of long bone knitting-needles No. 10, and two spare needles, six buttons, and a small strip of sateen for the button band.

SIZE AND TENSION.—Working at a tension to produce 7 stitches to the inch in width, the following measurements should be attained after light pressing : Length from shoulder to hem, 26 inches; width all round, including plain knitted bands, 41 inches.

ABBREVIATIONS.—K., knit ; p., purl ; tog., together ; sl., slip ; st., stitch. To decrease 1 at the beginning of a knitted row, k. the first st., then k. 2 tog. To decrease 1 at the end of a knitted row, work until 3 st. remain, then sl. 1, k. 1, pass the sl. st. over, k. the last st. Stocking-stitch is k. 1 row and p. 1 row alternately. Garter-stitch is produced by knitting every row plain.

The Pocket Linings

Cast on 35 st. in dark wool and work in stocking-stitch for 4 inches, the last row being a knitted row. Cut the wool leaving enough to sew three sides of pocket to

garment later. Slip these st. on a spare needle and work the second pocket lining in the same way.

Now cast on 258 st. in dark wool for all round the lower edge of garment.

K. 1 row into the back of cast-on stitches.

K. 11 more rows in garter-stitch and p 1 row. Now work in the pattern as follows :

The Two-Colour Pattern

1st row : K. 3 dark, 2 light, * 4 dark, 2 light ; repeat from *, finishing with 1 dark.

2nd row : P. 2 dark, 2 light, * 4 dark, 2 light ; repeat from *, finishing with 2 dark.

3rd row : K. 1 dark, 2 light, * 4 dark, 2 light ; repeat from *, finishing with 3 dark.

4th row : P. 6 dark, 2 light, * 4 dark, 2 light ; repeat from *, finishing with 4 dark.

5th row : K. 5 dark, 2 light, * 4 dark, 2 light ; repeat from *, finishing with 5 dark.

6th row : P. 4 dark, 2 light, * 4 dark, 2 light ; repeat from *, finishing with 6 dark.

Work 4 rows all dark in stocking-stitch.

11th row : K. 1 dark, 2 light, * 2 dark, 2 light ; repeat from *, finishing with 3 dark.

12th row : P. 1 dark, 2 light, * 2 dark, 2 light ; repeat from *, finishing with 3 dark.

Repeat 11th and 12th rows once more.

Using dark wool, work 4 rows in stocking-stitch.

These 18 rows complete one pattern ; now work from the 1st row to the 15th row, inclusive.

Pocket Row

With dark wool, p. 21, sl. the next 35 st. on a safety-pin, and, in place of these, p. 35 pocket-lining st. from spare needle, p. 146, sl. next 35 on a safety-pin, and in place of these p. 35 pocket-lining st., p. remaining 21 st.

K. 1 row and p. 1 row all dark.

Now repeat the 18 pattern rows 4 times more, then work next pattern to the end of the 4th row.

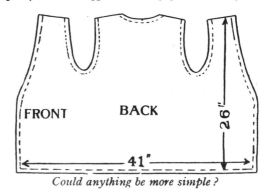

FRONT   BACK   41"   26"

Could anything be more simple ?

FOR SIR OR MADAM!

EITHER WAY

5th pattern row : K. 1, k. 2 tog., k. 60 in pattern. Now sl. these 62 st. on a spare needle for right front, cast off 6 st. for armhole ; k. next 120 st. in pattern and slip on a spare needle for back. Cast off 6 st., k. 60 st. in pattern, sl. 1, k. 1, pass the sl.-st. over, k. 1 (62 st. for left front).

The Left Front

WORK on these 62 st., beginning with the 6th pattern row.

At armhole end of work cast off 2 st. at beginning of every k. row for 5 decreasings, then decrease 1 st. at beginning of every k. row for 5 further decreasings. At the front edge end of k. rows) decrease 1 st. at end of 2 following k. rows. Do not decrease at end of the next k. row. This will give 2 decreasings at front edge in every 6 rows. Take care to follow the pattern correctly while decreasing ; it is quite easy at this stage of the work with such a small pattern. After the armhole decreasings are completed, this end of row can be followed from the two-colour pattern given above.

Continue the front edge decreases until the st. are reduced to 24, then work to end of 14th row of next pattern and cast off.

The Right Front

JOIN wool on purl side of work at armhole end of 62 st. left for the right front, and work the 6th pattern row. Now work to correspond with left front, the armhole decreasings being at end of k. rows and front decreasings at beginning of k. rows.

The Back

JOIN wool on purl side of work to first of 120 st. left for back, and work the 6th pattern row. Continue in pattern, casting off 2 at beginning of every row for next 10 rows. Decrease 1 st. at each end of every k. row for 5 decrease rows. There should now be 90 st. Complete the pattern to end of 18th row, then work the 18 pattern rows twice more. Now work the first 6 pattern rows. Continue in pattern and cast off 5 st. at the beginning of each of the next 8 rows ; then cast off the remaining 50 st.

Pocket Tops

REJOIN the dark wool to 35 st. left on a safety-pin, k. 10 rows, and cast off.

Work the other pocket top in the same way.

The Garter-Stitch Borders

FOR neck and front strip, cast on 8 st. in dark wool and k. 4 rows garter-stitch.

* Next row : K. 3, cast off 2, k. 3

Next row : K. 3, cast on 2, k. 3.

Please forgive us ! She looked so charming, and we were so interested in arranging the cardigan so that the pattern looked well —that nobody noticed she had fastened it up the wrong side over.

K. 24 rows, and repeat from * until 6 buttonholes have been worked.

Now k. for about 31 inches, then work 6 more buttonholes at intervals as before. Work 4 more rows and cast off.

For the armhole borders, cast on 8 st. in dark wool and k. in garter-stitch for about 19 inches, or enough to go round armhole, slightly stretching it. Cast off and work another piece in the same way.

To Make Up

PRESS all parts on the right side (except the neck and armhole garter-stitch strips), using a moderately hot iron over a damp cloth. Sew shoulder seams and sew pocket linings to wrong side and pocket tops to right side of garment. Join up the ends of the short strips and sew one to each armhole putting the join at the under arm and slightly stretching the band at that point. This will press out quite flat if a damp cloth be used. Pin centre of neck border to centre-back of neck, and pin in position at intervals down the fronts : then sew neatly, stretching slightly at back of neck to give a good fit. Make a narrow strip of double sateen, about 16 inches long, and sew the buttons to this at equal distances to correspond with buttonholes. Pass the buttons through the buttonholes on the correct side (according to the wearer) and secure at the two narrow ends of the band.

Press all seams on the wrong side.

A Patterned –
All-over Pull-Over

130 stitches, and work the first 6 rows in garter-stitch. Change the needles to No. 7 and work with the fawn wool in stocking-stitch for 5 rows, then the 1st pattern is started.

FIRST PATTERN

1st row: Plain row, 1 fawn. * 1 blue, 1 fawn, 1 blue, 2 fawn ; repeat from * to the end of the row, ending with 1 fawn.

2nd row : Purl row, 1 fawn, * 1 blue, 1 fawn, 1 blue, 2 fawn ; repeat from * to the end of the row, ending with 1 fawn.

3rd row: Plain row, same as the 1st row.
4th row : Purl row, same as the 2nd row.
5th row : Plain row, same as the 1st row.
6th row : Purl row, same as the 2nd row.
7th row : Plain row, same as the 1st row.
8th row: Purl row, 2 fawn, * 1 blue, 4 fawn ; repeat from * to the end of the row, ending with 2 fawn.

The next 5 rows are worked in the fawn wool in stocking-stitch, then the 2nd pattern starts.

SECOND PATTERN

1st row: Purl row, join on the green wool, and purl with this wool for the whole row.

2nd row : Plain row, * 3 flame, 3 green, 3 flame, 4 green, 1 flame, 4 green ; repeat from * to the end of the row, ending with 1 green.

3rd row: Purl row,* 2 flame, 1 green, 1 flame, 3 green, 1 flame, 1 green, 1 flame, 3 green, 1 flame, 1 green, 2 flame, 1 green ; repeat from * to the end of the row, ending with 1 flame.

4th row : Plain row, * 3 flame, 3 green, 3 flame, 2 green, 1 flame, 3 green, 1 flame, 2 green ; repeat from * to the end of the row, ending with 1 green.

5th row : Purl row, 1 flame, * 1 brown, 1 flame, 2 brown, 1 flame, 1 brown, 1 flame, 1 brown, 1 flame, 1 brown, 1 flame, 2 brown, 1 flame, 1 brown, 3 flame ; repeat from * to the end of the row, ending with 1 brown.

6th row: Plain row, * 3 brown, 1 flame, 1 brown, 1 flame, 3 brown, 1 flame, 3 brown, 1 flame, 3 brown, 1 flame ; repeat from * to the end of the row, ending with 1 flame.

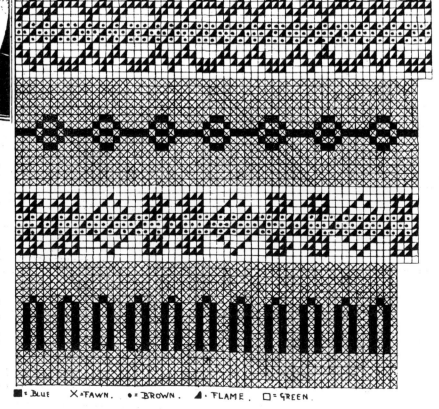

■ =BLUE   X =FAWN.   • =BROWN.   ▲ =FLAME.   □ =GREEN.

MATERIALS

Six ounces of Baldwin & Walker's 4-ply Ladyship Scotch Fingering (fawn) were used to make the " pull-over " pictured on this page, 2 oz. of flame, 2 oz. of saxe-blue, 1 oz. of brown, 2 oz. of green, and a pair of No. 8 needles, also a set of No. 10 needles.

MEASUREMENTS

The " pull-over " measures from the shoulder to the lower edge 25 inches, the sleeves 21½ inches, width, at the lower edge, 41 inches.

TENSION

The stocking-stitch is worked at a tension to produce about 13½ stitches to 2 inches in width, and about 16 rows to 2 inches in depth. The whole of the " pull-over " is worked in stocking-stitch, with the exception of the first and last 6 rows (these are in garter-stitch) and the band for the V neck.

THE BACK

Commence at the lower edge of the back with the fawn wool and the No. 10 needles by casting on

See colour plate on page 136

7th row: Purl row, same as the 5th row.

8th row: Plain row, same as the 4th row.

9th row: Purl row, same as the 3rd row.

10th row: Plain row, same as the 2nd row.

11th row: Purl row, same as the 1st row.

THIRD PATTERN

1st row: Plain row, join on the fawn wool, and knit for the whole row.

2nd row: Purl with the fawn wool for the whole row.

3rd row: Knit with the fawn wool for the whole row.

4th row: Purl with the fawn wool for the whole row.

5th row: Knit with the fawn wool for the whole row.

6th row: Purl row, join on the blue wool, 4 fawn, * 2 blue, 6 fawn; repeat from * to the end of the row, ending with 4 fawn.

7th row: Plain row, 3 fawn, * 1 blue, 2 fawn, 1 blue, 4 fawn; repeat from * to the end of the row, ending with 4 fawn.

8th row: Purl row, 3 blue, * 1 fawn, 2 blue, 1 fawn, 4 blue; repeat from * to the end of the row, ending with 3 blue.

9th row: Plain row, same as the 7th row.

10th row: Purl row, same as the 6th row.

11th row: Plain row, same as the 5th row.

12th row: Purl row, same as the 4th row.

13th row: Plain row, same as the 3rd row.

14th row: Purl row, same as the 2nd row.

15th row: Plain row, same as the 1st row.

FOURTH PATTERN

1st row: Purl row, join on the green wool, and purl with this wool for the whole row.

2nd row: Plain row, 2 green, * 1 flame, 3 green, 3 flame, 3 green; repeat from * to the end of the row, ending with 1 green.

3rd row: Purl row, * 5 flame, 1 green, 3 flame, 1 green; repeat from * to the end of the row, ending with 1 green.

4th row: Plain row, 2 flame, * 1 green, 3 flame, 3 green, 3 flame; repeat from * to the end of the row, ending with 1 flame.

5th row: Purl row, * 5 green, 1 flame, 3 green, 1 flame; repeat from * to the end of the row, ending with 1 flame.

6th row: Plain row, * 1 brown, 1 flame, 1 brown, 1 flame, 1 brown, 1 flame, 3 brown, 1 flame; repeat from * to the end of the row, ending with 1 flame.

7th row: Purl row, 1 brown, * 1 flame, 1 brown, 1 flame, 3 brown, 1 flame, 3 brown; repeat from * to the end of the row, ending with 2 brown.

8th row: Plain row, same as the 6th row.

9th row: Purl row, same as the 5th row.

10th row: Plain row, same as the 4th row.

11th row: Purl row, same as the 3rd row.

12th row: Plain row, same as the 2nd row.

13th row: Purl row, same as the 1st row.

This completes the 4th pattern.

Now repeat the 3rd pattern, then the 2nd pattern, then the 3rd pattern, then the 4th pattern (only work to the centre of the 4th pattern, then work the armhole. At the beginning and the end of the next row cast off 3 stitches either end of the work, then decrease 1 stitch at both ends of the work every third row twice; this to reduce the stitches to 120. Now continue with the 3rd pattern, then the 2nd pattern, and lastly the 3rd pattern. Now the stitches will be cast off for the back of the neck. With right side of the work towards you knit the first 44 stitches, cast off the following 32, and knit the remaining 44 to the end of the row. Now continue over the left shoulder first, leaving the other 44 stitches on the end of your needle. The patterns are carried on down the front, increasing 1 stitch at the neck edge of the work every fourth row, until the stitches number 60, but working the patterns all the time in the same order as the back. Repeat the 3rd pattern again, then the 2nd, then the 3rd, and don't forget to work your armhole increasings to correspond with the back of your work. Then work the 4th pattern; after this is done, leave that side and start to work the other side to correspond. When both sides of

the V neck are worked to the same point, slip all the stitches on to the one needle, and work right across 130 stitches. Now repeat the patterns to match the back of the "pull-over."

THE SLEEVES

Commence at the wrist, with the No. 10 needles, with the fawn wool by casting on 50 stitches, and work the first 6 rows in garter stitch, then change the needle to the No. 7, and work in stocking stitch, increasing 1 stitch at both ends of the work every seventh row until the stitches number 98, then continue without increasing until the sleeve measures 21½ inches, or the length required knitting the pattern all the time in the same order as on the main part of the work; cast off loosely.

The other sleeve is worked in exactly the same manner.

THE BAND FOR NECK

With the set of No. 10 needles pick up 124 stitches round the neck with the fawn wool, commencing in the centre of the V, and work round. Knit in ribs of 2 plain and 2 purl for 7 rows, but always taking the first and last 2 stitches together at the centre of the V. This will form a mitre.

TO MAKE UP

Sew the sleeves in the armholes, then seam up the underarm and side seams.

Press the whole of the garment on the wrong side with a moderately hot iron, especially the seams.

Man's Sweater.

(Medium Size.)

MATERIALS : 1¼ lbs. (20 ozs.) of Paton's Rose Wheeling ; 4 bone needles No. 7 ; 2 steel needles No. 12, for the cuffs.

Measurements : Shoulder to lower edge, 27 inches ; sleeves, including 6-inch cuff, 24½ inches ; neck opening, 21½ inches, without stretching ; width round lower edge of garment at ribbing, 36 inches.

The body part is knitted in stocking-web knitting, in one piece. Sleeves are worked separately and sewn into armholes. The straight collar is knitted on to neck opening in a ribbing to match the lower edge and cuffs.

Do not slip the first stitch of any row unless directed to do so.

Commence at lower edge of front. Use 2 No. 7 needles, cast on 96 stitches, and knit 1 row plain, taking up the back part of each cast-on stitch to make a firm edge.

FIRST 18 ROWS OF RIBBING—* Knit 1, purl 1, repeat from * to end. Ribbing should measure 3 inches. Now commence knitting in stocking-web stitch (that is, 1 row plain, 1 row purl, alternately), as follows : 19TH ROW—Knit plain to end. 20TH ROW—Purl to end. Repeat these 2 rows, ending on a purl row, until work measures 27 inches altogether from commencement. NEXT ROW (neck opening begins)—Knit 24 stitches, cast off loosely next 48 stitches, knit remaining stitches. (Two groups of 24 stitches on the needle with the 48 cast-off stitches between.) NEXT ROW—Purl 24, cast *on* 48 stitches to replace those cast off in previous row, purl last 24 stitches. (96 stitches again on needle.) Continue in stocking-web stitch upon these 96 stitches until a length of 24 inches has been worked, then knit in the ribbing of knit 1, purl 1, alternately, for 3 inches more (18 rows) and cast off.

THE SLEEVES (both alike)—Use No. 7 needles. Cast on 72 stitches. Knit in stocking-web stitch for 10 rows without decrease, ending on a purl row. 11TH ROW—* Decrease at each end of row thus : Knit 1, knit 2 together, knit until 3 stitches remain, then knit 2 together, knit 1. Knit 9 rows without decrease * Repeat from * to * 6 times more. (58 stitches on needle, 80 rows from commencement.) Knit on in stocking-web stitch for 40 rows more without decrease. 120 rows in all. Change to No. 12 needles and commence the ribbing for the cuffs, thus : * Knit 1, purl 1, repeat to end. Repeat this row until 46 rows of ribbing are knitted, measuring 6 inches ; cast off loosely.

THE COLLAR—Commence at centre front of neck-opening, pick up 96 stitches on to *three* No. 7 needles, 32 on each needle. Now work backwards and forwards along the needles in the same ribbing as in cuffs for 30 rows, or until collar measures 5 inches deep. Cast off very loosely.

To MAKE UP—Sew up the side seams as far as 19 inches (leaving an armhole of about 16 inches), join up sleeve seams, reversing the join at the latter part of the cuffs. Sew sleeves into armhole on wrong side of garment, placing seam to seam. Press all seams well with a moderately hot iron. Roll collar over halfway at back, bringing points well down in front, and slightly press. Turn up cuffs 3 inches and also press slightly.

Tie in Open-Work Stitch.

Abbreviations : k., knit ; m., make ; p., purl.

COMMENCE at centre of back. Cast on 18 stitches, and work 1 row plain and 1 row purl alternately for 6 inches. In the last purl row increase to 35 stitches by making 1 between every stitch, thus : * K. 1, m. 1 (by bringing thread forward between needles, and knitting next stitch in usual way), repeat from * until 1 stitch remains, k. 1. 1ST PATTERN ROW—K. 3, * k. 1, m. 1, k. 2 tog., repeat from * until 2 stitches remain, k. 2. 2ND PATTERN ROW—** K. 2, * p. 1, m. 1, p. 2 tog., repeat from * until 3 stitches remain, k. 3. Repeat these 2 pattern rows twice more, then increase each end of row thus : NEXT ROW—K. 2, k. 2 into next stitch (by knitting into back as well as front of stitch before slipping it off needle), * k. 1, m. 1, k. 2 tog., repeat from * until 2 remain, k. 2 into next, k. 1. NEXT ROW (2nd pattern row)— K. 3, * p. 1, m. 1, p. 2 tog., repeat from * until 4 remain, k. 4. NEXT ROW—K. 4,

* k. 1, m. 1 k. 2 tog., repeat from * until 3 remain, k. 3. Work 3 more rows without increase. NEXT ROW—K. 2, k. 2 into next stitch, k. 1, * k. 1, m. 1, k. 2 tog., repeat from * until 3 remain, k. 2 into next, k. 2. NEXT Row (2nd pattern row)—K. 4, * p. 1, m. 1, p. 2 tog., repeat from * until 5 remain, k. 5. NEXT ROW—K. 5, * k. 1, m. 1, k. 2 tog., repeat from * until 4 remain, k. 4. Work 3 more rows without increase. NEXT ROW—K. 2, k. 2 into next stitch, k. 2, * k. 1, m. 1, k. 2 tog., repeat from * until 4 remain, k. 1, k. 2 into next, k. 2 **. Repeat from ** to ** once more. (47 stitches on needle.) Work 2nd pattern row without increase, then repeat the 2 pattern rows without increasing until 13 inches of pattern have been worked. NEXT ROW—Now decrease for shaping to point. K. 3, k. 2 tog., work in pattern until 5 stitches remain, k. 2 tog., k. 3. Decrease thus in every row until there are only 3 stitches left. Cast off. Pick up the 18 stitches at centre back. Work 6 inches in stocking-web knitting, and proceed with pattern as described for the other end, only keeping to the 35 stitches all the way down. No increasings at all (as this is the under side) for 11 inches, then shape for point as described for other end. Cast off.

To MAKE UP—Take a piece of tape about 12 inches long, turn over each side of neckband, and sew to tape, and press all under a slightly damp cloth, pinning ends out to shape.

Materials :
2 ozs. of Pearsall's
Fedora Artificial
Silk.
2 Steel Needles,
No. 16.

Neck Part in Stocking-Web Knitting and the ends in Open Work.

Knee-Caps.

Materials Required.

3 or 4 ozs. Greenock Fingering or Super Fingering, 5-ply. 2 Knitting Needles, size 10 or 11.

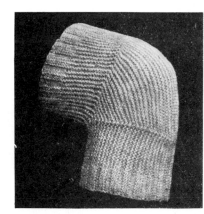

Cast on 49 stitches, and knit the first row plain.

2nd row—Purl 10, knit 29, purl 10.

3rd row—Plain.

4th row—Plain.

5th row—Purl 10, knit 29, purl 10.

6th row—Plain.

Repeat these six rows twice more.

19th row—Knit 24, increase 1, knit 1, increase 1 as before, knit 24.

20th row—Purl 10, knit 31, purl 10.

21st row—Knit 24, increase 1, knit 3, increase 1, knit 24. Now continue thus, always increasing every second row, after knitting the 24th stitch at the commencement, and just before the last 24th on the needle, working the sides in the ribbing until 21 ribs are done ; then knit 6 rows without any increase, still continuing the ribbing, and henceforth in every second row knit 2 together after the first 24 stitches and before the last 24 on the needle so as to decrease in the same way as you before increased. When the 49 stitches are attained, knit 18 rows to correspond with the beginning and cast off. Sew the cast-on to the cast-off stitches, when the knee cap will be complete. Make the other knee cap in the same manner.

Super-soft Fair Isle · For pattern see page 66

Deep-textured crews · For patterns see page 130 (left) and page 139 (right)

Big Aran cardigan · For pattern see page 150

Basket stitch zipper · For pattern see page 142

the 30s

'Never was there a time when so many hand-made garments are knitted for both men and women. Nowadays, if a man has not the choice of two or three pullovers and cardigans, to say nothing of scarves etc. he might quite fairly consider himself to be neglected.' *Bestway Magazine*, 1934.

The Thirties man had to be broad-shouldered, virile and tall. His new silhouette followed the same lines as the woman's. She had changed hers. He must do the same. She emphasized her shoulders with puffed sleeves and accentuated her long legs and slender hips by raising the waistline. Fitted garments showed her curves and revealed her bust. A man now had fullness in the chest. His trousers were cut high-waisted with pleats that fell straight down with a slight taper towards the cuff, while his sweater was very short to tuck into the waistband of trousers or plus fours. The Prince preferred a shaped 'tuck-in' which was 'quite the newest thing'. The V-neck was lowered to look 'athletic'; the low, roomy armholes emphasized the chest. The woolly was a fitted, lightweight affair that required little material, banishing the shapeless tubular garment 'whose excessive warmth was the only excuse for its inelegance'.

Because he was discreet in behaviour and restrained in manner, the well-bred man chose neat patterns and quiet colours of brown, blue and grey. Effeminacy and weakness were scorned. Conversely, 'courage, among all masculine characteristics, gains most admiration and applause from the female of the human species'. A man could no longer 'gad about'; he had to be a good father, a family man. Cary Grant was the best-loved actor—he looked as if he would be 'quite at home sitting with your family round the dinner table'.

A good wife was able to knit her husband all kinds of homely jerseys with names like 'The David Jumper' or 'Jeffrey'. She was now a practised knitter, making difficult garments in fancy stitches to beat the Depression. The favourite type was a sleeveless slipover in cable stitch, which the authorities on men's dress decreed was 'correct' for wear with flannels and plus fours. Though there were many who thought a sleeveless sweater too informal for work, slipovers crept in to replace the waistcoat. Inconspicuous designs that gave a matted effect, in unassuming colours of fawn, old heather or grey, were chosen by most office workers, but adventurous men in the West End of London preferred to wear the new reversible slipover, which displayed a distinct check on one side and diamonds on the other.

'Very mannish' to wear 'when there's some tinkering to be done with the car or the wireless set' was a cardigan fashioned in the new waisted style in grey-blue, fawn or brown. This could also be worn as a lounge jacket when sitting down in the evening with the newspaper. The older men still preferred a straight-sided jacket as a cosy garment 'for golfing, gardening, or just pottering about'. The younger men thought these unwaisted garments cumbersome, 'fitting everywhere yet fitting nowhere'. But both versions had to have a pocket for the pipe.

Canary or hunting yellow was the only intense colour allowed for knitwear. It invaded not only pullovers—a fashion favoured by the university men—but also waistcoats, sleeveless sweaters, cardigans, gloves, scarves, shirts and even woolly combinations. The few black sweaters which appeared around Chelsea and Bloomsbury were worn only because the people there had 'artistic leanings'. Even the long-sleeved Fair Isles, or the slipover version with fitted sleeves, were subdued.

When they knitted 'for the menfolk', women realized that although items of a modern man's wardrobe might have the very latest shapings, they must be strictly conventional in style, 'a feature so important and necessary from the masculine point of view'. But what they lacked in colour could be made up in variety, and just as women had different jerseys 'to rush about town in', 'for Tea-time', or 'the Cinema Jumper', so, too, could a man have a jersey for each occasion.

With the new thirty-hour week, leisure-time for sport was on the increase. Sportswear burgeoned. Women knew that 'no other type of gift is as acceptable as the one that is the result of the patient plying of knitting needles in the hands of mother, friend or fiancée'. For riders and athletes 'who are generally particular about their clothes', a polo-necked pullover, close-fitting but decidedly warm, would be perfect. 'Make it for your own particular hero in cream wool in plain stocking-stich, and let it have a pocket.'

In the early Thirties, the greatest outdoor craze was hiking. 'Everyone is smitten. These people are neither walkers nor ramblers, but something in between. They represent a new spirit in the country which is refreshing to see.' The craze demanded new lightweight clothing that would allow the air to circulate freely. The result was 'absorbant' underwear beneath shorts, and a pullover of basket-stitch. 'Man has realized that weight is not necessarily essential to warmth, and following the Fair Sex, is reducing the weight of his apparel to a minimum.' The new pullovers were well-fitting tuck-ins, knitted in tweed wool to match the socks. Scottish wool in soft marls, mixtures, pastel or two-tones, was considered 'the ideal medium for making a garment destined to keep you in perfect health when you become overheated at your games in a temperature that is below normal.'

Although hikers and cyclists wore 'shorts', the garment only became acceptable on the tennis courts after Bunny Austin appeared so attired in 1934. Correct for both cricket and tennis was a white cable-stitch pullover with club colours banding neck-edge, cuffs and hem. 'With the playing fields and their green grass forming an effective background, HE will appreciate a woollen pullover in bold cream cable patterning. Knit it for him to wear when he slips into flannels and win his appreciative thanks.'

For tennis, badminton and squash, a knitted sports shirt was something new. Made in a fine, soft, close-textured wool such as cashmere, it was styled with a turned-down collar and buttons at the neck. Sleeves were elbow-length, and the whole garment was drawn in with deep ribbing to emphasize the waist. The Prince of Wales often wore a small-collared knitted sports shirt for golf, with the fashionable blue beret pulled well forward. In 1934, golfers in Palm Beach wore navy blue knitted polo-shirts and tan slacks, while those in France chose bright solid-coloured cable pullovers.

The zip-fastener was appearing with great success on a number of modern knitted garments, and in 1934, Prince George and the Prince of Wales started yet another fashion for men when they pioneered the use of zip-fasteners for fly-fronts. Lord Louis Mountbatten is understood to have recommended the idea to the Princes. Their lead was soon followed by thousands in Britain and the United States. The zip-fastener was found to be 'very masculine in style when forming the front opening for the new woollen moss-stitch golfing jacket'. This had a ribbed welt and cuffs, and two pockets to carry safely 'any number of tees'. It could be worn tucked into or outside the trousers. A practical golfing cardigan in tweed wool with a shawl collar and new belted waistline had a 'lightening' zip-fastener front and could be 'slipped on in seconds without the disadvantage of disarranging a well-brushed head of hair'.

Trousers were beginning to deal the death blow to plus fours, though the handsome novelist Mr Frank Swinnerton described them as 'monstrous deflated bags ... why men should wish their legs to resemble the legs of chickens I haven't a notion.' The Prince of Wales stuck to his plus fours, especially those in a prominent check, declaring, 'I believe in bright checks for sportsmen. The louder they are the better I like them.' Meanwhile women adopted plus fours for motor-cycling and other sports, buying sweaters and caps from men's shops to go with them. Both men and women wore grey flannel suits in Hyde Park, and it was not uncommon to see girls and their boyfriends dressed exactly alike.

Today, especially for evening wear, 'men are as vain and as touchy about their clothes as women and as anxious as to the features of style'. Women had changed their hair and eyelashes from straight to curly and admired a man who had curly hair. Many young 'buds', as 'Flappers' were now termed in America, had their hair permanently waved, and encouraged their boyfriends to do the same. The well-groomed man was still clean-shaven, but he might sport a moustache, as that was considered 'very masculine'.

To look slim was now essential. One had to be as slender as a movie-star to go on the fashionable summer cruises or sunbathe on the beach. No longer could a man wear an old mac. or top-coat on the beach without seriously spoiling a holiday or wrecking a romance. He had to look presentable. A man could appear at the seaside in a vivid multi-striped knitted wrap and one-piece bathing suit with a skirt-attachment to cover the trunks. The back of the costume was in Y-formation, a cut-away shape that resembled a pair of braces and was referred to as the 'crab-back'. These suits were made in a special new type of wool that resisted the action of bright sunshine and seawater. Dark browns, black or navy were used for the lower part of the suit, with stripes of red and white for the top. Because a man was still required to cover his chest for swimming, the top part of the costume could be made entirely separate by means of a strap that fastened between the legs and a webbing belt at the waist, all of which could be removed for sun-bathing. Soon the new zip-fasteners could help convert the suit for swimming, by zipping off the top part at the waist.

The Jubilee year of King George V in 1935 saw a fashion for wine-coloured pullovers with flannels of a silvery grey, while the Prince of Wales (to become Edward VIII in that year) was resplendent in checked black-and-yellow plus fours and a glowing yellow roll-necked jersey. Prosperity returned in the second half of the Thirties, bringing with it a wealth of goods to catch a young man's fancy. Fashion was fickle: 'The younger men of today are restless and discontented, which they express in whims and fancies. They turn to dress for stimulation; they tire more quickly of things than they used to.' Fair Isle sweaters appeared in muted shades of rust, natural or dark brown. Cardigans and jackets had a tailored look with patch pockets, knitted half-belts and zip-fastened fronts. The sports shirts with collar attached was knitted in cashmere in soft shades of green, blue or brown—or it might be in silk, 'as chosen by the King' when hunting with the Quorn. In summer, the knitted shirt was of a light unshrinkable crepe wool. Such was a favourite for hot Florida days on the links. Cooler days brought pullovers of cashmere, Shetland or alpaca, in tan, yellow, white or light blue.

Suddenly, Royal influence on fashion ceased. In December of 1936, King Edward abdicated and his younger brother ascended the throne as George VI. *The Tailor and Cutter* commented optimistically: 'the late Monarch was responsible for many innovations ... the new King's tastes may be quieter, but it is likely that they will show a more original trend at a later date.' This was not to be. To celebrate the new Coronation, people knitted slipovers in navy blue with red, white and blue flecks or horizontal stripings. But after that, 'good taste' and a sense of restraint prevailed. Before long, men's fashion in England was unadventurous, and any innovation in dress came from the Continent or the United States.

In America the mood was relaxed and sporty. Sweaters often had leather or rayon fronts with knitted backs and sleeves, or were in a luxurious cashmere, camel hair or alpaca. Zips, pockets and belts adorned the fashionable jacket. At the sea-side in California, sea-slips or 'trunks' could now be worn if one had a good chest, knitted of coarse-knit or alpaca with a herringbone pattern. In Britain, too, trunks made their appearance, as men who objected to a stripey suntan managed to persuade sea-side resorts and public swimming-pools to lift restrictions on exposure of the chest.

Heavy pullovers in quick-to-knit soft wools were the most fashionable mode to come from the Continent. Very exciting and very stylish, they arrived in deep shades of blue, oxblood and mustard. They were worn for anything and everything. On the ski-slopes at St Moritz, big white crew-necked pullovers with knitted skull-caps to match vied with Norwegian flecked or 'reindeer' patterns. On the Riviera in summer, where the mood was informal, knitted jackets had no collars or lapels. The Americans took up the thick-knits for their 'vestovers' which were shaped like a waistcoat but without buttons.

In Britain, too, a more relaxed atmosphere crept in with sportswear. The great craze in the latter part of the Thirties was riding. Tens of thousands of people of moderate means took to horseback in fancy canary waistcoats or slipovers. Or it was 'in order' to leave off the jacket to display a chunky cable polo-neck of bright delphinium blue, green and navy, with handknit gloves to match.

Classic, tailored shapes gained interest with neat, small, honeycombed, diamond or barred designs. Production was in full swing in 1939, and the British were just inventing an intriguing mottled woollen waistcoat that *smelled* of tweed to match the famous Harris tweed suits, when war was declared. Knitting attentions were at once turned elsewhere...

A GIFT FOR A GOLFER

WINDPROOF, AND THE VERY SMARTEST THING IN SPORTSWEAR, IS THE EXTRA THICK WOOL WHICH MAKES THIS JACKET

Undaunted by the wind and the rain is the man who golfs! So see that he is comfortable and well protected in this neat jacket, "Lightning" fastened and ribbed at wrists and waist. It is knitted all in moss-stitch in a new, extra thick wool which works up delightfully quickly.

GOLF JACKET IN CHUBBY WOOL

You will require 1 lb. 12 oz. of Baldwin & Walker's Ladyship Chubby Wool, 2 pairs of knitting needles, Nos. 7 and 11, a 6-inch "Lightning" Fastener, and 2 bone buttons to match the colour of the wool.

MEASUREMENTS

The jacket measures from the shoulder to the lower edge 20 inches, the sleeve seam 20½ inches, and the chest measurement is 41 inches. The moss-stitch is worked at a tension to produce about 9 stitches to 2 inches in width and about 15 rows to 2 inches in depth.

THE BACK

Commence at the lower edge of the back with the No. 7 needles by casting on 80 stitches, then change to the No. 11 needles and work in ribbing of 1 plain and 1 purl for 4 inches.

Now change to the No. 7 needles and work in moss-stitch (1 stitch plain and 1 stitch purl alternately to the end of the row, then on the return row reverse the order of the stitches so that a plain stitch comes over a purl stitch, and vice versa), increasing by working twice into every 8th stitch all along the row, thus increasing the stitches to 90.

Continue in moss-stitch on these 90 stitches until the work measures 13 inches from the start, then the shaping for the armholes will be started.

At the beginning of the next 2 rows cast off 4 stitches, then decrease 1 stitch at both ends of the work every alternate row for 3 times (76 stitches on your needle).

Continue on these 76 stitches, all the time in moss-stitch, without shaping for 5½ inches, then shape for the shoulders as follows:

Next row : Moss-stitch to within 5 stitches from end of row ; turn (always slipping the first stitch after turning).

Next row: Moss-stitch to within 5 stitches from end of row : turn.

Next row: Moss-stitch to within 10 stitches from end of row; turn.

Next row : Moss-stitch to within 10 stitches from end of row ; turn.

Continue working, leaving 5 more stitches unworked at each end until 26 stitches remain in the centre of the work ; then turn, and work to the end of the row ; cast off.

THE FRONT

This is worked exactly the same as for the back as far as the armholes (13 inches from the start).

Next row : Cast off 4 stitches, moss-stitch 40, cast off 2 stitches (for neck opening), moss-stitch to end of row.

Next row : Cast off 4 stitches, moss-stitch 40 ; turn.

Now work on these stitches this half of the neck, decreasing 1 stitch at the sleeve edge of the work every other row for 3 times, then continue without further shaping until the front opening edge measures 6 inches deep.

Now at the neck edge of the work cast off the first 10 stitches. Work to the end of the row. Continue working in moss-stitch, decreasing 1 stitch at the neck edge of the work twice.

Next row : Commencing at the neck edge, work to within 5 stitches from end of row ; turn, work back over the 20 stitches just worked.

Next row : Moss-stitch to within 10 stitches from end of row ; turn, and work back over the 15 stitches just worked.

Next row : Moss-stitch to within 15 stitches from end of row ; turn, and work back over the 10 stitches just worked.

Next row : Moss-stitch 5 ; turn, and work back over the 5 stitches just worked and now cast off.

Rejoin the wool to the neck edge of the other side and work to match.

THE SLEEVES

Commence at the top of the sleeves, with the No. 7 needles, by casting on 18 stitches. Work all the time in moss-stitch, casting on 2 stitches at the beginning of every row until the stitches number 66.

Now decrease 1 stitch at both ends of the work on every 16th row until 50 stitches remain. Then work 10 rows without shaping.

Now change to the No. 11 needles and work in ribbing of 1 plain and 1 purl for 24 rows, then cast off loosely.

Work the second sleeve to match.

THE POCKETS

With the No. 7 needles cast on 25 stitches. Work in moss-stitch for 32 rows without shaping, then decrease 1 stitch at both ends of the work every other row for 3 times (19 stitches on your needle.) Then cast off rather tightly. Work the second pocket to match.

THE POCKET FLAP

With the No. 7 needles cast on 26 stitches and work in moss-stitch for 10 rows.

Next row : Knit 2 together, moss-stitch 9, cast off 4 stitches (for buttonhole), moss-stitch 9, knit 2 together.

Next row : Knit 2 together, moss-stitch 8, cast on 4 stitches, moss-stitch 8, knit 2 together.

Now continue working in moss-stitch, decreasing 1 stitch at both ends of the work every row until only 8 stitches remain, then cast off.

Work the second flap to match.

THE COLLAR

Before picking up the stitches for the collar, join the shoulders together, using cotton to match the wool. Pick up 65 stitches round the neck with the No. 7 needles, and work in moss-stitch, increasing 1 stitch at the end of every row until the stitches number 81, then cast off fairly loosely.

TO MAKE UP

Press all the knitting well on the wrong side with a hot iron over a damp cloth, sew the sleeves flat into the armholes, tack the pockets into position about 2¾ inches from the centre front and 1½ inches above the waist ribbing. Then machine round 3 sides of the pocket, and also machine the flap into position across the top of the pocket. Sew the button to correspond with the button-hole. Sew the "Lightning" fastener to the front opening, then sew up the under-arm and side seams. Press all the seams very flat on the wrong side.

Pockets are important to a golfer. This jacket has two flap ones, to carry safely any number of tees and

To ensure snugness at waist and wrists, thinner needles are used for the ribbing than for the rest of the garment.

THE SORT OF CARDIGAN FATHER LIKES

THE father of the family often feels happier in a knitted coat than anything. He will be certain to like this ribbed cardigan, trim and smart because of its extreme simplicity. In grey, or a soft shade of brown, it will look well with his lounge suits and sports clothes alike.

You will require 17 oz. of Baldwin & Walker's 4-ply Ladyship Konort Fingering, two pairs of knitting needles Nos. 10 and 12, also 6 bone buttons about the size of a shilling to match the wool, and a reel of buttonhole twist also to match the wool.

MEASUREMENTS

The cardigan measures from the shoulder to the lower edge 23½ inches, the sleeve seam 21 inches, and the chest measurement is 37 inches. The knitting, worked with the No. 10 needles and after pressing, produces about 18 stitches to 2½ inches in width and about 17 rows to 2 inches in depth.

To increase, knit into the front and then into the back of a stitch before slipping it off.

To decrease, knit 2 stitches together.

Always work into the back of all cast-on stitches.

Always slip the first stitch of a row when possible.

THE BACK

With the No. 12 needles commence at the lower edge of the back by casting on 180 stitches. Knit in ribbing of 1 plain and 1 purl for 20 rows, working into the back of the stitches for the first row.

Now change to the No. 10 needles.

Next row : * Knit 2, knit 2 together ; repeat from * to the end of the row (you will now have 135 stitches on your needle).

Next row : All purl.

1st pattern row : Slip 1, knit 3, purl 1, * knit 8, purl 1 ; repeat from * until 4 stitches remain, then knit 4.

2nd pattern row : Slip 1, purl 3, knit 1, * purl 8, knit 1 ; repeat from * until 4 stitches remain, then purl 4.

Continue repeating the 2 pattern rows until the work measures 15 inches in depth. Now begin the armholes by casting off 8 stitches at the beginning of each of the next 2 rows, then decrease 1 stitch at both ends of alternate rows for 8 times.

Now work 55 rows without shaping, and end with the 2nd of the 2 pattern rows. Here start the shoulder shaping by casting off 5 stitches at the beginning of every row for 12 rows, then loosely cast off the remaining stitches.

THE POCKET PIECES

With the No. 10 needles cast on 33 stitches and work in stocking-stitch (1 row plain and 1 row purl alternately) for 34 rows. Cut the wool and slip these stitches on to a spare needle.

Work another piece to match and then put both of them aside for the moment.

THE LEFT FRONT

With the No. 12 needles commence at the lower edge by casting on 90 stitches. Work in ribbing of 1 plain and 1 purl for 20 rows.

Now change to the No. 10 needles.

Next row : Knit 2 together for 10 times, knit 2, * knit 2 together, knit 2 ; repeat from * to the end of the row (63 stitches on your needle).

Next row : All purl.

Now work as described in the 2 pattern rows of the back for 34 rows.

Next row : Work the 15 stitches in pattern, slip off the next 33 stitches on to a stitch-holder for the pocket. Now knit in one of the pocket pieces and then finish the remaining 15 stitches in pattern.

Continue in pattern until your work matches in length (by number of rows) the back from the lower edge to the beginning of the armhole, and end with the 2nd pattern row.

Next row : With the right side of the work towards you, cast off 8 stitches for the armhole. Work in pattern until 2 stitches remain, then decrease for the neck opening.

Continue working in pattern and decrease at the neck edge in every 4th row for 17 times altogether, then work this edge straight. Meanwhile, decrease at the armhole edge in alternate rows for 8 times altogether, and then work this edge straight for 64 rows, ending with the wool at the armhole edge. Now cast off 3 stitches from the armhole end in alternate rows until no stitches remain, then fasten off.

With the No. 12 needles take off the 33 stitches left for the pocket.

Next row : With the right side of the work towards you, * knit 2, increase in the next stitch ; repeat from * to the end of the row (44 stitches). Now work 10 rows in ribbing of 1 plain and 1 purl, then cast off rather firmly in ribbing.

THE RIGHT FRONT

Commence and work the ribbing as described for the left front and then with the No. 10 needles work as follows :

Next row : Knit 2, * knit 2 together, knit 2 ; repeat from * until 20 stitches remain, then knit 2 together for 10 times (63 stitches on your needle).

Next row : All purl.

Now work the rest of the front to correspond with the left front, but work the shapings in rows with the wrong side of the work towards you to avoid getting both fronts for the same side.

THE SLEEVES

Commence at the cuff edge with the No. 12 needles by casting on 60 stitches, and work in ribbing of 1 plain and 1 purl for 40 rows.

Now change to the No. 10 needles and knit plain, increasing 1 stitch at the beginning of the row, 1 stitch in the centre, and 1 stitch at the end, so as to make the stitches number 63.

Next row : All purl.

Now work the rest of the sleeve in pattern as described for the two pattern rows of the back, but increase 1 stitch at both ends of every 6th row for 24 times (111 stitches on your needle).

Work 5 rows more after the 24th increasing row, then decrease at both ends of every row for 40 rows, then cast off the remaining stitches.

Work the second sleeve to match.

THE STRAPPING

With the No. 12 needles cast on 16 stitches. Work in ribbing of 1 plain and 1 purl until the strap is 46 inches long.

1st buttonhole row : Work 8 stitches in ribbing, cast off 6, work in ribbing to the end of the row.

2nd buttonhole row : Work 2 stitches in ribbing, cast on 6 stitches, work remaining 8 stitches in ribbing.

* Now work 24 rows in ribbing, then repeat the two buttonhole rows.

Repeat from * until you have 6 buttonholes altogether.

Now work 14 rows of ribbing and then firmly cast off in ribbing.

TO MAKE UP

Lay each piece downwards and pin out the edges, normally stretching to a good shape and the correct size. Press well with a hot iron over a damp cloth, but omit the ribbing. After making up, press all the seams on the wrong side. Work round the buttonholes with the twist.

Extra simple in making as well as in style, this coat is knitted in ribbing which fits perfectly without the aid of underarm decreasings.

FOR GOLFING, GARDENING OR JUST "POTTERING AROUND." THE OLDER MAN PREFERS A SIMPLE KNITTED JACKET

"JEFFREY" Design

Every man needs a polo-necked sweater for sports wear. Knit this in White for tennis and the river, in a colour for golf and riding, and the result will be just what is wanted. The rib is both unusual and attractive, but simplicity itself to follow.

MEASUREMENTS:
Round Chest, 38 inches.
Length from shoulder, 23 inches.
Sleeve seam, 21 inches (with cuff turned back).

MATERIALS.
12 ozs. "Femina" Botany Fingering Wool, 4 ply.
2 No. 8 Bairns-Wear Knitting Needles.
Set of 4 No. 10 Needles pointed at both ends.

ABBREVIATIONS.
K. = knit, p. = purl, st. = stitch, tog. = together.

TENSION.
$6\frac{1}{2}$ sts. to one inch.

BACK. Cast on 120 sts. and work in (k. 2, p. 2) rib for 2 inches. Now change to the following pattern :—

1st row. (Wrong side of work.) Slip 1 knitways, p. 2, * k 4, p. 2, k. 2, p. 2, repeat from * to the last 7 sts., k. 4, p. 2, k. 1.

2nd row. Slip 1 knitways, k. 2, * p. 4, k. 2, p. 2, k. 2, repeat from * to the last 7 sts., p. 4, k. 3.

3rd row. Slip 1 knitways, * p. 2, k. 2, repeat from * to the last 3 sts., p. 2, k. 1.

4th row. Slip 1 knitways, * k. 2, p. 2, repeat from * to the last 3 sts., k. 3.

These 4 rows form the pattern. Repeat them until the work measures 15 inches including the rib. Now shape the armholes by casting off 10 sts. at the beginning of each of the next 2 rows, then knitting 2 sts. tog. at the beginning and end of every row until there are 92 sts. Continue on these sts. until the work measures $22\frac{1}{2}$ inches from the commencement. Now cast off 7 sts. at the beginning of every row until there are 36 sts. Cast off.

FRONT. Cast on and work as for the back until the sts. have been reduced to 92 at the armholes. Continue without

further shaping until the work measures 20 inches from the commencement. Now shape the neck as follows :—Work 33 sts., cast off 26, work to the end. Leave the other 33 sts. on a holder until later and work on the last 33 sts., knitting 2 tog. at the neck edge on every row until there are 28 sts. Then work without further shaping until the armhole is the same depth as the back armhole. Now cast off 7 sts. at the armhole edge on every other row until there are no sts. left. Return to the other side and work to correspond.

SLEEVES. Cast on 60 sts. and work in (k. 2, p. 2) rib for 6 inches. Change to the pattern and increase 1 st. at the beginning and end of the first and every following 8th row until there are 96 sts. Continue without shaping until the work measures 24 inches including the cuff. To shape the top, k. 2 sts. tog. at the beginning and end of the next 6 rows, then k. 2 tog. at the beginning and end of every 2nd row until there are 40 sts. Cast off. Work a second sleeve in the same way.

COLLAR. Join the shoulder seams. Knit up 116 sts. evenly round the neck on 3 No.

14 needles, 40 on 2 and 36 on the 3rd, and work in (k. 2, p. 2) rib for 6 inches. Cast off loosely in rib.

TO MAKE UP. Do not press the work. Join side and sleeve seams. Sew in sleeves, placing seam to seam. Turn back the cuffs and turn down the collar.

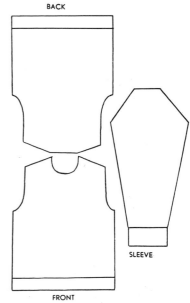

This diagram is given to show the shape of each part of the garment.

RIGHT WITH TOWN OR COUNTRY CLOTHES

THE MAN WHO PREFERS A PULLOVER TO A WAISTCOAT WILL LIKE THE NEAT SHAPING OF THIS DESIGN

THE pullover that is to replace a waistcoat must be well fitting and unobtrusive. Here is an ideal design for the purpose—plus that "extra little something" in its clever fancy stitching which will appeal to the young man of to-day. Grey, grey-blue, and brown are colours which will be likely to tone with several suits, and look equally smart with workaday lounge suits and country tweeds.

You will require 6 oz. of Baldwin & Walker's 4-ply Ladyship Scotch Fingering and a pair of No. 10 and No. 12 knitting needles.

MEASUREMENTS

The pullover measures from the shoulder to the lower edge 24 inches, round the chest 36 inches (unstretched).

The knitting is worked at a tension to produce about 6½ stitches to 1 inch in width and about 10 rows to 1 inch in depth.

THE BACK

With the No. 10 needles commence at the lower edge of the back by casting on 100 stitches. Work in ribbing of 1 plain and 1 purl for 3 inches.

Now work 10 rows in garter-stitch (plain knitting).

11th row : * Knit 5, purl 5 ; repeat from * to the end of the row.

12th row : Purl 1, * knit 5, purl 5 ; repeat from * to the end of the row, ending with purl 4.

13th row : Knit 3, * purl 5, knit 5 ; repeat from * to the end of the row, ending with knit 2.

14th row : Purl 3, * knit 5, purl 5 ; repeat from * to the end of the row, ending with purl 2.

15th row : Knit 1, * purl 5, knit 5 ; repeat from * to the end of the row, ending with knit 4.

16th row : * Purl 5, knit 5 ; repeat from * to the end of the row.

17th row : Knit 1, * purl 5, knit 5 ; repeat from * until 4 stitches remain, then knit 4.

18th row : Purl 3, * knit 5, purl 5 ; repeat from * until 2 stitches remain, then purl 2.

19th row : Knit 3, * purl 5, knit 5 ; repeat from * until 2 stitches remain, then knit 2.

20th row : Purl 1, * knit 5, purl 5 ; repeat from * until 4 stitches remain, then purl 4.

21st row : * Knit 5, purl 5 ; repeat from * to the end of the row.

Now repeat from the 12th to the 16th rows, then knit 10 rows in garter-stitch.

37th row : * Knit 9, purl 1 ; repeat from * to the end of the row.

38th row : Knit 2, * purl 7, knit 3 ; repeat from * until 8 stitches remain, then purl 7, knit 1.

39th row : Purl 2, * knit 5, purl 5 ; repeat from * until 8 stitches remain, then knit 5, purl 3.

40th row : Knit 4, * purl 3, knit 7 ; repeat from * until 6 stitches remain, then purl 3, knit 3.

41st row : Purl 4, * knit 1, purl 9 ; repeat from * until 6 stitches remain, then knit 1, purl 5.

42nd row : Knit 4, * purl 3, knit 7 ; repeat from * until 6 stitches remain, then purl 3, knit 3.

43rd row : Purl 2, * knit 5, purl 5 ; repeat from * until 8 stitches remain, then knit 5, purl 3.

44th row : Knit 2, * purl 7, knit 3 ; repeat from * until 8 stitches remain, then purl 7, knit 1.

45th row : Knit 9, * purl 1, knit 9 ; repeat from * until 10 stitches remain, then knit 9, purl 1.

46th row : Knit 2, * purl 7, knit 3 ; repeat from * until 8 stitches remain, then purl 7, knit 1.

47th row : Purl 2, * knit 5, purl 5 ; repeat from * until 8 stitches remain, then knit 5, purl 3.

48th row : Knit 4, * purl 3, knit 7 ; repeat from * until 6 stitches remain, then purl 3, knit 3.

49th row : Purl 4, * knit 1, purl 9 ; repeat from * until 6 stitches remain, then knit 1, purl 5 **

Now repeat from the 42nd row to the 45th row, then work 10 rows in garter-stitch.

Now repeat from ** to **, then work 4 rows in garter-stitch.

Here you commence to shape for the armholes, keeping to the pattern all the time, and knitting 2 stitches together at both ends of the work every row for 10 times. Then continue all the time in pattern as for the commencement of the pullover until the work measures 8½ inches from the start of the armhole shaping.

Next row : Knit to within 8 stitches from end of row ; turn, knit back to within 8 stitches from end of row.

Next row : Knit to within 16 stitches from end of row ; turn, knit back to within 16 stitches from end of row.

Next row : Knit to within 24 stitches from end of row ; turn, knit back to within 24 stitches from end of row.

Next row : Knit across all the stitches.

Next row : Cast off the first 29 stitches, knit 22, cast off the remaining 29 stitches. Slip the centre 22 stitches on to a stitch-holder ready to pick up for the neckband.

THE FRONT

With the No. 10 needles commence at the lower edge of the front by casting on 120 stitches. Work in ribbing of 1 plain and 1 purl for 3 inches. Now continue in pattern as for the back until the work is the same depth as the back till the armhole, is reached.

Here you see how simple the design really is—just patterns in plain and purl, separated by rows of garter-stitch.

Next row : Knit 1, knit 2 together. Knit to within 3 stitches from end of row then knit 2 together, knit 1.

Repeat the last row 3 times more (4 rows in all).

Next row : Knit 1, knit 2 together, knit 53. Now join on another ball of wool to work the other side of the V front, knit 53, knit 2 together, knit 1.

Next row : Knit 1, knit 2 together, knit 49, knit 2 together, knit 1. Now the other side of the V, knit 1, knit 2 together, knit 49, knit 2 together, knit 1.

Next row : Purl 1, purl 2 together, purl 2, * knit 5, purl 5 ; repeat from * to within 3 stitches of the end, purl 3. Now the other side of the V, * knit 5, purl 5 ; repeat from * to within 3 stitches of the end, knit 2 together, knit 1.

Next row : Purl 1, purl 2 together, * knit 5, purl 5 ; repeat from * to V, ending with purl 4. The other side of the V, knit 4, * purl 5, knit 5 ; repeat from * to within 3 stitches of the end, knit 2 together, knit 1.

Next row : Knit 1, knit 2 together, knit 3, * purl 5, knit 5 : repeat from * to V, ending with purl 5. The other side of the V, knit 3, * purl 5, knit 5 ; repeat from * to within 3 stitches of the end, knit 2 together, knit 1.

Next row : Purl 1, purl 2 together, * knit 5, purl 5 ; repeat from * to V, ending with purl 2. The other side of the V, purl 1, * knit 5, purl 5 ; repeat from * to within 3 stitches of the end, purl 2 together, purl 1.

Next row : Knit 1, purl 2 together, purl 4, * knit 5, purl 5 ; repeat from * to within 3 stitches of V, knit 2 together, knit 1. The other side of the V, purl 1, purl 2 together, purl 3, * knit 5, purl 5 ; repeat from * to within 3 stitches of the end, knit 2 together, knit 1.

Next row : Purl 1, purl 2 together, * knit 5, purl 5 : repeat from * to V, ending with knit 4. The other side of the V, purl 2, * knit 5, purl 5 ; repeat from * to within 3 stitches of the end, knit 2 together, knit 1.

Next row : Purl 1, purl 2 together, purl 2, * knit 5, purl 5 ; repeat from * to V, ending with knit 1. The other side of the V, * purl 5, knit 5 : repeat from * to within 3 stitches of the end, purl 2 together, purl 1.

Next row : Knit 1, knit 2 together, knit 1, * purl 5, knit 5 : repeat from * to V, ending with purl 1. The other side of the V, * knit 5, purl 5 ; repeat from * to within 3 stitches of the end, knit 2 together, knit 1.

Next row : * Purl 5, knit 5 ; repeat from * to V, ending with purl 4. The other side of the V, knit 2, * purl 5, knit 5 ; repeat from * to end.

Next row : Knit 1, * purl 5, knit 5 ; repeat from * to V, ending with purl 2 together, purl 1. The other side of the V, knit 1, knit 2 together, * purl 5, knit 5 ; repeat from * to end.

Next row : Knit 2, * purl 5, knit 5 ; repeat from * to V, ending with purl 1. The other side of the V, knit 3, * purl 5, knit 5 ; repeat from * to end.

Next row : Knit 1, * purl 5, knit 5 ; repeat from * to V. The other side of the V, knit 2, * purl 5, knit 5 ; repeat from * to end of row.

Next row : * Purl 5, knit 5 ; repeat from * to V. The other side of the V, knit 1, * purl 5, knit 5 ; repeat from * to end of row.

Next row : Knit 3, * purl 5, knit 5 ; repeat from * to centre. The other side of the V, knit 4, * purl 5, knit 5 ; repeat from * to end of row.

Next row : Purl 3, * knit 5, purl 5 ; repeat from * to V, ending with purl 2 together, purl 1. The other side of the V, purl 1, purl 2 together, purl 1, * knit 5, purl 5 ; repeat from * to end of row.

Next row : * Knit 5, purl 5 ; repeat from * to V. The other side of the V, * knit 5, purl 5 ; repeat from * to end of row.

Next row : Knit plain both sides of the V.

Next row : Knit plain both sides of the V.

Next row : Knit plain both sides of the V.

Next row : Knit plain to within 3 stitches from the centre, then knit 2 together, knit 1. Now on the other side of the V, knit 1, knit 2 together, knit to end of row.

Next row : Knit plain both sides of the V.

Next row : Knit plain both sides of the V.

Next row : Knit plain both sides of the V.

Next row : Knit plain both sides of the V.

Next row : Knit plain to within 3 stitches of the centre, then knit 2 together, knit 1. Now on the other side of the V, knit 1, knit 2 together, knit to end of row.

Next row : Knit plain both sides of the V.

Next row : Knit 6, * purl 1, knit 9 ; repeat from * to the centre. Now on the other side of the V, knit 4, ** purl 1, knit 9 ; repeat from ** to the end of the row.

Next row : Purl 4, * knit 3, purl 7 ; repeat from * to the centre. Now on the other side of the V, purl 2, ** knit 3, purl 7 ; repeat from ** to the end of the row.

Next row : Knit 4, * purl 5, knit 5 ; repeat from * to the centre. Now on the other side of the V, knit 2, ** purl 5, knit 5 ; repeat from ** to the end of the row.

Next row : Purl 2, * knit 7, purl 3 ; repeat from * to within 3 stitches from the centre, then knit 2 together, knit 1. Now on the other side of the V, knit 1, knit 2 together, knit 4, ** purl 3, knit 7 ; repeat from ** to the end of the row.

Now continue in pattern, decreasing 1 stitch at the neck edge every 5th row until only 29 stitches remain. Then shape for the shoulders, working all the time in garter-stitch on one side of the V.

Next row : Knit to within 8 stitches from the armhole end of the row ; turn.

Next row : Knit to the neck edge.

Next row : Knit to within 16 stitches from armhole edge of work ; turn.

Next row : Knit to the neck edge.

Next row : Knit to within 24 stitches from the armhole edge of work ; turn.

Next row : Knit to the neck edge, then cast off.

Work the other side of the neck to correspond. Join the shoulders together back and front, also the side seams.

THE NECKBAND

Join the wool to the centre of the V neck and with the set of No. 12 needles pick and knit 85 stitches on one side of the V. Now slip the 22 stitches from the stitch-holder on to another needle, and with the second needle knit these 22 stitches, with the third needle pick up and knit 85 stitches the other side of the V.

Next round : Work in ribbing of 2 plain and 2 purl all round.

Next 8 rounds : Work in ribbing of 2 plain and 2 purl, knitting 2 stitches together twice in the centre of the V, then cast off.

Sew together the shoulder and side seams.

THE ARMHOLE BAND

With the set of No. 12 needles pick up and knit 148 stitches round each armhole, and work in ribbing of 2 plain and 2 purl for 8 rounds, then cast off.

Press on the wrong side with a hot iron over a damp cloth.

TWO-WAY PULLOVER

You Can Make it with a Polo Collar or with a V-neck Opening

SOME men find a polo-necked pullover a most comfortable garment to wear when motoring, riding, cycling or playing golf. Others like a pullover to have a simple V-necked opening.

Here are given the instructions for making a warm pullover in whichever style is preferred. The polo collar and neck inset can be omitted in favour of a simple ribbed band at the V neckline. The patterned surface of the garment gives it distinction.

MATERIALS REQUIRED

11 oz. Baldwin and Walker's 4-ply Ladyship Scotch Fingering.
1 pair knitting needles, No. 8.
1 pair knitting needles, No. 11.

Measurements. — Length, from shoulder to lower edge, 21 inches. Length of sleeve, from shoulder, 25 inches. Length of sleeve seam, including cuff, 21 inches. Width all round below the underarms, without stretching, should be 38 inches.

To fit a 38 to 41 chest measurement.

Tension.—Pattern on No. 8 needles, before pressing, seven stitches to 1 inch in width; 8 rows to 1 inch in depth.

Alteration in Size.—For a larger garment use thicker needles, or a size which produces fewer stitches to the inch. For a smaller garment use finer needles, or a size which produces more stitches to the inch.

Abbreviations.—K, knit; P, purl; sts., stitches; tog., together; pat., pattern; inc., increase; dec., decrease; beg., beginning.

THE BACK.

Using the No. 11 needles, begin at the lower edge of the back by casting on 126 sts., and work in the rib of K 1, P 1 for 2⅜ inches, working into the back of all the *knit* sts.

Change to the No. 8 needles and the pat., as follows : —

1st row.—* K 9, P 9. Rep. from * to end of row. Rep. this row 8 times more.

10th row.—* P 9, K 9. Rep. from * to end of row. Rep. this row 8 times more.

These 18 rows form the pattern.

Continue in the pat. until you have worked 5 patterns in all, when the work should measure 13¼ inches from the cast-on edge.

To Shape the Armholes.—Keeping the pattern correct throughout, cast off 3 sts. from the beg. of each of the next 8 rows.

Continue in the pat. on the remaining 102 sts. until the armhole measures 7 inches on the straight, *i.e.,* from where the first 3 sts. were cast off.

To Shape the Neck.—Work in the pat. over 42 sts., cast off 18 sts., pat. 42.

Work on the last 42 sts. in the pat., casting off 3 sts. from the beg. of every neck edge row until 30 sts. remain.

To Shape the Shoulder.—Cast off 10 sts. from the beg. of each armhole end row until all are cast off.

Join the wool to the neck edge of the remaining 42 sts., and work to correspond with the first shoulder.

THE FRONT.

Using the No. 11 needles, begin at the lower edge by casting on 126 sts., and work in exactly the same way as stated for the back, until the armhole shaping is completed and 102 sts. remain on the needle.

Work in the pat. over 51 sts., and place the remaining 51 sts. on a spare needle.

Work on the first 51 sts. in the pat., decreasing 1 st. at the neck edge on every alternate row, until 30 sts. remain, then work without dec. until the armhole measures the same as for that of the back, *i.e.,* 7 inches on the straight.

Shape the shoulder by casting off 10 sts. from the beg. of each armhole end row, until all are cast off.

Join the wool to the neck edge of the remaining 51 sts., and work to correspond.

THE SLEEVES (both alike).

Using the No. 11 needles, begin at the cuff edge by casting on 63 sts., and work in the rib of K 1, P 1—working into the back of all knit sts.—for 2⅜ inches.

Change to the No. 8 needles and the pat., as follows : —

1st row.—K 5, * P 9, K 9. Rep. from * to the last 4 sts., P 4.

2nd row.—K 4, * P 9, K 9. Rep. from * to the last 5 sts., P 5.

Rep. these 2 rows 3 times more, then the 1st row again.

10th row.—P 4, * K 9, P 9. Rep. from * to the last 5 sts., K 5.

11th row.—P 5, * K 9, P 9. Rep. from * to the last 4 sts., K 4.

Rep. these 2 rows 3 times more, then the 10th row again.

These 18 rows complete 1 pat.

Continue to work in the pat., increasing 1 st. at both ends of the needle on the next, then every following 9th row, until the sts. are increased to 91, taking care to work the increased sts. in the pat. as the work proceeds.

Continue in the pat. without increase until the sleeve seam measures 20 inches, then cast off 2 sts. from the beg. of every row until 15 sts. remain.

Cast off.

THE INSET COLLAR.

Using the No. 11 needles, begin by casting on 130 sts., and work in the rib of K 1, P 1 for 4 inches, working into the back of all knit sts.

To Shape Inset. — *1st row.*—* Rib 6 (K 1, P 1, K 1) all into the next st., rib 6. Rep. from * to the end of row. (150 sts. on the needle.)

Work in the rib for 7 rows.

9th row.—Cast off 36 sts., rib to end of row.

10th row.—Cast off 36 sts., rib to end of row.

Continue to work on the remaining 78 sts. in the rib, decreasing 1 st. at both ends of the needle on every alternate row until 6 sts. remain, then dec. 1 st. at both ends of the needle on every row until all the sts. are worked off.

FOR "V" NECK.

If the garment is preferred with the ordinary "V" neck, omit the instructions for the Inset Collar, and, in place of these, work as follows : —

Using a set of four No. 11 needles, with the right side of work towards you, work up 51 sts. down the left side of front neck opening, beginning at the shoulder seam. With a second needle, work up 51 sts. up the other side of neck opening; and, with a third needle, work up 54 sts. from shoulder to shoulder across the back of the neck, making 156 sts. in the round.

Work in the rib of K 1, P 1—working into the back of all knit sts—and, on the first round, pick up and P 1 st. at the centre "V" of neck. (This st. should be purl on every round.)

Work 11 rounds in the rib, decreasing 1 st. on each side the centre "V" st. on every round.

Cast off loosely, still continuing to work in the rib.

TO MAKE UP.

Press on the wrong side with a hot iron over a damp cloth, but do not press any of the ribbed parts, or you will find that they slightly stretch and lose their neat appearance and good fit.

Sew up the shoulder seams, and sew the sleeves into the armholes. Press these seams, then sew up the side and sleeve seams.

Neatly sew in the "Inset" and the collar to the neck, and carefully press the seams.

Knit-Wear for MEN

Next row : Knit 6, * purl 2, knit 2 ; repeat from * until 6 stitches remain, then knit 6.

Next row : Knit 8, * purl 2, knit 2 ; repeat from * until 8 stitches remain, then knit 8.

Repeat these last 2 rows 7 times more.

Next row : All plain.

Next row : Knit 6, purl 38, knit 6.

Repeat the last 2 rows for 50 inches, ending with the row knit 6, purl 38, knit 6.

For the next 16 rows work the centre 38 stitches in ribbing of 2 purl and 2 plain, keeping the first and last 6 stitches of every row in garter-stitch, and finish the scarf with 8 rows of garter-stitch ; cast off rather loosely.

Below you see a close-up of the muffler that is knitted in stocking-stitch for the main part.

THE SCARF

You will require 4 oz. of Baldwin & Walker's 4-ply Ladyship Konort Fingering and a pair of No. 8 needles.

MEASUREMENTS

The scarf measures 55 inches long and about 8¼ inches wide.

The stocking-stitch is worked at a tension to produce about 12 stitches to 2 inches in width and about 15 rows to 2 inches in depth after pressing.

Commence by casting on 50 stitches. Knit into the back of the stitches for the first row, then work 8 rows in garter-stitch (plain knitting).

AN INGENIOUS SUIT FOR SUN AND SEA

A "LIGHTNING" FASTENER AT THE WAIST QUICKLY CONVERTS THESE TRUNKS FOR SUNNING INTO A SUIT FOR SWIMMING

You will require 8 oz. of Baldwin & Walker's Ladyship Holiday Wool in royal blue, two pairs of knitting needles Nos. 10 and 11, also a "Lightning" Fastener 6 inches long.

THERE is just as much thrill in planning next summer's swim suits as in discussing next summer's holidays. Here is a clever design which will meet with hearty approval from the modern man. He will so much prefer just "zipping off" the top to wearing a wet, clammy costume round his waist after his swim.

MEASUREMENTS
The shorts, all round the widest part, 38 inches; from the waist to the lower edge of leg, 14 inches; the waist 25 to 30 inches. The top part, from the shoulder to the fastener, 16½ inches; all round the body, 28 inches. The stocking-stitch is worked at a tension to produce about 7 stitches to 1 inch in width and about 9 rows to 1 inch in depth, worked with the No. 10 needles and after pressing.

To increase, knit into the front and then into the back of a stitch before slipping it off.

To decrease, knit 2 stitches together.

Always work into the back of all cast-on stitches.

Always slip the first stitch of a row when possible.

THE FRONT OF SHORTS
With the No. 11 needles commence at the lower edge of one leg by casting on 64 stitches. Knit in ribbing of 1 plain and 1 purl for 14 rows, working into the back of the stitches for the first row.

Now change to the No. 10 needles.

Continue in stocking-stitch (1 row plain and 1 row purl alternately) for 30 rows ending with a purl row. Cut the wool and slip these stitches on a spare needle while you work another piece to match.

Next row : Knit across the work you have just done, and then across the piece first worked, making 128 stitches on one needle, thus joining them together.

Next row : All purl.

Now work 26 rows in stocking-stitch, without shaping, ending with a purl row.

Next row : Knit 4, slip 1, knit 1, pass slipstitch over. Now knit until only 6 stitches remain, then knit 2 together, knit 4.

Next row : All purl.

Next row : All plain.

Next row : All purl.

Repeat the last 4 rows 9 times more, making 10 decreasings at each end of the work altogether.

Next row : * Knit 10, knit 2 together ; repeat from * 7 times more, knit 12.

Now change to the No. 11 needles and work 20 rows in ribbing of 1 plain and 1 purl, then cast off loosely in ribbing.

THE BACK OF SHORTS
This is worked exactly as for the front.

THE GUSSETS
With the No. 10 needles, commence by casting on 1 stitch, then knit twice into it. Now knit 2 into each of these stitches.

Next row : All purl.

Next row : Knit 2 into the first stitch, knit 1, knit 2 into the next stitch, knit 1.

Next row : All purl.

Next row : Knit 2 into the first stitch, knit until 2 stitches remain, increase into the next stitch, knit 1.

Next row : All purl.

Repeat the last 2 rows until you have 36 stitches, ending with a purl row.

Next row : Knit plain, but knit 2 together at both ends of the row.

Next row : All purl.

Repeat the last 2 rows until no stitches remain, then fasten off.

THE BELT LOOPS
With the No. 11 needles cast on 6 stitches. Work in ribbing of 1 plain and 1 purl for 24 rows, then cast off.

Work 4 more pieces in the same way.

THE TOP PART
With the No. 10 needles cast on 46 stitches. Knit a plain row into the backs of the stitches.

Next row : * Knit 1, purl 1; repeat from * twice, knit to within 6 stitches from end of row, then ** purl 1, knit 1; repeat from ** twice.

Next row : * Purl 1, knit 1; repeat from * twice, purl to within 6 stitches from end of row, then ** knit 1, purl 1; repeat from ** twice.

Next row : Work the first 6 stitches in ribbing as before, knit 1 into front and 1 into the back of the next stitch, knit plain until 8 stitches remain, then knit 2 into the next stitch, knit 1, working the remaining 6 stitches in ribbing.

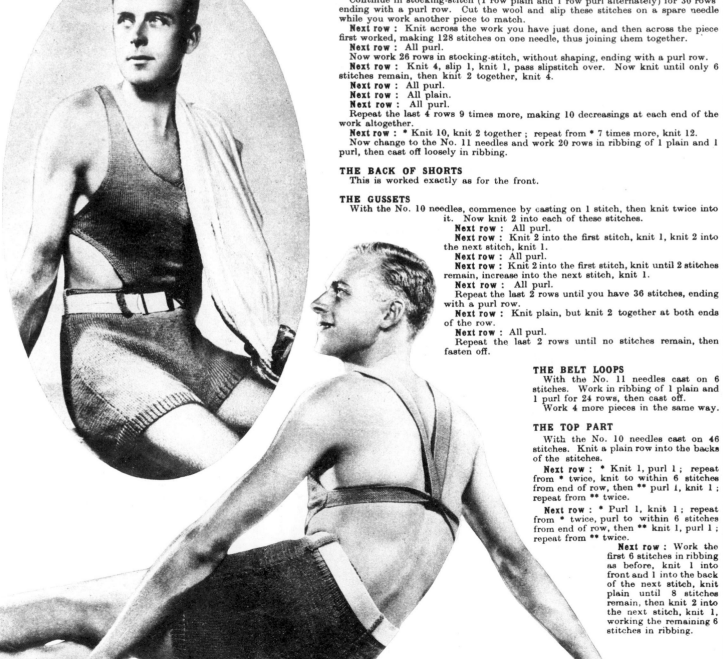

Next row : Work 6 stitches in ribbing, purl to within 6 stitches from end of row rib to end of row.

Repeat the last 2 rows 11 times more.

Next row : Work 6 stitches in ribbing, increase as before in the next stitch, knit to within 8 stitches from end of row, increase in the next stitch ; work in ribbing to the end.

Next row : Work 6 stitches in ribbing, purl 1 into the front and 1 into the back of the next stitch, purl to within 8 stitches from end of row, then purl 2 into the next stitch as before, purl 1 ; work the remaining 6 stitches in ribbing.

Repeat the last 2 rows 5 times more. Now work 10 rows in stocking-stitch, discontinuing ribbing and increasings at the edges for these 10 rows.

Next row : Work 6 stitches in ribbing, slip 1, knit 1, pass slipstitch over, knit until 8 stitches remain, knit 2 together, work in ribbing the last 6 stitches.

Next row : Work 6 stitches in ribbing, purl to within 6 stitches from end, then rib to the end.

Repeat the last 2 rows 4 times more, then continue repeating these 2 rows for 24 rows more, but decrease only in every 4th row—that is in every second *plain* row. When you are ready to work the 24th row (a purl row), proceed as follows :

Next row : Work 6 stitches in ribbing, purl 25, cast off 10, purl 25, work in ribbing the last 6 stitches.

Now work one side of the neck first.

Next row : Work 6 stitches in ribbing, knit plain to within 8 stitches, then knit 2 together, work in ribbing the last 6 stitches.

Next row : Work 6 stitches in ribbing, purl to within 6 stitches, then rib the last 6 stitches.

Repeat the last 2 rows until only 15 stitches remain for the strap.

Next row : With the right side of the work towards you, knit 1, purl 1, wool back, * slip 1 purlwise, purl 1, wool back ; repeat from * to the last stitch, knit 1.

Next row : Knit 1, * wool forward, slip 1 purlwise, wool back, knit 1 ; repeat from * to the end of the row.

Repeat the last 2 rows for 15 inches, then cast off tightly.

Rejoin the wool to the neck edge of the other side and work to match, but on this side of the neck work the decreasings thus : With the right side of the work towards you, work 6 stitches in ribbing, slip 1, knit 1, pass slipstitch over, finish the row as usual.

THE STRAP FOR BACK

With the No. 10 needles cast on 15 stitches, and knit a row into the back of the stitches. Now repeat the 2 rows described for the shoulder-straps until this strip measures 15 inches in length, then cast off tightly.

TO MAKE UP

Well pin out each part face downwards, normally stretching the edges to the correct shape and size. Firmly press with a hot iron over a damp cloth, but do not iron the ribbing of the shorts.

The sewing together needs no description, except that the slider half of the separable " Lightning " Fastener would be attached to the top part of the suit and the other half should be sewn across the centre of the waist ribbing of the shorts, about 1¼ inches from the top edge.

The ribbing should be slightly stretched, too.

Press the seams on the wrong side, and through the loops at the waist thread a webbing belt.

A Knitted Sports Shirt in a Simple Stitch

TENSION

Seven-and-a-half sts. and 10 rows to 1 in.

THE *Back*.—Using fawn wool, cast on 150 sts. and work in st.-st. for 2 ins., working into the backs of the sts. on the first row and ending with a p. row. Turn the work up on the wrong side and k. through a st. on the needle tog. with the corresponding st. on the cast-on edge all across, thus forming a hem. P. 1 row.

Now continue in st.-st. and work in the following stripes : 6 rows fawn, * 2 rows brown, 4 rows natural, 8 rows brown, 4 rows natural, 2 rows brown, 12 rows fawn, (2 rows brown, 2 rows natural) twice, 2 rows brown, 12 rows fawn. Repeat from * for the length required.

When work measures 18 ins. from the beginning, shape the armholes by casting off 6 sts. at the beginning of the next 2 rows and then dec. at both ends of the following 4 rows. Continue straight in st.-st. in the stripes as before until work measures 25 ins. from the beginning. Shape the shoulders by casting off 11 sts. at the beginning of the next 8 rows. Place the remaining sts. on a holder.

The Front.—Work as for the back till work measures 17¼ ins from the beginning, ending with a p. row. Leave this part of the work and start the plastron as follows : Using brown wool, cast on 1 st. and work 3 times into it, then work in k. 1, p. 1 rib and inc. at both ends of every row until there are 13 sts. on the pin.

Return to the main part and k. across 75 sts., then work in k. 1, p. 1 rib with brown wool across the 13 plastron sts., turn and place the remaining 75 sts. on a holder.

Continue in the sts. on the pin, working 75 sts. in the stripes as before and the 13 sts. of the plastron in brown wool, and always twisting the wools round each other when changing colour

When work measures 18 ins. from the beginning shape the armhole by casting off 6 sts. at the beginning of the next k. row and dec. at the same edge of the following 4 rows. Continue straight

TO GREET THE SUNSHINE

with the sts. arranged as before until work measure 19 ins. from the beginning, then work a buttonhole in the plastron as follows : K. 65, rib 5, cast off 4, rib to end. On the following row cast on 4 sts. to take the place of those cast off.

Work two more buttonholes in the same way at 2-inch intervals, and when ½ inch has been worked above the 3rd buttonhole, shape the neck as follows : Cast off 17 sts. at the beginning of the next row which starts at the centre front. Dec. at the same edge of the following 12 rows, and then dec. at the same edge of the following 5 alternate rows. Shape the shoulder by casting off 11 sts. at the beginning of the next 4 k. rows.

Return to the sts. on the holder, join the wool to the centre front and cast on 13 sts. Now work across all sts. in the stripe pattern. When work measures 18 ins. from the beginning shape the armhole by casting off 6 sts. at the beginning of the next p. row, and then dec. at the same edge of the following 4 rows. Continue straight till work measures 23½ ins. from the beginning.

Shape the neck by casting off 17 sts. at the beginning of the next k. row, then dec. at the same edge of the following 12 rows, and then at the same edge of the following 5 alternate rows. Shape the shoulder by casting off 11 sts. at the beginning of the next 4 p. rows.

The Sleeves.—Using fawn wool, cast on 98 sts. and work in st.-st. for 2 ins., working into the backs of the sts. on the first row and ending with a p. row. Turn up the work on the wrong side, and work a hem as for the back. Now continue in stripes as for the back from *, and inc. at both ends of every 6th row until there are 110 sts. on the pin. Continue in the stripes till work measures 7 ins. from the beginning, then shape the top by casting off 6 sts. at the beginning of the next 2 rows, and then dec. at both ends of every row until 64 sts. remain. Dec. at both ends of every alternate row until 30 sts. remain. Cast off.

The Collar.—Join the shoulder seams, then with brown wool pick up the sts. round the neck, working twice into every 4th st. (144 on original model.) Now work in k. 1, p. 1 rib with brown wool for 2½ ins., and inc. at both ends of every alternate row. Cast off.

To Make Up.—Press the st.-st. part of the work on the wrong and then on the right side with a hot iron over a damp cloth. Sew the sleeves into the armholes and join the side and sleeve seams. Catch down the bottom of the plastron and the under-flap, and sew on buttons to correspond with button-holes. Press all seams.

a fair-isle pullover

MATERIALS
Paton's Real Shetland Wool, 2-ply in the following colours : 5 ozs. drab, shade 648 ; 3 ozs. natural, shade 633 ; 2 ozs. dark brown, shade 671 ; 2 ozs. green, shade 672 ; 2 ozs. rust, shade 649. A pair of No. 8 knitting pins ; a pair of No. 12 knitting pins.

MEASUREMENTS
Round the chest—40 ins. Length from shoulder to lower edge—24 ins. Sleeve, from shoulder seam to edge of cuff—26 ins. Sleeve under-arm seam to edge of cuff—22 ins.

TENSION
After pressing the Fair Isle fabric, 6 sts. make 1 inch in width, and 7 rows make 1 inch in depth.

COLOUR ABBREVIATIONS
D., drab ; n., natural ; b., brown ; g., green ; r., rust.

COMMENCE at the lower edge of the back by casting 110 sts. with d. wool on No. 12 needles. Work in a rib of k. 1, p. 1 for 3½ ins., which is about 40 rows. Cast on 1 st. at the end of the last row.

Now change to No. 8 needles and st.-st.

1st row : * 2 g., 2 b., repeat from * to the end of the row.

2nd row : P. each st. in the same colour as in 1st row.

3rd row : * 2 n., 2 g., repeat from * to the end of the row.

4th row : P. each st. in the same colour as in the 3rd row.

5th–8th rows : As the 1st–4th.

9th row : * 2 r., 3 d., 1 r., 3 d., 1 r., repeat from * to the end of the row, and work the last st. of *every row* the same as the first st.

10th row : * 1 r., 4 d., repeat from *.

11th row : * 4 d., 3 r., 3 d., repeat from *.

12th row : P. each st. in the same colour as in the 11th row.

13th row : * 3 n., 2 r., 1 n., 2 r., 2 n., repeat from *.

14th row : * 3 n., 1 r., 3 n., 1 r., 2 n., repeat from *.

15th row : * 2 n., 2 r., 3 n., 2 r., 1 n., repeat from *.

16th row : * 2 n., 1 b., 5 n., 1 b., 1 n., repeat from *.

17th row : * 1 n., 2 b., 5 n., 2 b. repeat from *.

18th–25th rows : As the 16th–9th rows, inclusive, worked in their reverse order. This completes the pattern once.

Work the 25 pattern rows 3 times, then work the first 13 rows. When the pattern is repeated for the 2nd, 4th or the 6th time, the k. rows become p. rows, and the p. rows become k. rows. If a longer pull-over be required, work the extra rows here.

The Armhole.—At the beginning of the next 10 rows, cast off 4 sts ; 71 sts. now remain. Continue in the pattern until it has been repeated 5 times, then work the first 12 rows.

The Shoulder.—Work till 6 sts. remain, turn. *Next row :* Work till 6 sts. remain, turn.

Next row : Work till 12 sts. remain, turn.

Continue in this way until 24 sts. remain unworked at either end. Place each set of shoulder sts. on a safety-pin. On the 23 middle sts. work 12 rows of ribbing with d. wool on No. 12 needles. Cast off. Cast off each set of shoulder sts. with d. wool.

The Front.—Cast 130 sts. on No. 12 needles with d. wool and continue as for the back (increasing the sts. to 131 at the end of the ribbing) until 84 rows have been worked in the pattern.

Next row : K 65 sts. in pattern for the left front. Place the remaining 66 sts. on a holder. Work 3 more rows on the 65 sts. Now shape the neck and armhole. Cast off 4 sts. at the beginning of the row for the armhole, then k. till 2 sts. remain ; k. 2 tog. for the V neck. Cast off 4 sts. at the commencement of alternate rows 4 more times for the armhole. For the V neck, decrease at the end of every 4th row until 15 decreases have been made.

When the pattern has been repeated 5 times, and 18 rows of the next repetition have been worked, shape for the shoulder as follows :

Next row : P. till 6 sts. remain, turn.
Next row : S. 1, k. to the end.

Continue in this way, working 6 sts. fewer in alternate rows, until the row with 6 sts. has been completed. Cast off with d. wool.

Return to the 66 sts. for the right front. Commence with a k. row, and work the 2 first sts. tog., to make 65 sts. K. to the end. Work 3 more rows.

Next row : S 1, k. 1, p.s.s.o., k. to the end.

Next row : Cast off 4, p. to the end.

Make this side correspond with the left side by casting off 4 sts. at the commencement of alternate rows, 4 more times, and by decreasing at the commencement of every 4th row for the V neck 14 more times. When the shoulder is reached, commence the shaping with a k. row, as follows :

Next row : K. till 6 sts. remain, turn.
Next row : P. to the end.

In every k. row work 6 sts. less until only 6 sts. have been worked in the row. Turn and p. these sts., then cast off with d. wool.

The Neck Edge.—Along one side of the V neck pick up a st. for every row of knitting with d. wool on a No. 12 needle. There should be about 68 sts. Work 12 rows of ribbing, and decrease in every row at the point of the V by taking 2 sts. tog. Work a similar edge along the other side of the V.

The Sleeves.—Commence at the cuffs by casting 60 sts. with d. wool on No. 12 needles. Work in ribbing for

3½ ins. Change to No. 8 needles and proceed in st.-st.

Start with the 9th pattern row. In every 6th row m. 1 st. at either end until there are 20 increases on either side of the sleeve. When 126 rows have been worked in the pattern, begin the shaping for the top.

127th row : K. 1, s. 1, k. 1, p.s.s.o., k. till 3 sts. remain, k. 2 tog., k. 1.

128th row : P. in the pattern.

Repeat the last 2 rows 5 more times.

139th row : Decrease as in the 127th row. *140th row :* P. 1, p. 2 tog., p. in the pattern till 3 sts. remain, p. 2 tog., p. 1. Repeat the last 2 rows 4 more times.

Next row : Cast off 4 sts., work to the end. Repeat the last row 9 more times. Cast off and make the second sleeve.

TO MAKE UP
Press the parts, except the ribbing, under a damp cloth. Make the shoulder, side and sleeve seams, and join the parts of the neck edging. Press the seams. Sew the sleeves in the armholes, with the sleeve seam about 2 ins. in front of the side seam. Give the garment a final pressing.

TENNIS PULLOVER

Curved Line and Straight Line.

Materials Required:

9-ozs. White "Wendy" Swiftnit Wool.
(Long Sleeve) 15-ozs. White "Wendy" Swiftnit Wool.

1-oz. Navy "Wendy" Swiftnit Wool.

1-oz. Pale Blue "Wendy" Swiftnit Wool.

1 pair No. 8 needles.

1 pair No. 4 needles.

This design can also be knitted from WENDY "Highland Tweed" Heavyweight.

Measurements: Length of body, 21 inches; Long Sleeve, 21 inches.

Tension: 5 sts. to one inch; 6 rows to one inch.

Front: Cast on 82 sts. with No. 8 needles. Do 12 rows of ribbing 1 plain 1 purl in White. Do 4 rows of ribbing 1 plain 1 purl in Navy. Do 4 rows of ribbing 1 plain 1 purl in Pale Blue. Do 4 rows of ribbing 1 plain 1 purl in Navy. Change to No. 4 needles. Purl 1, knit 3, purl 6.

1st row: * K 2, P 1, K 3, P 6 * repeat to end of row.

2nd row: * K 6, P 3, K 1, P 2 * repeat to end of row (less last purl 2).

3rd row: P 2, K 3, P 5 * K 2, P 2, K 3, P 5 * repeat to end of row.

4th row: * K 5, P 3, K 2, P 2 * to end of row (less last P 2).

5th row: P 3, K 3, P 4 * K 2, P 3, K 3, P 4 * repeat to end.

6th row: * K 4, P 3, K 3, P 2 * repeat to end of row (less last P 2).

7th row: P 4, K 3, P 3 * K 2, P 4, K 3, P 3 * repeat to end of row.

8th row: * K 3, P 3, K 4, P 2 * repeat to end of row (less last P 2).

9th row: P 5, K 3, P 2 * K 2, P 5, K 3, P 2 * repeat to end of row.

10th row: * K 2, P 3, K 5, P 2 * repeat to end of row ending with K 5.

11th row: P 6, K 3, P 1 * K 2, P 6, K 3, P 1 * repeat to end of row.

12th row: * K 1, P 3, K 6, P 2 * repeat to end of row ending with P 6.

13th row: Purl 6, K 3, P 1 * K 2, P 6, K 3, P 1 * repeat to end of row.

14th row: As 12th row.

15th row: As 9th.

16th row: As 10th.

17th row: As 7th.

18th row: As 8th.

19th row: As 5th.

20th row: As 6th.

21st row: As 3rd.

22nd row: As 4th.

23rd row: As 1st.

24th row: As 2nd.

Continue in pattern until work measures 12 inches.

Armhole: Cast off 4 sts. each end of needle. Knit 1 row in pattern. Divide for vest opening. Decrease at beginning of next row and every other row at armhole edge until there are 4 decreasings. Decrease at vest edge every 4th row for 11 times. When work measures 20½ inches, decrease for shoulder. Cast off 6 sts. at armhole edge. Knit back. Cast off 8 sts., knit back. Cast off 8 sts.

Back: Work back as front. Decrease armholes as front, then continue until shoulders are reached. Cast off shoulder as front shoulder and remaining stitches for neck last.

Sleeves (both alike): Cast on 50 sts. with No. 8 needles. Knit 1 plain 1 purl for 12 rows in White. Knit 1 plain 1 purl for 4 rows in Navy. Knit 1 plain 1 purl for 4 rows in Pale Blue. Knit 1 plain 1 purl for 4 rows in Navy. Change to No. 4 needles.

Work in pattern, increasing every 8 rows until sleeve measures 19 inches. Cast off 2 sts. each end of needle every other row until 50 sts. remain. Cast off 10 sts. each end of needle every other row. Sew jumper seams. Pick up 42 sts. on front side of vest, holding right side of jumper to you.

Pick up 20 sts. across back of neck and 42 on left side.

Turn. Knit 2 together in purl stitch with Navy wool. Purl right round to last 2 sts., purl together.

Turn. Knit 2 together, purl 1 knit right round to last 2 sts., K 2 together.

Continue in Navy until 3 rows are worked in Navy (knitting 2 together each end).

Continue in Pale Blue until 3 rows are worked in Pale Blue (knitting 2 together each end).

Continue in Navy until 3 rows are worked in Navy (knitting 2 together at each end).

Continue in White for 1 row. Cast off in ribbing st.

Pick up 72 sts. round armhole in White; rib 1 purl 1 plain for 5 rows. Cast off in ribbing st.

Do not press garment.

The "WIMBLEDON"
Tennis Sweater

N° 130

Price Twopence

WENDY Swiftnit WOOL

the 40s

'Wool is scarce and precious now and there's a general feeling that, even apart from reasons of economy, one cannot lightly turn last year's jumper into this year's floor cloth – not without exploring every possibility of giving it a new lease of life. Now one can use cunning devices to rejuvenate old friends and bring them forth as good as new. It's amazing what radiant creations can be contrived from two pairs of father's old socks, an old beret and a ball of string!' *Knitting For All Illustrated*, 1941.

War came to Britain in September 1939, and once more women were making 'comforts for the troops'. 'Never, since the last war, have we taken up our knitting needles with so much enthusiasm as we are doing now. Every woman throughout the length and breadth of the land, whether she is engaged on National Service or merely sticking to her part as housewife, is spending every spare minute with needles clicking, doing that 'extra bit' of duty to her country' (*Bestway Magazine*, 1939). Jerseys were adapted to fit the regulation patterns for the Forces. For example, British naval jerseys had three-quarter-length sleeves to free the wrists. Likewise a wide armhole was preferred to allow unrestricted movement. A cable pattern was good – chunky looking and warm but not too bulky to wear beneath the 'duffel coat' which was now an Admiralty issue. Special 'steering' gloves were needed, and long woollen socks to wear with sea-boots.

For the Home Front, knitting booklets called 'Woollies for Wardens' and 'Shelter Knitwear' gave patterns for zipped polo-neck sweaters or lumber-jackets. These useful garments were to go beneath a 'siren suit', a protective garment made popular by Winston Churchill. Warm woollen underwear in a simple rib was essential, though nowadays it might be briefer and 'American in style'. Knitted skull caps went beneath tin hats, and a woollen muffler-helmet was very suitable for a 'careless' man because the scarf was attached and could not be left behind. Garments which could serve both military and civilian purposes were always a clever idea. The balaclava (cold weather hood) could be for any man who had to 'face up to the weather' – fighting the wind on the allotment as well as the parade ground; or a pair of mittens was useful 'for soldier, sailor, tinker, tailor alike'. To be practical, a pullover must look business-like as well as sporting, 'ready to do battle with the weeds in the garden' and to be worn in town. Typical was a grey sleeveless pullover with a deep V-neck in stocking-stitch, for 'hard service'. Only the British tie must be different for work and leisure. It was straight for the City and shaped for sport; though a straight silk tie to match the tweed suit was permissable.

The coming of war sobered man's already conservative taste in clothes. Said *Knitting For All Illustrated*: 'Men don't care for new ideas in dress. Fashion means nothing to them.' They chose the classic cardigan as the most pleasing garment to place in the week-end case, as well as the 'kit' bag. Easy to slip on, long-sleeved and buttoned up the front, with pockets that 'gave an air of comfort', the cardigan-jacket might be knitted in a variety of stitches.

The lumber-jacket with a turned-down collar, knitted in a strong four ply rib, was also highly prized, because the zip-fastener made it 'very informal'. 'Being restrained and unobtrusive and most workmanlike, he will want it plain, but if it is exclusively for off-duty days, you could persuade him to let himself go a bit and wear it in a variegated check pattern in navy and white.' Only the knitted waistcoats had to be as 'tailored as the smartest from Savile Row', and not home-made looking. A fine stocking-stitch would be streamlined under a fitted jacket, as well as hard-wearing. Small neat stitches of an unusual sort that gave the appearance of cloth were right, 'for men these days are very conscious of the comfort of their well-fitting garments which they used to take so much for granted'.

Across the Atlantic, the scene was brighter. The best British knitwear was being exported there to help the war effort – luxurious alpacas in soft pastels, slipovers in fancy diamonds or rough rib. In 1940 *Menswear* magazine stated that 'bold colours will be worn more extensively than before by the men of this country.' The growing demand for sportswear sparked off new fabrics, new colours, new designs and novelty stitches. The 'finger-tip' coat was the 'big shot'. Single breasted with fly-front and the popular raglan sleeves, it was fashioned in wool and gaberdine. In Princeton, crew-necked pullovers, or those part-knitted and part made from materials like leather, suede or woven cloth, were the newest thing. Cardigans were popular, too, in camel or brown with buttons or slide-fasteners. Fred Astaire liked a cardigan-sweater in natural jersey almost as long as his jacket. Sleeveless sweaters, with or without buttons, were the most popular garments of all.

In summer, blue-and-yellow checks or stripes of all sizes patterned knitwear. And at Nassau in the Bahamas, green, navy and orange cross-stripes, or blue and red stripes on a white ground, were knitted in lightweight English wool for sports shirts that were comfortable to wear beneath the casual sports jacket.

In winter, European designs were prominent on the American ski-slopes. There were open-knit plaids, snowflake designs and raised rib pullovers. Dick Durance, the skier from Vermont, wore a Norwegian snowflake sweater of vivid red-white-and-green over navy, with socks to match.

'Cambridge in wartime is more colourful than most places,' noted Americans in England. Elsewhere, 'odd heavy trousers are worn with woollies of any form'. Even in Cambridge, plus fours were no longer ordered: 'the day of the baggy knickers is over'. With flannels, corduroys or trousers of patterned worsted went heavy cabled slipovers, or chunky crew-necked jerseys in French mustard, lacquer or Air Force blue. Mufflers matched the jerseys or were in club colours.

On 1 June 1941, rationing came into force in Britain. Every man, woman and child received forty clothing coupons which were to last for twelve months. With this coupon allowance, a man could afford to buy a pullover once in every five years. One clothing coupon equalled two ounces (about 50 grams) of knitting wool. Usually the man was favoured when it came to the family knitting. Most new wool went to make the solid-colour sweater he needed for his job, while the women made do with two-tone checks or stripes made from odd balls of wool.

In the wartime knitting-books and magazines, 'adventures in knitting' beckoned from every page, alluring women to knit for the War effort. Learning how to utilize every scrap of wool was important, as was knowing how to repair so that 'a new lease of life can be given to all those knitteds you resigned yourself to giving up as hopeless'. Of the many yarns available (cotton, silk, linen, jute, hair, rayon, or a combination of these), wool was considered the best; for 'it will wear for years if it is carefully washed and it can be un-picked and re-used again and again'.

From 1942 onwards, the wool shortage in Britain was drastic. 'There's likely to be a wholesale starvation of moth larvae before long, so scarce is becoming their favourite food – wool,' warned *Menswear* magazine. Some very heavy, long-sleeved sweaters with roll-necks in rib were to be found in navy, khaki and Air Force blue, as well as a few sombre, plain-coloured turtle-neck shirts, worn for golf. Apart from stripes and diamonds, patterning disappeared in favour of solid colours.

America, too, was 'feeling the pinch'. 'Although our machines are humming night and day turning out sweaters for Uncle Sam's fighting men ... there are not enough to go round.' The mills had been experimenting with substitutes for wool, and the percentage of blends greatly increased. Few of the non-service sweaters were of pure wool; mostly they were half-rayon. To help the situation, a home knitting 'fad' began, along with the slogan: 'Made in America'. Long- or short-sleeved pullovers became by far the most popular garment for the Home Front.

'Austerity now for stability later,' said the British Board of Trade. At the end of the war, soldiers in Britain were issued with a hurriedly made de-mob suit of inferior fabric. The pullover became a much-needed gift for Christmas or birthday. New square and block patterns joined the wartime cable-stitches, for 'nothing is more sensible for any man working on the farm than a crew-necked pullover in small block patterns of knit two purl two'. Some new shapes emerged. Sweaters with straight-across necks came in dark reds or greys. 'V-necks' with raglan sleeves were comfortable and warm in the new link-stitch. Pullovers with mock-cables used less wool. Best liked for the office, because it was really two garments in one, was the reversible slipover or cardigan in neat patterns of two quiet colours, such as beige and brown.

In America, though the shortage of yarn continued after the war, sweaters had 'a dash of something new' in either colour or pattern, especially picture motifs which 'cut a keen caper' on the college Campus. Bright Norwegian designs leavened the more conservative pastels and greys. For the Twentieth Annual Los Angeles Golf Tournament on 4 January 1946, the sweaters 'reached into the paint pot for interesting new grape and plum shades, soft tones of sage and deep moss green and yellow'.

In 1946 the 'American Look' reflected a return to better conditions. Rich fabrics, new styles, bright colours and 'patterns galore' came and stayed. The look included double-breasted jackets with wide shoulders and big drapes, white shirts with long-pointed collars and colourful hand-painted ties. The object was to appear 'dressed up'. Pullovers were long and heavy, in blues, browns and greys; jackets were chosen with pleated pockets and high-buttoning fronts, and if they had Argyle patterning in beige, blue and brown to match the socks, so much the better. For sports, cabled V-necks of Australian 'Zephyr' wool appeared in maize, scarlet, rust and silver; or a three-colour Fair Isle made a cheerful garment in navy, natural and green.

British suits, although styled with the American Look, fitted more tightly, probably because rationing regulated the amount of material used, and to wear with them, the classic knits were the most admired. Sleeveless cardigans were worn to the office; buttoned waistcoats with low pockets were smart. For riding, fishing and other sports, fancy polo-necks were more cheerfully coloured. In summer, knitted shirts with stripes on white were the most sought-after garments; and, for the beach, knitted trunks in navy, grey and Air Force blue four-ply were secured with webbing belts.

The 'Bold Look' for knitwear arrived in America in 1948. *Esquire* magazine stated that it was 'as new as a fin-tailed Cadillac'. The aim was a broad-shouldered, deep-chested effect, and it set a completely new trend in pullovers. Necks were cut low and wide to show off the shirt-front. Emphasis at this point might be given with a wide kipper tie in a loud Hawaiian or East Indian print. Ribbed sweaters with turned-up cuffs could be 'as rugged as the Rockies', while the long cardigan jackets with expansive pockets had to be 'easy-fitting', for it is always 'comfort that counts'. Designs were bold and patterns strong. Large Jacquard-panel effects were 'having a field day'.

Picture motifs, from lighthouses to heraldic beasts, appeared on winter pullovers, seahorses and birds on summer cotton sweaters in cactus or grey. America's longer weekend and shorter working day had created a great new demand for leisure clothes. Knitted polo-necks were favourites to wear with shorts. Yellow polo-necks could be worn for tennis, but the professionals still chose white cabled sweaters with bands of light, dark-blue and red at neck and hem. Varsity sweaters had striking plaids or wavy lines. A new Campus craze was 'Sweetheart Sweaters'–identical boy-and-girl designs–with massive shoulder stripes and all manner of cheerful motifs. Ski-sweaters were bigger and bolder than ever before.

Perhaps because wool was still scarce there, in Britain most sweaters stayed tailored. Novelty designs of stags or ducks might appear on the front of casual wear. Argyle or plaid designs had the sleeves in plain colours and the pattern in rust, light- and dark-green, yellow and navy. Large star patterns in navy and grey were popular for every garment, and bold Norwegian designs in navy, white, brown and fawn centred around the yoke. The British claimed their inspiration came from Norwegian refugees to the Shetlands during the war, and not from the Bold Look.

The most popular designs in Britain in the late Forties were the classic Fair Isles, because, in a neat three-colour pattern, they could be 'as sporting or as formal as a man could wish'. Men and women alike wore trimly tailored Fair Isles of 'sophisticated effect' that would fit under their tailored suits. In winter, sets of scarf, socks and gloves were highly approved. For golf, a plain ribbed sweater, an all-over pattern, or a polo-shirt of a deep rich shade would be warm under a 'parka' jacket. In summer, a natural or coloured cashmere sweater over a knitted polo-shirt in red, white or navy, was almost uniform. Exciting designs were fishermen's sweaters with smocking-stitch yokes across back and chest.

Bold Look or classic design, the trend was towards informality. At the close of Forties a new type of sweater-wearer was about to be invented–the 'Teenager'...

SERVICE WOOLLIES FOR AIR, LAND AND SEA.

ABBREVIATIONS:—K.=Knit plain; P.=Purl; tog.=together; wl. fwd.=wool forward; p.s.s.o.=pass slip-stitch over; t.b.l.=through the back of the loops.

JERSEY

MATERIALS:—1 lb. 5 ozs. BEEHIVE, or CYCLE, DOUBLE KNITTING (or PATONS SUPER Wheeling, 3-ply). Two No. 7 and two No. 8 "BEEHIVE" Knitting Needles (or "INOX," if Metal preferred), and four No. 8 "BEEHIVE" Knitting Needles, with points at both ends, measured by the Beehive gauge. A Beehive Stitch-holder.

ACTUAL MEASUREMENTS:—Length from top of shoulder, 28 ins. Width all round at under-arm, 40 ins. Length of sleeve from under-arm, 19 ins.

TENSION:—5½ stitches to the inch in width (not stretched) must be obtained to give a garment of the above-mentioned size.

RECIPE:—THE FRONT.—Using the No. 8 Needles, cast on 108 stitches.

1st row.—K. 2, * P. 1, K. 1, repeat from * to the end of the row. Repeat this row nineteen times. Using the No. 7 Needles, proceed as follows:—

1st row.—Knit plain.

2nd row.—K. 1, purl to the last stitch, K. 1.

Repeat these two rows until the work measures 19 inches from the commencement, ending with a purl row. Proceed as follows:—

1st row.—K. 2, * P. 2, K. 2, P. 2, K. 8, repeat from * to the last 8 stitches, (P. 2, K. 2) twice.

2nd row.—K. 1, P. 1, * K. 2, P. 2, K. 2, P. 8, repeat from * to the last 8 stitches, K. 2, P. 2, K. 2, P. 1, K. 1. Repeat the 1st and 2nd rows twice.

7th row.—K. 2, * P. 2, K. 2, P. 2, take a third needle and slip the next 4 stitches on to it, letting this needle fall to the back of the work, knit the next 4 stitches, bring the 4 stitches forward and slip them back on to the needle again, knit these 4 stitches (the crossing of these 8 stitches will now be termed "twist" throughout), repeat from * to the last 8 stitches, (P. 2, K. 2) twice.

8th row.—Like the 2nd row.

9th row.—Cast off 6 stitches, K. 1, P. 1, * K. 8, P. 2, K. 2, P. 2, repeat from * to the last 2 stitches, K. 2.

10th row.—Cast off 6 stitches, K. 2, * P. 8, K. 2, P. 2, K. 2, repeat from * to the last 10 stitches, P. 8, K. 2.

11th row.—K. 1, K. 2 tog., K. 7, * P. 2, K. 2, P. 2, K. 8, repeat from * to the last 16 stitches, P. 2, K. 2, P. 2, K. 7, K. 2 tog., K. 1.

12th row.—K. 1, * P. 8, K. 2, P. 2, K. 2, repeat from * to the last 9 stitches, P. 8, K. 1.

13th row.—K. 1, K. 2 tog., K. 6, * P. 2, K. 2, P. 2, K. 8, repeat from * to the last 16 stitches, K. 6, K. 2 tog., K. 1.

14th row.—K. 1, P. 7, * K. 2, P. 2, K. 2, P. 8, repeat from * to the last 14 stitches, K. 2, P. 2, K. 2, P. 7, K. 1.

15th row.—K. 1, K. 2 tog., K. 5, * P. 2, K. 2, P. 2, K. 8, repeat from * to the last 14 stitches, P. 2, K. 2, P. 2, K. 5, K. 2 tog., K. 1.

16th row.—K. 1, P. 6, * K. 2, P. 2, K. 2, P. 8, repeat from * to the last 13 stitches, K. 2, P. 2, K. 2, P. 6, K. 1.

17th row.—K. 1, K. 2 tog., K. 4, * P. 2, K. 2, P. 2, twist, repeat from * to the last 13 stitches, P. 2, K. 2, P. 2, K. 4, K. 2 tog., K. 1.

18th row.—K. 1, P. 5, * K. 2, P. 2, K. 2, P. 8, repeat from * to the last 12 stitches, K. 2, P. 2, K. 2, P. 5, K. 1.

19th row.—K. 1, K. 2 tog., K. 3, * P. 2, K. 2, P. 2, K. 8, repeat from * to the last 12 stitches, P. 2, K. 2, P. 2, K. 3, K. 2 tog., K. 1.

20th row.—K. 1, P. 4, * K. 2, P. 2, K. 2, P. 8, repeat from * to the last 11 stitches, K. 2, P. 2, K. 2, P. 4, K. 1.

21st row.—K. 1, K. 2 tog., K. 2, * P. 2, K. 2, P. 2, K. 8, repeat from * to the last 11 stitches, P. 2, K. 2, P. 2, K. 2, K. 2 tog., K. 1.

22nd row.—K. 1, P. 3, * K. 2, P. 2, K. 2, P. 8, repeat from * to the last 10 stitches, K. 2, P. 2, K. 2, P. 3, K. 1.

23rd row.—K. 1, K. 2 tog., K. 1, * P. 2, K. 2, P. 2, K. 8, repeat from * to the last 10 stitches, P. 2, K. 2, P. 2, K. 1, K. 2 tog., K. 1.

24th row.—K. 1, P. 2, * K. 2, P. 2, K. 2, P. 8, repeat from * to the last 9 stitches, (K. 2, P. 2) twice, K. 1.

25th row.—K. 3, * P. 2, K. 2, P. 2, K. 8, repeat from * to the last 9 stitches, P. 2, K. 2, P. 2, K. 3.

26th row.—Like the 24th row.

27th row.—K. 3, * P. 2, K. 2, P. 2, twist, repeat from * to the last 9 stitches, P. 2, K. 2, P. 2, K. 3.

28th row.—K. 1, P. 2, * K. 2, P. 2, K. 2, P. 8, repeat from * to the last 9 stitches, (K. 2, P. 2) twice, K. 1.

29th row.—K. 3, * P. 2, K. 2, P. 2, K. 8, repeat from * to the last 9 stitches, P. 2, K. 2, P. 2, K. 3.

Repeat 28th and 29th rows three times, then 28th row once **. Repeat from ** to ** three times. In the next row K. 3, P. 2, K. 2, P. 2, twist, K. 2, P. 2, K. 4, turn.

Work on these 27 stitches as follows:—

1st row.—K. 1, P. 3, K. 2, P. 2, K. 2, P. 8, (K. 2, P. 2) twice, K. 1.

2nd row.—K. 3, P. 2, K. 2, P. 2, K. 8, P. 2, K. 2, P. 2, K. 1, K. 2 tog., K. 1.

3rd row.—K. 1, P. 2, K. 2, P. 2, K. 2, P. 8, K. 1, turn. **4th row.**—P. 1, K. 8, P. 2, K. 2, P. 2, K. 2 tog., K. 1.

5th row.—K. 1, P. 1, K. 2, P. 2, K. 2, P. 1, turn.

6th row.—K. 1, (P. 2, K. 2) twice. Cast off.

Commencing again on the stitches which were left, slip the first 28 stitches on to a stitch-holder and work across the remaining stitches as follows:—

1st row.—K. 4, P. 2, K. 2, P. 2, twist, (P. 2, K. 2) twice, K. 1. **2nd row.**—K. 1, (P. 2, K. 2) twice, P. 8, (K. 2, P. 2) twice, K. 1, P. 1, K. 1.

3rd row.—K. 1, K. 2 tog., K. 1, P. 2, K. 2, P. 2, K. 8, P. 1, turn.

4th row.—K. 1, P. 8, (K. 2, P. 2) twice, K. 1.

5th row.—K. 1, K. 2 tog., P. 2, K. 2, P. 2, K. 1, turn. **6th row.**—P. 1, K. 2, P. 2, K. 2, P. 1, K. 1.

7th row.—(K. 2, P. 2) twice, K. 8, (P. 2, K. 2) twice, K. 1. Cast off.

THE BACK.—Using the No. 8 Needles, cast on 108 stitches. Work exactly as given for the Front, until the 26th row of pattern has been worked.

Repeat from ** to ** as given for the Front, four times. In the next row K. 3, * P. 2, K. 2, P. 2, twist, repeat from * to the last 9 stitches, P. 2, K. 2, P. 2, K. 3.

In the following row K. 1, P. 2, * K. 2, P. 2, K. 2, P. 8, repeat from * to the last 9 stitches, (K. 2, P. 2) twice, K. 1. Shape for the shoulders as follows:—

1st row.—K. 3, * P. 2, K. 2, P. 2, K. 8, repeat from * to the last 9 stitches, P. 1, turn.

2nd row.—K. 1, * P. 8, K. 2, P. 2, K. 2, repeat from * to the last 17 stitches, P. 8, K. 1, turn.

3rd row.—P. 1, * K. 8, P. 2, K. 2, P. 2, repeat from * to the last 17 stitches, K. 1, turn.

4th row.—P. 1, * K. 2, P. 2, K. 2, P. 8, repeat from * to last 23 stitches, K. 2, P. 2, K. 2, P. 1, turn.

5th row.—K. 1, * P. 2, K. 2, P. 2, K. 8, repeat from * to last 37 stitches, P. 2, K. 2, P. 2, K. 6, turn.

6th row.—P. 6, * K. 2, P. 2, K. 2, P. 8, repeat from * to last 37 stitches, K. 2, P. 2, K. 2, P. 6, turn.

7th row.—K. 6, * P. 2, K. 2, P. 2, K. 8, repeat from * to the last 9 stitches, P. 2, K. 2, P. 2, K. 3.

8th row.—Cast off 25 stitches, P. 6, * K. 2, P. 2, K. 2, P. 8, K. 2, P. 2, K. 2, P. 6, cast off 25 stitches. Sew up the shoulder seams.

THE COLLAR.—Using the No. 8 Needles, with points at both ends and with the right side of the work facing, join in the wool and knit up 8 stitches evenly along the left side of the neck; (K. 1, P. 1) nine times across the stitches of the Front; taking a second needle (K. 1, P. 1) five times, knit up 8 stitches evenly along the right side of the neck, (K. 1, P. 1) three times across the stitches of the Back; taking a third needle (K. 1, P. 1) thirteen times (there should now be 76 stitches in the round). Work 6 inches in rounds in rib of (K. 1, P. 1). Cast off loosely.

THE SLEEVES.—Using the No. 7 Needles, cast on 24 stitches. Work in plain, smooth fabric, casting on 2 stitches at the end of every row until there are 76 stitches on the needle.

Continue in plain, smooth fabric, decreasing once at each end of the needle in the 13th and every following 8th row until 64 stitches remain, then in every following 6th row until 52 stitches remain. Continue without shaping until the work measures 18½ inches from the commencement, ending with a purl row. In the next row K. 5, * K. 2 tog., K. 6, repeat from * to the last 7 stitches, K. 2 tog., K. 5. Using the No. 8 Needles, in the following row K. 2, * P. 1, K. 1, repeat from * to the end of the row. Repeat this row twenty-four times. Cast off. Work another Sleeve in the same manner.

TO MAKE UP THE JERSEY.—With a damp cloth and hot iron press carefully. Sew up side, shoulder and sleeve seams, joining seams of each piece by sewing together the corresponding ridges (formed by the stitch knitted at each end of every row). Sew in sleeves, placing seam to seam.

AERO CAP

MATERIALS:—5 ozs. BEEHIVE, or CYCLE, DOUBLE KNITTING (or PATONS SUPER Wheeling, 3-ply). Two No. 7 "BEEHIVE" Knitting Needles (or "INOX," if Metal preferred), measured by the Beehive gauge. Three Buttons.

ACTUAL MEASUREMENT:—Width all round brim, 20 ins.

TENSION:—5½ stitches to the inch in width (not stretched) must be obtained to give a garment of the above-mentioned size.

For abbreviations, see page 3.

RECIPE:—Cast on 52 stitches.

1st row.—(K. 1, increase once in the next stitch, K. 22, increase once in the next stitch) twice, K. 2.

2nd and alternate rows.—K. 1, purl to the last stitch, K. 1.

3rd row.—(K. 1, increase once in the next stitch, K. 24, increase once in next stitch) twice, K. 2.

5th row.—(K. 1, increase once in the next stitch, K. 26, increase once in the next stitch) twice, K. 2.

Continue increasing in this manner, until there are 104 stitches on the needle. Work 7 inches in plain, smooth fabric, ending with a purl row. Shape for the crown as follows:—

1st row.—K. 1, (K. 2 tog.t.b.l., K. 47, K. 2 tog.) twice, K. 1. **2nd and alternate rows.**—K. 1, purl to the last stitch, K. 1.

3rd row.—K. 1, (K. 2 tog.t.b.l., K. 45, K. 2 tog.) twice, K. 1. **5th row.**—K. 1, (K. 2 tog.t.b.l., K. 43, K. 2 tog.) twice, K. 1.

Continue decreasing in this manner, until 52 stitches remain, ending with a purl row. Cast off.

THE FRONT-BAND.—Cast on 72 stitches.

1st row.—K. 2, * P. 1, K. 1, repeat from * to end of row. Repeat this row for 3 inches. Cast off.

THE BACK-BAND.—Cast on 96 stitches.

1st row.—K. 2, * P. 1, K. 1, repeat from * to the end of the row. Repeat this row for 3 inches. In the next row K. 2, (P. 1, K. 1) fifteen times, cast off 32 stitches, (P. 1, K. 1) sixteen times.

Work in rib on the last 32 stitches, decreasing once at each end of the needle in the 3rd and every row until 12 stitches remain.

Proceed as follows:—

1st row.—K. 1, K. 2 tog., K. 1, P. 1, cast off 2 stitches, K. 1, P. 1, K. 2 tog., K. 1.

2nd row.—K. 1, K. 2 tog., P. 1, cast on 2 stitches (thus forming a button-hole), K. 1, P. 2 tog., K. 1.

3rd row.—K. 1, P. 2 tog., K. 1, P. 1, K. 2 tog., K. 1. **4th row.**—K. 1, K. 2 tog., P. 2 tog., K. 1.

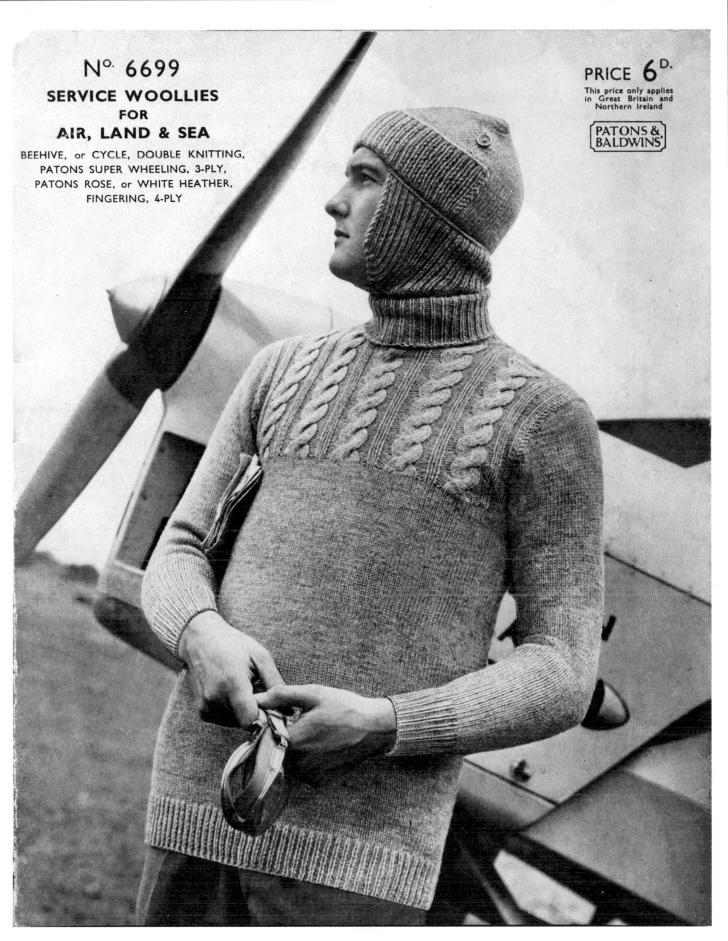

N°: 6699
SERVICE WOOLLIES
FOR
AIR, LAND & SEA

BEEHIVE, or CYCLE, DOUBLE KNITTING,
PATONS SUPER WHEELING, 3-PLY,
PATONS ROSE, or WHITE HEATHER,
FINGERING, 4-PLY

5th row.—(K. 2 tog.) twice. Cast off.
Join in the wool and work on the remaining 32 stitches in the same manner.

TO MAKE UP THE CAP.—With a damp cloth and hot iron press carefully. Fold the cap with the wrong sides together, placing the cast-on edge to the cast-off edge, sew up the side seam and across the top, through the four thicknesses. Sew the front-band firmly in position, along the lower edge of the front, leaving 7 inches plain at the back. Sew the ends of the band to the cap.

Sew the back-band in position, over-wrapping the front-band at the sides and leaving 5½ inches plain at the front. Sew buttons on the cap to correspond with button-holes. Sew another button immediately below the button-hole inside the right point.

FATIGUE CAP

Materials.—*4 oz. of Jaeger "Super-Spun" ("J.S." Quality) Fingering, 3-ply, (9d. per oz.), and 1 set of No. 10 Jaeger knitting needles with points at both ends.*

Measurements.—*Length, 36 inches ; width across 8 inches.*

Tension.—*7 stitches to 1 inch in width, and 10 rows to 1 inch in depth.*

Abbreviations.—*St.-st. = stocking stitch; sts. = stitches.*

Casting-on.—*Work into the back of all cast on sts.*

CAST on 111 sts. using three needles (37 sts. on each needle), and with the fourth needle work 36 inches in st.-st. Cast off.

THE MAKING UP

Press the work on the wrong side with a warm iron and damp cloth. Join one end and press the seam. Turn the work to the right side and slip-stitch the other end. Press the seam.

THE LOWER PHOTOGRAPH SHOWS THE CAP WHEN FINISHED, THE TOP PHOTOGRAPH SHOWS THE CAP WHEN FOLDED. THIS GARMENT CAN BE WORN AS A SCARF, AND HAS MANY OTHER USES

VEST OR PULL-ON GARMENT

"TOMMY" CAN WEAR THIS GARMENT UNDER HIS SHIRT, IN PLACE OF A SHIRT, OR EVEN AS A PULLOVER

Materials.—*8 oz. of Jaeger "Classic" Superfine Scotch Fingering, 3-ply (7d. per oz.), 1 pair of No. 10 Jaeger knitting needles, and a medium crochet hook.*

Measurements.—*Length from shoulder, 26 inches; width all round under the arms, 36 inches; length of sleeve seam, 9 inches.*

Tension.—*7 stitches to 1 inch in width, and 10 rows to 1 inch in depth.*

Abbreviations.—*K. = knit; p. = purl; sts. = stitches; st.-st. = stocking-stich; inc. = increase or increasing; dec. = decrease or decreasing; d.c. = double crochet.*

Casting on.—*If you cast on with two needles work into the back of all cast-on sts. to produce firm edges, but if you use the thumb method this is not necessary.*

THE BACK

BEGIN at the lower edge. Cast on 126 sts. and work 3 inches in k. 1, p. 1 rib. Change to st.-st. and continue until the work measures 18 inches from the beginning, finishing after a p. row.

The Armhole Shaping.—Dec. 1 st. at both ends of every row until 114 sts. remain. Continue without dec. until the armholes measure 6 inches on the straight, finishing after a p. row.

The Neck Shaping.—**Next row**—K. 39, cast off 36, k. to end. Continue on the last 39 sts., dec. 1 st. at the neck edge on every alternate row until 34 sts. remain. Continue without dec. until the armhole measures 8 inches on the straight. Cast off. Join the wool to the inside edge of the other side and work up this to match the first.

THE FRONT

Work this exactly like the back.

THE SLEEVES

Begin at the lower edge. Cast on 84 sts. and work 3 inches in k. 1, p. 1 rib. Change to st.-st., inc. 1 st. at both ends of the 5th row, then on every alternate row until there are 124 sts. on the needle.

Continue without inc. until the work measures 8½ inches from the beginning, measured down the centre. Now shape the top by dec. 1 st. at both ends of every row until 114 sts. remain. Cast off.

THE MAKING UP

Press the work on the wrong side with a warm iron and damp cloth. Join the shoulders, sew in the sleeves and press the seams. Sew up the side and sleeve seams and press them. Work 1 row of d.c. round the neck edge.

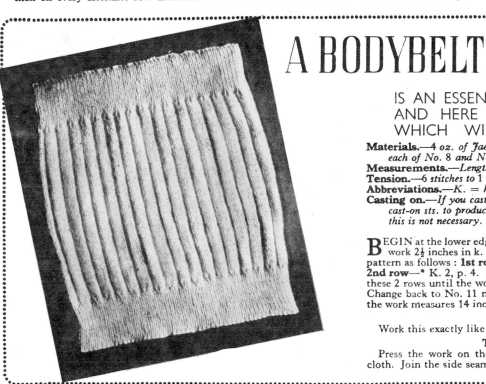

A BODYBELT

IS AN ESSENTIAL GARMENT, TOO, AND HERE IS A RIBBED DESIGN WHICH WILL KEEP ITS SHAPE

Materials.—*4 oz. of Jaeger "Spiral-Spun" (7d. per oz.), and 1 pair each of No. 8 and No. 11 Jaeger knitting needles.*

Measurements.—*Length, 14 inches; width all round, 37 inches.*

Tension.—*6 stitches to 1 inch in width, and 15 rows to 2 inches in depth.*

Abbreviations.—*K. = knit; p. = purl; sts. = stitches; rep. = repeat.*

Casting on.—*If you cast on with two needles work into the back of all cast-on sts. to produce firm edges, but if you use the thumb method this is not necessary.*

THE BACK

BEGIN at the lower edge. Cast on 110 sts. using No. 11 needles and work 2½ inches in k. 1, p. 1 rib. Change to No. 8 needles and the pattern as follows : **1st row**—* P. 2, k. 4. Rep. from * finishing p. 2. **2nd row**—* K. 2, p. 4. Rep. from * finishing k. 2. Continue to rep. these 2 rows until the work measures 11¼ inches from the beginning. Change back to No. 11 needles and k. 1, p. 1 rib, and continue until the work measures 14 inches from the beginning. Cast off.

THE FRONT

Work this exactly like the back.

THE MAKING UP

Press the work on the wrong side with a warm iron and damp cloth. Join the side seams, and press them.

HELMET WITH CAPE PIECES
see Fig. A

MATERIALS:—5 ozs. BEEHIVE, or CYCLE, DOUBLE KNITTING (or PATONS SUPER Wheeling, 3-ply). Two No. 6 "BEEHIVE" Knitting Needles (or "INOX," if Metal preferred), and four No. 6 "BEEHIVE" Knitting Needles, with points at both ends, measured by the Beehive gauge. A Beehive Stitch-holder.

TENSION:—5 stitches to the inch in width (not stretched), measured over the plain knitting, must be obtained.

For abbreviations, see page 3.

RECIPE:—Using the No. 6 Needles, cast on 24 stitches.

1st row.—K. 1, increase once in the next stitch, knit plain to the last 3 stitches, increase once in the next stitch, K. 2.

2nd row.—Knit plain. Repeat the 1st and 2nd rows until there are 44 stitches on the needle. Work 5 inches in plain knitting.

Leave these stitches on a stitch-holder and work another piece in the same manner.

Using the No. 6 Needles, with points at both ends, K. 28 on the first needle; taking a second needle, K. 16, and K. 14 from the stitch-holder on to the same needle; taking a third needle, K. 30.

Work 4 inches in rounds in rib of (K. 2, P. 2).

Proceed as follows:—K. 13, slip the next 18 stitches on to a stitch-holder, leaving these stitches for the face opening, turn. Work 58 rows in plain knitting on the remaining stitches. Proceed as follows:—

1st row.—K. 46, slip 1, K. 1, p.s.s.o., turn.

2nd row.—K. 23, slip 1, K. 1, p.s.s.o., turn.

Repeat the 2nd row until all the stitches are worked on to one needle (24 stitches).

Break off the wool.

Commencing again on the 18 stitches which were left, K. 1, (P. 2, K. 2) four times, P. 1, knit up 15 stitches; taking a second needle, knit up 14 stitches along the edge of the plain knitted rows, (K. 2, P. 2) six times across the 24 stitches on the needle; with a third needle, knit up 29 stitches along the edge of the plain knitted rows (there should now be 100 stitches in the round).

Work 11 rounds in rib of (K. 2, P. 2). Cast off. With a damp cloth and hot iron press carefully.

RIBBED HELMET see Fig. B

MATERIALS:—6 ozs. PATONS SUPER Wheeling, 3-ply (or BEEHIVE, or CYCLE, DOUBLE KNITTING). Four No. 6 "BEEHIVE" Knitting Needles, with points at both ends, measured by the Beehive gauge.

TENSION:—5 stitches to the inch in width (measured flat) must be obtained.

RECIPE:—Cast on 100 stitches, 36 on first needle and 32 on each of the second and third needles.

1st round.—* K. 2, P. 2, repeat from * to end of round. Repeat this round for twelve inches.

In the next round K. 2, cast off 22 stitches (this makes the opening for the face), work in pattern to end of round. Work backwards and forwards in rows on remaining 78 stitches as follows:—

1st row.—K. 1, P. 1, * K. 2, P. 2, repeat from * to the last 4 stitches, K. 2, P. 1, K. 1.

2nd row.—* K. 2, P. 2, repeat from * to the last 2 stitches, K. 2. Repeat the 1st and 2nd rows five times, casting on 22 stitches at the end of last row. Divide stitches on to three needles, as before.

Continue working in rounds in rib of (K. 2, P. 2) for four inches. Shape for the crown as follows:—

1st round.—* K. 18, K. 2 tog., repeat from * to the end of the round. **2nd and alternate rounds.**—Knit plain. **3rd round.**—* K. 17, K. 2 tog., repeat from * to the end of the round. **5th round.**—* K. 16, K. 2 tog., repeat from * to end of round. Continue in this manner, decreasing in every alternate round until 25 stitches remain. Break off the wool and run the end through the remaining stitches, draw up and fasten off securely. With a damp cloth and hot iron press carefully.

SLEEPING CAP see Fig. C

MATERIALS:—2 ozs. PATONS SUPER Wheeling, 3-ply (or BEEHIVE, or CYCLE, DOUBLE KNITTING). Four No. 6 "BEE-HIVE" Knitting Needles, with points at both ends, measured by the Beehive gauge.

TENSION:—5 stitches to the inch in width (not stretched) must be obtained.

RECIPE:—Cast on 100 stitches, 36 on first needle and 32 on each of the second and third needles.

1st round.—* K. 2, P. 2, repeat from * to the end of the round. Repeat this round seventeen times.

19th round.—Knit plain.

Repeat this round for four inches.

Shape for the crown as follows:—

1st round.—* K. 18, K. 2 tog., repeat from * to the end of the round.

2nd and alternate rounds.—Knit plain.

3rd round.—* K. 17, K. 2 tog., repeat from * to the end of the round.

5th round.—* K. 16, K. 2 tog., repeat from * to the end of the round. Continue decreasing in this manner, until 25 stitches remain.

Break off the wool and run the end through the remaining stitches, draw up and fasten off securely. With a damp cloth and hot iron press carefully. Turn back the brim.

SPORTS CAP see Fig. D

MATERIALS:—4 ozs. BEEHIVE, or CYCLE, DOUBLE KNITTING (or PATONS SUPER Wheeling, 3-ply). Two No. 7 "BEEHIVE" Knitting Needles (or "INOX," if Metal preferred), measured by the Beehive gauge.

TENSION:—5½ stitches to the inch in width (not stretched) must be obtained.

RECIPE:—Cast on 60 stitches.

1st row.—Knit plain. **2nd row.**—K. 44, turn.

3rd and alternate rows.—Knit plain.

4th row.—K. 46, turn. **6th row.**—K. 48, turn.

8th row.—K. 50, turn. **10th row.**—K. 52, turn.

12th row.—K. 54, turn. **14th row.**—K. 56, turn.

16th row.—K. 58, turn. **18th row.**—Knit plain **. Repeat from ** to ** three times.

In the next row K. 32, cast off 14 stitches, K. 14. Work 47 rows in plain knitting on the last 14 stitches. Break off the wool.

Commencing again on the stitches which were left, join in the wool and proceed as follows:—

*** **1st row.**—K. 16, turn.

2nd and alternate rows.—Knit plain.

3rd row.—K. 18, turn. **5th row.**—K. 20, turn.

7th row.—K. 22, turn. **9th row.**—K. 24, turn.

11th row.—K. 26, turn. **13th row.**—K. 28, turn.

14th row.—Knit plain. **15th row.**—K. 30, turn.

16th, 17th and 18th rows.—Knit plain ***.

Repeat from *** to *** once, then from the 1st to the 14th row once, casting on 14 stitches at the end of the last row and knitting across the 14 stitches which were left. Proceed as follows:—

1st row.—K. 58, turn.

2nd and 3rd rows.—Knit plain.

Repeat from ** to ** four times, then knit 1 row plain. Cast off.

THE NEB.—Cast on 28 stitches.

1st row.—K. 1, K. 2 tog., knit plain to the last 3 stitches, K. 2 tog., K. 1. **2nd row.**—Knit plain. Repeat 1st and 2nd rows until 14 stitches remain. Cast off. Work another piece in the same manner.

TO MAKE UP THE CAP.—With a damp cloth and hot iron press carefully. Sew up the seam of the cap. Sew together the two pieces of the neb, leaving the cast-on edges open. Turn inside out and sew together the two straight sides, then sew the straight side to the top of the front opening.

See colour plate on page 99

A ROUND - NECKED PULLOVER

is a garment "Tommy" needs for colder days

Materials.—11 oz. of Carter & Parker's "Wendy" Super Botany Wool, 4-ply, and 1 pair each of No. 8 and No. 11 "Stratnoid" knitting needles.

Measurements.—Length from shoulder at armhole edge, 21 inches; width all round under the arms, 38 inches; length of sleeve seam, 19½ inches.

Tension.—13 stitches to 2 inches in width, and 8 rows to 1 inch in depth.

Abbreviations.—K. = knit; p. = purl; sts. = stitches; rep. = repeat; sl. = slip; inc. = increase or increasing; dec. = decrease or decreasing.

Casting-on.—If you cast on with two needles work into the back of all cast-on sts. to produce firm edges, but if you use the thumb method this is not necessary.

THE BACK

BEGIN at the lower edge. Cast on 124 sts. using No. 11 needles and work 3½ inches in k. 1, p. 1 rib. Change to No. 8 needles and the pattern as follows : **1st row**—Sl. 1, k. 3, * p. 4, k. 4. Rep. from * to end. **2nd row**—Sl. 1, p. 3, * k. 4, p. 4. Rep. from * finishing p. 3, k. 1. Rep. these 2 rows once more.

5th row—Like the 2nd row. **6th row**—Like the 1st row. Rep. the last 2 rows once more.

These 8 rows form the pattern and are rep. throughout. Continue in pattern until the work measures 13 inches from the beginning, finishing with the work right side towards you.

The Armhole Shaping.—Cast off 4 sts. at the beginning of the next 8 rows (92 sts.). Continue on these sts. until the armholes measure 6 inches on the straight, finishing with the work right side towards you.

The Neck Shaping.—Next row—Pattern 40, cast off 12, pattern to end. Continue on the last 40 sts., dec. 1 st. at the neck edge on every row until 24 sts. remain, finishing with the work wrong side towards you.

The Shoulder Shaping.—Cast off 8 sts. at the beginning of the next row, then on every alternate row until all sts. are cast off. Join the wool to the inside edge of the other side and work up this to match the first.

THE FRONT

Work this exactly like the back until the armholes measure 5 inches on the straight, finishing with the work right side towards you.

The Neck Shaping.—Next row—Pattern 40, cast off 12, pattern to end. Continue on the last 40 sts., dec. 1 st. at the neck edge on every row until 24 sts. remain. Continue without dec. until the armhole measures 8 inches on the straight, finishing with the work wrong side towards you.

The Shoulder Shaping.—Cast off 8 sts. at the beginning of the next row, then on every alternate row until all sts. are cast off. Join the wool to the inside edge of the other side and work up this to match the first.

THE SLEEVES

Begin at the lower edge. Cast on 60 sts. using No. 11 needles and work 2½ inches in k. 1, p. 1 rib. Change to No. 8 needles and the pattern, inc. 1 st. at both ends of the 7th row, then on every 8th row following until there are 90 sts. on the needle. Continue without inc. until the work measures 19 inches from the beginning, measured down the centre. Now shape the top by casting off 2 sts. at the beginning of every row until 10 sts. remain. Cast off.

THE NECK BAND

Cast on 150 sts. using No. 11 needles and work 1½ inches in k. 1, p. 1 rib. Cast off rather tightly in rib.

THE MAKING UP

Press the work on the wrong side with a warm iron and damp cloth. Join the shoulders, sew in the sleeves and press the seams. Sew up the side and sleeve seams and press them. Join the neck band, then place the join to the centre back and sew the band round the neck edge. Press the seam.

This SERVICE Polo-neck Jumper

casting off 10 stitches at arm hole edge on following 3 alternate rows. Return to remaining stitches, leave centre 20 stitches on spare needle, and work remaining 34 stitches to correspond with left shoulder.

Needles 3+5

MATERIALS: 12 ozs. Diana Non-Shrink Knitting, 4-ply. A pair No. 10 and No. 8 "Beehive" needles, and a set of four No. 8 needles, pointed both ends.

MEASUREMENTS: To fit 37–39-inch chest; length from top of shoulder to lower edge, 23 inches; sleeve seam, 19 inches.

TENSION: 6 stitches to an inch.

FRONT

With No. 10 needles, cast on 116 stitches and work 3 inches in k. 1, p. 1 rib. Change to No. 8 needles and pattern:—1ST ROW: (k. 1, p. 1) 12 times, k. 12, (p. 1, k. 1) 8 times, k. 12, (k. 1, p. 1) 8 times, k. 12, (p. 1, k. 1) 12 times. 2ND ROW: k. 24, (p. 12, k. 16) twice, p. 12, k. 24. Repeat these 2 rows 3 times more.

9TH ROW: (k. 1, p. 1) 12 times, double-cable the next 12 stitches (*i.e.*, slip next 3 stitches on to spare needle at back, knit next 3 stitches, then k. 3 stitches from spare needle; slip next 3 stitches on to spare needle at front, knit next 3 stitches, then knit 3 stitches from spare needle), (p. 1, k. 1) 8 times, double-cable, (k. 1, p. 1) 8 times, double-cable, (p. 1, k. 1) 12 times. 10TH ROW: As 2nd.

These 10 rows form pattern. Repeat them 8 times more. Now shape armholes:—Cast off 6 stitches at beginning of next 2 rows, then k. 2 tog., at each end of next 8 rows (88 stitches). Now continue in pattern till 15 patterns have been done from commencement. Here shape neck:—

NEXT ROW: Work across 34 stitches, turn, leaving remaining stitches on a spare needle. Now k. 2 tog. at neck on every alternate row 4 times. Shape shoulder by

BACK

Work to correspond with front to end of armhole shapings. Work straight till length equals that of front, then shape shoulders by casting off 10 stitches at beginning of next 6 rows. Leave remaining 28 stitches on a spare needle.

SLEEVES

With No. 10 needles, cast on 48 stitches and work 3½ inches in k. 1, p. 1 rib. Change to No. 8 needles and pattern, having 1 double-cable up centre and 18 stitches either side [thus: k. 2, (k. 1, p. 1) 8 times, k. 12, (p. 1, k. 1) 8 times, k. 2], increasing at each end of next and every following 6th row till there are 88 stitches on the needle. (Keep increased stitches in stocking-stitch until you have sufficient to start a new cable at each end.)

Work straight till sleeve measures 19 inches, then shape top by k. 2 tog. at each end of every row till 26 remain. Cast off.

COLLAR

Join shoulder seams, then with the set of four No. 8 needles and right side facing, pick up and knit 18 stitches down left shoulder, work across the 20 stitches left at front, pick up and knit 18 stitches down right shoulder, and work across the 28 stitches left at back (84 stitches). Work in rounds of k. 1, p. 1 rib for 6 inches. Cast off loosely in rib.

TO MAKE UP

Press carefully with a damp cloth and warm iron. Join side and sleeve seams and sew in sleeves.

——THE——
WONDER-SOCK
. . . Ever New—no darning !

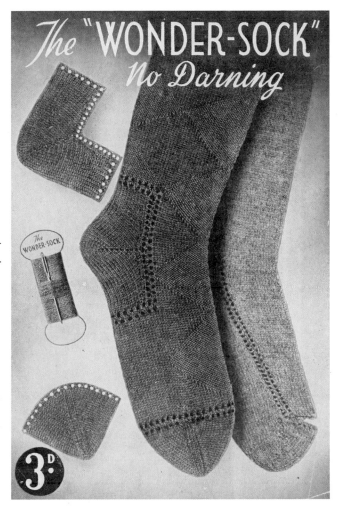

Any good Standard Wool can be used successfully.

5-ozs. 4-ply Wool—A set of No. 12 Needles (school & heavy wear).

4-ozs. 3-ply Wool—A set of No. 14 Needles (gentlemen's socks).

1 Wool Needle.

INSTRUCTIONS

GENTLEMAN'S SOCK, 10-inch foot.

4-ozs. 3-ply Wool.   A set of Needles No. 14.

Cast on 88 stitches (80 stitches for 4-ply wool), knit border of 3 inches 1 purl 1 plain. Turn work inside-out to reverse the fabric, work 4 inches in stocking-stitch or design chosen. Decrease 8 stitches in two's each 8th row down leg either side of centre back. At the 10-inch length there should be 80 stitches. Put half these into the front needle, *i.e.* 40, on the 2 back needles, 20 on each needle.

Next row—Commencing from end of Front Needle, make a stitch by passing wool over needle and knit 2 together. Repeat to end of 2nd needle ; knit to your design on front needle.

Next row—Commencing 1st back needle cast off very, very loosely, the 2 back needles, making the PERFORATED EDGE of 20 holes.

Commencing front needle, knit 1, make 1, knit 2 together. Knit design to end of needle.

Next row—Front only. Purl 1, make 1, purl 2 together. Reverse design as usual on single needles. Purl to end.

Next row—Repeat these two rows till 22 perforated holes border the front half of sock each side.

Last row—Cast on loosely 40 stitches, use 3 needles in circular form again, knit front needle to design, then first back needle commencing make 1, knit 2 together, through the new cast-on stitches making 20 perforated holes.

Next row—Work design on front needle as usual, plain on underfoot till 4 inches deep.

Next Row—Commencing from CENTRE BACK make 1, knit 2 together ; repeat all round.

Next row—Cast off very, very loosely.

TOE.
Cast on 80 stitches on 3 needles.

First row—Make 1, knit 2 together ; repeat the round.

Second row—Knit plain.

Third row—Knit plain.

Fourth row—Knit plain.

Fifth row—Knit plain, knit 18th–19th stitches together, knit 2 plain, knit 22nd–23rd together, knit 34 stitches, knit 2 together, knit 2 plain, knit 2 together, knit remaining 17.

Sixth row—Knit plain.

Seventh row—Decrease 4 stitches at same decreasings, repeat 6th and 7th row till only 20 stitches remain, cast off.

HEEL.
Cast on 40 stitches, using 2 needles.

First row—Purl 1, make 1, purl 2 together ; repeat, make 1, purl 2 together to end, purl last stitch.

Second row—Knit 2 together, knit to end.

Third row—Purl 1, make 1, purl 2 together, purl to end.

Fourth row—Knit 1, make 1, knit 2 together, knit to end.

Fifth row—Purl 1, make 1, purl 2 together, purl to end.

Sixth row—Knit 1, make 1, knit 2 together, make 1 extra stitch, knit to 4th stitch from end, make 1 stitch, knit to end : you now have 42 stitches.

Seventh row—Purl 1, make 1, purl 2 together, purl to end.

Eighth row—Knit 1, make 1, knit 2 together, knit to end.

Ninth row—Purl 1, make 1, purl 2 together, purl to end.

Repeat *Sixth, Seventh, Eighth* and *Ninth* rows three times. There should now be 48 stitches on the needles. *Next row*—knit 1, make 1, knit 2 together, knit to end. *Next Row*—Purl 1, make 1, purl 2 together, purl to end. There will now be 11 perforated holes on either side of heel.

Now make heel by leaving the three border stitches on needle ; knit to end less three border stitches ; turn, slip first stitch and purl to end, less three border stitches ; turn, slip first stitch, knit to end, less four stitches (including border stitches) ; turn, slip first stitch, purl to end, less 1 stitch ; turn, repeat till 18 stitches are left for centre ; then pick up stitches each side by picking up stitch of last row and placing on right-hand needle, slipping last stitch over and knitting one extra stitch on left needle ; repeat till all the stitches are again on one needle. Make second half of heel similarly, but decrease instead of increase till 40 stitches are on needles. Knit till 21 holes on border. *Next row*—knit 1, make 1, knit 2 together ; repeat, make 1, knit 2 together, to end ; cast off loosely. Pass the wool-needle through the perforated holes and link the toe and heel. Press with damp cloth to shape. Make extra heels and toes.

MAN'S PULLOVER

With or Without Sleeves.

*TO OBTAIN THE BEST RESULTS BE SURE
TO USE "WENDY" WOOL AS DIRECTED.*

MATERIALS REQUIRED.

WENDY "SUPER BOTANY" Wool, 4-ply.
    With sleeves—**11 ozs.**
    Without sleeves—**8 ozs.**
1 pair each No. 10 and 8 needles. *3 + 5 needles*
Or
WENDY Wool, 4-ply.
    With sleeves—**12 ozs.**
    Without sleeves—**9 ozs.**
1 pair each No. 11 and 9 needles. *5 + 5 needles*
1 stitch holder.

TENSION.

7 sts. and 8 rows to 1in.

THE BACK.

Using No. 10 (11) needles, cast on 124 sts.
Work in K.1, P.1, rib for 29 rows.
30th row. Rib 3, (inc. rib 8) 13 times, inc. rib 3. (138 sts.)
Optional Cut off 16in. of the WENDY ELASTIC RIBBING, 2¼in. width, and using No. 10 (11) needles, commence in the 5th hole with the right side facing, to pick up 124 sts.
Next row. P.3, (inc., P.8) 13 times, inc., P.3 (138 sts.)
Change to No. 8 (9) needles, and commence pattern.
1st row. (K.3, P.6) 15 times, K.3.
2nd row. P.2, (K.6, P.3) 7 times, K.8, (P.3, K.6) 7 times, P.2.
3rd row. K.1, (P.6, K.3) 7 times, P.10, (K.3, P.6) 7 times, K.1.
4th row. (K.6, P.3) 7 times, K.12, (P.3, K.6) 7 times.
5th row. As 3rd row.
6th row. As 2nd row.
These 6 rows form the pattern. Rep. pattern 17 times more
Shape Armholes.
1st row. Cast off 6 sts., P.2, (K.3, P.6) 14 times, K.3.
2nd row. Cast off 6 sts., K.1, P.3, (K.6, P.3) 6 times, K.8, (P.3, K.6) 6 times, K.3, K.2.
3rd row. Cast off 6 sts., P.3, K.3, (P.6, K.3) 5 times, P.10, (K.3, P.6) 6 times, K.3, P.1.
4th row. Cast off 6 sts., K.2, P.3, (K.6, P.3) 5 times, K.12, (P.3, K.6) 5 times, P.3, K.3.
5th row. K.2 tog., P.2, K.3, (P.6, K.3) 5 times, P.10, (K.3, P.6) 5 times, K.3, P.2, K.2 tog.
6th row. K.2 tog., K.2, P.3, (K.6, P.3) 5 times, K.8, (P.3, K.6) 5 times, P.3, K.2, K.2 tog.
7th row. K.2 tog., P.2, (K.3, P.6) 11 times, K.3, P.2, K.2 tog.
8th row. K.2 tog., P.3, (K.6, P.3) 5 times, K.8, (P.3, K.6) 5 times, P.3, K.2 tog.
9th row. K.2 tog., K.1, (P.6, K.3) 5 times, P.10, (K.3, P.6) 5 times, K.1, K.2 tog.
10th row. K.2 tog., K.5, P.3, (K.6, P.3) 4 times, K.12, (P.3, K.6) 4 times, P.3, K.5, K.2 tog. (102 sts.)
11th row. K.1, (P.6, K.3) 5 times, P.10, (K.3, P.6) 5 times, K.1.
12th row. P.2, (K.6, P.3) 5 times, K.8, (P.3, K.6) 5 times, P.2.
13th row. (K.3, P.6) 11 times, K.3.
14th row. P.2, (K.6, P.3) 5 times, K.8, (P.3, K.6) 5 times, P.2.
15th row. K.1, (P.6, K.3) 5 times, P.10, (K.3, P.6) 5 times, K.1.
16th row. (K.6, P.3) 5 times, K.12, (P.3, K.6) 5 times.
17th row. As 15th row.
18th row. As 14th row.
Rep. the 13th to the 18th rows inclusive, 5 times more.
Cast off if WENDY ELASTIC RIBBING is used. If not

Next 6 rows. Work in K.1, P.1, rib.
Cast off.

THE FRONT.

Work exactly as for the Back, until the 13th to the 18th rows have been repeated 4 times more, only.
Shape Neck.
Next row. (K.3, P.6) 3 times, K.3, P.4, cast off 34 sts., P.3, (K.3, P.6) 3 times, K.3, work on the last 34 sts. as follows:—
1st row. P.2, (K.6, P.3) 3 times, K.3, K.2 tog.
2nd row. K.2 tog., P.3, K.3, (P.6, K.3) twice, P.6, K.1.
3rd row. (K.6, P.3) 3 times, K.3, K.2 tog.
4th row. K.2 tog., P.1, K.3, (P.6, K.3) twice, P.6, K.1.
5th row. P.2, (K.6, P.3) twice, K.6, P.2, K.2 tog.
6th row. K.2 tog., (P.6, K.3) 3 times.
Leave these sts. on st. holder. Join wool to rem. 34 sts. and work as follows :—
1st row. K.2 tog., K.3, (P.3, K.6) 3 times, P.2.
2nd row. K.1, P.6 (K.3, P.6) twice, K.3, P.3, K.2 tog.
3rd row. K.2 tog., K.3, (P.3, K.6) 3 times.
4th row. K.1, P.6, (K.3, P.6) twice, K.3, P.1, K.2 tog.
5th row. K.2 tog., P.6, K.6, (P.3, K.6) twice, P.2.
6th row. (K.3, P.6) 3 times, K.2 tog.
With right side of work facing, and on the same needle, pick up and K. 46 sts. Slip 28 sts. left on st. holder on to same needle. (102 sts.)
Cast off if WENDY ELASTIC RIBBING is used. If not:
Next 6 rows. Work in K.1, P.1, rib.
Cast off.

THE SLEEVES (Both alike).

Using No. 10 (11) needles, cast on 66 sts. Work in K.1, P.1, rib for 30 rows.
Optional. Cut off 9in. of the WENDY ELASTIC RIBBING, 2¼in. width and using No. 10 (11) needles, commence in the 5th hole with the right side facing, to pick up 66 sts.
Next row. P.
Change to No. 8 (9) needles, and commence pattern.
1st row. (K.3, P.6) 7 times, K.3.
2nd row. P.2, (K.6, P.3) 3 times, K.8, (P.3, K.6) 3 times, P.2.
3rd row. K.1, (P.6, K.3) 3 times, P.10, (K.3, P.6) 3 times, K.1.
4th row. (K.6, P.3) 3 times, K.12, (P.3, K.6) 3 times.
5th row. As 3rd row.
6th row. As 2nd row.
Rep. these 6 rows 4 times more.
31st row. Inc. K.2, P.6, (K.3, P.6) 6 times, K.2, inc.
32nd row. P.3, (K.6, P.3) 3 times, K.8, (P.3, K.6) 3 times, P.3.
33rd row. K.2, (P.6, K.3) 3 times, P.10, (K.3, P.6) 3 times, K.2.
34th row. P.1, (K.6, P.3) 3 times, K.12, (P.3, K.6) 3

MAN'S PULLOVER
(WITH OR WITHOUT SLEEVES)
in 4 ply

No. 277

PRICE 2ᴰ

times, P.1.

35th row. As 33rd row.

36th row. As 32nd row.

37th row. Inc., (K.3, P.6) 7 times, K.3, inc.

38th row. K.1, P.3, (K.6, P.3) 3 times, K.8, (P.3, K.6) 3 times, P.3, K.1.

39th row. K.3, (P.6, K.3) 3 times, P.10, (K.3, P.6) 3 times, K.3.

40th row. P.2, (K.6, P.3) 3 times, K.12, (P.3, K.6) 3 times, P.2.

41st row. As 39th row.

42nd row. As 38th row.

43rd row. Inc., P.1, (K.3, P.6) 7 times, K.3, P.1, inc.

44th row. K.2, P.3, (K.6, P.3) 3 times, K.8, (P.3, K.6) 3 times P.3 K.2.

45th row. P.1, K.3, (P.6, K.3) 3 times, P.10, (K.3, P.6) 3 times K.3, P.1.

46th row. P.3, (K.6, P.3) 3 times, K.12, (P.3, K.6) 3 times P.3.

47th row. As 45th row.

48th row. As 44th row.

49th row. Inc., P.2, (K.3, P.6) 7 times, K.3, P.2, inc.

50th row. K.3, P.3, (K.6, P.3) 3 times, K.8, (P.3, K.6) 3 times P.3, K.3.

51st row. P.2, K.3, (P.6, K.3) 3 times, P.10, (K.3, P.6) 3 times K.3 P.2.

52nd row. K.1, P.3, (K.6, P.3) 3 times, K.12, (P.3, K.6) 3 times, P.3, K.1.

53rd row. As 51st row.

54th row. As 50th row.

55th row. Inc., P.3, (K.3, P.6) 7 times, K.3, P.3, inc.

56th row. K.4, P.3, (K.6, P.3) 3 times, K.8, (P.3, K.6) 3 times, P.3, K.4.

57th row. P.3, K.3, (P.6, K.3) 3 times, P.10, (K.3, P.6) 3 times, K.3, P.3.

58th row. K.2, P.3, (K.6, P.3) 3 times, K.12, (P.3, K.6) 3 times, P.3, K.2.

59th row. As 57th row.

60th row. As 56 throw.

61st row. Inc., P.4 (K.3, P.6) 7 times, K.3, P.4, inc.

62nd row. K.5, P.3, (K.6, P.3) 3 times, K.8, (P.3, K.6) 3 times, P.3, K.5.
63rd row. P.4, K.3, (P.6, K.3) 3 times, P.10, (K.3, P.6) 3 times, K.3, P.4.
64th row. K.3, P.3, (K.6, P.3) 3 times, K.12, (P.3, K.6) 3 times, P.3, K.3.
65th row. As 63rd row.
66th row. As 62nd row.
67th row. Inc., P.5, (K.3, P.6) 7 times, K.3, P.5, inc.
68th row. (K.6, P.3) 4 times, K.8, (P.3, K.6) 4 times.
69th row. P.5, K.3, (P.6, K.3) 3 times, P.10, (K.3, P.6) 3 times, K.3, P.5.
70th row. K.4, P.3, (K.6, P.3,) 3 times, K.12, (P.3, K.6) 3 times, P.3, K.4.
71st row. As 69th row.
72nd row. As 68th row.
73rd row. Inc., P.6, (K.3, P.6) 8 times, inc.
74th row. P.1, (K.6, P.3) 4 times, K.8 (P.3, K.6) 4 times, P.1.
75th row. (P.6, K.3) 4 times, P.10, (K.3, P.6) 4 times.
76th row. K.5, P.3, (K.6, P.3) 3 times, K.12, (P.3, K.6) 3 times, P.3, K.5.
77th row. As 75th row.
78th row. As 74th row.
79th row. Inc., K.1, P.6, (K.3, P.6) 8 times, K.1., inc.
80th row. P.2, (K.6, P.3) 4 times, K.8, (P.3, K.6) 4 times, P.2.
81st row. K.1, (P.6, K.3) 4 times, P.10, (K.3, P.6) 4 times, K.1.
82nd row. (K.6, P.3) 4 times, K.12, (P.3, K.6) 4 times.
83rd row. As 81st row.
84th row. As 80th row.
85th row. Inc., K.2, P.6, (K.3, P.6) 8 times, K.2, inc.
86th row. P.3, (K.6, P.3) 4 times, K.8, (P.3, K.6) 4 times, P.3.
87th row. K.2, (P.6, K.3) 4 times, P.10, (K.3, P.6) 4 times, K.2.
88th row. P.1, (K.6, P.3) 4 times, K.12, (P.3, K.6) 4 times, P.1.
89th row. As 87th row.
90th row. As 86th row.
91st row. Inc., (K.3, P.6) 9 times, K.3, inc.
92nd row. K.1, P.3, (K.6, P.3) 4 times, K.8, (P.3, K.6) 4 times, P.3, K.1.
93rd row. K.3, (P.6, K.3) 4 times, P.10, (K.3, P.6) 4 times, K.3.
94th row. P.2, (K.6, P.3) 4 times, K.12, (P.3, K.6) 4 times, P.2.
95th row. As 93rd row.
96th row. As 92nd row.
97th row. Inc., P.1, (K.3, P.6) 9 times, K.3, P.1, inc.
98th row. K.2, P.3, (K.6, P.3) 4 times, K.8, (P.3, K.6) 4 times, P.3, K.2.
99th row. P.1, K.3, (P.6, K.3) 4 times, P.10, (K.3, P.6) 4 times, K.3, P.1.
100th row. P.3, (K.6, P.3) 4 times, K.12, (P.3, K.6) 4 times, P.3.
101st row. As 99th row.
102nd row. As 98th row.
103rd row. Inc. P.2, (K.3, P.6) 9 times, K.3, P.2, inc.
104th row. K.3, P.3, (K.6, P.3) 4 times, K.8, (P.3, K.6) 4 times, P.3, K.3.
105th row. P.2, K.3, (P.6, K.3) 4 times, P.10, (K.3, P.6) 4 times, K.3, P.2.
106th row. K.1, P.3, (K.6, P.3) 4 times, K.12, (P.3, K.6) 4 times, P.3, K.1.
107th row. As 105th row.
108th row. As 104th row.
109th row. Inc., P.3, (K.3, P.6) 9 times, K.3, P.3, inc.
110th row. K.4, P.3, (K.6, P.3) 4 times, K.8, (P.3, K.6) 4 times, P.3, K.4.
111th row. P.3, K.3, (P.6, K.3) 4 times, P.10, (K.3, P.6) 4 times, K.3, P.3.
112th row. K.2, P.3, (K.6, P.3) 4 times, K.12, (P.3, K.6) 4 times, P.3, K.2.
113th row. As 111th row.
114th row. As 110th row.
115th row. Inc. P.4, (K.3, P.6) 9 times, K.3, P.4, inc.
116th row. K.5, P.3, (K.6, P.3) 4 times, K.8, (P.3, K.6) 4 times, P.3, K.5.
117th row. P.4, K.3, (P.6, K.3) 4 times, P.10, (K.3, P.6) 4 times, K.3, P.4.
118th row. K.3, P.3, (K.6, P.3) 4 times, K.12, (P.3, K.6) 4 times, P.3, K.3.
119th row. As 117th row.
120th row. As 116th row.
121st row. Inc. P.5, (K.3, P.6) 9 times, K.3, P.5, inc.
122nd row. (K.6, P.3) 5 times, K.8, (P.3, K.6) 5 times.
123rd row. P.5, K.3, (P.6, K.3) 4 times, P.10, (K.3, P.6) 4 times, K.3, P.5.

124th row. K.4, P.3, (K.6, P.3) 4 times, K.12, (P.3, K.6) 4 times, P.3, K.4.
125th row. As 123rd row.
126th row. As 122nd row.
127th row. Inc. P.6, (K.3, P.6) 10 times, inc.
128th row. P.1, (K.6, P.3) 5 times, K.8, (P.3, K.6) 5 times, P.1.
129th row. (P.6, K.3) 5 times, P.10 (K.3, P.6) 5 times.
130th row. K.5, P.3, (K.6, P.3) 4 times, K.12, (P.3, K.6) 4 times, P.3, K.5.
131st row. As 129th row.
132nd row. As 128th row.
133rd row. Inc., K.1, P.6, (K.3, P.6) 10 times, K.1, inc.
134th row. P.2, (K.6, P.3) 5 times, K.8, (P.3, K.6) 5 times, P.2.
135th row. K.1, (P.6, K.3) 5 times, P.10, ((K.3, P.6) 5 times, K.1.
136th row. (K.6, P.3) 5 times, K.12, (P.3, K.6) 5 times.
Shape Top.
137th row. K.2 tog., P.5, K.3, (P.6, K.3) 4 times, P.10, (K.3, P.6) 4 times, K.3, P.5, K.2 tog.
138th row. K.2 tog., K.5, P.3, (K.6, P.3) 4 times, K.8, (P.3, K.6) 4 times, P.3, K.5, K.2 tog.
139th row. K.2 tog., P.5, (K.3, P.6) 9 times, K.3, P.5, K.2 tog.
140th row. K.2 tog., K.3, P.3, (K.6, P.3) 4 times, K.8, (P.3, K.6) 4 times, P.3, K.3, K.2 tog.
141st row. K.2 tog., P.1, K.3, (P.6, K.3) 4 times, P.10, (K.3, P.6) 4 times, K.3, P.1, K.2 tog.
142nd row. K.2 tog., P.2, (K.6, P.3) 4 times, K.12, (P.3, K.6) 4 times, P.2, K.2 tog.
143rd row. K.2 tog., K.2, (P.6, K.3) 4 times, P.10, (K.3, P.6) 4 times, K.2, K.2 tog.
144th row. K.2 tog., P.2, (K.6, P.3) 4 times, K.8, (P.3, K.6) 4 times, P.2, K.2 tog.
145th row. K.2 tog., K.2, P.6, (K.3, P.6) 8 times, K.2, K.2 tog.
146th row. K.2 tog., (K.6, P.3) 4 times, K.8, (P.3, K.6) 4 times, K.2 tog.
147th row. K.2 tog., P.4, K.3, (P.6, K.3) 3 times, P.10, (K.3, P.6) 3 times, K.3, P.4, K.2 tog.
148th row. K.2 tog., K.2, P.3, (K.6, P.3) 3 times, K.12, (P.3, K.6) 3 times, P.3, K.2, K.2 tog.
149th row. K.2 tog., P.2, K.3, (P.6, K.3) 3 times, P.10, (K.3, P.6) 3 times, K.3, P.2, K.2 tog.
150th row. K.2 tog., K.2, P.3, (K.6, P.3) 3 times, K.8, (P.3, K.6) 3 times, P.3, K.2, K.2 tog.
151st row. K.2 tog., P.2, (K.3, P.6) 7 times, K.3, P.2, K.2 tog.
152nd row. K.2 tog., P.3, (K.6, P.3) 3 times, K.8, (P.3, K.6) 3 times, P.3, K.2 tog.
153rd row. K.2 tog., K.1, (P.6, K.3) 3 times, P.10, (K.3, P.6) 3 times, K.1, K.2 tog.
154th row. K.2 tog., K.5, P.3, (K.6, P.3) twice, K.12, (P.3, K.6) twice, P.3, K.5, K.2 tog.
155th row. K.2 tog., P.5, K.3, (P.6, K.3) twice, P.10, (K.3, P.6) twice, K.3, P.5, K.2 tog.
156th row. K.2 tog., K.5, P.3, (K.6, P.3) twice, K.8, (P.3, K.6) twice, P.3, K.5, K.2 tog.
157th row. K.2 tog., P.5, (K.3, P.6) 5 times, K.3, P.5, K.2 tog.
158th row. K.2 tog., K.3, P.3, (K.6, P.3) twice, K.8, (P.3, K.6) twice, P.3, K.3, K.2 tog.
159th row. K.2 tog., P.1, K.3, (P.6, K.3) twice, P.10, (K.3, P.6) twice, K.3, P.1, K.2 tog.
160th row. K.2 tog., P.2 ,(K.6, P.3) twice, K.12, (P.3, K.6) twice, P.2, K.2 tog.
161st row. K.2 tog., K.2, (P.6, K.3) twice, P.10, (K.3, P.6) twice, K.2, K.2 tog.
162nd row. K.2 tog., P.2, (K.6, P.3) twice, K.8, (P.3, K.6) twice, P.2, K.2 tog.
163rd row. K.2 tog., K.2, P.6, (K.3, P.6) 4 times, K.2, K.2 tog. (48 sts.)
Cast off.

ARMHOLE RIBBING. (Without sleeves)
Sew up 26 sts. of rib for shoulders, with right side facing, using No. 8 needles, pick up 124 sts. round armhole.
Work 6 rows in K.1, P.1, rib.
Cast off loosely.
Work the other armhole to correspond.

To MAKE UP.
Press each part lightly with a warm iron under a damp cloth.
If sleeves are worked, join 26 sts. of rib for shoulder
Sew side and sleeve seams. Insert sleeves.
Press all seams.
Optional. Sew 16in. of ⅜in. width WENDY ELASTIC RIBBING across neck and shoulders of both Back and Front. Sew together the equivalent of 26 sts. for each shoulder. Sew over ends of WENDY ELASTIC RIBBING with a run-and-fell seam.

Big-knit jacket · For pattern see page 164

Slipover and socks to match · For pattern see page 140

Norwegian knit and real silk scarf · For jersey pattern see page 158, for scarf pattern see page 65

Smart sweater · For pattern see page 80

Evening Scarf

MATERIALS

4 oz. of real silk.
2 No. 10 knitting needles.
A crochet hook to make the fringe.

MEASUREMENTS

Length, 52 ins.
Width, 10½ ins.

TENSION

One complete patt. measures about 1¾ ins.

Cast on 80 sts. and work in patt. thus:—
1st row.—K. 1, (p. 1, k. 1) twice, *k. twice into next st., k. 4, (k. 2 tog.) twice, k. 3, k. twice into next st., k. 1; rep. from * to last 5 sts., (k. 1, p. 1) twice, k. 1.

2nd row.—K. 1, (p. 1, k. 1) twice, p. to last 5 sts., (k. 1, p. 1) twice, k. 1.

Rep. these 2 rows until work measures 52 ins. Cast off.

The Fringe.—Cut lengths of yarn about 3½ ins. long. Take 4 strands and fold in half, draw the loop through the edge of the fabric, then draw the ends through the loop and pull tight. Continue thus in every alternate stitch all along.

Top hats and tail coats may be ruled out these days, but the festive feeling that goes with a special occasion can be helped a lot by this elegant white silk scarf. It's knitted in a rib that gives a wide arrow-head effect.

The young don't believe in over-coats—a woollen scarf is all they'll submit to. Then let the scarf be a worthy one, both warm and easy to wear. Here is the silk scarf knitted in wool. It's longer by eight inches. You can add school or club colours if you wish.

The sports scarf is made in wool, using the same instructions, but with these differences in materials and measurements.

MATERIALS

6 oz. 4-ply wool.
2 No. 9 knitting needles.

MEASUREMENTS

Length, 60 ins.
Width, 10½ ins.

For the sports scarf repeat the patt. until the work measures 60 ins. instead of 52 ins. for the silk scarf.

See colour plate on page 63

Man's Fair Isle Pullover

FEATURING A ROUND NECK

This good-looking classic pullover, knitted in an effective three-colour Fair Isle pattern, is neat without being bulky and will fit comfortably under a coat. The round neck, deep welt and cuffs are in plain ribbing.

MATERIALS

7 oz. 4-ply wool in a dark colour.
4 oz. 4-ply wool in a light colour.
2 oz. 4-ply wool in a medium colour.
2 No. 8 and 2 No. 12 knitting needles.

MEASUREMENTS

Length, 21½ ins.
Chest, 38 ins.
Sleeve, 22½ ins. including cuff.

TENSION

7 sts. to 1 in. on No. 8 needles.

ADDITIONAL ABBREVIATIONS

Dk. =dark; lt. =light; md. =medium.

The Back.—With No. 12 needles and dk. wool cast on 108 sts. and work in k. 2, p. 2 rib for 4 ins.

Next row.—Rib 6, * inc. in next st., rib 2; rep. from * to last 6 sts., rib 6 (140 sts.).

Change to No. 8 needles and work in patt. as shown on chart.

The odd number rows are k. rows and are worked from right to left, the even number rows are p. rows and are worked from left to right.

A guide to the colours is given on the chart. Thus the first 2 rows will read:—

1st row.—K. * 2 lt., 1 md., 1 lt.; rep. from * to end.

2nd row.—P. * 3 md., 1 lt.; rep. from * to end.

Rows 1 to 48 form the patt.

Continue in patt. until 1 complete patt. and 16 rows of the 2nd patt. have been worked and work measures about 13 ins. from lower edge.

Shape Armholes thus: Cast off 6 sts. at beg. of next 2 rows, then k. 2 tog. at both

See colour plate on page 25

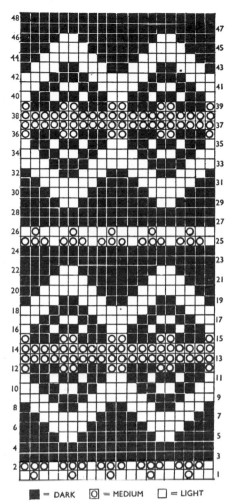

■ = DARK	◎ = MEDIUM	□ = LIGHT

Key to the Fair Isle pattern.

The Front.—Work to match back until armhole shaping has been completed and 104 sts. remain.

Continue without shaping until work measures 19 ins.

Shape Neck thus:—

Patt. 44, turn, work on these sts. only, dec. 1 st. at neck edge on every row until 32 sts. remain, then work without further shaping until the work measures 21½ ins., ending at the armhole edge.

Shape Shoulder thus:—

1st row.—Cast off 8, patt. to end.
2nd row.—Patt. to end.
Rep. these 2 rows twice.
Cast off.
Sl. centre 16 sts. on to spare needle, work to end, then shape to match first side.

The Sleeves.—With No. 12 needles and dk. wool cast on 60 sts. Work in k. 2, p. 2 rib for 3 ins.

Change to No. 8 needles and work in patt. inc. 1 st. both ends of 3rd row and every following 4th row until 118 sts. are on the needle.

Continue without shaping until 2 complete patts. and 36 rows of 3rd patt. have

been worked and work measures about 22½ ins.

Shape Top thus: K. 2 tog. at both ends of every row until 60 sts. remain.
Cast off.

The Back Neck Band.—With No. 12 needles and dk. wool, and with right side of work facing, knit up 7 sts. along one side of neck edge, k. 30 sts. from spare needle, then k. up 7 sts. along other side of neck (44 sts.).

Work in k. 2, p. 2 rib for 1 in.
Cast off in rib.

The Front Neck Band.—With No. 12 needles and dk. wool, and with right side of work facing, knit up 36 sts. down one side of neck, k. 16 sts. from spare needle, then knit up 36 sts. along other side of neck (88 sts.).

Work in k. 2, p. 2 rib for 1 in.
Cast off.

Make-up.—Press work carefully on the wrong side under a damp cloth with a very hot iron.

Join side, sleeve and shoulder seams with back stitch.

Sew in sleeves. Press all seams.

ends of alternate rows until 104 sts. remain.

Continue without shaping until work measures 21½ ins.

Shape Neck and Shoulders thus:—

1st row.—Cast off 8, patt. to last 67 sts., turn, work on these 29 sts. for one shoulder.

2nd row.—K. 2 tog., patt. to end.
3rd row.—Cast off 8, patt. to last 2 sts., k. 2 tog.
Rep. last 2 rows once, then 2nd row again.
Cast off.
Sl. centre 30 sts. on to spare needle and leave for the present, then work one row in patt. across remaining 37 sts.
Continue thus for second shoulder:—
1st row.—Cast off 8, patt. to last 2 sts., k. 2 tog.
2nd row.—K. 2 tog., patt. to end.
Rep. last 2 rows once then 1st row again.
Cast off.

Any man who appreciates ease and comfort and a smart appearance will value this "all occasions" sports sweater—it can be as sporting or as formal as a man could wish.

GENT'S PULLOVER
with or without Sleeves

MATERIALS REQUIRED
7 ozs. "Secil" 3-ply Merino Wool (Sleeveless); 12 ozs. "Secil" 3-ply Merino Wool (with Sleeves); 1 pair No. 9 "Secil" needles; 1 (set of 4) No. 11 needles double pointed.

MEASUREMENTS
Length, 21½ ins.; Chest, 38 ins. to 40 ins.

ABBREVIATIONS
K., Knit; P., Purl; sts., stitches; patt., pattern; tog., together.

THE BACK
With No. 9 needles cast on 110 sts.
Knit into the back of each st. unless the thumb method of casting on is used, when this is not necessary.
Change to No. 11 needles and work in rib (K.1, P.1) for 40 rows.
Purl the next row, but increase the sts. by purling into the front and then into the back of every 3rd st. until 14 sts. remain. P.14. (142 sts.).
Change to No. 9 needles and the pattern.
1st patt. row—K.4, * P.2, K.4, P.2, K.6; repeat from * to the end, ending K.4.
2nd patt. row—K.6, * P.4, K.10; repeat from * to the end, ending K.6.
Repeat the last 2 rows twice more.
7th patt. row—K.4, * P.2, slip the next 2 sts. on to a double pointed needle and let it fall to the back of the work, knit the next 2 sts. and then knit the 2 sts. from the spare needle. (This will be referred to as Cable 4), P.2, K.6; repeat from * to the end, ending with P.2, Cable 4, P.2, K.4.
8th patt. row—Repeat the 2nd row.
9th patt. row—Repeat the 1st row.
10th patt. row—P.4, * K.2, P.4, K.2, P.6; repeat from * to the end, ending P.4.
Repeat the last 2 rows twice more.
15th patt. row—Repeat the 7th row.
16th patt. row—Repeat the 10th row.
These 16 rows complete one patt. and are repeated throughout.
Work until there are 6 complete patterns from the ribbing.

ARMHOLE SHAPING
Cast off 4 sts. at the beginning of each of the next 6 rows.
Then work 2 sts. tog. at each end of the next 5 rows.
Care must be taken to keep the patt. sequence correct as these decreases are made.
Continue working without further shaping until there are 10 complete patts. of 16 rows from the beginning.
Then work the first 10 rows of another patt.

SHOULDER SHAPING
Cast off 10 sts. at the beginning of each of the next 6 rows. Leave the remaining 48 sts. on a spare needle.

THE FRONT
Work exactly as instructed for the Back until the armhole shaping is reached.

ARMHOLE SHAPING AND LEFT SIDE OF NECK
1st row—Cast off 4 sts., * P.2, K.4, P.2, K.6; repeat from * 3 times more, P.2, K.4, P.2, K.1, K.2 tog., turn.
2nd row—P.2, K.2, * P.4, K.10; repeat from * to the end, ending K.2.
3rd row—Cast off 4 sts., K.2, P.2, K.6, * P.2, K.4, P.2, K.6; repeat from * twice more, P.2, K.4, P.2, K.2.
4th row—P.2, K.2, * P.4, K.10; repeat from * 3 times, P.2.
5th row—Cast off 4 sts., * K.6, P.2, K.4, P.2; repeat from * to the end, but knit the last 2 sts. tog.
6th row—P.1, K.2, * P.4, K.10; repeat from * to the end, ending P.4, K.8.
Continue now working in patt., but work 2 sts. tog. at the armhole edge on each of the next 5 rows. At the same time work 2 sts. tog. at the neck edge on every 4th row until there are 10 complete patterns of 16 rows from the beginning.
Now work 10 rows of another patt., but decrease at the neck edge on every alternate row. (32 sts.).

SHOULDER SHAPING
1st row—Cast off 10 sts., work in patt. to last 2 sts., K.2 tog.
2nd row—Work in patt.
Repeat the last 2 rows once.
Cast off the remaining sts.

RIGHT ARMHOLE AND RIGHT SIDE OF NECK
Join in the wool at the centre front.
1st row—K.2 tog., K.1, * P.2, K.4, P.2, K.6; repeat from * to the end, ending K.4.
2nd row—Cast off 4 sts., K.2, * P.4, K.10; repeat from * 3 times more, P.4, K.2, P.2.
3rd row—K.2, * P.2, K.4, P.2, K.6; repeat from * to the end, ending P.2, K.4, P.2.
4th row—Cast off 4 sts., P.2, * K.10, P.4; repeat from * 3 times more, K.2, P.2.
5th row—K.2 tog., * P.2, K.4, P.2, K.6; repeat from * to the end, ending P.2, K.2.
6th row—Cast off 4 sts., K.8, * P.4, K.10; repeat from * twice more, P.4, K.2, P.1.
Continue working the patt., decreasing 1 st. at the armhole edge on each of the next 5 rows, and also decreasing 1 st. at the neck edge on every 4th row until there are 10 complete patts. from the beginning.
Work 11 rows of the next patt. but now decrease on alternate rows at the neck edge. End at the armhole edge.

SHOULDER SHAPING
Cast off 10 sts. at the beginning of the next 2 alternate rows and work 2 sts. tog. at the neck edge.
Cast off the remaining 10 sts.

THE NECK BAND
Join up the shoulder seams and with the right side of the work towards you, using the set of 4 double pointed needles and starting at centre front, pick up 72 sts. up the right side of the neck. Slip the sts. left at the back of the neck on to another needle, and then pick up 72 sts. down the left side of the neck on another needle.
Work for 8 rows in rib (K.1, P.1), turning at the centre front, and work 2 sts. tog. at the centre front at the beginning and end of every row. Cast off loosely in rib with a No. 9 needle.

THE ARMBANDS (Not required if sleeves are worked)
With No. 11 needles pick up 172 sts. along the armhole edges.
Work in rib (K.1, P.1) for 8 rows.
Cast off in rib with a No. 9 needle.

THE SLEEVES (both alike)
With No. 11 needles cast on 58 sts.
Work in rib (K.1, P.1) for 40 rows.
Change to No. 9 needles and the pattern as instructed for the Back.
Work 8 rows in patt., and then increase 1 st. at each end of the next and every following 6th row until the work measures 19 inches from the beginning. The length of sleeve can be regulated here and more or less rows worked as required.
Take care to keep the patt. correct whilst the increased sts. are being worked.

SLEEVE SHAPING
Work 2 sts. tog. at each end of every row until 30 sts. remain. Cast off.

TO MAKE UP
Press with hot iron and DRY cloth. Sew up the seams and join the neck band neatly at the centre front. Darn all ends in neatly and give the seams a final press.

SECIL
REGISTERED TRADE MARK

**KNITTING
WOOLS**

No. 366
4ᴰ

Golf Club Covers

KNITTED IN MIXED COLOURS

MATERIALS

1 oz. 4-ply wool (mixed colours).
2 No. 10 and 2 No. 12 knitting needles.

MEASUREMENTS

Length about 11½ ins.

ABBREVIATIONS

K. knit, p. purl, sts. stitches, rep. repeat, ins. inches, tog. together, st. st. stocking stitch, (1 row K., 1 row P).

With No. 12 needles cast on 48 sts. and work in k. 2, p. 2 rib for 7 ins.

Change to No. 10 needles and st.st. and continue straight until work measures 10½ ins., ending with a p. row.

Shape top thus :—

1st row.—*K. 6, k. 2 tog., rep. from* to end. **2nd and alternate rows.**—P.

3rd row.—* K. 5, k. 2 tog., rep. from * to end.

5th row.—*K. 4, k. 2 tog., rep. from * to end.

7th row.—* K. 3, k. 2 tog., rep. from * to end.

9th row.—*K. 2 tog., rep. from * to end. **10th row.**—P.

Break wool, thread end through sts., draw up and fasten off. Join side edges.

Make a tassel and sew to top securely.

FOR THE GOLFER. *He will welcome these gay little covers to protect his golf clubs. The originals were knitted in rows of different coloured wool, and were about eleven inches in length with a tassel fixed to the top.*

Diamond Stitch Pullover

MATERIALS: Of Patons Fair Isle Fingering, 4 ozs. navy and 3 ozs. grey. A pair each Nos. 9 and 12 "Beehive" needles.

MEASUREMENTS: To fit 36–38-inch chest; length from top of shoulders, 22½ inches.

TENSION: 8 stitches and 8 rows to an inch.

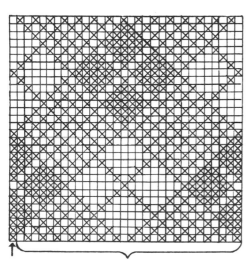

Last st. K. rows   30 Pattern sts.
First st. P. rows

BACK

With No. 12 needles and navy, cast on 151 sts. and work 3½ inches k. 1, p. 1 rib, rows on right side having a k. 1 at each end.

Change to No. 9 needles and diamond pattern in stocking-stitch, working the 30 rows from chart, reading knit rows from right to left, purl rows from left to right. Work the 30 pattern sts. 5 times across and last stitch on knit rows and first stitch on purl rows as indicated. Work the 30 rows twice, then the first 16 rows again.

Shape armholes: Cast off 5 sts. at beginning of next 6 rows, *i.e.*, you have decreased half a diamond, 15 sts., up each armhole and 121 sts. remain.

Work straight to end of 24th row of 5th pattern from start, then shape shoulders by casting off 10 sts. at beginning of next 6 rows; this completes 5th pattern and 61 sts. remain. Cast off.

FRONT

Work as for back to end of 16th row of 3rd pattern.

Shape armholes and divide for neck: Cast off 5, k. 70 in pattern, turn and continue on these 70 sts., leaving remaining 76 on a spare needle. * NEXT ROW (wrong side facing): Purl in pattern to end. NEXT ROW: Cast off 5, knit in pattern to last 2 sts., k. 2 tog. Repeat from * once more (58 sts. remain).

Keep armhole edge straight and k. 2 tog. at neck edge on every knit row until 30 sts. remain. Work straight to end of 24th row of 5th pattern, then shape shoulder by casting off 10 sts. at beginning of next and following 2 alternate rows.

Return to sts. on spare needle. With right side facing, join in wool at neck edge, cast off 1 for centre V., k. 75 in pattern. NEXT ROW: Cast off 5, purl in pattern to end. NEXT ROW: k. 2 tog., knit in pattern to end. Now complete to correspond with first half.

TO MAKE UP

Press back and front carefully under a damp cloth, taking care not to spoil rib. NECK RIB: With navy, No. 12 needles and right side facing, pick up and k. 60 sts. across back of neck. Work 1¼ inches k. 1, p. 1 rib; cast off in rib. Similarly pick up 64 sts. down left side of neck, 1 from centre V. and 64 up right side. Work 1¼ inches rib, decreasing at either side of centre st. on alternate rows. Cast off in rib. *Armhole rib:* Join shoulder seams and press on wrong side. Pick up 140 sts. round each armhole as for neck; work 1¼ inches rib and cast off in rib. Join side seams and press on wrong side. Press ribbed bands very lightly.

man's knitted waistcoat

neat under a coat

MATERIALS

5 oz. 4-ply wool in main colour.
5 oz. 4-ply wool in contrasting colour.
2 No. 11 and 2 No. 13 knitting needles.
7 buttons.

MEASUREMENTS

Length at back, 18½ ins. (including border).
Chest, 38 ins.

TENSION

8 sts. to 1 in. on No. 11 needles.

ADDITIONAL ABBREVIATIONS

Mn. = main colour; c. = contrasting colour.

The Back.—With No. 13 needles and mn. wool cast on 144 sts. and work in patt. thus:—

1st row.—* K.5 mn., 1 c., rep. from * to end.

2nd row.—* P.1 mn., 1 c., 3 mn., 1 c., rep. from * to end.

3rd row.—* K.1 mn., 1 c., 1 mn., 1 c., 2 mn., rep. from * to end.

4th row.—* P.3 mn., 1 c., 2 mn., rep. from * to end.

5th row.—* K.1 mn., 1 c., 1 mn., 1 c., 2 mn., rep. from * to end.

6th row.—* P.1 mn., 1 c., 3 mn., 1 c., rep. from * to end.

These 6 rows form the patt.

Continue in patt. until work measures 2 ins., ending on the wrong side.

Change to No. 11 needles and continue in patt., inc. 1 st. at both ends of the next and every 10th row until there are 156 sts.

Continue straight until work measures 8½ ins., ending with a row on the wrong side.

Shape Armholes thus:—Cast off 4 sts. at beg. of next 2 rows, then dec. 1 st. at both ends of every row until 108 sts. remain.

Continue straight until work measures 17½ ins., ending on the wrong side.

Shape Shoulders thus: Cast off 8 sts. at beg. of next 8 rows.

Cast off remaining sts.

The Left Front.

The Pocket Linings.—With No. 11 needles and mn. wool cast on 30 sts. and work in st.st. for 3 ins., ending with a p. row.

Leave these sts. on a spare needle.

Work another pocket lining in the same way.

With No. 11 needles and mn. wool cast on 3 sts.

Now work in patt. as for back, making the centre st. of the cast-on sts. the base of diamond patt. and inc. to shape point thus:—

1st row.—K.1 mn., 1 c., with mn. k. twice in the last st.

2nd row.—With mn., p. twice in first st., p.1 c., 1 mn., 1 c.

3rd row.—With mn. cast on 4 sts., k.1 mn., 1 c., 1 mn., 1 c., 3 mn., 1 c., with mn., k. twice in the last st.

4th row.—With mn. p. twice in the first st., p.1 c., 5 mn., 1 c., 2 mn.

5th row.—With mn. cast on 4 sts. patt. to last st., k. twice in last st.

6th row.—With mn. p. twice in first st., patt. to end.

Continue thus, inc. 1 st. at beg. of every wrong side row and end of every right side row, and casting on 4 at beg. of every right side row, working the extra sts. into patt. until there are 70 sts., thus ending with a row on the right side.

Next row.—Work twice in first st., patt. to end.

Next row.—Work to last st., work twice in last st.

Change to No. 13 needles and continue straight in patt. for a further 2 ins., ending with a row on the wrong side.

Change to No. 11 needles and continue in patt., inc. 1 st. at the beg. of the next and every following 10th row until work measures 2½ ins. measured from beg. of work on No. 13 needles, and ending with a 6th patt. row.

Insert Pocket Lining thus:—

Next row.—Patt. to last 48 sts., slip the next 30 sts. on a spare needle.

Now with the right side of the pocket lining facing, work in patt. across the 30 sts. of lining on a spare needle, patt. to end.

Continue in patt., still inc. 1 st. at beg. of every 10th row until there are 78 sts.

Continue straight until work measures 8½ ins. (measured from beg. of work on No. 13 needles), ending with a row on the wrong side.

Shape Armholes thus: Cast off 4 sts.

at beg. of next row, then dec. 1 st. at armhole edge in every row until work measures 9 ins., ending with a 6th patt. row.

Insert Top Pocket Lining thus:—

Next row.—Work 2 tog., patt. to last 48 sts., slip next 30 sts. on a spare needle, now with right side of pocket lining facing work in patt. across the 30 sts. of pocket lining, patt. to end.

Next row.—Work to last 2 sts., work 2 tog.

Continue in patt., still dec. 1 st. at armhole edge in every row, and dec. 1 st. at neck edge in the next and every following 4th row, until 24 sts. have been dec. at armhole edge, including the 4 sts. cast off at beg. of armhole shaping.

Continue in patt., dec. 1 st. at front edge only in every 4th row, until 32 sts. remain.

Continue straight on these 32 sts. until work measures 17½ ins., ending at armhole edge.

Shape Shoulder thus:—

Next row.—Cast off 8 sts., work to end.

Next row.—Work to end.

Rep. these 2 rows twice more.

Cast off.

The Right Front.—Work pocket linings as for left front.

With No. 11 needles and mn. wool cast on 3 sts.

Now making the centre cast-on st. the base of diamond patt. as for left front, shape for front thus:—

1st row.—With mn. work twice in first st., k.1 c., with mn. k. to end.

2nd row.—With mn. cast on 4 sts., p.1 c., 3 mn., 1 c., 1 mn., 1 c., with mn. p. twice in last st.

3rd row.—With mn. work twice in first st., k.1 c., 3 mn., 1 c., 1 mn., 1 c., 1 mn.

4th row.—With mn. cast on 4 sts., p.1 c., 5 mn., 1 c., 5 mn., 1 c., with mn. p. twice in last st.

Continue thus inc. at beg. of wrong side rows, and end of right side rows and casting on 4 sts. at beg. of every wrong side row, until there are 70 sts., thus ending with a row on the right side.

Next row.—Work to last st., work twice in last st.

Next row.—Work twice in first st., work to end.

Change to No. 13 needles and continue in patt. for a further 2 ins., ending with a row on the wrong side.

Change to No. 11 needles and continue in patt., inc. 1 st. at the end of the next and every following 10th row, until work measures 2½ ins. (measured from beg. of work on No. 13 needles), ending with a 6th patt. row.

Insert Pocket Lining thus:—

Next row.—Patt.18, slip next 30 sts. on a spare needle, now with right side of pocket lining facing, work in patt. across the 30 sts. on spare needle of lining, patt. to end.

Continue in patt., inc. 1 st. at end of every 10th row as before until there are 78 sts.

Continue straight on these 78 sts. until work measures 8¼ ins., ending with a row on the right side.

Shape Armhole thus: Cast off 4 sts. at beg. of next row, then dec. 1 st. at armhole edge in every row until work measures 9 ins., ending with a 6th patt. row.

Insert Pocket Lining thus:

Next row.—Patt.18, slip next 30 sts. on a spare needle, now with right side of pocket lining facing, patt. across the 30 sts. of lining on a spare needle, patt. to last 2 sts., work 2 tog.

Continue in patt., dec. 1 st. at front edge in next and every 4th row, still dec. in every row at armhole edge, until 24 sts. have been dec. at armhole edge.

Continue in patt., dec. 1 st. at front edge in every 4th row, until 32 sts. remain. Complete to match left side.

The Pocket Borders.—Using No. 13 needles and c. wool work in g.st. on the 30 sts. on spare needles at pocket tops, for ½ in.

Cast off.

The Front Border.—With No. 13 needles and c. wool cast on 3 sts. and work in g.st., casting on 2 sts. at the beg. of every alternate row until there are 9 sts.

Work in g.st. for 4½ ins. (length of front point), now work a buttonhole thus:—

Next row.—K.3, cast off 3, k. to end.
Next row.—K.3, cast on 3, k.3.

Continue in g.st., making further buttonholes in the same way at intervals of 1½ ins. from the last buttonhole worked, until 7 buttonholes have been worked.

Continue straight in g.st until shortest edge of border is of sufficient length to fit round front edges, along back of neck, to end of right front point when slightly stretched.

Cast off 2 sts. on alternate rows at

Grey and tan was the colour scheme for this knitted waistcoat, and the design gives a neatness of appearance that cannot help but be popular. The pattern makes a firm but not too thick fabric, and will not be bulky when worn under a jacket.

shaped edge, until 3 sts. remain.

Cast off.

The Lower Edge Border.—With No. 13 needles and c. wool cast on 3 sts., and work in g.st., casting on 2 sts. on alternate rows until there are 9 sts.

Continue straight in g.st. until lower border is long enough to reach all round lower edge, from left front point to right front point.

Cast off 2 sts. at shaped edge on alternate rows until 3 sts. remain.

Cast off.

The Sleeve Borders.—With No. 13 needles and c. wool cast on 9 sts. and work in g.st. until border is long enough to reach all round armhole edge.

Cast off.

Work a second border in the same way.

Make-up.—Press work lightly on wrong side with hot iron and a damp cloth.

Join side and shoulder seams.

Sew down pocket borders neatly on the wrong side, and sew linings into position.

Sew lower edge border all round lower edge, sewing shortest edge of border to garment, with shaped edges from the left front point to the right front point.

Sew front borders all round front edges and back of neck, matching the shaped edges of borders, to shaped edges of lower borders, and placing buttonholes on left-hand side.

Sew on buttons to match the buttonholes.

man's long-sleeved pullover

in two-colour fair isle

Designed especially for the man who spends most of his spare time on the golf-links, this Fair Isle sports pullover simply cannot fail to please. In a two-colour all-over pattern, the original garment was made up in a smart combination of black and grey. The deep welt, cuffs and neckline are in plain rib.

MATERIALS
6 oz. 3-ply in main colour.
4 oz. 3-ply in contrasting colour.
2 No. 12, 2 No. 9 knitting needles and 4 No. 12 knitting needles with points both ends.

MEASUREMENTS
Length, 22 ins.
Chest, 40 ins.
Sleeve seam, 19 ins.

TENSION
7 sts. to 1 in. on No. 9 needles.

ADDITIONAL ABBREVIATIONS
Mn. = main; c. = contrasting.

The Back.—With 2 No. 12 needles and mn. wool cast on 120 sts. and work in k.1, p.1 rib for 4 ins.

Next row.—Work twice in the first st., rib 3, work twice in the next st., * rib 4, work twice in the next st., rep. from * to end. (145 sts.) Change to No. 9 needles.

Now work in Fair Isle patt.

The patt. is worked from the chart on page **75** across all sts.

Where more than 6 sts. are worked in one colour, do not weave wools, but catch up wool not in use once or twice on the wrong side.

The odd numbered rows are k. rows and are worked from right to left, the even numbered rows are p. rows and are worked from left to right.

Each square represents 1 st. The white squares are mn. wool and the dark squares are c. wool.

Thus the first 2 rows will be:—

1st row.—* K.1 mn., 1 c., rep. from * to last st., k.1 mn.

2nd row.—P.1 mn., * (1 mn., 1 c.) 8 times, 2 mn., rep. from * to end.

Continue working in patt. until work measures 13 ins., ending with a row on the wrong side.

Shape Armholes thus: Cast off 5 sts. at beg. of next 2 rows, then dec. 1 st. at both ends of every row until 109 sts. remain.

Continue straight on these 109 sts. until work measures 22 ins., ending with a row on the wrong side.

Divide for Neck thus:—

Next row.—Patt.38, cast off 33 sts., patt. to end.

Now work on the 2nd set of 38 sts. for one side of neck only, thus:—

Next row.—Cast off 8 sts., patt. to last 2 sts., work 2 tog.

Next row.—Work 2 tog., patt. to end.

Rep. these 2 rows twice more.

Cast off.

Rejoin wools at neck edge to remaining 38 sts.

Next row.—Patt. to end.

Now work to match other side.

The Front.—Work exactly as given for the back until armhole shapings are completed and 109 sts. remain.

Continue straight on these 109 sts. until work measures 19½ ins., ending with a row on the wrong side.

Shape Neck thus:—

Next row.—Patt.44, cast off next 21 sts., patt. to end.

Now work on the 2nd set of 44 sts. for one side of neck only thus:—

Continue in patt., dec. 1 st. at neck edge in every row until only 32 sts. remain.

Continue straight on 32 sts. until work measures 22 ins., ending at armhole edge.

Shape Shoulder thus: Cast off 8 sts.

ALTERNATIVE INSTRUCTIONS FOR SLEEVELESS VERSION

5 oz. of mn. colour and 3 oz. of c. will be needed.

Work as given, but omit sleeves.

With right side of work facing, using No. 12 needles and mn. colour wool, pick up and k.160 sts. round armhole. (80 sts. either side of shoulder seam.)

Work in k.1, p.1 rib for 1 in. Cast off in rib.

Join side seams.

Press seams.

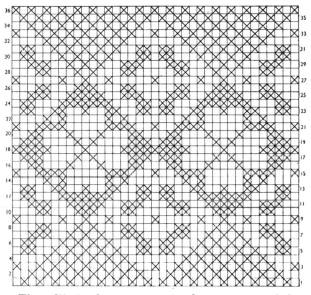

These 37 sts. show two repeats plus one extra stitch.

The attractive two-colour Fair Isle is shown here without sleeves. Instructions for knitting the plain ribbed armhole borders are on this page. The diamond-shaped pattern is new and effective.

at beg. of next and alternate rows until all sts. are cast off.

Rejoin wools at neck edge to remaining sts. and work to match.

The Sleeves.—With No. 12 needles and mn. wool cast on 72 sts. and work in k.1, p.1 rib for 3 ins., inc. 1 st. at the end of the last row. (73 sts.)

Change to No. 9 needles, and continue in patt. as for back until the 8th patt. row has been worked.

Continue in patt., inc. 1 st. at both ends of the next and every following 4th row, working the extra sts. into the patt., until there are 127 sts.

Continue straight on these 127 sts. until work measures 19 ins. from cast-on

edge, ending on the wrong side.

Shape Top thus: Dec. 1 st. at both ends of the next and every row until 59 sts. remain. Cast off.

The Neck Border.—Join shoulder seams.

With right side of work facing, using the 4 No. 12 needles and mn. wool, and starting at right shoulder seam, pick up and k.112 sts. evenly all round neck edge. Arrange these sts. on 3 needles and work in k.1, p.1 rib for 1 in. Cast off loosely in rib.

Make-up.—Press work lightly on the wrong side, using a warm iron and a damp cloth.

Join side and sleeve seams.

Sew sleeves into armholes, matching seams. Press all seams.

little boys' jerseys

Materials: 5 ozs. "Greenock" Super Fingering 3-ply natural or 5 ozs. "Greenock" Fair Isle Fingering natural ; balls of red, black, blue, yellow, green, white and flesh in a similar weight of wool for the Drummer Boys and of brown and royal blue for the Teddy Bears ; 1 pair each knitting needles nos. 10 and 12 ; 4 buttons.

Tension: 7½ stitches to one inch in width and 10 rows to one inch in depth on no. 10 needles.

Measurements: length from shoulder 15½ inches, chest 24 inches, sleeve seam 12 inches.

Abbreviations:

k knit
p purl
sts stitches
rep repeat
beg beginning
inc increase, by working into the back and front of a stitch
dec decrease, by taking two stitches together
wfd wool forward
ss stocking stitch (knit one row, purl one row alternately)

Back

With no. 12 needles cast on 90 sts and rib—k1, p1—for 2 inches. Change to no. 10 needles and work in ss for 9 inches, ending with a p row.

To shape armholes: cast off 5 sts at beg of next 2 rows and dec at beg and end of the following 5 rows (70 sts). Continue without further shaping until the armholes measure 4½ inches (measuring straight).

To slope shoulders : cast off 8 sts at the beg of the next 6 rows. Cast off remainder.

Front

Work as back until the armhole shaping is completed, then divide for front opening.
1st row : k37, turn (leaving the other 33 sts on a spare needle meantime).
2nd row : k4, p33.
3rd row : k.
** 4th row : k2, wfd, k2tog, p33.
5th row : k.
Rep 2nd and 3rd rows 3 times. Rep from ** twice, then rep from 4th to 7th rows.

To shape for neck : cast off 10 sts at beg of next row and dec at same end of the following 3 rows. Continue until armhole measures the same depth as on back, ending at armhole edge.

To slope shoulder : Cast off 8 sts at beg of the next and the following 2 alternate rows. Cast on 4 sts and with same needle k the sts on spare needle. Work right side to correspond with left side, reversing shaping and omitting buttonholes.

Sleeves, both alike

With no. 12 needles cast on 46 sts and rib—k1, p1 for 2 inches. Change to no. 10 needles and work in ss. Inc at beg and end of the 7th row and every following 6th row until there are 68 sts on the needle. Continue without further shaping until the sleeve measures 12 inches from the cast-on edge, then shape top of sleeve. Dec at beg and end of every k row until 54 sts remain, then dec at beg and end of every row until 22 sts remain. Cast off.

Collar

With no. 12 needles cast on 124 sts and rib—k1, p1—for 4 rows. Dec at beg and end of the next row and every following 4th row until 114 sts remain. Work 3 rows after the last dec, then cast off 8 sts at the beg of the next 8 rows. Cast off remainder.

To make up

Press the knitting—except ribbing—with a hot iron over a damp cloth. Join shoulder seams, sew sleeves into armholes, join side and sleeve seams. Sew cast-off edge of collar to neck edge, beg and ending inside garter st border at front. Sew buttons on right side of opening.

Each **Drummer Boy** requires 28 sts for the complete motif, so run a thread between the 30th and 31st sts and the 60th and 61st sts as a guide when working the motifs, which are worked in Swiss darning thus :

Bring the needle up through the centre of a stitch, take the needle under the stitch above and pull thread through, put the needle down through the centre of stitch where the work commenced and bring it up through the stitch to the left. Take the needle under the stitch above, pull wool through, put needle through the centre of the stitch underneath and bring it up through the stitch to the left.

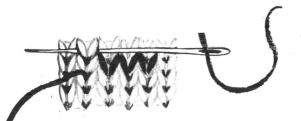

Complete row of stitches in this manner. For next row work backwards. Bring the needle up through the centre of the coloured stitch at end of row, take the needle from left to right across the top of stitch, put needle down through centre

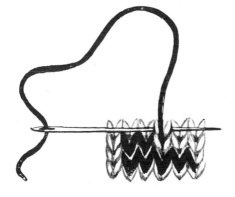

of stitch and bring it up through the centre of stitch to the right. Work backwards and forwards in this way, having the tension of the darning correspond with the knitting. The chart gives the complete background of the figure and the drumsticks. These last are worked in stem and satin stitches. The features and the red lines on drum and trousers are added on top of the Swiss darning.

The Teddy Bears require 23 sts for the complete motif, so 6 sts are left between the motifs, 4 sts at one end and 5 sts at the other.

Press the embroidery and seams on the wrong side.

O PINK
X BLACK
⟋ SCARLET
✚ YELLOW
• BLUE
● GREEN

X BROWN
● BLUE

Muffler Helmet

HELMET AND SCARF IN ONE

MATERIALS
9 oz. 4-ply wool, to be used double.
2 No. 5 and 2 No. 8 knitting needles.

TENSION
4 sts. to 1 in.

Using No. 5 needles and double wool cast on 52 sts. and work in following patt.:—

This helmet and muffler combined means complete protection for the head in the bitterest weather.

On the lookout! Many of you have been looking for just this type of muffler helmet. It does mean that both the head and the throat are properly protected, and the careless man can't leave his scarf behind just when he needs it most.

1st row.—* K. 1, p. 2, k. 1; rep. from * to end.
2nd row.—K.
Rep. these 2 rows until work measures 42 ins., ending with a k. row. Change to No. 8 needles.
Next row.—*K. 1, p. 2, k. 1; rep. from * to end.
Next row.—K. 1, * k. 2, p. 2; rep. from * to last 3 sts., k. 3.
Rep. the last 2 rows for 6 ins.
Shape as follows:—
Next row.—K. 2 tog., work in rib to last 2 sts., k. 2 tog.
Rep. this row until 18 sts. remain.
Work 1 row without shaping.
Next row.—Inc. in first st., work in rib to last 2 sts., inc. in next st., k. 1.
Rep. the last row until there are 52 sts. on the needle.
Work 6 ins. in rib.
Cast off loosely in rib.
Make-up.—Press work carefully on wrong side using a warm iron and damp cloth. Join side seams of the cap.
Press the seams.

A SET IN FAIR ISLE

Materials: PATONS BEEHIVE FINGERING, 3-ply ("Patonised" shrink-resist finish). *Pullover:* Sleeveless: 4 oz. main shade, grey, and 4 oz. assorted shades; original used 1½ oz. each, dark green and wine, and ½ oz. each, yellow and royal blue. Long sleeves: 6 oz. grey; 2 oz. each green and wine, and 1 oz. each yellow and royal blue. *Gloves:* 2 oz. main shade, and odd balls of four diffent shades. *Scarf:* 4 oz. main shade and 1½ oz. each, green and wine; ½ oz. each, yellow and royal blue. A pair each No. 9, 11 and 13 "Beehive" needles.

¶If you prefer you can work the Fair Isle in two colours only, reversing the stripes as in the long-sleeved pullover and scarf. Pullover takes 6 oz. light shade and 5 oz. dark shade with long sleeves; 4 oz. light and 3 oz. dark shades for sleeveless copy; scarf, 3 oz. each of two shades.

Measurements: *Pullover:* To fit 36–38-inch chest; length from top of shoulders, 22 inches; sleeve seam, 21 inches. *Scarf:* 36 inches; width, 6½ inches. *Gloves:* All round hand, 8 inches; length from tip of middle finger to lower edge of cuff, 11 inches.

Tension: 7½ sts. to an inch; 9½ sts. over gloves. Be very careful about this and see that you twist your wools at the back of work when changing colour, otherwise there will be no elasticity in the knitting.

N.B. –Remarks and figures in brackets apply to long sleeved pullover. Where these do not appear, the instructions apply to both long-sleeved and sleeveless models.

BACK. With No. 11 needles, cast on 128 sts. and work 3 inches k. 1, p. 1 rib, increasing 1 st. at end of last row (129). Change to No. 9 needles and fair-isle pattern, working from chart, in stocking-stitch knit rows, read from right to left, and purl rows left to right. Increase at each end of 13th and every following 10th row until there are 135 sts., taking new sts. into pattern as they are made.

Work straight until side edge measures 12½ (13) inches, then shape armholes by casting off 7 sts. at beginning of next 2 rows and decrease at each end of every alternate row until 99 (105) sts. remain.

Work straight in pattern until back measures 21 inches, then shape shoulders by casting off 12 (14) sts. at beginning of next 6 rows. Cast off.

FRONT. Work as for back until 113 sts. remain, then divide for neck. Work in pattern on first 55, k. 2 tog., turn; continue on these 56 sts., decreasing at front edge on every 3rd, still decreasing arm-hole edge every alternate row, 7 (4) more times, until 36 (42) remain. Work straight until front is same length as back on top of shoulder, then cast off 12 (14) at beginning of next 3 alternate rows, armhole edge.

Join wool at neck edge to remaining sts. and work to correspond.

SLEEVES.

With No. 11 needles, cast on 62 sts. and work 3 inches k. 1, p. 1 rib, increasing in last st. to 63. Change to No. 9 needles and fair-isle pattern, increasing at each end of 9th and every following 6th row until there are 99 sts. Work straight until side edge measures 21 inches or required length. Shape top, by decreasing at each end of every alternate row until 29 remain. Cast off.

RIBBING.

With front of work facing and No. 11 needles, pick up and knit 41 sts. across back of neck. Work

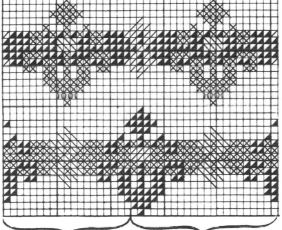

Work last 19 sts. on rows thus

Repeat 5 times across on Back
" twice " Sleeve
" 4 times " Scarf

KEY
◨ WINE
⊠ GREEN
⧄ BLUE
⧅ YELLOW
☐ GREY

1 inch k. 1, p. 1 rib, then cast off in rib, using double wool to strengthen.

Similarly, pick up and k. 72 down left front, 1 from centre front and 72 up right front. Work 1 inch k. 1, p. 1 rib, taking 2 tog. each side of centre st. on every alternate row. Cast off in rib using double wool.

Join shoulder seams on sleeveless model and with front of work facing and No. 11 needles, pick up and k. 144 sts. round each armhole. Work 1 inch k. 1, p. 1 rib; cast off in rib using double wool.

TO MAKE UP

Press pieces carefully under a damp cloth. Join all seams and sew in sleeves.

SCARF

With No. 9 needles cast on 107 sts. and work straight in pattern until scarf measures 36 ins., or required length. Press

• pullover— sleeveless or long-sleeved
• gloves
• scarf

carefully. Fold work in half and join side seam. Finish off with fringes at lower edges.

GLOVES

LEFT HAND. *Gloves:* With No. 13 needles, cast on 56 sts. and work 2½ inches k. 1, p. 1 rib, increasing 7 sts. equally across last row. Change to pattern and work 3 stripes of Fair-isle, casting on 4 sts. at end of 37th row. Take these 4 sts. into pattern.

Using main shade, decrease to 57 sts. across next row. NEXT ROW: Purl. NEXT ROW: Knit to last 21 sts., cast on 3, turn, p. 18. Work 26 rows stocking-stitch on these 18 sts. 27TH ROW: (k. 1, k. 2 tog.) to end. 28TH ROW: Purl. 29TH ROW: As 27th. Run wool through remaining sts., pull up and fasten off.

2ND FINGER: Right side facing, knit up 4 sts. from the 3 cast-on sts., k. 6, cast on 3, turn, p. 19. Work 34 rows on these 19 sts. and finish as before.

3RD FINGER: Right side facing, knit up 4, k. 7, cast on 3, turn, p. 21. Work 38 rows on these 21 sts. Finish as before.

4TH FINGER: Right side of work facing, knit up 3 sts. from the 4 cast-on sts., knit remaining sts., turn and purl back. Work 34 rows. Finish as before.

THUMB: Cast on 2 sts. Increase at each end of next and every 4th row until there are 20 sts. Work 27 rows straight. Finish as for fingers. Press carefully. Join finger and side seams.

RIGHT HAND. Work as for left hand, casting on the sts. for gusset at thumb at the end of the 36th row, and for fingers at opposite sides.

See colour plate on page 134

man's sports sweater

in wide rib with cable yoke

MATERIALS

12 oz. 4-ply wool.
2 No. 8 and 2 No. 12 knitting
needles. A spare needle with points
both ends for cable.

MEASUREMENTS

Length, 23 ins.
Chest, 38 to 40 ins.
Sleeve seam, 19 ins.

TENSION

6 sts. to 1 in. measured over st.st.

The Back.—Using No. 12 needles
cast on 98 sts. and work in k.1, p.1 rib
for 4 ins., dec. 1 st. at end of last row.
(97 sts.)

Change to No. 8 needles and work
in patt. thus:—

1st row.—Moss st.3, p.3, * k.10, p.3,
moss st.9, p.3, rep. from * to last 16 sts.,
k.10, p.3, moss st.3.

2nd row.—Moss st.3, k.3, * p.10,
k.3, moss st.9, k.3, rep. from * to last
16 sts., p.10, k.3, moss st.3.

These 2 rows form the patt.

Continue in patt. inc. 1 st. at both
ends of 9th row and every following
6th row until there are 123 sts. on
needle.

Continue in patt. on these sts. until
work measures 14½ ins. from cast-on
edge.

Shape Armholes thus: Cast off 7 sts.
at beg. of next 2 rows, then dec. 1 st.
at both ends of every row until 93 sts.
remain, ending with a row on wrong
side.

Now work in cable patt. thus:—

1st row.—K.1, p.3, * k.10, p.3,
moss st.9, p.3, rep. from * to last 14 sts.,
k.10, p.3, k.1.

2nd row.—K.4, * p.10, k.3, moss st.9,
k.3, rep. from * to last 14 sts., p.10, k.4.

3rd row.—K.1, p.3, * cable next
10 sts. thus: slip the first 5 sts. on to a
spare needle and leave at front of work,
k.5, k.5 from spare needle, p.3, moss st.
9, p.3, rep. from * to last 14 sts., cable
10, p.3, k.1.

4th row.—As 2nd row.

Rep. the 1st and 2nd rows 3 times
more.

These 10 rows form the cable patt.

Continue in patt. until work measures
23 ins. from cast-on edge, ending with
a row on wrong side.

Shape Neck and Shoulders thus:—

Next row.—Patt.38, cast off next
17 sts., patt. to end.

Work on this 2nd set of 38 sts. for
one side of neck thus:—

Next row.—Cast off 8, work to last
2 sts., work 2 tog.

Next row.—Work 2 tog., work to end.
Rep. these 2 rows twice more.
Cast off.

Rejoin wool to remaining sts. at
neck edge and work to end.

Complete to match first side.

The Front.—Work as given for back
(changing to cable patt. when armhole
shaping is completed) until work
measures 20½ ins. from cast-on edge,
ending with a row on wrong side.

Shape Neck thus:—

Next row.—Patt.41, cast off next
11 sts., patt. to end.

Work on this 2nd set of 41 sts. only,
dec. 1 st. at neck edge on every row
until 32 sts. remain.

Continue without shaping on these
sts. until work measures 23 ins. from
cast-on edge ending at armhole edge.

Shape Shoulders thus:—

Next row.—Cast off 8, work to end.
Next row.—Work to end.
Rep. these 2 rows twice more.
Cast off.

Rejoin wool to remaining sts. at
neck edge and work to match first side.

The Sleeves.—Using No. 12 needles
cast on 72 sts. and work in k.1, p.1 rib
for 3 ins.

Change to No. 8 needles and work in
patt. thus:—

1st row.—Moss st.3, p.3, * k.10, p.3,
moss st.9, p.3, rep. from * to last 16 sts.,
k.10, p.3, moss st.3.

*Here is the sleeveless version of the long-sleeved pullover which makes it ideal for
wearing under a jacket.*

See colour plate on page 64

For week-ends in the open air; ideal for riding or cycling, any man would welcome this neat ribbed pullover with its cable-rib yoke, round neck and long sleeves. It has a deep ribbed welt which helps it to fit comfortably at the waist.

2nd row.—Moss st.3, k.3, * p.10, k.3, moss st.9, k.3, rep. from * to last 16 sts., p.10, k.3, moss st.3.

These 2 rows form the patt., continue in patt. for 3 ins., then inc. 1 st. at both ends of next row and every following 8th row until there are 90 sts. on needle, working extra sts. into patt.

Continue without further shaping until work measures 19 ins. from cast-on edge.

Shape Top thus: Dec. 1 st. at both ends of alternate rows until 54 sts. remain.

Cast off 5 sts. at beg. of next 6 rows.

Cast off remaining sts. Work a second sleeve in the same way.

The Neck Borders.—With right side of work facing, using No. 12 needles, pick up and k.78 sts. evenly along neck edge of front.

Work in k.1, p.1 rib for 1 in.

Cast off in rib.

With right side of work facing, using No. 12 needles, pick up and k.42 sts. evenly along neck edge of back.

Work in k.1, p.1 rib for 1 in.

Cast off in rib.

Make-up.—Press work lightly on wrong side, using a warm iron and a damp cloth.

Join side, sleeve and shoulder seams.

Sew in sleeves matching seams to side seams. Press all seams.

ALTERNATIVE INSTRUCTIONS FOR SLEEVELESS PULLOVER

Work as given but omit sleeves.

The Sleeve Borders.—Join shoulder seams.

With right side of work facing, using 2 No. 12 needles, pick up and k.140 sts. round armhole, 70 sts. either side of shoulder seams.

Work 1 in. in k.1, p.1 rib.

Cast off in rib.

BATHING TRUNKS IN 2 SIZES

MATERIALS

6 oz. PATONS PURPLE HEATHER Fingering 4-ply, Patonised, for large size; 5 oz. for small size. A pair No. 13 "BEEHIVE" needles.

ACTUAL MEASUREMENTS

Large size to fit 36–38-inch hips, 33-inch waist; small size to 34–36-inch hips, 29-inch waist.

TENSION

9 sts. and 11 rows to one square inch on No. 13 needles in smooth fabric.

13th row—Knit.
14th row—Purl to last 6 sts., turn.
15th row—Knit.
16th row—Purl to last 9 sts., turn.
17th row—Knit.
Continue thus, working 3 sts. less at end of every purl row until 3 (2) remain.
Change to K.1, P.1 rib and work over all 66 (62) sts. for 12 (12) rows.
Cast off loosely in rib, using double wool.
Join wool to sts. on spare needle with right side facing, working the 3 sts. less at end of every **knit** row until 3 (2) remain.

BACK

Work rib as for front and continue thus:—
1st row—K.63 (52), turn.
2nd row—P.18 (14), turn.
3rd row—K.24 (20), turn.
4th row—P.30 (26), turn.
5th row—K.36 (32), turn.
6th row—P.42 (38), turn.
Continue thus, working 6 more sts. on every row until all are in stocking-stitch.
Now work exactly as for Front, starting leg shapings when stocking-stitch measures 7¾ (6¾) ins. at side edge.

GUSSET

Cast on 3 sts. and work in stocking-stitch, increasing at each end of needle on every knit row until there are 53 (47) sts.
Now decrease at each end of every alternate row until 3 remain.
Cast off and make another piece the same.

TABS

Cast on 8 sts. and work 1¾ inches K.1, P.1. rib.
Cast off and make 3 more the same.

FRONT

Cast on 114 (92) sts. very loosely and work 2½ ins. K.1, P.1, rib.

Change to stocking-stitch and increase at each end of next and every following 4th row until there are 132 (124) sts.

Work straight until front measures 10¼ (9¼) ins. from start, ending with a purl row.

Continue thus:—
1st row—Knit to last 4 sts., turn.
2nd row—Purl to last 4 sts., turn.
3rd row—Knit to last 7 sts., turn.
4th row—Purl to last 7 sts., turn.
5th row—Knit to last 9 sts., turn.
6th row—Purl to last 9 sts., turn.
7th row—Knit to last 12 sts., turn.
8th row—Purl to last 12 sts., turn.
9th row—Knit to last 15 sts., turn.
10th row—Purl to last 15 sts., turn.
11th row—Knit 51 (47) turn, leaving remaining sts. on a spare needle.
12th row—Purl to last 3 sts., turn.

TO MAKE UP

Press work lightly on wrong side under a damp cloth, avoiding rib, then join side seams. Sew together gusset pieces, back to back, then insert gusset so that bottom of fold comes just below top of rib. Turn down waist rib to make a hem and stitch, allowing for stretch. Run in a plait of thread elastic. Sew on tabs.

The Story of the Cable

Pullover in long cable.

Pullover in simple spaced cable.

Pullover in tight cable.

According to an old story, the cable was invented by the women of fishing villages when knitting guernseys for their men. The cable is an attempt to copy the pattern of the ropes which play so important a part in the life of a fisherman. Not only are they part of the tackle of his boat, and of his fishing gear, but they are to him a symbol of life itself; for a rope thrown to a sinking man, or the ropes to which the fisherman clings to prevent his being swept overboard in a storm, are truly called "life lines." No wonder that the women folk of these fishermen wanted to weave the pattern of the rope into the clothes the men wore.

As time went on, the cable patterns grew more elaborate, and the village, or sometimes even the family, had a design of its own, so that you could tell by the pattern of his guernsey from where a man came.

That is the story of how the cable stitch orginated. Now, if you're interested enough, you can make up your own particular designs if you know the basic process by which the cable is formed. It is made by the twisting and knitting out of order of two or more stitches. The working method is as follows: working in stocking stitch, the group to be cabled is divided in half, and the first half left on a spare needle while the second half is knitted. Then the stitches on the spare needle are knitted. Several rows of stocking stitch, according to the required depth of the cable, are knitted, and the twist process repeated.

Striped Shirt

FOR SUMMER SPORTS WEAR

MATERIALS

5 oz. 3-ply wool.
4 oz. fine knitting cotton.
2 No. 9 knitting needles pointed at both ends and 2 No. 12 knitting needles.
3 buttons.

MEASUREMENTS

Chest, 40 ins.
Length, 27 ins.
Sleeve seam, 6 ins.

TENSION

7 sts. to 1 in.

The main part of garment is worked in st.st. stripes of 1 row wool, 1 row cotton.

Work the stripes as follows to avoid unnecessary ends: K. 1 row in wool, sl. sts. back again to other end of needle and k. 1 row in cotton; now p. 1 row in wool, then sl. sts. back again to other end of needle and p. 1 row in cotton.

Detail of the stripe stitch.

Continue in this way throughout except for shoulder shapings and last 8 rows of top of sleeve shaping; work these in usual way, breaking off thread at end of rows, or use 2 balls of wool and 2 balls of cotton.

The Back.—With No. 9 needles and wool cast on 140 sts. Work ¾ in. in k. 1, p. 1 rib.

Join in cotton and continue in st.st. stripes (as above) until work measures 19 ins., finishing with 1 k. row.

Shape Armholes thus: Continue in stripes, cast off 6 sts. beg. of next 2 rows, then dec. 1 st. both ends of every row until 104 sts. remain.

Continue straight until work measures 27 ins., finishing p. rows.

Shape Shoulders thus:—

Cast off 9 sts. beg. of next 6 rows, cast off 8 sts. beg. of next 2 rows.

Cast off remaining sts.

The Front. The Pocket Lining.—With No. 9 needles and wool cast on 28 sts. Join in cotton and work in st.st. stripes for 4 ins., finishing 2 k. rows.

Leave sts. on spare needle.

Now work for front exactly as given for back until work measures 19 ins., finishing with 1 k. row.

Shape Armholes and Divide for Opening thus: Continue in stripes, cast off 6 sts. beg. of next 2 rows, then dec. 1 st. both ends of next 5 rows, thus finishing with 2 p. rows.

Next row.—K. 2 tog., k. 54, turn. Leave remaining sts. on spare needle.

Continue in st.st. stripes on these 55 sts., dec. 1 st. at armhole edge on every row until 49 sts. remain.

Continue straight until work measures 21¼ ins., finishing with 1 k. row.

Next row.—K. 10, cast off 28 sts. for pocket, k. to end.

Next row.—P. 11, p. 28 sts. for pocket lining, p. 10.

Continue straight on 49 sts. until work measures 25 ins., finishing front opening edge.

Shape Neck and Shoulder thus:—Cast off 3 sts. beg. of next row, then dec. 1 st. both ends of every row until 38 sts. remain, then dec. on every alternate row until 35 sts. remain.

Continue straight until work measures 27 ins., finishing armhole edge.

Next row.—Cast off 9, work to end.

Next row.—Work to end.

Rep. last 2 rows twice.

Cast off remaining sts.

Return to remaining sts., sl. centre 6 sts. on to a safety-pin and leave for front border, rejoin wool and continue in stripes on remaining 56 sts., dec. 1 st. at armhole edge on every row until 49 sts. remain.

Cotton and wool in two colours combine to make a striped shirt that, with short sleeves and adaptable neckline, is perfect for summer sportswear.

Continue straight until work measures 25 ins., finishing front opening edge.

Shape Neck and Shoulder as for first side.

The Left-front Border.—Slip the 6 sts. from safety-pin on to a No. 12 needle and with right side of work facing and using wool throughout, work thus:—

1st row.—K. twice into first st., k. 1, p. 1, k. twice into next st., k. 1, p. 1.

Work ¾ in. in rib on 8 sts., finishing row on wrong side.

Next row.—Rib 3, cast off 3 sts. for a buttonhole, rib to end.

Next row.—Rib 2, cast on 3, rib 3.

* Continue in rib for 2 ins., then make another buttonhole in next 2 rows.

Rep. from * once then continue in rib until border is same length as front edge when slightly stretched. Cast off in rib.

The Right Front Border.—With No. 12 needles and wool k. up 8 sts. at back of left front border at lower edge.

Work in k. 1, p. 1 rib until this border is same length as first.   Cast off in rib.

The Sleeves.—With No. 9 needles and wool cast on 106 sts. and work ¾ in. in k. 1, p. 1 rib. Join in cotton and continue in st.st. stripes until work measures 6 ins., finishing with 1 k. row.

Shape Top thus: Cast off 6 sts. beg. of next 2 rows, dec. 1 st. both ends of every row until 74 sts. remain.

Cast off 8 sts. beg. of next 8 rows.

Cast off remaining sts.

The Collar.—With No. 12 needles and wool cast on 189 sts.

Work 2 rows in k. 1, p. 1 rib, beg. and finishing 1st row with k. 1.

3rd row.—K. 1, p. 1, sl. 1, k. 1, p.s.s.o., work in rib to last 4 sts., k. 2 tog., p. 1, k. 1.

4th row.—Work in rib.

Rep. last 2 rows until work measures 2½ ins.

Cast off 30 sts. beg. of next 2 rows, then cast off 6 sts. beg. of next 4 rows.

Cast off remaining sts.

The Pocket Border.—With No. 12 needles and wool and with right side of work facing, k. up 32 sts. evenly along cast-off edge of pocket.

Work ¾ in. in k. 1, p. 1 rib.

Cast off loosely in rib.

Make-up.—Press work lightly on wrong side with hot iron over damp cloth.

Join side, shoulder and sleeve seams.

Backstitch sleeves into armholes, matching seams.

Sew front borders to front edges.

Sew round pocket lining on wrong side and down side edges of pocket border.

Pin centre of cast-off edge of collar to centre back of neck and sew collar round neck edge, finishing in centre of front border.

Sew on buttons to match buttonholes. Press seams.

Elvis Presley in the film *Jailhouse Rock*, 1957

the 50s

'The pullover has now become a friend ... whether it is worn on the back, over the shoulders, wrapped around the waist, or slung over the arm, thrown in the car, tied to a bicycle, it seems indispensable.' *Menswear*, 1953.

Roger Moore and Michael Bentley were two of the young men who modelled the fashion jumpers in the Fifties. They epitomized the rugged 'clean-limbed' look that was the aspiration of every man, and showed all the new 'separates' in the relaxed American manner. The accent was on youth, and the young dictated the fashions. The older man wore single-breasted suits with natural shoulders and trousers with two pleats at the waist, but the young drew their inspiration from the 'Teds', or from American film stars, and preferred to adopt the Tough Look. Hair was worn longer so that the top could be swept up in a Tony Curtis quiff with the sides combed back towards the centre –all held in place with a little grease. Sideboards were allowed, but moustaches thought 'too conventional', and beards 'nothing but a deplorable lapse into bohemianism'.

The modern woman wore a red, yellow or green 'twinset' knitted in a fine two-, three- or four-ply and styled so that it fitted at the bust, framed a natural waist and continued further to flatter shapely hips. The stiffness of her 'wartime' shoulders had melted into rounded adolescent curves. Helen Temple described this young look as 'freshness–a clean-little-girl-straight-from-the-bath look; it's partly a smooth simple way of wearing your clothes and your hair. Cool, crisp and uncluttered.'

Casual clothing was the prerogative of the young, and it was to America that the teenager looked for relaxed dressing, even though it might be disapproved of by Mum and Dad. Jeans worn with a jumper was the new image of freedom, and the jumper was worn 'any way you liked'. The freshest, most exciting colour to knit it in was pink. Soon pink, from light to bright, appeared in most items of men's apparel. 'Strangely,' said *Menswear*, 'this extreme colour, daring in a way for men, is liked and almost worn with a challenge.' By 1954, Gary Cooper was wearing at the Beach Club in Southampton, USA, a pink knit polo-shirt and pink linen slacks with his black alligator belt and black espadrilles.

In the United States, a man would spend more time at leisure than at work (roughly 55 hours, compared to 50), and casual clothing had 'tremendous appeal', especially now it could be made from orlon, dacron, acrilan and dynel–powerful competitors to pure wool which was expensive.

Britain, too, brought out nylon-wool mixtures to compete with pure yarns. 'Wendy's' new 'nylonette' stated that it was 'the fastest most exciting thing in knitting wools'. In 1951, the Festival of Britain marked the beginning of the end of an era of austerity. To celebrate the occasion, yellow round-necked pullovers were knitted with the Festival emblem on the front.

The British man was still very reluctant to indulge in colours other than grey, beige and brown, when it came to the pullover worn to work. These and slipovers knitted in fine plies were still shaped to the body in small, neat self-patterns or modest cables. But for leisure-wear, he went to the other extreme. Vying with snowflake sweaters, Fair Isles were on the 'up and up' and achieved extremely complex designs in 'a gay assortment of colours'. A slipover might have five shades such as lemon, bright green, rust, fawn and stone; a long-sleeved V-neck, nine colours including turquoise. Some V-necks came in bright solid colours or showed a Fair Isle border at neck, sleeves and hem. The most successful garment was the modern knitted waistcoat. So popular did these become that by 1953 'no man's wardrobe is complete without one or more'. The favourite was plaid in red, black and yellow–Roger Moore modelled one in red, green and yellow. The Tattersall style, with two pointed fronts and two lower pockets, appeared in bold Argyles, plaids and double overchecks. It was worn with a bow tie. Plainer varieties, fashioned on cardigan lines with coloured trim, were worn to work.

In America the Campus men, who had refrained from wearing the very padded shoulders, nipped in waist and over-long jackets from England, were unable to resist the new 'fancy London vest'. Abandoning their usual garb of crew-necked long-sleeved sweaters, the brave students took to waistcoats. 'At the main entrance to any of the Eastern University stadiums any Saturday afternoon this Fall, thousands upon thousands of fancy waistcoats pass before your eyes—all worn for style not for warmth; dress up, not utility.' (*Menswear*, 1954). With them went Tyrolean hats and bow ties.

As the fancy vests were making their way to the United States, so the new Bermuda shorts arrived in Britain. In America they were worn with knitted Bermuda-length socks that ended just below the knee. If the shorts were made of a linen-like rayon that did not crease, and were cut well, they could be worn for business. For really informal occasions, no socks were worn at all—just knitted shirts and sandals. The British teenager was no exception in picking up this latest relaxation in dress. A correspondent from Plymouth wrote to his Sunday newspaper in 1952: 'I recently watched an open-air dance on Plymouth Hoe. Jive was the order of the day. Youths in gaudy American-style shirts joined forces with girls who appeared to be wearing father's trousers chopped off below the knee. The ensuing contortions were remarkable to behold.'

It was thought that these and other American 'habits' had been picked up from the new British television sets, six million of which were owned by 1950. Patriotism returned as the nation tuned in to see the Queen crowned on 2 June 1953. 'There dignity went hand in hand with modesty, simplicity, gravity, and with a charm like crystal.' A million new aerials sprung up over the rooftops for the occasion, and Coronation jerseys were knitted up in red, white and blue, or gold, scarlet and black.

The American influence in dress was soon to give way to stronger forces from the Continent. A brand new knitted sports shirt had arrived with a 'floating' sleeve. This was achieved by knitting the sleeve and shirt all in one piece, thus giving a completely 'easy' shoulder. It was fashioned like a fisherman's blouse with fullness in the waist. There were no buttons. The new shirts were nearly always horizontally striped with red, light-blue or yellow over a white ground, or were in the latest charcoal grey.

By 1954 the Continental shirts reached Cannes, Monte Carlo, Nice and Rome. Sleeves were worn pushed up to just below the elbow; hems tucked in or worn outside the lightweight trousers. Such nonchalance dazzled Mr Perkins of *Menswear*: 'They wear it with confidence and ease that is casually distinguished.' The floating-shouldered shirt continued popular throughout the Fifties, acquiring a zipped or buttoned front. The buttonless models developed flaps or overlaps to the neck-placket to shield from sight a too-hairy chest.

The influence of the floating shoulder was evident in every knitted style. Even golfers took up a lacy, shell-stitch pullover for 'easy swing', while Bing Crosby made a 'jaunty' figure in a loose-fitting cashmere golf-shirt with his Madagascar straw cap and grey flannels.

By 1955 a Too Big chunky, thick-knit style emerged from the Continent. So right and different was it that it set the style for every jumper for the rest of the decade. Its influence is still with us today. It was designed on easy lines with easy stitches, and was knitted in double-quick wool. The idea was to give a 'big top' athletic look to the torso, made more evident by wearing slim straight slacks below. The bulkiness was 'planned and calculated', so that where the garment hugged the body it should 'respond to a man's every movement—act as if almost part of him'. Because the sleeves and body were made all-in-one, when the wearer moved the whole jumper seemed alive.

Before long, these 'sloppy joes', as the jerseys were affectionately termed, became the most important item in the wardrobe for both men and women. Worn with jeans, they became the teenager's ultimate in casual wear. Suddenly everyone was in a hurry to knit a sloppy joe, in white, pink or yellow, black or emerald green. It was not important to put the sweaters on, as long as they accompanied you as an auxiliary item. They could be tied round the shoulder or knotted round the waist; worn to cover you up completely, with a large polo neck; or worn scruffily, with the welt and sleeves pushed up. They were good for rock and roll—Elvis Presley wore a chunky-knit cable sweater with open stand-up collar with his slacks or blue denim jeans. On the British 'Ban the Bomb' march in 1956, loose charcoal-grey hand-knits were worn beneath duffel coats of the same hue.

The chest had now become the focal point of knitwear for both men and women. The 'top heavy' look was emphasized with patterns on or around that area. The women wore fine-ply jumpers with V- or low rounded necklines, and brassières beneath which were 'guaranteed to mould the breast into any desired position'–even 'falsies', if nature was ungenerous. Jane Russell and Marilyn Monroe were the two 'sweater girls'.

By 1955 the 'loosened' form of knitwear had altered every garment. V-neck sweaters, crew-necks in 'popcorn' stitch and turtle necks were all getting the 'big stitch' treatment. For tennis, bold and chunky cables had monograms or personal insignia 'to add a distinctive touch'. Golfers, discovering 'porous and wonderfully easy' cardigans with low bell- or batwing-sleeves, decided they would have no others. In Britain men favoured shawl-collared cardigans, easy-fitting windjammers with zips, or Arans with gussets giving fullness under the arm.

Nowadays the modern skier looked 'tall, lean, efficient and workmanlike' in the new elasticated ski pants that gave the much sought-after 'taut' look, worn with supple, all-in-one pullovers in the big style with a Greek key pattern running from cuff to cuff. A bulky ski sweater with some dramatic Scandinavian pattern could be good for every leisure activity. In Britain, 'there's no limit to the use of stripes. They can be bold or conservative, but the bolder the better'.

Menswear hailed 1957 as 'The year of the big stitch, the bulky look, the beefy texture to sweaters, and they're here on a volume basis.' Giant mohairs, soft, lavish and luxurious, with V-necks and big roll collars, had arrived in America in vibrant orange or pure white. They were worn with very slim slacks–their top-bulk more apparent than real owing to the coarseness of their stitches. There was no season for this knitwear. Big plaid jackets worn in winter were exchanged for equally big white jackets in summer, their sleeves pushed up with the right degree of unconcern.

Big knits next developed an 'outerwear' look. Most of them had the bulk of an overcoat and the weight of a feather. Extravagant amounts of hem held in the bulk that bloused above. Athletic men chose sporty raised cable-stitches.

Icelandic wools were the latest yarns to knit up a ski jumper. The thickness of the ply produced exceptionally 'hefty' stitches. So 'smart' were these sweaters with their

bold patterned borders and dropped sleeves that they raced off the slopes and made their way to Campus and town. 'Hot red' was the liveliest colour, but they were pleasing in chartreuse or blue and white, with big-stitch socks to match.

In 1957 the neglected cardigan had been given a 'shot in the arm' when Rex Harrison popularized it by wearing one of the raglan-sleeve shawl-collared variety. It was in the new loose fit and much longer. In 1958 Kirk Douglas chose a bulky-rib blue raglan-sleeved cardigan that buttoned up to the neck. Suddenly cardigans came in every shape and form.

By 1958 knitwear of all kinds had reached an all time high. 'As busy and tortuous as possible', jumpers were made to look rugged by means of texture. Varied surfaces could be achieved by clever use of colour and pattern as well as by using the new textured yarns. Added depth was given to the mohair sweaters with Jacquard patterns. Fancy yarns gave an exciting 'tree bark' effect to jerseys; wool shirts showed rough textures in charcoal grey and blond-tobacco. Texture was produced from the stitch itself, by rack stitch, deep basket-weaves, box patterns, panels of contrast ribs. In Britain, the Aran patterns covered all shapes–polo-, crew- and turtle-necks–and suited all occasions. So chic had the fashion-jumpers for men become that by the end of the Fifties they were star items in all the big Collections. James Norbury, the great authority on knitting, observed in 1960: 'Knitting has moved into the salons of Bond Street, couture houses of Paris, palaces of Rome and the penthouses of New York.' Wrote *Knitting Review* in 1958: 'Dior's boutique in Paris carries very 'baggy' looking heavy knit sweaters in lovely warm shades of burgundy, and lighter red, a very pale yellow and navy. Necklines are generously open ... to allow the wearing of a scarf, open-necked shirt or even a polo sweater.'

The high fashion hand-knitted woollen was here to stay, but by the Sixties, the innovative pace of the past four decades had slackened. The Seventies and Eighties rediscovered the fine quality of the hand-made garment, the inventiveness of the original designs, and the pleasures of hand-knitting.

MAN'S PULLOVER
(ADAPTATION FROM FLAMBOROUGH FISHERMAN'S JERSEY)

TENSION

The tension for this garment is 7 sts. to one inch measured over the stocking stitch.

ABBREVIATIONS

K, knit ; p, purl ; sts, stitches ; tog., together ; sl.1, slip one stitch knitways ; t.b.l., through back of loops.
After casting off stitches for shaping, one stitch will remain on the right hand needle which is not included in the instructions that follow.

No. 2   **MATERIALS**

8 ozs. Sirdar Crochet Wool.

1 pair No. 9 and No. 11 Knitting Needles.

1 spare needle with points at both ends.

MEASUREMENTS

Width all round at underarm	...	38 inches
Length from top of shoulder	...	21 inches

The Back

Using the No. 11 needles cast on 129 sts.

1st ROW. Sl.1, k.1, * p.1, k.1, repeat from * to the last st., k.1.

2nd ROW. Sl.1, * p.1, k.1, repeat from * to end of row.

Repeat the 1st and 2nd rows 15 times then the 1st row once.

34th ROW. Sl.1, * increase once in the next st. purlways, (k.1, p.1) 3 times, increase once in the next st., (p.1, k.1) 3 times, repeat from * to the last 2 sts., increase once in the next st. purlways, k.1. (148 sts.).

Change to No. 9 needles and proceed as follows:

1st ROW. Sl.1, * p.1, k.9, p.2, k.6, p.2, k.9, repeat from * to the last 2 sts., p.1, k.1.

2nd ROW. Sl.1, * k.1, p.9, k.2, p.6, k.2, p.9, repeat from * to the last 2 sts., k.2.

3rd ROW. Sl.1, * k.1, p.1, k.8, p.2, k.6, p.2, k.8, p.1, repeat from * to the last 2 sts., k.2.

4th ROW. Sl.1, * p.1, k.1, p.8, k.2, p.6, k.2, p.8, k.1, repeat from * to the last 2 sts., p.1, k.1.

5th ROW. Sl.1, * p.1, k.1, p.1, k.7, p.2, slip the next 3 sts. on to the spare needle and let this fall to the back of the work, k.3, then knit the 3 sts. from the spare needle, this will in future be termed "cable", p.2, k.7, p.1, k.1, repeat from * to the last 2 sts., p.1, k.1.

6th ROW. Sl.1, * k.1, p.1, k.1, p.7, k.2, p.6, k.2, p.7, k.1, p.1, repeat from * to the last 2 sts., k.2.

7th ROW. Sl.1, * (k.1, p.1) twice, (k.6, p.2) twice, k.6, p.1, k.1, p.1, repeat from * to the last 2 sts., k.2.

8th ROW. Sl.1, * (p.1, k.1) twice, (p.6, k.2) twice, p.6, k.1, p.1, k.1, repeat from * to the last 2 sts., p.1, k.1.

9th ROW. Sl.1, * (p.1, k.1) twice, p.1, k.5, p.2, k.6, p.2, k.5, (p.1, k.1) twice, repeat from * to the last 2 sts., p.1, k.1.

10th ROW. Sl.1, * (k.1, p.1) twice, k.1, p.5, k.2, p.6, k.2, p.5, (k.1, p.1) twice, repeat from * to the last 2 sts., k.2.

11th ROW. Sl.1, * (k.1, p.1) 3 times, k.4, p.2, k.6, p.2, k.4, (p.1, k.1) twice, p.1, repeat from * to the last 2 sts., k.2.

12th ROW Sl.1, * (k.1, p.1) 3 times, p.4, k.2, p.6, k.2, p.4, (k.1, p.1) twice, k.1, repeat from * to the last 2 sts., p.1, k.1.

13th ROW. Sl.1, * (p.1, k.1) 3 times, p.1, k.3, p.2, "cable", p.2, k.3, (p.1, k.1) 3 times, repeat from * to the last 2 sts., p.1, k.1.

14th ROW. Sl.1, * (k.1, p.1) 3 times, k.1, p.3, k.2, p.6, k.2, p.3, (k.1, p.1) 3 times, repeat from * to the last 2 sts., k.2.

15th ROW. Sl.1, * (k.1, p.1) 4 times, k.2, p.2, k.6, p.2, k.2, (p.1, k.1) 3 times, p.1, repeat from * to the last 2 sts., k.2.

16th ROW. Sl.1, * (p.1, k.1) 4 times, p.2, k.2, p.6, k.2, p.2, (k.1, p.1) 3 times, k.1, repeat from * to the last 2 sts., p.1, k.1.

17th ROW. Sl.1, * (p.1, k.1) 3 times, p.1, k.3, p.2, k.6, p.2, k.3, (p.1, k.1) 3 times, repeat from * to the last 2 sts., p.1, k.1.

Repeat the 14th, 11th and 12th rows once.

21st ROW. Sl.1, * (p.1, k.1) twice, p.1, k.5, p.2, "cable", p.2, k.5, (p.1, k.1) twice, repeat from * to the last 2 sts., p.1, k.1.

Repeat the 10th, 7th and 8th rows once.

25th ROW. Sl.1, * p.1, k.1, p.1, k.7, p.2, k.6, p.2, k.7, p.1, k.1, repeat from * to the last 2 sts., p.1, k.1.

26th ROW. Sl.1, * k.1, p.1, k.1, p.7, k.2, p.6, k.2, p.7, k.1, p.1, repeat from * to the last 2 sts., k.2.

Repeat the 3rd and 4th rows once.

29th ROW. Sl.1, * p.1, k.9, p.2, "cable", p.2, k.9, repeat from * to the last 2 sts., p.1, k.1.

Repeat the 2nd row once.

31st ROW. Sl.1, * k.10, p.2, k.6, p.2, k.9, repeat from * to the last 2 sts., k.2.

32nd ROW. Sl.1, * p.10, k.2, p.6, k.2, p.9, repeat from * to the last 2 sts., p.1, k.1.

These 32 rows form the pattern.

Repeat from the 1st to the 32nd row (inclusive) once then from the 1st to the 26th row (inclusive) once.

Shape the Armholes

Keeping the continuity of the pattern, cast off 11 sts. at the beginning of each of the next 2 rows.

Decrease once at each end of the next 18 rows, (90 sts.).

Repeat from the 15th to the 32nd row (inclusive) once, from the 1st to the 32nd row (inclusive) once then from the 1st to the 12th row (inclusive) once.

Shape the Shoulders

Keeping the continuity of the pattern, cast off 10 sts. at the beginning of each of the next 6 rows. Cast off the remaining 30 sts.

The Front

Using the No. 11 needles cast on 129 sts.

Work exactly as given for the Back until the armholes are reached.

Shape the Armholes

Keeping the continuity of the pattern, cast off 11 sts. at the beginning of each of the next 2 rows.

Decrease once at each end of the next 2 rows.

Shape the Neck

1st ROW. K.2 tog., k.4, p.2, k.19, p.2, k.6, p.2, k.19, p.2, k.1, k.2 tog., turn.

Work on these 59 sts. as follows :—

1st ROW. Sl.1, p.1, k.2, p.19, k.2, p.6, k.2, p.19, k.2, p.3, k.2 tog.

2nd ROW. K.2 tog., k.2, p.2, k.9, p.1, k.9, p.2, k.6, p.2, k.9, p.1, k.9, p.2, k.2.

3rd ROW. Sl.1, p.1, k.2, p.9, k.1, p.9, k.2, p.6, k.2, p.9, k.1, p.9, k.2, p.1, k.2 tog.

Keeping the continuity of the pattern decrease once at the armhole edge in each of the next 12 rows, at the same time decreasing once at the neck edge in the next and every following 4th row. (41 sts.).

Keeping the continuity of the pattern decrease once at the neck edge only in the next and every following 4th row until 30 sts. remain.

Work 21 rows in pattern without shaping.

Shape the Shoulder

1st ROW. Cast off 10 sts., work in pattern to the last st., k.1.

2nd ROW. Sl.1, work in pattern to end of row.

Repeat the 1st and 2nd rows once. Cast off the remaining 10 sts.

With the right side of the work facing, rejoin the wool to the remaining 61 sts. and proceed as follows :—

1st ROW. K.2 tog., k.1, p.2, k.19, p.2, k.6, p.2, k.19, p.2, k.4, k.2 tog.

2nd ROW. K.2 tog., p.3, k.2, p.19, k.2, p.6, k.2, p.19, k.2, p.1, k.1.

3rd ROW. Sl.1, k.1, p.2, k.9, p.1, k.9, p.2, k.6, p.2, k.9, p.1, k.9, p.2, k.2, k.2 tog.

4th ROW. K.2 tog., p.1, k.2, p.9, k.1, p.9, k.2, p.6, k.2, p.9, k.1, p.9, k.2, p.1, k.1.

Keeping the continuity of the pattern, decrease once at the armhole edge in each of the next 12 rows, at the same time decreasing once at the neck edge in the next and every following 4th row. (41 sts.).

Keeping the continuity of the pattern, decrease once at the neck edge only in the next and every following 4th row until 30 sts. remain.

Work 22 rows in pattern without shaping.

Sirdar
No. 1402
CROCHET WOOL
Chest 38 inches
6^d

Shape the Shoulder

1st ROW.   Cast off 10 sts., work in pattern to the last st., k.1.

2nd ROW.   Sl.1, work in pattern to end of row.

Repeat the 1st and 2nd rows once.   Cast off the remaining 10 sts.

Sew up the right shoulder seam.

The Neck Band

Using the No. 11 needles and with the right side of the work facing, pick up and knit 71 sts. evenly along the left side of the neck, 1 st. from the centre of the V, 71 sts. evenly along the right side of the neck and 30 sts. from the 30 cast off sts. at the back of neck.   (173 sts.).

1st ROW.   Sl.1, * p.1, k.1, repeat from * to end of row.

2nd ROW.   Sl.1, (k.1, p.1) 34 times, k.2 tog. t.b.l., k.1, k.2 tog., (p.1, k.1) 49 times, k.1.

3rd ROW.   Sl.1, p.1, (k.1, p.1) 48 times, p.2 tog., p.1, p.2 tog. t.b.l., (p.1, k.1) 34 times.

4th ROW.   Sl.1, (k.1, p.1) 33 times, k.2 tog. t.b.l., k.1, k.2 tog., (p.1, k.1) 48 times, k.1.

5th ROW.   Sl.1, p.1, (k.1, p.1) 47 times, p.2 tog., p.1, p.2 tog. t.b.l., (p.1, k.1) 33 times.

6th ROW.   Sl.1, (k.1, p.1) 32 times, k.2 tog. t.b.l., k.1, k.2 tog., (p.1, k.1) 47 times, k.1.

7th ROW.   Sl.1, p.1, (k.1, p.1) 46 times, p.2 tog., p.1, p.2 tog. t.b.l., (p.1, k.1) 32 times.

8th ROW.   Sl.1, (k.1, p.1) 31 times, k.2 tog. t.b.l., k.1, k.2 tog., (p.1, k.1) 46 times, k.1.

9th ROW.   Sl.1, p.1, (k.1, p.1) 45 times, p.2 tog., p.1, p.2 tog. t.b.l., (p.1, k.1) 31 times.

Cast off loosely in rib.

Sew up the left shoulder seam.

The Armhole Bands (both alike)

Using the No. 11 needles and with the right side of the work facing, pick up and knit 149 sts. evenly round the armhole edge.

1st ROW.   Sl.1, * p.1, k.1, repeat from * to end of row.

2nd ROW.   Sl.1, k.1, * p.1, k.1, repeat from * to the last st., k.1.

Repeat the 1st and 2nd rows 3 times then the 1st row once.   Cast off loosely in rib.

TO MAKE UP THE PULLOVER

Press carefully on the wrong side under a damp cloth with a hot iron.   Sew up the side seams.

Press all seams.

No. 1001
Price 5d

A Templeton Design

Man's Waistcoat

In Templeton's Double Knitting Wool

(Two sizes)

MATERIALS.—8 or 10 ozs. Templeton's Double Knitting Wool in medium shade; 2 ozs. dark shade; 2 ozs. light shade. 1 pr. No. 10 needles; 1 pr. No. 8 needles. 7 medium shade buttons.

TENSION.—5 stitches=1 inch; 8 rows=1 inch.

MEASUREMENTS.—

	Size 1	Size 2
Length from shoulder....	21½ inches	22½ inches
Width round underarm	38 - 40 inches	40 - 42 inches

ABBREVIATIONS.—K=knit; P=purl; tog.=together; alt.=alternate; dec.=decrease; m=medium; d=dark; l=light; beg.=beginning.

NOTE.—As this garment is knitted in heavy wool, it is advisable not to weave the various colours across the back of work, as in ordinary Fair Isle, as this will make the garment too heavy, and will require extra wool. A very simple method is to use short strands of wool for each colour, about 42 inches long should work one complete square. The strand can, of course, be woven across the single stitches in the centre of each square. In this way, the wools do not become entangled, although care must be taken to twist the wools together once when changing colours, in order to avoid making holes.

Pocket Underlaps (both alike) — Using No. 8 needles, cast on 25 sts. Work in stocking st. for 24 rows. Place stitches on stitch holder.

The Right Front — Using No. 10 needles, and m colour wool, cast on 54 (58) sts. Work in rib of K1, P1 for 23 rows. Change to No. 8 needles, and work as follows:—

1st row.—Rib 8m, * K2d, 1l, 2d, 2m, 1d, 2m *. Rep. from * to * 3 times, ending K2d, 1l, 3d (K2d, 1l, 2d, 2m, 1d, 2m).

2nd row.—P3d, 1l, 2d (P2m, 1d, 2m, 2d, 1l, 2d) * P2m, 1d, 2m, 2d, 1l, 2d *. Rep. from * to * 3 times. Rib 8m. Rep. the 1st and 2nd rows twice.

7th row.—Rib 8m. Join on l wool, and K across row (remembering to twist each strand of coloured wool at back of work).

8th row.—P across row in l wool to last 8 sts. Rib 8m. Rep. the first and 2nd rows 3 times.

15th row.—Rib 8m * K2m, 1l, 2m, 2l, 1d, 2l *. Rep. from * to * 3 times ending K2m, 1l, 3m (K2m, 1l, 2m, 2l, 1d, 2l).

16th row.—P3m, 1l, 2m (P2l, 1d, 2l, 2m, 1l, 2m) * P2l, 1d, 2l, 2m, 1l, 2m *. Rep. from * to * 3 times. Rib 8m.
Rep. the 15th and 16th rows twice.

21st row.—Rib 8m. Join on d wool and K across row (twisting wools at back as on 7th row).

22nd row.—P across row in d wool to last 8 sts. Rib 8m.
Rep. the 15th and 16th rows 3 times. These 28 rows complete one pattern.
Rib 8m. Work next 10 sts. in pattern (as 1st row).
Place these 18 sts. on stitch holder. Now break off all strands of wool at back of next 25 sts., leaving ends about 2 inches long to fasten off. Join on m wool and K next 25 sts. Place remaining sts. on 2nd st. holder.
Work on 25 sts. thus:—

Next row.—(K1, P1) 12 times, K1.

Next row.—(P1, K1) 12 times, P1.

Rep. the last 2 rows 3 times. Cast off loosely in rib. Now place 18 sts. from holder on to needle. Then take one pocket underlap with right side facing, and work these 25 sts. from holder in pattern, as on 1st row. Then

The Pocket

work sts. from 2nd st. holder and complete pattern across row. Now continue in pattern across all sts. until the 12th (18) row of the 3rd pattern has been worked.

Neck Shaping

Rib 7. Now rib the last st. of front rib border and the 1st st. of pattern tog. with m wool. Then keeping pattern correct, work to end of row. Continue to rep. this dec. row on every following 4th row, taking care to keep the pattern correct at centre edge until the 21st (27th) row of the 3rd pattern has been worked.

Armhole Shaping

Continue to dec. at centre edge on every 4th row. Cast off 7 (8) sts. at the beg. of the next row. Then dec. 1 st. at armhole edge on every alt. row 3 times. (This completes the armhole shaping.) Now continue in pattern, dec. at centre edge as before until there are 35 (38) sts. on needle. Now make dec. at centre edge on every 6th row until there are 30 (32) sts. on needle. Work straight until armhole measures 8½ inches (9 inches) ending with right side of work facing.

Shoulder Shaping

Cast off 6 sts. at armhole edge on every alt. row 2 (4) times. Then 5 (-) sts. 2 (-) times. Work on remaining sts. in m colour for 2¾ inches. Cast off in rib.

The Left Front — Work as given for right front, taking care to make pattern correspond on both sides, and placing the pocket in correct position, and reversing shaping for neck, armholes and shoulder, working 1st buttonhole on the 5th row of rib welt thus:—

Rib 3, cast off 2. Rib to end of row. On the next row cast on 2 over 2 cast off on previous row. The 2nd buttonhole is worked on the 23rd or last row of rib welt and 1st row of pattern. The 3rd buttonhole on the 14th and 15th rows of pattern, the 4th buttonhole on the 28th and 1st pattern rows, and so on until 7 in all have been worked.

The Back — Using No. 10 needles and m wool cast on 94 (102) sts. Work in rib of K1, P1 for 23 rows. Change to No. 8 needles, and work in stocking st. until work measures the same as front to armholes.

Armhole Shaping

Cast off 6 (7) sts. at the beg. of the next 2 rows. Then dec. 1 st. at both ends of every alt. row 3 times. Continue straight until armhole measures 8½ (9) inches.

Shoulder Shaping

Cast off 6 sts. at the beg. of the next 4 (8) rows. Then 5 (-) sts. at the beg. of the next 4 (-) rows. Cast off remainder.

Armbands

Join shoulder seams, then with right side of work facing, using No. 8 needles, pick up and K 104 (110) sts. round armholes. Work in rib of K1, P1 for 8 rows. Cast off in rib. Work other armhole to match.

To Make Up — Fasten off all short ends at back of work. Then carefully pin out each part to correct measurements, and press with a damp cloth and hot iron. Join side seams. Sew down underlap of pockets, taking care not to let stitches show on right side. Then sew side edges of rib at top of pockets, to waistcoat. Join ends of neck band, then sew band to back of neck, keeping seam as flat as possible. Sew on buttons to correspond with buttonholes, and press all seams.

Father and Son Special

Instructions are given for 36 ins. chest and any alterations for larger sizes are given in brackets thus 36 ins. (38 ins., 40 ins., 42 ins., 44 ins., 46 ins.) chest.

MATERIALS—8 ozs. (8, 9, 9, 9, 10) MARRINER "Heritage" 4-ply wool.
1 pair No. 11 and 1 pair No. 9 knitting needles.
1 set of four double pointed No. 12 knitting needles.

MEASUREMENTS—To fit 36 ins. (38 ins., 40 ins., 42 ins., 44 ins., 46 ins.) chest.
Length from top of shoulder 22½ ins. (23 ins., 23½ ins., 24 ins., 24½ ins., 25 ins.).

TENSION—6½ sts. and 8½ rows to one inch.

ABBREVIATIONS—K.=knit; P.=purl; sts.=stitches; inc.=increase; dec.=decrease; tog.=together.

BOY'S SLEEVELESS PULLOVER

Instructions are given for 26 ins. chest and any alterations for larger sizes are given in brackets thus 26 ins. (28 ins., 30 ins., 32 ins., 34 ins.). chest.

MATERIALS—4 ozs. (5, 5, 5, 6) MARRINER "Heritage" 4-ply wool.
1 pair No. 11 and 1 pair No. 9 knitting needles.
1 set of 4 double pointed No. 12 knitting needles.

MEASUREMENTS—To fit 26 ins. chest (28 ins., 30 ins., 32 ins., 34 ins.).
Length from top of shoulder 15 ins. (16 ins., 17 ins., 18 ins., 19 ins.).

TENSION—As for man's pullover.

ABBREVIATIONS—As for man's pullover.

The Man's Pullover

THE BACK

Reminder—have you checked your tension?

With No. 11 needles cast on 126 (132, 138, 144, 150, 156) sts. and work 30 rows in stocking stitch. Now make hem by folding work in half and knitting next row together with the cast on sts. Purl 1 row, then change to No. 9 needles and continue in stocking stitch until work measures 14½ ins. (14¾ ins., 15 ins., 15¼ ins., 15½ ins., 15¾ ins.) ending with a purl row.

Shape Armholes

Cast off 4 (5, 5, 5, 6, 6) sts. at the beginning of the next 4 rows, then cast off 3 (2, 3, 4, 3, 4) sts. at the beginning of the following 2 rows, after which cast off 2 (2, 2, 2, 2, 2) sts. at the beginning of the following 2 rows. Dec. 1 st. at each end of the next two rows. There should now be 96 (100, 104, 108, 112, 116) sts. on the needle. Continue in stocking stitch without further shaping until work measures 21 ins. (21½ ins., 22 ins., 22½ ins., 23 ins., 23½ ins.) ending with a purl row, then inc. 1 st. at each end of the next and following 4th row. Continue without further shaping until work measures 22½ ins. (23 ins., 23½ ins., 24 ins., 24½ ins., 25 ins.) ending with a purl row.

Shape Shoulders

Cast off 8 (8, 8, 8, 8, 8) sts. at the beginning of the next 6 rows, then cast off 6 (7, 8, 9, 10, 11) sts.

at the beginning of the following 2 rows. Cast off remaining 40 (42, 44, 46, 48, 50) sts. for back of neck.

THE FRONT

Work exactly as given for back until front measures 14½ ins. (14¾ ins., 15 ins., 15¼ ins., 15½ ins., 15¾ ins.) ending with a purl row.

Shape armholes and Vee neck.

1st row—Cast off 4 (5, 5, 5, 6, 6) sts., K.59, (61, 64, 67, 69, 72) sts., including stitch on needle, turn. Work on this group of sts. only as follows:—

2nd row—Purl.

3rd row—Cast off 4 (5, 5, 5, 6, 6) sts., knit to the last 2 sts., K.2 tog.

4th row—Purl.

5th row—Cast off 3 (2, 3, 4, 3, 4) sts., knit to end of row.

6th row—P.2 tog., purl to end of row.

7th row—Cast off 2 (2, 2, 2, 2, 2) sts., knit to end of row.

8th row—Purl.

9th row—K.2 tog., knit to the last 2 sts., K.2 tog.

10th row—Purl to the last 2 sts., P.2 tog.

11th row—Knit.

12th row—P.2 tog., purl to end of row.

Now keep armhole edge straight but continue to dec. 1 st. at front edge every 3rd row until 20 (21, 22, 23, 24, 25) decreases in all have been made, **but at the same time** when front measures 21 ins. (21½ ins., 22 ins., 22½ ins., 23 ins., 23½ ins.) ending with a purl row, increase 1 st. at the beginning of the next

Marriner

Heritage 4-ply

26, 28, 30, 32, 34, in.

and

36, 38, 40, 42, 44, 46 in.

6ᵈ MARRINER Knitting Wools

524

and following 4th row, then keep armhole edge straight until work measures as back to shoulder ending at shoulder edge. Cast off 8 (8, 8, 8, 8, 8) sts. at the beginning of the next and following 2 alternate rows. Work 1 row. Cast off remaining 6 (7, 8, 9, 10, 11) sts.

With right side of work facing rejoin wool to remaining sts. and knit to the end of the row. Continue:—

1st row—Cast off 4 (5, 5, 5, 6, 6) sts., purl to end of row.

2nd row—K.2 tog., knit to end of row.

3rd row—Cast off 4 (5, 5, 5, 6, 6), purl to end of row.

4th row—Knit.

5th row—Cast off 3 (2, 3, 4, 3, 4) sts., purl to the last 2 sts., P.2 tog.

6th row—Knit.

7th row—Cast off 2 (2, 2, 2, 2, 2) sts., purl to end.

8th row—K.2 tog., knit to the last 2 sts., K.2 tog.

9th row—P.2 tog., purl to end of row.

10th row—Knit.

11th row—Purl to the last 2 sts., P.2 tog.

Now keep armhole edge straight but continue to dec. 1 st. at front edge every 3rd row until 20 (21, 22, 23, 24, 25) decreases in all have been made, **but at the same time** when front measures 21 ins. (21½ ins., 22 ins., 22½ ins., 23 ins., 23½ ins.) ending with a purl row, inc. 1 st. at the end of the next and following 4th row, then keep armhole edge straight until work measures as back to shoulder ending at shoulder edge. Cast off 8 (8, 8, 8, 8, 8) sts. at the beginning of the next and following 2 alternate rows. Work 1 row. Cast off the remaining 6 (7, 8, 9, 10, 11) sts.

The Armbands

Press each piece with a warm iron over a damp cloth. Join shoulder and side seams with narrow backstitch. With right side of work facing and set of four double pointed No. 12 needles pick up and knit 166 (170, 174, 178, 182, 186) sts. all round armhole and arrange these on three needles. Work 12 rounds in K.1, P.1, rib. Turn and cast off knitwise on wrong side of work fairly tightly. Work second armband in similar manner.

The Neckband

With right side of work facing and set of four double pointed No. 12 needles commence at left shoulder and pick up and knit 71 (75, 79, 83, 87, 91) sts. to centre front, pick up loop and knit into the back of centre, then pick up and knit 71 (75, 79, 83, 87, 91) sts. to right shoulder and 38 (40, 42, 44, 46, 48) sts. across back of neck. Arrange these sts. on three needles and work 12 rounds in K.1, P.1, rib, keeping centre front st. knitted in every row and dec. 1 st. at each side of it in every row. Turn and cast off knitwise on wrong side of work fairly tightly.

TO COMPLETE

Neaten end of round of armband and neckband. Press all seams.

Boy's Sleeveless Pullover

THE BACK

Reminder—have you checked your tension?

With No. 11 needles cast on 92 (98, 104, 110, 116) sts. and work 20 rows in stocking stitch. Now make hem by folding work in half and knitting the next row together with the cast on sts. Purl 1 row, then change to No. 9 needles and continue in stocking stitch until back measures 9½ ins. (10 ins., 10½ ins., 11 ins., 11½ ins.) ending with a purl row.

Shape Armholes

Cast off 5 (5, 6, 6, 7) sts. at the beginning of the next two rows, then cast off 4 (5, 5, 6, 6) sts. at the beginning of the following 2 rows. Dec. 1 st. at each end of the next 3 rows, then continue in stocking stitch without further shaping until back measures 15 ins. (16 ins., 17 ins., 18 ins., 19 ins.) ending with a purl row.

Shape Shoulders

Cast off 6 (6, 6, 6, 6) sts. at the beginning of the next 4 rows, then cast off 7 (8, 9, 10, 11) sts. at the beginning of the following 2 rows. Cast off remaining 30 (32, 34, 36, 38) sts. for back of neck.

THE FRONT

Work exactly as given for back until work measures 9½ ins. (10 ins., 10½ ins., 11 ins., 11½ ins.) ending with a purl row.

Shape Armholes and Vee Neck

1st row—Cast off 5 (5, 6, 6, 7) sts., K.41 (44, 46, 49, 51) sts., including stitch on needle, turn. Work on this group of sts. as follows:—

2nd row—P.2 tog., purl to end of row.

3rd row—Cast off 4 (5, 5, 6, 6) sts., knit to end.

4th row—Purl.

5th row—K.2 tog., knit to the last 2 sts., K.2 tog.

6th row—Purl to the last 2 sts., P.2 tog.

7th row—K.2 tog., knit to end of row.

Now keep armhole edge straight but continue to dec. 1 st. at front edge of next and every following 3rd row until 15 (16, 17, 18, 19) decreases in all have been made. When work measures 15 ins. (16 ins., 17 ins., 18 ins., 19 ins.) ending at shoulder edge, shape shoulder. Cast off 6 (6, 6, 6) sts. at the beginning of the next and following alternate row, work 1 row then cast off remaining 7 (8, 9, 10, 11) sts.

With right side of work facing rejoin wool to remaining sts. and knit to end of row. Continue:—

1st row—Cast off 5 (5, 6, 6, 7) sts., purl to the last 2 sts., P.2 tog.

2nd row—Knit.

3rd row—Cast off 4 (5, 5, 6, 6) sts., purl to end of row.

4th row—K.2 tog., knit to the last 2 sts., K.2 tog.

5th row—P.2 tog., purl to end of row.

6th row—Knit to the last 2 sts., K.2 tog.

Now keep armhole edge straight but continue to dec. 1 st. at front edge of next and every following 3rd row until 15 (16, 17, 18, 19) decreases in all have been made. When work measures 15 ins. (16 ins., 17 ins., 18 ins., 19 ins.) ending at armhole edge, shape shoulder. Cast off 6 (6, 6, 6) sts. at the beginning of the next and following alternate row. Work 1 row. Cast off remaining 7 (8, 9, 10, 11) sts.

The Armbands

Press each piece with a warm iron over a damp cloth. Join shoulder and side seams with narrow backstitch. With right side of work facing and set of four No. 12 double pointed needles pick up and knit 104 (112, 120, 128, 136) sts. all round armhole. Arrange these sts. on three needles and work 10 rounds in K.1, P.1, rib. Turn and cast off knitwise on wrong side of work fairly tightly.

The Neckband

With right side of work facing commence at left shoulder and with a set of four double pointed No. 12 needles pick up and knit 51 (55, 59, 63, 67) sts. to centre front, pick up loop and knit into the back of it at centre front, then pick up and knit 51 (55, 59, 63, 67) sts. to right shoulder and 28 (30, 32, 34, 36) sts. across back of neck. Arrange these sts. on three needles and work 10 rounds in K.1, P.1, rib, keeping centre front st. knitted in every row, and dec. 1 st. each side of it in every row. Turn and cast off knitwise on wrong side.

TO COMPLETE

As for man's pullover.

Nine-colour slipover · For pattern see page 120

Classic slipover · For pattern see page 137

Foul weather helmets · For pattern see page 54

Soft cable slipover · For pattern see page 101

Sleeveless Cable Pullover

In Templeton's "AYRBEAM"
Super Scotch Fingering, 4-ply

MATERIALS. 8 oz. Templeton's "Ayrbeam" Super Scotch Fingering, 4-ply. A pair of No. 9 knitting needles. A pair and set of No. 11 knitting needles.

MEASUREMENTS.—Length from the top of the shoulder, 23 ins. Width all round below armholes, 38-40 ins.

TENSION.—8 sts. to 1 in. in width.

ABBREVIATIONS.—K.=knit ; P.=purl ; sts.=stitches ; ins.=inches.

The Back

Using No. 11 knitting needles begin at the lower edge by casting on 132 sts.

Work a depth of 3½ ins. in K. 1, P. 1 rib, working into the backs of the knit sts. on the first row.

Change to No. 9 needles and the following pattern :—

1st row.—* P. 2, K. 8, P. 2, and repeat from * all across.

2nd row.—* K. 2, P. 8, K. 2, and repeat from * all across.

3rd row.—As for the 1st row.

4th row.—As for the 2nd row.

5th row.—* P. 2, cable 8, leaving the spare needle at the front, P. 4, K. 8, P. 2, and repeat from * to the last 12 sts., then P. 2, cable 8, P. 2.

6th row.—As for the 2nd row.

7th row.—As for the 1st row.

8th row.—As for the 2nd row.

9th row to 12th rows.—Repeat the 5th to 8th rows inclusive once.

13th to 16th row.—Repeat the 5th to 8th rows inclusive once.

17th row.—* P. 2, K. 8, P. 4, cable 8, leaving the spare needle at the back, P. 2, and repeat from * to the last 12 sts., then P. 2, K. 8, P. 2.

18th row.—As for the 2nd row.

19th row.—As for the 1st row.

20th row.—As for the 2nd row.

21st to 24th rows.—Repeat the 17th to 20th rows inclusive once.

25th to 28th rows.—Repeat 17th to 20th rows inclusive once.

The last 24 rows, that is the 5th to the 28th rows inclusive form the pattern.

Continue in the pattern, increasing at both ends of the needle on the next and every following 6th row until there are 12 increases at each side, and 156 sts. on the needle.

Work all added sts. into the correct pattern as the work proceeds.

Continue straight until the work measures a depth of 15 ins. from the beginning, finishing at the end of the 12th row of the pattern.

Shape the Armholes by casting off 10 sts. at the beginning of each of the next 2 rows, then 4 sts. on the next 2 rows, followed by 2 sts. on each of the next 8 rows, leaving 112 sts. on the needle.

Work a depth of 6 ins. straight.

Shape the Shoulders by casting off 8 sts. at the beginning of the next 8 rows.

Cast off the remaining 48 sts. for the back of the neck.

The Front

Work this in the same way as for the back until the armhole shaping is completed—112 sts. on the needle.

Work a depth of 3 ins. straight.

Shape the Neck.

On the next row work over 50 sts., cast off 12 sts. and complete the row.

Continue over the last 50 sts., casting off 3 sts. at the beginning of each

of the next 6 rows commencing at the neck edge, and leaving 32 sts. for the shoulder.

Continue straight on these sts. for a depth of 6 rows longer than that of the back at the armhole edge.

Shape the Shoulder by casting off 8 sts. at the beginning of the next 4 rows commencing at the armhole edge.

Join the wool to the front edge of the opposite side and complete this side to match the first.

To Complete

Press the work on the wrong side with a hot iron over a damp cloth.

Use a thick pad as the pressing cloth so that the pattern will not be stamped out.

Sew the shoulders together.

Using No. 11 needles and holding the right side of the work towards you pick up and knit through all sts. along the armhole edge.

Work a depth of 1 in. in K. 1, P. 1 rib.

Cast off.

Complete the second armhole in the same way,

The Neck

Holding the right side of the work towards you and using the set of No. 11 needles, pick up and knit through all sts. round the neck.

Work in K. 1, P. 1 rib for the same depth as on the armhole edges.

Sew up the side seams and press these.

Give a final pressing on the wrong side, avoiding the ribbing.

See colour plate on page 100

STITCHCRAFT

Knitting for a Coronation summer

Materials: Of Patons Moorland Double Knitting, 14 (13) ozs. White, 4 ozs. Black, 1 oz. each Scarlet 55 and Straw 1037. A pair each No. 9 and No. 8 "Beehive" needles.

"Club colours"

Measurements: To fit 41–43 (38–40) inch chest; length from top of shoulders, 25 (25) inches; sleeve seam, 19 (19) inches.

Tension: 5½ sts. and 7½ rows to an inch.

N.B.—Instructions for small size in brackets thus ( ). Where one set of figures is given, this applies to both sizes.

Abbreviations: W.= White. R.= Red. Y.= Yellow. B.= Black.

FRONT

Start by winding 3 balls of white, 2 of red, 2 of yellow and 4 of black.

With No. 9 needles and black wool, cast on 110 (102) sts. and work 3 inches k. 2, p. 2 rib, rows on right side having a k. 2 at each end. Decrease 1 stitch at end of last row to 109 sts. (On small size increase 1 stitch to 103 sts.)

Change to No. 8 needles and white wool and continue straight in stocking-stitch until work measures 11½ (11½) inches.

With right side facing, start V stripes as follows:—

1ST ROW: Knit, 54 (51) W., join in 1st ball of black, 1 B., join in 2nd ball of white, 54 (51) W. 2ND ROW: Purl, 54 (51) W., 1 B., 54 (51) W. (Twist wools at back of work when changing colour to avoid a hole.) 3RD ROW: Knit, 53 (50) W., 3 B., 53 (50) W. 4TH ROW: Purl, 53 (50) W., 3 B., 53 (50) W.

5TH ROW: Knit, 52 (49) W., 5 B., 52 (49) W. 6TH ROW: Purl, 52 (49) W., 5 B., 52 (49) W. 7TH ROW: Knit, 51 (48) W., 7 B., 51 (48) W. 8TH ROW: Purl, 51 (48) W., 7 B., 51 (48) W. 9TH ROW: Knit, 50 (47) W., 4 B., join in 1st ball of yellow, 1 Y., join in 2nd ball of black, 4 B., 50 (47) W. 10TH ROW: Purl, 50 (47) W., 4 B., 1 Y., 4 B., 50 (47) W.

11TH ROW: Knit, 49 (46) W., 4 B., 3 Y., 4 B., 49 (46) W. 12TH ROW: Purl, 49 (46) W., 4 B., 3 Y., 4 B., 49 (46) W. 13TH ROW: Knit, 48 (45) W., 4 B., 2 Y., join in 1st ball of red, 1 R., 2 Y., 4 B., 48 (45) W. 14TH ROW: Purl, 48 (45) W., 4 B., 2 Y., 1 R., 2 Y., 4 B., 48 (45) W.

15TH ROW: Knit, 47 (44) W., 4 B., 2 Y., 3 R., 2 Y., 4 B., 47 (44) W. 16TH ROW: Purl, 47 (44) W., 4 B., 2 Y., 3 R., 2 Y., 4 B., 47 (44) W. 17TH ROW: Knit, 46 (43) W., 4 B., 2 Y., 2 R., 1 Y., 2 R., 2 Y., 4 B., 46 (43) W. 18TH ROW: Purl, 46 (43) W., 4 B., 2 Y., 2 R., 1 Y., 2 R., 2 Y., 4 B., 46 (43) W.

19TH ROW: Knit, 45 (42) W., 4 B., 2 Y., 2 R., 3 Y., 2. R., 2 Y., 4 B., 45 (42) W. 20TH ROW: Purl, 45 (42) W., 4 B., 2 Y., 2 R., 3 Y., 2 R., 2 Y., 4 B., 45 (42) W. 21ST ROW: Knit, 44 (41) W., 4 B., 2 Y., 2 R., 2 Y., join in 3rd ball of black, 1 B., join in 2nd ball of yellow, 2 Y., join in 2nd ball of red, 2 R., 2 Y., 4 B., 44 (41) W. 22ND ROW: Purl, 44 (41) W., 4 B., 2 Y., 2 R., 2 Y., 1 B., 2 Y., 2 R., 2 Y., 4 B., 44 (41) W.

23RD ROW: Knit, 43 (40) W., 4 B., 2 Y., 2 R., 2 Y., 3 B., 2 Y., 2 R., 2 Y., 4 B., 43 (40) W. 24TH ROW: Purl, 43 (40) W., 4 B., 2 Y., 2 R., 2 Y., 3 B., 2 Y., 2 R., 2 Y., 4 B., 43 (40) W. 25TH ROW: Knit, 42 (39) W., 4 B., 2 Y., 2 R., 2 Y., 5 B., 2 Y., 2 R., 2 Y., 4 B., 42 (39) W. 26TH ROW: Purl, 42 (39) W., 4 B., 2 Y., 2 R., 2 Y., 5 B., 2 Y., 2 R., 2 Y., 4 B., 42 (39) W.

27TH ROW: Knit, 41 (38) W., 4 B., 2 Y., 2 R., 2 Y., 7 B., 2 Y., 2 R., 2 Y., 4 B., 41 (38) W. 28TH ROW: Purl, 41 (38) W., 4 B., 2 Y., 2 R., 2 Y., 7 B., 2 Y., 2 R., 2 Y., 4 B., 41 (38) W.

Here shape armholes. 29TH ROW: Cast off 8 (8), knit, 32 (29) W., 4 B., 2 Y., 2 R., 2 Y., 4 B., join in 3rd ball of white, 1 W., join in 4th ball of black, 4 B., 2 Y., 2 R., 2 Y., 4 B., 40 (37) W. 30TH ROW: Cast off 8 (8), purl, 32 (29) W., 4 B., 2 Y., 2 R., 2 Y., 4 B., 1 W., 4 B., 2 Y., 2 R., 2 Y., 4 B., 32 (29) W.

31ST ROW: k. 2 tog., knit, 29 (26) W., 4 B., 2 Y., 2 R., 2 Y., 4 B., 3 W., 4 B., 2 Y., 2 R., 2 Y., 4 B., 29 (26) W., k. 2 tog. 32ND ROW: Purl, 30 (27) W., 4 B., 2 Y., 2 R., 2 Y., 4 B., 3 W., 4 B., 2 Y., 2 R., 2 Y., 4 B., 30 (27) W. 33RD ROW: k. 2 tog., knit, 27 (24) W., 4 B., 2 Y., 2 R., 2 Y., 4 B., 5 W., 4 B., 2 Y., 2 R., 2 Y., 4 B., 27 (24) W., k. 2 tog.

34TH ROW: Purl, 28 (25) W., 4 B., 2 Y., 2 R., 2 Y., 4 B., 5 W., 4 B., 2 Y., 2 R., 2 Y., 4 B., 28 (25) W. 35TH ROW: k. 2 tog., knit, 25 (22) W., 4 B., 2 Y., 2 R., 2 Y., 4 B., 7 W., 4 B., 2 Y., 2 R., 2 Y., 4 B., 25 (22) W., k. 2 tog. 36TH ROW: Purl, 26 (23) W., 4 B., 2 Y., 2 R., 2 Y., 4 B., 7 W., 4 B., 2 Y., 2 R., 2 Y., 4 B., 26 (23) W.

37TH ROW: Knit, 25 (22) W., 4 B., 2 Y., 2 R., 2 Y., 4 B., 9 W., 4 B., 2 Y., 2 R., 2 Y., 4 B., 25 (22) W. 38TH ROW: Purl, 25 (22) W., 4 B., 2 Y., 2 R., 2 Y., 4 B., 9 W., 4 B., 2 Y., 2 R., 2 Y., 4 B., 25 (22) W.

Here divide for neck. 39TH ROW: Knit, 24 (21) W., 4 B., 2 Y., 2 R., 2 Y., 4 B., 5 W., turn and leave remaining stitches on a spare needle. 40TH ROW: Purl, 5 W., 4 B., 2 Y., 2 R., 2 Y., 4 B., 24 (21) W. 41ST ROW: Knit, 24 (21) W., 4 B., 2 Y., 2 R., 2 Y., 4 B., 5 W. 42ND ROW: Purl, 5 W., 4 B., 2 Y., 2 R., 2 Y., 4 B., 24 (21) W.

43RD ROW: Knit, 23 (20) W., 4 B., 2 Y., 2 R., 2 Y., 4 B., 4 W., k. 2 tog. W. 44TH ROW: Purl, 5 W., 4 B., 2 Y., 2 R., 2 Y., 4 B., 23 (20) W. 45TH ROW: Knit, 23 (20) W., 4 B., 2 Y., 2 R., 2 Y., 4 B., 5 W. 46TH ROW: Purl, 5 W., 4 B., 2 Y., 2 R., 2 Y., 4 B., 23 (20) W. 47TH ROW: Knit, 22 (19) W., 4 B., 2 Y., 2 R., 2 Y., 4 B., 4 W., k. 2 tog. W.

Continue in pattern thus, shaping neck by decreasing 1 stitch at neck edge on every following 4th row and at the same time slope coloured stripes on every 4th row until 30 (27) sts. remain. Purl back in pattern, then with right side facing, shape shoulder by casting off 10 (9) sts. at beginning of next and following 2 alternate rows, armhole edge.

With right side facing, rejoin W. to remaining stitches at centre, k. 2 tog. W., knit, 4 W., 4 B., 2 Y., 2 R., 2 Y., 4 B., 24 (21) W. Work last 43 (40) sts. to correspond with first.

BACK

With No. 9 needles and black wool cast on 110 (102) sts. and work 3 inches k. 2, p. 2 rib, rows on right side having a k. 2 at each end. Decrease 1 stitch at end of last row to 109 sts. (on small size increase 1 stitch to 103 sts.).

Change to No. 8 needles and white wool and continue straight in stocking-stitch until back measures same as front at armhole edge. With right side facing, shape armholes by casting off 8 (8) sts. at beginning of next 2 rows, then k. 2 tog. at each end of next 3 knit rows [87 (81) sts.]. Work straight until back matches front.

With right side facing, shape shoulders by casting off 10 (9) sts. at beginning of next 6 rows; cast off remaining stitches fairly tightly.

SLEEVES

With No. 9 needles and black wool, cast on 42 sts. and work 2 inches k. 2, p. 2 rib as before. Change to No. 8 needles and stocking-stitch and work a band of stripes as follows:—8 rows white, 8 rows black, 4 rows yellow, 4 rows red, 8 rows black, and *at the same time* shape sides by increasing 1 stitch at each end of 3rd and every following 6th row. When stripes are done, continue in white, still increasing at each end of every 6th row until there are 70 sts. Work straight until sleeve measures 19 inches or required length.

With right side facing, shape top by k. 2 tog. at beginning of every row until 20 sts. remain. Cast off.

TO MAKE UP

Press work on wrong side under a damp cloth. Join right shoulder seam. With No. 9 needles, black wool and right side facing, pick up and k. 64 sts. down left side of neck, 1 from centre, 64 sts. up right side of neck and 26 sts. across back of neck. Work 1¼ inches k. 1, p. 1 rib, decreasing 1 stitch at each side of centre knit stitch on every row. Cast off in rib. Join left shoulder, side and sleeve seams; insert sleeves. Press seams.

For "Him and Her"

(In 3 sizes to fit: Man's 35 - 36 and 37 - 38 inch Chest
Lady's 33 - 34 and 35 - 36 inch Bust)

IMPORTANT:

As different dye-lots should not be worked into the same garment, it is most important that you should make sure of having sufficient wool from the one dye-lot to complete the garment. Each dye-lot has a separate letter which is shown on the band or skein ticket.

MATERIALS REQUIRED: **Man's 11 [12] ozs., Lady's 9 [10] ozs. BALDWIN & WALKER'S LADYSHIP 4-ply BELINDA WOOL AND NYLON. One pair each Knitting Needles Nos. 10 and 12.**

MEASUREMENTS: **Length from top of shoulder—Man's 23½ [24] ins. Lady's—19 [19½] ins.**
Length of sleeve seam—Man's 19 ins., Lady's 16½ ins.
Details for larger size are given in square brackets.
Where only one set of figures is given, this applies to all sizes.

TENSION: Rib 11½ sts. and 9½ rows to one square inch on No. 10 needles, unpressed. Smooth fabric 8 sts. and 10 rows to one square inch on No. 10 needles.
Note: If the needles stated do not produce these tensions, try different sizes until you get them correct.

ABBREVIATIONS: K., knit; P., purl; st., stitch; inc., increase by working into front and back of same st.; dec., decrease; tog., together; beg., beginning; rep., repeat; ins., inches; L., Lady's; M., Man's.

BACK

Using No. 10 needles, for L., cast on 153 [163] sts.; M., 163 [173] sts.
1st row. K.2, *P.1, K.1, rep. from * to last st., K.1.
2nd row. *K.1, P.1, rep. from * to last st., K.1.
Rep. 1st and 2nd rows until work measures 14 [14½] ins. for L.; 17½ [17¾] ins. for M., ending with 1st row. (When pressed, this length is reduced by approximately ¾ ins.).
Proceed as follows:
1st row. For L. only. K.1, P.3 [K.1, P.1], *P.2 tog., P.5, P.2 tog., P.4, rep. from * to last 6 [5] sts., P.2 tog., P.3 [2], K.1. (130 [138] sts.).
1st row. For M. K.1, P.1 [K.1], *P.2 tog., P.5, P.2 tog., P.4, rep. from * to last 5 [3] sts., P.2 tog., P.2, K.1 [P.2 tog., K.1]. (138 [146] sts.).
2nd row. Cast off 5 [6] sts., for L.; 6 [7] sts. for M., K. to end.
3rd row. Cast off 5 [6] sts., for L.; 6 [7] sts. for M., P. to last st., K.1.
Continue in smooth fabric, dec. at each end of needle in every row until 110 [116] sts. for L.; 116 [122] for M., remain, then in every alternate row until 102 [108] sts. for L.; 108 [114] sts. for M. remain.**
Work 29 rows for L.; 39 for M., without shaping.
In next row. K.41 [43] for L.; K.43 [45] for M., turn.
Work on these sts. as follows:
***1st row.* Cast off 3 sts., work to end.
2nd row. Work to end.
Rep. 1st and 2nd rows once.
5th row. Cast off 2 sts., work to end.
6th row. Work to end.
Rep. 5th and 6th rows 3 times.
13th row. Cast off 1 st., work to end.
14th row. Work to end.
Rep. 13th and 14th rows 4 [5] times.***
Work 8 rows for L.; 10 rows for M. without shaping. Cast off.
Slip next 20 [22] sts. for L., 22 [24] sts. for M., on to a length of wool, join in wool and K.41 [43] for L., 43 [45] for M., across remaining sts.
In next row. K.1, P. to end.
Rep. from *** to *** as given for other side once.
Work 7 rows for L., 9 rows for M., without shaping. Cast off.

BACK YOKE

Using No. 10 needles, with right side of work facing, join in wool at right shoulder and knit up 38 [39] sts. for L., 40 [41] sts. for M., down side of neck; K.9 [10], K.2 tog., K.9 [10] for L., K.10 [11], K.2 tog., K.10 [11] for M., across sts. of centre back; knit up 38 [39] sts. for L., 40 [41] sts. for M., along other side of neck. (95 [99] sts. for L., 101 [105] for M.).
Proceed as follows:
1st row. *K.1, P.1, rep. from * to last st., K.1.
2nd row. K.2, *P.1, K.1, rep. from * to last st., K.1.
Rep. 1st and 2nd rows twice, then 1st row once.
8th row. For L. only. K.2, P.1, K.1 [twice], *P.3 tog., (K.1, P.1) 4 times, K.1, rep. from * to last 7 [9] sts., P.3 tog., K.1, P.1, [twice], K.2. For M., K.2 (P.1, K.1) twice, [3 times], P.1, *K.3 tog., (P.1, K.1) 4 times, P.1, rep. from * to last 10 [12] sts., K.3 tog., (P.1, K.1) 3 [4] times, K.1.
Rep. 1st and 2nd rows 3 times, then 1st row once.

16th row. For L. only. K.2, P.1, [K.2, P.1, K.1, P.1], *K.3 tog., (P.1, K.1) 3 times, P.1, rep. from * to last 6 [8] sts., K.3 tog., P.1, K.2, [P.1, K.1, P.1, K.2]. For M., K.2, (P.1, K.1) twice [3 times], *P.3 tog., (K.1, P.1) 3 times, K.1, rep. from * to last 9 [11] sts., P.3 tog., (K.1, P.1) twice [3 times], K.2.
Rep. 1st and 2nd rows 4 times, then 1st row once.
Break off wool and leave these sts. on a length of wool.

FRONT

Using No. 10 needles, cast on 153 [163] sts. for L., 163 [173] sts. for M.
Work exactly as given for Back until ** are reached.
In next row. K.41 [43] for L., 43 [45] for M., then rep. from *** to *** as given for Back.
Work 14 rows for L., 16 rows for M., without shaping. Cast off.
Slip next 20 [22] sts. for L., 22 [24] sts. for M., on to a length of wool.
Join in wool and K.41 [43] for L., 43 [45] for M.
In next row. K.1, P. to end.
Rep. from *** to *** as given for Back.
Work 13 rows for L., 15 rows for M., without shaping. Cast off.

FRONT YOKE

Using No. 10 needles, with right side of work facing, join in wool at left shoulder and knit up 44 [45] sts. for L., 46 [47] sts. for M., down side of neck; K.9 [10], K.2 tog., K.9 [10] for L., K.10 [11], K.2 tog., K.10 [11] for M., across sts. of centre front, knit up 44 [45] sts. for L., 46 [47] sts. for M. along other side of neck. (107 [111] sts. for L., 113 [117] sts. for M.).
Proceed as follows:
1st row. *K.1, P.1, rep. from * to last st., K.1.
2nd row. K.2, *P.1, K.1, rep. from * to last st., K.1.
Rep. 1st and 2nd rows twice, then 1st row once.
8th row. For L. only, K.2, (P.1, K.1) 4 [5] times, *P.3 tog., (K.1, P.1) 4 times, K.1, rep. from * to last st., K.1. [3 sts., P.1, K.2]. For M., K.2, *K.3 tog., (P.1, K.1) 4 times, P.1, rep. from * to last 4 [6] sts., K.1, P.1, [twice], K.2.
Rep. 1st and 2nd rows 3 times, then 1st row once.
16th row. For L., K.2, (P.1, K.1) 3 [4] times, P.1, *K.3 tog., (P.1, K.1) 3 times, P.1, rep. from * to last 2 sts., K.2, [4 sts., K.1, P.1, K.2]. For M., K.2, (P.1, K.1) 5 [6] times, *P.3 tog., (K.1, P.1) 3 times, K.1, rep. from * to last 5 [7] sts., (P.1, K.1) twice [3 times], K.1.
Rep. 1st and 2nd rows 4 times, then 1st row once. Do not break off wool. Sew up Right shoulder seam.
Using No. 12 needles, in next row, K.2, *P.1, K.1, rep. from * to last st., P.1, of Front Neck, then K.2 tog., *P.1, K.1, rep. from * to last st., K.1 across back neck.
Work 17 rows in K.1, P.1 rib. Cast off loosely in rib.

SLEEVE

Using No. 12 needles, cast on 56 [60] sts. for L., 66 [70] sts. for M.
1st row. K.2, *P.1, K.1, rep. from * to end.
Rep. this row 31 times.
Change to No. 10 needles, and proceed as follows:
1st row. For L., K.3 [5], *inc. once in next st., K.6, rep. from * to last 4 [6] sts., inc. once in next st., K.3 [5]. (64 [68] sts.). For M., K.4 [6], *inc. once in next st., K.7, rep. from * to last 6 [8] sts., inc. once in next st., K.5 [7]. (74 [78] sts.).
2nd row. K.1, P. to last st., K.1.
3rd row. Knit.
Rep. 2nd and 3rd rows twice, then 2nd row once.
9th row. K.1, inc. once in next st., K. to last 3 sts., inc. once in next st., K.2.
Continue in smooth fabric, inc. once at each end of needle in every following 8th row until there are 94 [98] sts. for L., for M., inc. in every following 6th row until there are 114 [118] sts. on needle.
Continue without shaping until work measures 16½ ins. for L., 19 ins. for M., ending with a purl row.
Cast off 1 st. at beg. of each of next 8 rows.
Cast off 2 sts. at beg. of each of next 12 [14] rows.
Cast off 1 st. at beg. of each of next 2 rows.
Cast off 2 sts. at beg. of each of next 2 rows.
Rep. last 4 rows 5 times for L., 6 times for M.
Cast off 1 st. at beg. of each of next 2 rows. Cast off remaining sts.
Work another Sleeve in same manner.

TO MAKE UP

Using hot iron and damp cloth, press carefully on wrong side of work. Sew up left shoulder and neck-band seam. Sew up side and sleeve seams. Sew in sleeves, placing seam to seam. Turn up lower edge of Sweater for 2 inches on to wrong side to form hem, and sew in position. For L., using 4 strands of wool 130 ins. long, make a twisted cord and thread through ribbing evenly above hem, to tie in centre front, knotting each end.

3315

6d.
In 3 sizes to fit
33 - 34 and 35 - 36 inch Bust
35 - 36 and 37 - 38 inch Chest
9 or 10 or 11 or 12 ozs.
4-ply
BELINDA
WOOL & NYLON

Ladyship
WOOLS

Match Mates!

Plain pockets on checked yokes for this gay pair of sweaters

Materials: 7 ozs. Sirdar Majestic Wool 3-ply in main shade; 1 oz. in contrast; 1 pair each of Nos. 10 and 12 "Aero" knitting needles; set of 4 No. 12 needles; a small piece of material to line pocket flaps.

Measurements.—Bust, 34 ins.

Tension.—7½ sts. and 10 rows to 1 in.

Abbreviations.—K., knit; p., purl; st(s)., stitch(es); st.-st., stocking-stitch; alt., alternate; foll., following; rem., remain-(ing) in(s)., inch(es); inc., increase; dec., decrease; patt., pattern; rep., repeat; beg., beginning; tog., together; cont., continue; M., main; C., contrast.

BACK.—On No. 12 needles and M. cast on 120 sts. Rib 3 ins. k. 2, p. 2. On No. 10 needles in st.-st. inc. 1 st. at each end of 9th and every foll. 8th row until 130 sts. Cont. straight until work measures 12 ins., ending with a p. row. Patt. as follows:

1st row.—K. 7 M., (2 M., 3 C.) 9 times, 26 M. Join on another ball of C., (3 C., 2 M.) 9 times, 7 M.

2nd row.—P. 7 M., (2 M., 3 C.) 9 times, drop C., 26 M., (3 C., 2 M.) 9 times, 7 M.

3rd and 4th rows.—As 1st and 2nd rows.

5th row.—K. in M.

6th row.—P. in M.

These 6 rows form patt. Keeping patt. correct and centre panel of 26 sts. in M.

Shape Armholes.—Cast off 5 sts. at beg. of next 2 rows, dec. 1 st. at beg. of every row until 112 sts. rem. Cont. straight until work measures 20 ins.

Shape Shoulders.—Cast off 17 sts. at beg. of next 4 rows; cast off rem. sts.

FRONT (Pocket Linings).—On No. 10 needles and M., cast on 30 sts. Work in st.-st. for 40 rows. Cast off. Make another piece.

(Pocket Flaps).—On No. 10 needles and M., cast on 30 sts. Work in st. st. for 14 rows. Leave sts. on a st.-holder. Make another piece.

Work Front as given for Back until work measures 16 ins., ending with 4th patt. row. Make pocket openings thus:

Next row.—K. across 10 sts., cast off 30, k. 32, cast off 30, k. 10.

Next row.—P. 10, with a pocket flap wrong side facing, p. across sts. to replace cast-off ones of previous row, then p. to 2nd opening, work across 2nd pocket flap, p. 10. Cont. in patt. until work measures 18 ins., ending with p. row.

Shape Neck: Next row.—Work across 49 sts., cast off 14, work to end of row. Cont. in patt. on last set of sts., casting

off 2 sts. at neck edge on next 2 alt. rows. Dec. 1 st. at neck edge every alt. row until 34 sts. rem. Cont. straight until work measures same as Back to shoulder, ending side edge.

Shape Shoulder.—Cast off 17 sts. at beg. of next and foll. alt. row. Rejoin wool to neck edge of rem. sts., and work to match 1st side.

SLEEVES.—On No. 12 needles and M., cast on 60 sts. Rib 2½ ins. k. 2, p. 2. On No. 10 needles cont. in st.-st., inc. 1 st. each end of 7th and every foll. 6th row until there are 106 sts. Cont. straight until Sleeve measures 18½ ins.

Shape Top.—Cast off 5 sts. beg. of next 2 rows, dec. 1 st. beg. of every row until 56 sts. rem. Then dec. 1 st. at each end of every row until 26 sts. rem. Cast off.

Neck Border: Join shoulder seams. With right side of work facing, join M. wool to left shoulder and using set of No. 12 needles pick up and k. 34 sts. down left side of neck, 14 sts. across Front, 34 up right side and 42 across back neck. Rib 14 rows k. 2, p. 2. Cast off ribwise loosely.

TO MAKE UP.—Press work on wrong side avoiding all ribbing. Set in Sleeves. Stitch pocket linings in position on wrong side with small invisible stitches, the top edge to back of pocket flap where sts. were knitted across jumper. Line pocket flaps with piece of material to prevent flaps from curling up. Join side and Sleeve seams. Press seams.

MAN'S PULLOVER WITH CHECK-PATTERNED YOKE

Materials.—9 ozs. Sirdar Majestic Wool, 3-ply, in main shade and 1 oz. in contrasting shade. 1 pair each of No. 10 and 12 "Aero" knitting needles. A set of 4 No. 12 needles with double points. A small piece of material to line pocket flaps.

Measurements.—38-39-in. chest. Length, 22 ins. Sleeve seam, 20 ins.

Tension.—7½ sts. and 10 rows to 1 inch.

BACK.—With No. 12 needles and M. wool, cast on 136 sts. Work in k. 2, p. 2 rib for 3 ins.

Next row.—Rib 14, * (inc. in next st., rib 11). Rep. from * 8 times more, inc. in next st., rib 13 (146 sts.).

Change to No. 10 needles, cont. in st.-st. until work measures 18 ins. from beg.

Shape Armholes: Cast off 8 sts. at beg. of next 2 rows, then dec. 1 st. both ends of every row until 120 sts. rem. Then work

as follows:

1st row.—K. (2 M., 3 C.) 9 times, 30 M.; join on another ball of C. (3 C., 2 M.) to end of row.

2nd row.—P. (2 M., 3 C.) 9 times, drop C., 30 M., (3 C., 2 M.) to end of row.

3rd and 4th rows.—As 1st and 2nd rows.

5th row.—K. in M.

6th row.—P. in M.

These 6 rows form patt. Rep. them until work measures 22 ins.

Shape Shoulders.—Cast off 19 sts. at beg. of next 4 rows. Leave rem. sts. on a st.-holder.

Pocket Lining.—On No. 10 needles and M. wool, cast on 30 sts. Work in st.-st. for 40 rows. Cast off. Make another piece the same.

Pocket Flap.—On No. 10 needles and M. wool cast on 30 sts. Work in st.-st. for 16 rows. Leave sts. on a st.-holder. Make another piece the same.

FRONT.—Work as given for Back until work measures 18 ins., ending with a 4th patt. row. Make pocket opening thus:

Next row.—K. across 12 sts., cast off 30, k. 36, cast off 30, k. 12.

Next row.—P. 12, with a pocket flap wrong side facing, p. across these sts. to replace cast-off ones of previous row, then p. to second opening, work across second pocket flap, p. 12. Cont. in patt. until work measures 20½ ins., ending with a p. row.

Shape Neck.—Work across 52 sts., cast off 16, work to end of row. Cont. in patt. on last set of 52 sts., casting off 2 at neck edge on next 2 alt. rows, then dec. 1 st. at neck edge every alt. row until 38 sts. remain. Cont. straight until work measures same as Back to shoulder seam, ending at side edge.

Shape Shoulder.—Cast off 19 sts. at beg. of next row and foll. alt. row. Rejoin wool to neck edge of rem. sts., and work in same way.

SLEEVES.—With No. 12 needles and M. wool cast on 64 sts. Work in k. 2, p. 2 rib for 2½ ins. On No. 10 needles, cont. in st.-st., inc. 1 st. at both ends of 7th and every foll. 6th row until there are 112 sts. Cont. straight until sleeve measures 20 ins. Shape top. Cast off 8 sts. at beg. of next 2 rows, then dec. 1 st. at both ends of next 6 rows, then 1 st. at beg. of every row until 50 sts. rem. Dec. at both ends of every row until 28 sts. rem. Cast off.

Neck Border.—Join shoulder seams. With right side of work facing and using the set of No. 12 needles and M. wool, beg. at left shoulder seam, pick up and k. 34 sts. down left side of neck, 16 across front of neck, 34 up right side of neck and 48 across back of neck. Work 14 rows in k. 2, p. 2 rib. Cast off loosely ribwise, using a larger needle.

TO MAKE UP.—Press work on wrong side under a damp cloth with a hot iron, omitting all ribbing. Set in sleeves. Stitch pocket linings in position on wrong side, the top edge to back of pocket flap where sts. were knitted-in across Pullover. Line pocket flaps with a piece of material. Join side and sleeve seams. Press seams. ▲▲▲

MATCHING SET

Fair Isle Socks, Gloves and Scarf

SOCKS

MATERIALS

5 oz. Light, 2 oz. Dark PATONS PURPLE HEATHER Fingering 4-ply. One set of four No. 14 and one set of four No. 13 BEEHIVE needles, or QUEEN BEE if stainless rigid needles preferred, with points at both ends, measured by BEEHIVE gauge.

MEASUREMENTS

To fit 11-inch foot. (Adjustable to length required). Length of leg, 13½ ins.

ABBREVIATIONS

K.=Knit; P.=purl; st.=stitch; sl.=slip; p.s.s.o.=pass slip st. over; tog.=together; inc.=increase by working into front and back of st.; beg=beginning; rep.=repeat; patt.=pattern; incl.=inclusive; ins.=inches; L.=Light.

TENSION

The tension should be 9 stitches and 11 rows to 1 square inch in stocking stitch,

Using No. 14 needles and Light, cast on 79 sts. Working on 2 needles proceed as follows:—

1st row—K.2, * P.1, K.1, rep. from * to last st., K.1.

2nd row—K.1, * P.1, K.1, rep. from * to end.

Rep. these 2 rows until work measures 4 ins. from beg., finishing at end of a first row.

Next row—(K.1, P.1) 5 times, K.1, leave these 11 sts. on first safety pin, P.4, * inc. in next st., P.2, rep. from * to last 16 sts., P.3, leave remaining 13 sts. on 2nd safety pin (71 sts. on needle).

Change to No. 13 needles and work **from Chart** on page 4 (odd rows K., even rows P.) reading K. rows from right to left and P. rows from left to right.

Work rows 1–32 incl. twice, then rows 1–16 incl. once. Break off both wools.

With right side of work facing, slip first 11 sts. on to 3rd safety pin, join in wools and work next 49 sts. from row 17 of Chart (instep sts.). Slip next 11 sts. on to 4th safety pin.

Continue working from Chart rows 18–32 incl., then rows 1–6 incl. Break off Dark.

Change to No. 14 needles.

Next row—K.1, * K.2 tog., K.2, rep. from * to end (37 sts.).

Leave these sts. on one needle.

BACK PANEL

Slip sts. from first and 2nd safety pins on to one No. 14 needle (24 sts.). With **wrong** side of work facing, join in Light and using No. 14 needles work Back Panel as follows:—

Next row—(K.1, P.1) 6 times, K.2 tog., (P.1, K.1) 5 times (23 sts.).

Proceed in rib as on welt until panel matches Fair Isle panel up to instep sts.

With **right** side of work facing work across 11 sts. on 3rd safety pin as follows:—(K.2 tog., K.2) twice, K.2 tog., K.1 (31 sts.).

Next row—K.1, P.30, with **wrong** side of work facing, work across 11 sts. on 4th safety pin as follows:—(P.2 tog., P.2) twice, P.2 tog., K.1 (39 sts.).

Work "Aladdin" heel as follows:—

1st row—* K.1, sl. 1, rep. from * to last st., K.1.

2nd row—K.1, P. to last st., K.1,

Rep. these 2 rows until work measures 2½ ins. from beg., finishing with a first row.

Turn heel as follows:—

1st row—K.1, P.19, P.2 tog., P.1, turn.

2nd row—K.3, sl. 1, K.1, p.s.s.o., K.1, turn.

3rd row—P.4, P.2 tog., P.1, turn.

4th row—K.5, sl. 1, K.1, p.s.s.o., K.1, turn.

Continue in this manner working 1 st. more at beg. of each row as before until the row "K.19, sl. 1, K.1, p.s.s.o., K.1" has been worked. Break off wool.

With **right** side of work facing and using Dark **(leaving an end 8 ins. long)** K. across 21 heel sts. Break off wool leaving another end 8 ins. long.

Shape instep and make sole. With **right** side of work facing, rejoin Light to the 21 heel sts. Cast on 18 sts. K. these 18 sts. and K. across 21 heel sts. Cast on 18 sts. (57 sts.).

Next row—K.1, P. to last st., K.1.

Next row—K.1, K.2 tog., K. to last 3 sts., sl. 1, K.1, p.s.s.o., K.1.

Rep. last 2 rows until 37 sts. remain.

Continue in stocking stitch (1 row P., 1 row K.) knitting first and last st. on every row until work measures same as instep piece, finishing with a P. row.

Still using Light, proceed as follows:—
Next row—K.18 (this is 3rd needle). Using another needle K. across remaining 19 sts. (first needle). Using another needle K. across 37 instep sts. (2nd needle). Join up ready to work in rounds. K. across 3rd needle (sts. should now be divided as follows:—1st needle 19 sts., 2nd needle 37 sts., 3rd needle 18 sts.).

Continue in stocking stitch (every round K.) until work measures 6¼ ins. or length required (from where sts. were cast on for instep).

Shape toe as follows:—
1st round—First needle, K. to last 3 sts., K.2 tog., K.1; 2nd needle, K.1, sl.1, K.1, p.s.s.o., K. to last 3 sts., K.2 tog., K.1; 3rd needle, K.1, sl.1, K.1, p.s.s.o., K. to end.
2nd round—K.

Rep. these 2 rounds until 30 sts. remain.

K. the sts. of first needle on to end of 3rd needle. Break off wool.

Using a strand of **Dark** 12 ins. long, graft toe.

TO MAKE UP

1. With wrong side of work facing, block Fair Isle fabric by pinning out round edges.

2. Press, using a hot iron and wet cloth.

3. Press foot, using a **warm** iron and damp cloth.

4. Join seams.

5. Press all seams.

The row of Dark at the heel and the grafting in Dark at the toe, is to facilitate the working of new toes and heels when they wear out. To do this pull out the coloured thread which releases the sts. of foot and heel.

CHART FOR SOCKS

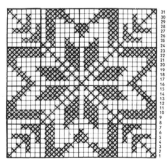

49 STS. FOR INSTEP
71 STS. FOR LEG

ODD ROWS K.
EVEN ROWS P.

KEY
⊠ DARK
☐ LIGHT

GLOVES

MATERIALS

3 oz. Light, oddment Dark PATONS PURPLE HEATHER Fingering 4-ply. One set of four No. 12 BEEHIVE needles, or QUEEN BEE if stainless rigid needles preferred, with points at both ends, measured by BEEHIVE gauge.

MEASUREMENTS

To fit average hand.

TENSION

8 sts. and 10 rows to one square inch measured over stocking stitch.

RIGHT GLOVE

Using Light cast on 64 sts. Proceed in rib as Socks for 3½ ins.

Next row—K.1, P.4, slip these 5 sts. on to a safety pin and leave for thumb gusset. P. across remaining sts. to last st., K.1. Work 5 rows in stocking stitch (1 row K., 1 row P.).

Next row—K.1, P.3, (inc. in next st., P.7) 3 times, inc. in next st., P. to last st., K.1 (63 sts.).

Next row—K.28, join in Dark, work from Chart across next 31 sts., K.4L.

Next row—K.1L., P.3L., work next 31 sts. from Chart, P.27L., K.1L.

Continue in this manner working 31 sts. from Chart and outside sts. in Light, until 25th row of Chart on page 5 has been worked.

Cast on 5 sts. at end of last row (68 sts.). Keeping these 5 sts. in stocking stitch in Light, continue until 31st row of Chart has been worked. Break off Dark.

Next row—K.1, P.8, (P.2 tog., P.7) 3 times, P.2 tog., P. to last st., K.1 (64 sts.).

Divide on 3 needles as follows:—
1st round—1st needle K.20, 2nd needle K.22, 3rd needle K.22. With right side of work facing join round, K. 5 rounds.

1st finger—Dividing sts. on to 3 needles, K.3, slip next 16 sts. on to a length of wool. Cast on 2 sts., K. remaining 15 sts. Join round (20 sts.). K. 3 ins. (or length required).

Shape top as follows:—
K.2 tog., 10 times. Break off wool. Thread end through remaining sts. Draw up and fasten off securely.

2nd finger—With right side of work facing, K. next 8 sts. of round from length of wool. Cast on 2 sts., K. last 8 sts. of round; **knit up** 2 sts. at base of first finger (20 sts.). K. 3½ ins. and complete as 1st finger.

3rd finger—K. next 8 sts. of round, cast on 2 sts. K. last 8 sts. of round; **knit up** 2 sts. at base of 2nd finger (20 sts.). Complete as 1st finger.

4th finger—K. remaining sts. from thread, **knit up** 2 sts. at base of 3rd finger (16 sts.). K. 2½ ins.
Next round—K.2 tog. 8 times. Finish off as 1st finger.

Thumb Gusset and Thumb—Slip the 5 sts. for Thumb Gusset on to one needle. With right side of work facing and using Light, proceed as follows:—
1st row—K.
2nd row—K.1, P. to last st., K.1.
3rd row—Inc. in first st., K. to last 2 sts., inc. in next st., K.1.

Continue in this manner inc. 1 st. at each end of every following 4th row until there are 19 sts. on needle.

Work 4 more rows. Cast on 5 sts. (24 sts.).

Divide these sts. on to 3 needles, Join round.
1st round—K.
2nd round—K. to 5 cast-on sts., sl.1, K.1, p.s.s.o., K.1, K.2 tog.
3rd round—K. to last 3 sts., sl.1, K.2 tog., p.s.s.o. (20 sts.), K. 2½ ins. and complete as 1st finger.

LEFT GLOVE

Work ribbing as Right Glove.
Next row—K.1, P. to last 5 sts., slip these 5 sts. on to a safety pin for thumb gusset. Work 5 rows in stocking stitch.
Next row—K.1, P.29 (inc. in next st., P.7) 3 times, inc. in next st., P.3, K.1 (63 sts.).
Next row—K.4, join in Dark, work from Chart across next 31 sts., K.28L.
Next row—K.1L., P.27L., work next 31 sts. from Chart, P.3L., K.1L.

Continue working to match Right Glove casting on 5 sts. at end of **24th** row instead of 25th. When 31st row of Chart has been completed, break off Dark.

Next row—K.1, P.29, (P.2 tog., P.7) 3 times, P.2 tog., P. to last st., K.1 (64 sts.).

Divide on 3 needles as follows:—
1st round—1st needle K.22, 2nd needle K.22, 3rd needle K.20. With right side of work facing, join round, K. 5 rounds.

1st finger—Dividing sts. on to 3 needles, K.15, slip next 46 sts. on to a length of wool. Cast on 2 sts., K. remaining 3 sts. Work as first finger of Right Glove.

Work remainder of Glove to match Right Glove.

TO MAKE UP

1. Sew down thumb gusset and join ribbing.

2. Press, using a warm iron and damp cloth.

SCARF

MATERIALS

3 oz. Light, 3 oz. Dark PATONS FAIR ISLE Fingering. One set of four No. 11 BEEHIVE needles, or QUEEN BEE if stainless rigid needles preferred, with points at both ends, measured by BEEHIVE gauge. One crochet hook.

MEASUREMENTS

Width, 7 ins. Length (without fringe), 44 ins.

TENSION

8½ sts. and 8½ rows to one square inch measured over stocking stitch.

Using Light, cast on 128 sts. (42, 42, 44 sts. on 1st, 2nd and 3rd needle respectively) K. 1 round.

Join in Dark and work from Chart, on page 5, reading **every** round from right to left working the 32 st. rep. 4 times.

Work in patt. until work measures approx. 44 ins. from beg., ending with 31st row of Chart. Break off Dark.

K. 1 round. Cast off.

TO MAKE UP

1. Press, using hot iron and wet cloth.
2. Fringe Scarf as follows:—
Using Light, wind wool over a piece of cardboard 2½ ins. wide and cut through one edge. Taking 2 strands tog., double them, and using crochet hook draw a loop through double end of Scarf. Pass the ends through the loop and knot firmly.
Repeat all across each end of Scarf. Trim evenly.

CHART FOR GLOVES

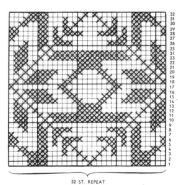

CHART FOR SCARF

32 ST. REPEAT

Wynnefield *Vest*

"When day is done" father can slip off his coat, enjoy his paper, smoke his pipe, and relax in comfort in this cosy knitted Vest. Made of Minerva Featherweight Knitting Worsted.

Sizes: 38, 40, 42 and 44

MATERIALS REQUIRED:

Minerva Featherweight Knitting Worsted
(2 ounce skein)
—OR—
Minerva Heather Featherweight Knitting Worsted
(2 ounce skein)

	Size 38	Size 40	Size 42	Size 44
Brown	3 Skeins	3 Skeins	4 Skeins	4 Skeins
Green	3 Skeins	3 Skeins	4 Skeins	4 Skeins

Knitting Needles: 1 Pair Standard Size 2—14 inch
1 Pair Standard Size 3—14 inch
Gauge: 7 Sts. to 1 inch (Size 3 Needles)
1 Composition Crochet Hook—Standard Size 3—6 inch

PATTERN STITCH: (for Front) Multiple of 4 Sts., plus 1.
Row 1—* Green K. 1, Brown K. 1, repeat from * across, end Green K. 1.
Row 2—Brown P. 1, * Green P. 3, Brown P. 1, repeat from * across.
Row 3—Brown K. 2, Green K. 1, * Brown K. 3, Green K. 1, repeat from * across, end Brown K. 2.
Row 4—Brown P. 2, * Green P. 1, Brown P. 3, repeat from * across, end Green P. 1, Brown P. 2.
Row 5—Same as Row 3.
Row 6—Same as Row 2.
Repeat the 6 rows for Pattern.

Sizes:	38	40	42	44

RIGHT FRONT: Pocket Facing—With Size 3 Needles and Brown cast on 26 Sts. Work in Stockinette St. for 4 inches, slip Sts. on St. Holder.
With Size 3 Needles and Green cast on

61 Sts.	65 Sts.	69 Sts.	73 Sts.

Join Brown and work in Pattern St. for 26 rows.
Row 27—(Row 3 of Pattern) Work across 19 Sts., bind off 26 Sts. for Pocket, work to end of row.
Row 28—Work Pattern to Pocket, continue in Pattern St. across 26 Sts. of Pocket Facing, work to end of row.
Continue even in Pattern St. until Front measures

11″	11½″	12″	12″

to underarm.

To Shape Armhole: Bind off 12 Sts. at side edge, then decrease 1 St. at same edge every other row 8 times, being careful to keep Pattern St. even.

To Shape Neck Edge: Decrease 1 St. at Front edge, then decrease 1 St. every 4th row

13 times	14 times	15 times	16 times

more.

When Armhole measures

8″	8½″	9″	9½″

(measured straight up from bound off Sts. at underarm).
To Shape Shoulders: Bind off

9 Sts.	10 Sts.	11 Sts.	12 Sts.

(from Armhole edge) every other row 3 times.

LEFT FRONT: Work to correspond with Right Front, having Pocket 19 Sts. from Front edge and decreases at opposite sides.

BACK: With Size 2 Needles and Brown cast on

96 Sts.	104 Sts.	112 Sts.	120 Sts.

Work in Ribbing of K. 1, P. 1, for 1½ inches, then work in Stockinette St. increasing 1 St. each side every 6th row 14 times, changing to Size 3 Needles when work measures 3½ inches from start. Work same length as Front to underarm.

To Shape Armholes: Bind off 12 Sts. at beginning of each of the next 2 rows, then decrease 1 St. each side every other row 8 times. When Armhole measures same as Front, bind off

9 Sts.	10 Sts.	11 Sts.	12 Sts.

at beginning of each of the next 6 rows, bind off remaining Sts. Sew Shoulder.

POCKET BORDER: With Brown pick up and K. 26 Sts. across Pocket Sts. Work in Ribbing of K. 1, P. 1, for 4 rows, bind off in Ribbing.
Sew Pocket Facings in place.

ARMHOLE BORDER: With Brown pick up Sts. around Armhole and work same as Pocket Border.

FRONT BAND: With Size 3 Needles and Green cast on 14 Sts. Work in Stockinette St. for 36 inches—to fit up right Front edge, across back of neck and to the first decrease of left Front edge. (Start of Buttonholes.)
Work double Buttonholes as follows: K. 2, bind off 3 Sts., K. 4, bind off 3 Sts. K. 2, on next row cast on 3 Sts. over the bound off Sts., work 5 more Buttonholes equal distances apart, having last Buttonhole 1 inch from end of band. Fold Band and sew to front edge and across back of neck.
With Green work 1 row of Single Crochet across lower edge of Fronts

HIS FAVOURITE SLIPOVER

MATERIALS

The original model was knitted from 5 ozs. of Sirdar Majestic Wool 3-ply in the main shade of natural, and a small quantity of the same make and ply of wool in 3 contrasting colours of red, blue, and green. Two pairs of knitting needles, Nos. 9 and 12.

MEASUREMENTS

The slipover measures from shoulder to lower edge, 20 ins. ; chest measurement, 38 ins.

TENSION

Using No. 9 needles, about 7½ sts. and 9 rows to 1 in.

ABBREVIATIONS

K., knit ; P., purl ; st., stitch ; sts., stitches ; tog., together ; dec., decrease (take 2 tog.) ; inc., increase (work into front and back of same st.) ; rep., repeat ; in., inch ; ins., inches ; sl., slip ; p.s.s.o., pass slipped st. over ; st.-st., stocking-stitch. (K. 1 row, P. 1 row alternately) ; N, natural ; B, blue ; R, red ; G, green.

THE BACK

*** Using No. 12 needles and N, cast on 133 sts.

1st row (right side) : P. 1, * K. 1, P. 1 ; rep. from * to end.

2nd row : K. 1, * P. 1, K. 1 ; rep. from * to end.

Rep. these 2 rows until 39 rows have been worked.

P. 1 row.

Change to No. 9 needles and work Fair Isle border.

1st row (right side) : K. thus : (2 G, 1 N) 7 times, * 3 G, 1 N, (2 G, 1 N) 6 times ; rep. from *, ending with 2 G.

2nd row : P. thus : 1 N, (2 G, 1 N) 3 times, * 3 G, 1 N, (2 G, 1 N) 6 times ; rep. from *, ending 3 G, 1 N, (2 G, 1 N) 3 times.

3rd row : K. in N.

4th row : P. thus : 1 N, * 2 B, 2 N, 1 R, 1 N, 2 B, 2 N, 1 R, 2 N, 2 B, 1 N, 1 R, 2 N, 2 B, 1 N ; rep. from * to end.

5th row : K. thus : 2 B, * 2 N, 1 R, 1 N, 2 B, 2 N, 3 R, 2 N, 2 B, 1 N, 1 R, 2 N, 3 B ; rep. from *, ending last rep. with 2 B, instead of 3 B.

6th row : P. thus : 1 B, * 2 N, 1 R, 1 N, 2 B, 2 N, 2 R, 1 N, 2 R, 2 N, 2 B, 1 N, 1 R, 2 N, 1 B ; rep. from * to end.

7th row : K. thus : 1 N, inc. in next st. in N, * 1 R, 1 N, 2 B, 2 N, 2 R, 1 N, 1 B, 1 N, 2 R, 2 N, 2 B, 1 N, 1 R, 3 N ; rep. from *, but instead of 3 N at end of last rep., only 2 sts. remain, and on these work inc. in N, 1 N. (135 sts.)

8th row : P. thus : 1 N, 1 B, * 2 N, 1 R, 1 N, 2 B, 2 N, 2 R, 1 N, 2 R, 2 N, 2 B, 1 N, 1 R, 2 N, 1 B ; rep. from *, ending 1 N.

9th row : K. thus : 3 B, * 2 N, 1 R, 1 N, 2 B, 2 N, 3 R, 2 N, 2 B, 1 N, 1 R, 2 N, 3 B ; rep. from * to end.

10th row : P. thus : 1 B, 1 N, * 2 B, 2 N, 1 R, 1 N, 2 B, 2 N, 1 R, 2 N, 2 B, 1 N, 1 R, 2 N, 2 B, 1 N ; rep. from *, ending 1 B.

11th row : K. in N.

12th row : P. thus : 1 G, 1 N, (2 G, 1 N) 3 times, * 3 G, 1 N, (2 G, 1 N) 6 times ; rep. from *, ending with 3 G, 1 N, (2 G, 1 N) 3 times, 1 G.

13th row : K. thus : * 3 G, 1 N, (2 G, 1 N) 6 times ; rep. from * ending 3 G.

This completes the Fair Isle border.

Cut R, B, and G wools, and work remainder of back in N.

P. 1 row.

Continue in st.-st. and inc. 1 st. into the 4th st. from each end of next and every following 8th row until the sts. number 145.

Work 19 rows without shaping after last inc. row, thus ending with a P. row. Now shape armholes.

Cast off 5 sts. at beginning of the next 2 rows. (135 sts.) ***

Dec. 1 st. at both ends of next 11 rows. (113 sts.)   Now dec. 1 st. at both ends of every 4th row 4 times. (105 sts.)

Work 59 rows without shaping after last dec. row, thus ending with a P. row.

Now shape shoulders.

Cast off 6 sts. at the beginning of next 10 rows, then cast off 5 sts. at beginning of next 2 rows.

Change to No. 12 needles and work 8 rows in ribbing of K. 1, P. 1 on remaining 35 sts.   Cast off in ribbing.

THE FRONT

Work as for back from *** to ***. (135 sts.)

Now dec. 1 st. at both ends of next 4 rows, thus ending with a P. row. (127 sts.)

Next row : K. 2 tog., K. 61, cast off next st., K. until 2 sts. remain, K. 2 tog.

Work on last set of 62 sts. for right side of front.

**** Still in st.-st., dec. 1 st. at armhole edge of next 6 rows, and at the same time dec. 1 st. at neck edge of 2nd, 4th, and 6th of these rows. (53 sts.)

* P. 1 row.   Dec. 1 st. at neck edge of next row.   P. 1 row.   Dec. 1 st. at both ends of next row.   P. 1 row, K. 1 row, P. 1 row.   Dec. 1 st. at both ends of next row.   Rep. last 8 rows from * once more.   (43 sts.)

** P. 1 row.   Dec. 1 st. at neck edge of next row.   P. 1 row.   Dec. 1 st. at neck edge of next row.   P. 1 row, K. 1 row, P. 1 row.   Dec. 1 st. at neck edge of next row.   Rep. last 8 rows from ** 6 times more. (22 sts.)

Work 4 rows in st.-st. (3 rows on left-front), ending at armhole edge.

Cast off 6 sts. at beginning of next and following alternate rows 3 times.   Work 1 more row, then cast off remaining 4 sts. ****

With wrong side of front facing, re-join wool to neck edge of other 62 sts. and work from **** to ****.

THE NECK BORDER OF FAIR ISLE

With wrong side of front facing, using a No. 12 needle and N wool, pick up purlwise 85 sts. from each side of V-neck. (170 sts.)

Change to No. 9 needles and commence Fair Isle pattern.

1st row (right side) : K. thus : * (1 N, 2 G) 6 times, 1 N, 3 G ; rep. from * twice more (1 N, 2 G) 5 times 1 N, 1 G, sl. 1, K. 1 G, p.s.s.o., K. 2 tog. G, 1 G, 1 N, (2 G, 1 N) 5 times, ** 3 G, 1 N, (2 G, 1 N) 6 times ; rep. from ** twice more. (168 sts.)

2nd row : P. thus : 1 G, (1 N, 2 G) twice, 1 N, 3 G, 1 N, * (2 G, 1 N) 6 times, 3 G, 1 N ; rep. from * twice more, 2 G, 1 N. 1 G, P. 2 tog. G, P. 2 tog. G through backs of loops, 1 G, 1 N, 2 G, ** 1 N, 3 G, (1 N, 2 G) 6 times ; rep. from ** twice more, 1 N, 3 G, 1 N, (2 G, 1 N) twice, 1 G.   (166 sts.)

3rd row : K. 80 N, sl. 2, K. 1 N, p.s.s.o., K. 3 tog. N, K. 80 N.   (162 sts.)

4th row : P. thus : 1 B, 2 N, * 1 R, 1 N, 2 B, 2 N, 1 R, 2 N, 2 B, 1 N, 1 R, 2 N, 2 B, 1 N, 2 B, 2 N ; rep. from * twice more, 1 R, 1 N, 2 B, 2 N, 1 R, 2 N, 1 B, P. 2 tog. B, P. 2 tog. B through backs of loops, 1 B, 2 N, 1 R, 2 N, 2 B, 1 N, 1 R, ** 2 N, 2 B, 1 N, 2 B, 2 N, 1 R, 2 N, 2 B, 1 N, 1 R ; rep. from ** twice more, 2 N, 1 B.   (160 sts.)

5th row : K. thus : * 2 N, 1 R, 1 N, 2 B, 2 N, 1 R, 2 N, 2 B, 1 N, 1 R, 2 N, 3 B ; rep. from * twice more, 2 N, 1 R, 1 N, 2 B, 2 N, 3 R, 1 N, sl. 1, K. 1 N, p.s.s.o., K. 2 tog. N, 1 N, 3 R, 2 N, 2 B, 1 N, 1 R, 2 N, ** 3 B, 2 N, 1 R, 1 N, 2 B, 2 N, 3 R, 2 N, 2 B, 1 N, 1 R, 2 N ; rep. from ** twice more.   (153 sts.)

BESTWAY 2125 3ᵈ

Man's Slipover with Fair Isle Borders
38-INCH CHEST
5 ozs. and oddments of 3-ply

6th row : P. thus : I N, * I R, I N, 2 B, 2 N, 2 R, I N, 2 R, 2 N, 2 B, I N, I R, 2 N, I B, 2 N ; rep. from * twice more, I R, I N, 2 B, 2 N, 2 R, I N, I R, P. 2 tog. R, P. 2 tog. R through backs of loops, I R, I N, 2 R, 2 N, 2 B, I N, I R, ** 2 N, I B, 2 N, I R, I N, 2 B, 2 N, 2 R, I N, 2 R, 2 N, 2 B, I N, I R ; rep. from ** twice more, I N. (156 sts.)

7th row : K. thus : * I R, I N, 2 B, 2 N, 2 R, I N, I B, I N, 2 R, 2 N, 2 B, I N, I R, 3 N ; rep. from * twice more, I R, I N, 2 B, 2 N, 2 R, I N, sl. 2, K. I B, p.s.s.o., K. 3 tog. B, I N, 2 R, 2 N, 2 B, I N, I R, ** 3 N, I R, I N, 2 B, 2 N, 2 R, I N, I B, I N, 2 R, 2 N, 2 B, I N, I R ; rep. from ** twice more. (152 sts.)

8th row : P. thus : I N, * I R, I N, 2 B, 2 N, 2 R, I N, 2 R, 2 N, 2 B, I N, I R, 2 N, I B, 2 N ; rep. from * twice more, I R, I N, 2 B, 2 N, I R, P. 2 tog. R, P. 2 tog. R through back of loops, I R, 2 N, 2 B, I N, I R, ** 2 N, I B, 2 N, I R, I N, 2 B, 2 N, I N, 2 R, 2 N, 2 B, I N, I R ; rep. from ** twice more, I N. (150 sts.)

9th row : K. thus : * 2 N, I R, I N, 2 B, 2 N, 3 R, 2 N, 2 B, I N, I R, 2 N, 3 B ; rep. from * twice more, 2 N, I R, I N, 2 B, I N, sl. I, K. I N, p.s.s.o., K. 2 tog. N, I N, 2 B, I N, I R, 2 N, ** 3 B, 2 N, I R, I N, 2 B, 2 N, 3 R, 2 N, 2 B, I N, I R, 2 N ; rep. from ** twice more. (143 sts.)

10th row : P. thus : I B, 2 N, * I R, I N, 2 B, 2 N, I R, 2 N, 2 B, I N, I R, 2 N, 2 B, I N, 2 B, 2 N ; rep. from * twice more, I R, I N, I B, P. 2 tog. B, P. 2 tog. B through backs of loops, I B, I N, I R, ** 2 N, 2 B, I N, 2 B, 2 N, I R, I N, 2 B, 2 N, I R, 2 N, 2 B, I N, I R ; rep. from ** twice more, 2 N, I B. (146 sts.)

11th row : K. 70 N, sl. 2, K. I N, p.s.s.o., K. 3 tog. N, K. 70 N. (142 sts.)

12th row : P. thus : I G, (I N, 2 G) twice, * I N, 3 G, (I N, 2 G) 6 times ; rep. from * once more, I N, 3 G, (I N, 2 G) 4 times, I N, I G, P. 2 tog. G, P. 2 tog. G through backs of loops, I G, I N, (2 G, I N) 4 times, 3 G, I N, ** (2 G, I N) 6 times, 3 G, I N ; rep. from ** once more, (2 G, I N) twice, I G. (140 sts.)

13th row : K. thus : * (I N, 2 G) 6 times, I N, 3 G ; rep. from * twice more, I N, I G, sl. I, K. I G, p.s.s.o., K. 2 tog. G, I G, I N, ** 3 G, I N, (2 G, I N) 6 times ; rep. from ** twice more. (138 sts.)

Cut R, B and G wools. Change to No. 12 needles and work in N. only.

14th row : P. 67, P. 2 tog., P. 2 tog. through backs of loops, P. 67. (136 sts.)

Next row : (K. I, P. I) 33 times, K. 2 tog., P. 2 tog., (K. I, P. I) 33 times. Work 7 more rows in ribbing, taking 2 sts. tog., ribwise, twice at centre-front in every row.

Cast off in ribbing.

THE ARMHOLE RIBBINGS

Sew up shoulder seams.

With right side facing, using No. 12 needles and N wool, pick up and K. 183 sts. along one armhole edge. Work 7 rows in ribbing of K. I, P. I. Cast off in ribbing.

Work along other armhole edge in the same way.

MAKING UP

Press work, avoiding all ribbing.

Sew up side seams, carefully matching Fair Isle border. Press seams.

BESTWAY LEAFLET No. 518

MAN'S PULLOVER
With or Without Sleeves

3d.

EVERY MAN NEEDS A PULLOVER!

MATERIALS.—6 *ounces of Patons Super, or Beehive, Scotch Fingering 3-ply for the sleeveless pullover, or 9 ounces of the same wool for the pullover with long sleeves, a pair each of No. 11 and No 13 knitting pins ; a short cable pin.*

TENSION AND MEASUREMENTS.—*Worked at a tension of 8 sts. to the inch in width with No. 11 pins, the measurements on the diagram are attained after light pressing.*

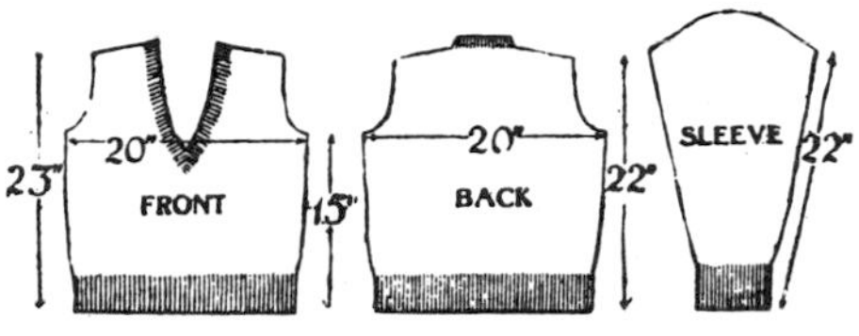

The shape and measurements of the pullover.

ABBREVIATIONS.—TO BE READ BEFORE WORKING. —*K., knit plain ; p., purl ; st., stitch ; tog., together ; inc., increase (by working into the front and back of the same st.) ; dec., decrease (by working 2 sts. tog.) ; a cable is worked on 3 sts. thus : slip the first 2 sts. on to the cable pin and leave it at the front of the work, k. the next st. along the row, then return the 2nd st. from the cable pin to the left-hand pin and p. it, still leaving the cable pin at the front of the work, and finally k. the remaining st. from the cable pin ; p. twist is worked thus : p. into the back of the 2nd st. from the point of the left-hand pin, but do not slip it off the pin, k. into the front of the 1st st., and slip both sts. off the pin together ; k. twist, k. into the front of the 2nd st. but do not let it off the pin, p. into the back of the 1st. st. and slip both sts. off the pin tog. ; k. 1 back, k. 1 through the back of the st. ; single rib is k. 1 and p. 1 alternately. Directions in brackets are worked the number of times stated after the brackets.*

TO WORK THE BACK

USING No. 13 pins cast on 180 sts. for the lower edge, and work 40 rows in single rib, working into the back of the sts. on the 1st row to give a neat edge.

Change to No. 11 pins.

Next row (wrong side).—P. 2, * k. 2, p. 1, k. 5, p. 1, k. 2, p. 4 ; repeat from * ending the last repeat with p. 2 instead of p. 4.

Now begin the main pattern as follows :

1st row.—K. 2, * p. 2, k. 1 back, p. 5, k. 1 back, p. 2, k. 4 ; repeat from * ending the last repeat with k. 2 instead of k. 4.

2nd row.—P. 2, * k. 2, p. 1, k. 5, p. 1, k. 2, p. 4, repeat from * ending the last repeat with p. 2 instead of p. 4.

Repeat these 2 rows once more.

5th row.—K. 2, * p. 2, p. twist, p. 3, k. twist, p. 2, k. 4 ; repeat from * ending the last repeat with k. 2.

6th row.—P. 2, * (k. 3, p. 1) twice, k. 3, p. 4 ; repeat from * ending the last repeat with p. 2.

7th row.—K. 2, * p. 3, p. twist, p. 1, k. twist, p. 3 k. 4 ; repeat from * ending the last repeat with k. 2.

8th row.—P. 2, * k. 4, p. 1, k. 1, p. 1, k. 4, p. 4 ; repeat from * ending the last repeat with p. 2.

9th row.—K. 2, * p. 4, cable, p. 4, k. 4 ; repeat from * ending the last repeat with k. 2.

10th row.—As 8th row.

11th row.—K. 2, * p. 3, k. twist, p. 1, p. twist, p. 3, k. 4 ; repeat from * ending the last repeat with k. 2.

12th row.—As 6th row.

13th row.—K. 2, * p. 2, k. twist, p. 3, p. twist, p. 2, k. 4 ; repeat from * ending the last repeat with k. 2.

14th row.—As 2nd row.

Repeat from the 5th row to the 14th row once more ; then repeat the 1st and 2nd rows 3 times more.

These 30 rows form the pattern, so repeat them twice more and the first 10 rows again, to the armholes.

TO SHAPE THE ARMHOLES.—1st row.—Cast off 9 (1 st. on pin), p. 3, * k. 4, p. 3, k. twist, p. 1, p. twist, p. 3 ; repeat from * until 2 sts. remain, k. 2.

2nd row.—Cast off 9 (1 st. on pin), k. 3, * p. 4, (k. 3, p. 1) twice, k. 3 ; repeat from * until 8 remain, p. 4, k. 3, p. 1.

3rd row.—Cast off 9 (1 st. on pin), * k. twist, p. 3, p. twist, p. 2, k: 4, p. 2 ; repeat from * until 2 sts. remain, k. twist.

4th row.—Cast off 9 (1 st. on pin), * p. 1, k. 5, p. 1, k. 2, p. 4, k. 2 ; repeat from * until 8 remain, p. 1. k. 5, p. 1, k. 1.

5th row.—K. 2 tog., p. 1, * p. 3, k. twist, p. 2, k. 4, p. 2, p. twist ; repeat from * until 6 remain, p. 4, p. 2 tog.

6th row.—P. 2 tog., k. 3, p. 1, * k. 3, p. 4, (k. 3, p. 1) twice ; repeat from * ending the last repeat with p. 2 tog.

7th row.—K. 2 tog., * p. 1, k. twist, p. 3, k. 4, p. 3, p. twist ; repeat from * until 3 remain, p. 1, k. 2 tog.

8th row.—K. 2 tog., * p. 1, k. 4, p. 4, k. 4, p. 1, k. 1 ; repeat from * ending the last repeat with k. 2 tog.

9th row.—K. 2 tog., p. 4, k. 4, * p. 4, cable, p. 4, k. 4 ; repeat from * until 6 remain, p. 4, k. 2 tog.

10th row.—K. 2 tog., k. 3, p. 4, * k. 4, p. 1, k. 1, p. 1. k. 4, p. 4 ; repeat from * until 5 remain, k. 3, k. 2 tog.

11th row.—P. 2 tog., p. 2, k. 4, * p. 3, k. twist, p. 1, p. twist, p. 3, k. 4 ; repeat from * until 4 remain, p. 2, p. 2 tog.

12th row.—K. 2 tog., k. 1, p. 4, * (k. 3, p. 1) twice, k. 3, p. 4 ; repeat from * until 3 remain, k. 1, k. 2 tog. (128 sts.)

Now work 62 rows in pattern without shaping, beginning with the 23rd pattern row, but note there will be 4 sts. extra at each end, so that the right side rows will begin with p. 2, k. 4 before the *, and finish with k. 4, p. 2.

TO SLOPE THE SHOULDERS.—Cast off 9 sts. at the beginning of the next 8 rows, then cast off 11 sts. at the beginning of the next 2 rows. (34 sts.)

THE BACK NECK-BAND.—Next row.—(K. 1 inc.) 17 times. (51 sts.)

Change to No. 13 pins and work 11 rows in single rib, then cast off in rib.

THE FRONT

WORK this the same as the back until 3 complete patterns have been worked altogether, then divide the sts. thus :

LEFT HALF FRONT.—1st row.—K. 2, * p. 2, k. 1 back, p. 5, k. 1 back, p. 2, k. 4 ; repeat from * 4 times more, p. 2, k. 1 back, p. 5, k. 1 back, p. 2, k. 2 tog., turn, leaving the remaining 90 sts. on a spare pin.

2nd row.—K. 2 tog., k. 1, p. 1, k. 5, p. 1, k. 2, (p. 4, k. 2, p. 1, k. 5, p. 1, k. 2) 5 times, p. 2.

3rd row.—K. 2, (p. 2, k. 1 back, p. 5, k. 1 back, p. 2, k. 4) 5 times, p. 2, k. 1 back, p. 5, k. 1 back, p. 2 tog.

4th row.—P. 2 tog., k. 5, p. 1, k. 2, (p. 4, k. 2, p. 1 k. 5, p. 1, k. 2) 5 times, p. 2.

5th row.—K. 2, (p. 2, p. twist, p. 3, k. twist, p. 2, k. 4) 5 times, p. 2, p. twist, p. 3, k. 2 tog.

6th row.—K. 2 tog., k. 2, p. 1, * k. 3, p. 4, (k. 3, p. 1) twice ; repeat from * 4 times more, k. 3, p. 2.

7th row.—K. 2, (p. 3, p. twist, p. 1, k. twist, p. 3, k. 4) 5 times, p. 3, p. twist, p. 2 tog.

8th row.—P. 2 tog., (k. 4, p. 4, k. 4, p. 1, k. 1, p. 1) 5 times, k. 4, p. 2.

9th row.—K. 2, (p. 4, cable, p. 4, k. 4) 5 times, p. 3, p. 2 tog.

10th row.—K. 2 tog., k. 2, (p. 4, k. 4, p. 1, k. 1, p. 1, k. 4) 5 times, p. 2.

TO SHAPE THE ARMHOLE.—11th row.—Cast off 9 (1 st. on pin), p. 3, k. 4, (p. 3, k. twist, p. 1, p. twist, p. 3, k. 4) 4 times, p. 1, p. 2 tog.

12th row.—K. 2 tog., * p. 4, (k. 3, p. 1) twice, k. 3 ; repeat from * 3 times more, p. 4, k. 3, p. 1.

13th row.—Cast off 9 (1 st. on pin), * k. twist, p. 3, p. twist, p. 2, k. 4, p. 2 ; repeat from *, ending the last repeat with k. 3, k. 2 tog.

14th row.—P. 4, k. 2, p. 1, k. 5, (p. 1, k. 2, p. 4, k. 2, p. 1, k. 5) 3 times, p. 1, k. 1.

15th row.—K. 2 tog., p. 1 (p. 3, k. twist, p. 2, k. 4, p. 2, p. twist) 3 times, p. 3, k. twist, p. 2, k. 2, k. 2 tog.

16th row.—P. 3, k. 3, p. 1, k. 3, (p. 1, k. 3, p. 4, k. 3, p. 1, k. 3) 3 times, p. 2 tog.

17th row.—P. 2 tog., p. 1, (k. twist, p. 3, k. 4, p. 3, p. twist, p. 1) 3 times, k. twist, p. 3, k. 1, k. 2 tog.

18th row.—P. 2, (k. 4, p. 1, k. 1, p. 1, k. 4, p. 4) 3 times, k. 4, p. 1, k. 2 tog.

19th row. K. 2 tog., (p. 4, k. 4, p. 4, cable) 3 times, p. 4, k. 2 tog.

20th row.—P. 1, (k. 4, p. 1, k. 1, p. 1, k. 4, p. 4) 3 times, k. 3, k. 2 tog.

21st row.—P. 2 tog., p. 2, * k. 4, p. 3, k. twist, p. 1, p. twist, p. 3 ; repeat from *, ending the last repeat with p. 2, p. 2 tog.

22nd row.—* (K. 3, p. 1) twice, k. 3, p. 4 ; repeat from * twice more, k. 1, k. 2 tog. (47 sts.)

** Now work from the 23rd to the 30th pattern row (but note that there will be 4 sts. more at the arm end and 2 sts. less at the neck end, than on the corresponding rows of pattern at the beginning), then work 2 complete patterns more to the shoulder. (Work 1 row more here on the Right Half Front.)

TO SLOPE THE SHOULDER.—Cast off 9 sts. at the beginning of the next row and following 3 alternate rows, then on the next alternate row cast off the remaining 11 sts.

THE RIGHT HALF FRONT. 1st row.—Beginning at the neck end of the remaining 90 sts., k. 2 tog., * p. 2, k. 1 back, p. 5, k. 1 back, p. 2, k. 4 ; repeat from *, ending the last repeat with k. 2.

2nd row.—P. 2, (k. 2, p. 1, k. 5, p. 1, k. 2, p. 4) 5 times, k. 2, p. 1, k. 5, p. 1, k. 1, k. 2 tog.

3rd row.—P. 2 tog., k. 1 back, p. 5, k. 1 back, (p. 2, k. 4, p. 2, k. 1 back, p. 5, k. 1 back) 5 times, p. 2, k. 2.

4th row.—P 2, (k. 2, p. 1, k. 5, p. 1, k. 2, p. 4) 5 times, k. 2, p. 1, k. 5, p. 2 tog.

5th row.—P. 2 tog., k. 1, p. 3, k. twist, p. 2, (k. 4, p. 2, p. twist, p. 3, k. twist, p. 2) 5 times, k. 2.

6th row.—P. 2, * (k. 3, p. 1) twice, k. 3, p. 4 ; repeat from * 4 times more, k. 3, p. 1, k. 2, k. 2 tog.

7th row.—P. 2 tog., k. twist, p. 3, (k. 4, p. 3, p. twist, p. 1, k. twist, p. 3) 5 times, k. 2.

8th row.—P. 2, (k. 4, p. 1, k. 1, p. 1, k. 4, p. 4) 5 times, k. 4, p. 2 tog.

9th row.—P. 2 tog., p. 3, (k. 4, p. 4, cable, p. 4) 5 times, k. 2.

10th row.—P. 2, (k. 4, p. 1, k. 1, p. 1, k. 4, p. 4) 5 times, k. 2, k. 2 tog.

11th row.—P. 2 tog., p. 1, (k. 4, p. 3, k. twist, p. 1, p. twist, p. 3) 5 times, k. 2.

TO SHAPE THE ARMHOLE.—12th row.—Cast off 9 (1 st. on pin), k. 3, * p. 4, (k. 3, p. 1) twice, k. 3 ; repeat from * 3 times more, p. 4, k. 2 tog.

13th row.—K. 2 tog., k. 3, (p. 2, k. twist, p. 3, p. twist, p. 2, k. 4) 4 times, p. 2, k. twist.

14th row.—Cast off 9 (1 st. on pin), (p. 1, k. 5, p. 1, k. 2, p. 4, k. 2) 3 times, p. 1, k. 5, p. 1, k. 2, p. 4.

15th row.—K. 2 tog., k. 2, (p. 2, p. twist, p. 3, k. twist, p. 2, k. 4) 3 times, p. 2, p. twist, p. 4, k. 2 tog.

16th row.—K. 2 tog., k. 3, p. 1, * k. 3, p. 4, (k. 3, p. 1) twice ; repeat from * twice more, k. 3, p. 3.

17th row.—K. 2 tog., k. 1, p. 3, (p. twist, p. 1, k. twist, p. 3, k. 4, p. 3) 3 times, p. twist, p. 1, k. 2 tog.

18th row.—K. 2 tog., (p. 1, k. 4, p. 4, k. 4, p. 1, k. 1) 3 times, p. 1, k. 4, p. 2.

19th row.—K. 2 tog., (p. 4, cable, p. 4, k. 4) 3 times, p. 4, k. 2 tog.

20th row.—K. 2 tog., k. 3, (p. 4, k. 4, p. 1, k. 1, p. 1, k. 4) 3 times, p. 1.

21st row.—P. 2 tog., p. 2, * k. twist, p. 1, p. twist, p. 3, k. 4, p. 3 ; repeat from *, ending the last repeat with p. 2, p. 2 tog.

22nd row.—K. 2 tog., k. 1, * p. 4, (k. 3, p. 1) twice, k. 3 ; repeat from * to the end. (47 sts.)

Now work from ** on the Left Half Front to the end.

THE FRONT NECK BORDER.—Using No. 13 pins, and holding the work with the right side facing, pick up and k. 166 sts. all round the front neck edge, and work 11 rows in single rib, taking tog. the 3 centre sts. at the point of the V on every row, then cast off in rib.

These rows can be continued further for a deeper band, and can be worked in different shades when club colours are wanted.

THE ARMHOLE BANDS FOR THE SLEEVELESS PULLOVER

FIRST join the shoulder seams, beginning at the arm end and taking 1 st. from each side at a time.

Using No. 13 pins and holding the work with the right side facing, pick up and k. 140 sts. all round one armhole, and work 11 rows in single rib, then cast off in rib.

Work the other armhole band in the same way.

THE SLEEVES.—Begin at the cuff, and with No. 13 pins cast on 75 sts. Work 40 rows in single rib.

Change to No. 11 pins and beginning with the 19th row of pattern as on the back, continue in pattern, increasing 1 st. at both ends of every 6th row, until the 26th inc. row has been worked and there are 127 sts.

(If there is any difficulty in working the increases into the pattern, the extra stitches may be worked in a rib of k. 4, p. 11—right side—until there are 15 sts. more at each end, making one more repeat of the pattern.)

TO SHAPE THE SLEEVE TOP.—Dec. 1 st., at both ends of the next 42 rows, then cast off the remaining sts.

Work another sleeve in the same way.

TO MAKE UP THE PULLOVER

FIRST press all parts except the ribbing very lightly on the wrong side, with a hot iron over a damp cloth.

For the sleeveless pullover, join the side seams and press these seams.

If sleeves have been worked, join the shoulder seams, beginning at the arm end and taking 1 st. from each side at a time. Set the sleeves into armholes and press these seams. Join the sleeve and side seams in one line and press.

See colour plate on page 133

PULL-OVER—TO FIT 37″ CHEST

MATERIALS

7 oz. PATONS BEEHIVE Fingering 3-ply, Patonised. Two No. 12 and two No. 10 BEEHIVE needles, or QUEEN BEE if stainless rigid needles preferred, measured by BEEHIVE gauge.

MEASUREMENTS

Chest 37 ins., Length 20½ ins.

ABBREVIATIONS

K.=knit; P.=purl; st.=stitch; tog.=together; wl. bk.=wool to back; ins. =inches.

TENSION

7½ stitches and 9½ rows to one square inch in stocking stitch

FRONT

Using No. 12 needles, cast on 128 sts.
1st row—K.2, * P.1, K.1, repeat from * to end of row.

Repeat this row forty times.

42nd row—K.2, (P.1, K.1) twice, P.1, increase once in next st., * (P.1, K.1) twice, increase once in next st., (K.1, P.1) twice, increase once in next st., repeat from * to last 10 sts., (P.1, K.1) five times (there should now be 151 sts. on needle).

Change to No. 10 needles.

****1st row**—K.1, * insert right-hand needle between 5th and 6th sts. to left, draw a loop between these two sts., slip loop on to left-hand needle and knit it together with next st. (this will now be termed ''knit left'' throughout), K.4, P.3, wl.bk., repeat from * to last 6 sts., knit left, K.5.

2nd row—K.1, * P.5, K.3, repeat from * to last 6 sts., P.5, K.1.

3rd row—K.1, * K.5, P.3, repeat from * to last 6 sts., K.6. Repeat 2nd and 3rd rows twice, then 2nd row once.

9th row—K.2, P.3, * wl. bk., knit left, K.4, P.3, repeat from * to last 2 sts., K.2.

10th row—K.1, P.1, * K.3, P.5, repeat from * to last 5 sts., K.3, P.1, K.1.
11th row—K.2, * P.3, K.5, repeat from * to last 5 sts., P.3, K.2.

Repeat 10th and 11th rows twice, then 10th row once**.

Repeat from ** to ** four times, from ** to 11th row once, then 10th row once.

Proceed as follows:—
1st row—Cast off 18 sts., K.1, P.2, * K.5, P.3, repeat from * to last 2 sts., K.2.
2nd row—Cast off 18 sts., * K.3, P.5, repeat from * to last 3 sts., K.3.

3rd row—K.1, P.2 tog., * K.5, P.3, repeat from * to last 8 sts., K.5, P.2 tog., K.1.
4th row—K.2, * P.5, K.3, repeat from * to last 7 sts., P.5, K.2.
5th row—K.1, K.2 tog., P.3, * wl. bk., knit left, K.4, P.3, repeat from * to last 3 sts., K.2 tog., K.1.
6th row—K.1, P.1, * K.3, P.5, repeat from * to last 5 sts., K.3, P.1, K.1.
7th row—K.1, P.2 tog., P.2, * K.5, P.3, repeat from * to last 10 sts., K.5, P.2, P.2 tog., K.1.
8th row—K.1, * K.3, P.5, repeat from * to last 4 sts., K.4.
9th row—K.1, P.2 tog., P.1, * K.5, P.3, repeat from * to last 9 sts., K.5, P.1, P.2 tog., K.1.
10th row—* K.3, P.5, repeat from * to last 3 sts., K.3.

Repeat from 3rd to 7th row once.

16th row—K.1, * K.3, P.5, repeat from * to last 4 sts., K.4.
17th row—K.1, P.2 tog., P.1, * K.5, P.3, repeat from * four times, K.5, P.2 tog., turn.

Work on these 49 sts. as follows:—
1st row—K.1, (P.5, K.3) six times.
2nd row—K.1, P.2 tog., (K.5, P.3) five times, K.6.
3rd row—K.1, P.5, (K.3, P.5) five times, K.2.
4th row—K.1, K.2 tog., (P.3, wl. bk., knit left, K.4) five times, P.2, P.2 tog., K.1.
Continue in pattern, decreasing once at neck edge in every following 4th row, until 28 sts. remain.

Work 2 rows without shaping.

Shape for shoulder as follows:—
1st row—K.1, P.2, (K.3, P.5) twice, turn.
2nd row—(K.5, P.3) twice, K.2 tog., K.1.
3rd row—K.1, P.1, K.3, P.4, turn.
4th row—K.4, P.3, K.2. Cast off.

Join in wool and work on remaining 50 sts. as follows:—
1st row—K.6, (P.3, K.5) five times, P.1, P.2 tog., K.1.
2nd row—(K.3, P.5) six times, K.1.
3rd row—K.6, (P.3, K.5) five times, P.2 tog., K.1.
4th row—K.2, (P.5, K.3) five times, P.5, K.1.
5th row—K.1, P.2 tog., P.2, (wl. bk., knit left, K.4, P.3) five times, K.2 tog., K.1.

Continue in pattern, decreasing once at neck edge in every following 4th row, until 28 sts. remain.
Work 1 row without shaping.

Shape for shoulder as follows:—
1st row—K.3, (P.3, K.5) twice, turn.
2nd row—(P.5, K.3) twice, P.2, K.1.
3rd row—K.1, K.2 tog., P.3, K.4, turn.
4th row—P.4, K.3, P.1, K.1.
5th row—K.2, (P.3, K.5) three times, K.1. Cast off.

BACK

Using No. 12 Needles, cast on 128 sts. Work exactly as given for Front, until 16th row of arm-hole has been worked.

Proceed as follows:—
1st row—K.1, P.2 tog., P.1, * K.5, P.3, repeat from * to last 9 sts., K.5, P.1, P.2 tog., K.1.

2nd row—* K.3, P.5, repeat from * to last 3 sts., K.3.
3rd row—K.1, P.2 tog., * K.5, P.3, repeat from * to last 8 sts., K.5, P.2 tog., K.1.
4th row—K.2, * P.5, K.3, repeat from * to last 7 sts., P.5, K.2.
5th row—K.1, K.2 tog., P.3, * wl. bk., knit left, K.4, P.3, repeat from * to last 3 sts., K.2 tog., K.1.

Work 73 rows without shaping.

Shape for shoulders as follows:—
1st and 2nd rows—Work in pattern to last 9 sts., turn.

3rd and 4th rows—Work in pattern to last 18 sts., turn.
5th and 6th rows—Work in pattern to last 27 sts., turn.
7th row—Work in pattern to end of row.
8th row—Cast off 27 sts., work in pattern to last 27 sts., cast off 27 sts.

Sew up Right Shoulder seam.

NECKBAND

Using No. 12 needles, with right side of work facing, join in wool and knit up 64 sts. evenly along left side of neck (knitting last st. from centre); knit up 63 sts. evenly along right side of neck; K.1, (P.1, K.1) twenty times across the 41 sts. of Back (there should now be 168 sts. on needle).
1st row—K.2, (P.1, K.1) fifty times, K.2 tog., P.1, K.2 tog., K.1, (P.1, K.1) thirty times.
2nd row—K.2, (P.1, K.1) twenty-nine times, (P.2 tog., K.1) twice, (P.1, K.1) fifty times.
3rd row—K.2, (P.1, K.1) forty-nine times, K.2 tog., P.1, K.2 tog., K.1, (P.1, K.1) twenty-nine times.
4th row—K.2, (P.1, K.1) twenty-eight times, (P.2 tog., K.1) twice, (P.1, K.1) forty-nine times.
5th row—K.2, (P.1, K.1) forty-eight times, K.2 tog., P.1, K.2 tog., K.1, (P.1, K.1) twenty-eight times.
6th row—K.2, (P.1, K.1) twenty-seven times, (P.2 tog., K.1) twice, (P.1, K.1) forty-eight times.
7th row—K.2, (P.1, K.1) forty-seven times, K.2 tog., P.1, K.2 tog., K.1, (P.1, K.1) twenty-seven times.
8th row—K.2, (P.1, K.1) twenty-six times, (P.2 tog., K.1) twice, (P.1, K.1) forty-seven times.
9th row—K.2, (P.1, K.1) forty-six times, K.2 tog., P.1, K.2 tog., K.1, (P.1, K.1) twenty-six times.
10th row—K.2, (P.1, K.1) twenty-five times, (P.2 tog., K.1) twice, (P.1, K.1) forty-six times.
11th row—K.2, (P.1, K.1) forty-five times, K.2 tog., P.1, K.2 tog., K.1, (P.1, K.1) twenty-five times.
12th row—K.2, (P.1, K.1) twenty-four times, (P.2 tog., K.1) twice, (P.1, K.1) forty-five times.
Cast off.

Sew up Left Shoulder seam.

ARMBANDS

Using No. 12 needles, with right side of work facing, knit up 164 sts. evenly round armhole.

1st row—K.2, * P.1, K.1, repeat from * to end of row.

Repeat this row eleven times. Cast off.

Work other Armband in same manner.

TO MAKE UP

With a damp cloth and hot iron press carefully. Sew up side seams, joining seams by sewing together corresponding ridges (formed by st. knitted at each end of every row).

Man's Pullover

Materials.

With Sleeves 15 ozs. ⎱ Lister's Lavenda
Sleeveless 9 ozs. ⎰ 4 ply.
Pair each needles, Nos. 9 and 11.
Small needles with points at both ends for cabling.
2 safety pins.

Measurements.

To fit 38/40 ins. Chest measurement.
Length from shoulder ... ... 22 ins.
Length of undersleeve seam ... 19 ins.

Abbreviations.

k = Knit.　　　p = Purl.
sts. = Stitches.
ins. = Inches.
tog. = Together.
C6 = Cable 6, slip next 3 sts. on to spare needle in front of work, k3, then knit 3 sts. off spare needle.
SKPO = Slip one, knit one, pass slipped st. over.
P2IN = Purl twice into same st., i.e. into front, and then into back of st.

Tension.

7 sts. and 9 rows equal one inch (No. 9 needles).

Sleeveless Pullover

BACK

** Using No. 11 needles, cast on 125 sts.
1st row.—* K1, p1. Repeat from * ending k1.
2nd row.—* P1, k1. Repeat from * ending p1.
Repeat these 2 rows for 3½ ins., finishing after a 1st row.
Increase row.—P5, * p4, P2IN. Repeat from * ending p5. (148 sts.)
Change to No. 9 needles.
Commence pattern as follows:
1st row.—* K5, C6. Repeat from * ending k5.
2nd row.—Purl.
3rd row.—Knit.
4th row.—Purl.
5th row.—K6, * C6, k5. Repeat from * ending k4.
Repeat 2nd to 4th rows inclusive.
9th row.—K7, * C6, k5. Repeat from * ending k3.
Repeat 2nd to 4th rows inclusive.
13th row.—K8, * C6, k5. Repeat from * ending k2.
Repeat 2nd to 4th rows inclusive.
Continue in pattern, moving the cable one st. to the left every 4th row until work measures 13 ins. from commencement.

SHAPE ARMHOLES

Right side facing and keeping in pattern:
Cast off 10 sts. at the beginning of the next 2 rows, then k2tog. at each end of following 7 rows, then k2tog. at the end of the following row. (113 sts.) **
Continue on these sts., still keeping in pattern, until work measures 22 ins.

SHAPE SHOULDERS

Cast off 9 sts. at beginning of next 8 rows.
Slip remaining sts. on to a safety pin.

FRONT

Work as Back from ** to **.
Continue in pattern on these sts. until work measures 17½ ins.

SHAPE NECK. Right side facing:

Work 45 sts. in pattern, turn.
Next row.—Work back in pattern.
Next row.—Work in pattern to within 3 sts. of division, k2tog., k1.
Repeat these 2 rows until 36 sts. remain.
*** Continue without shaping until work measures 22 ins.

SHAPE SHOULDERS. Commencing at armhole edge:

Cast off 9 sts. at beginning of next and each alternate row, four times. Return to remaining sts. and slip first 23 sts. on to a safety pin. Rejoin wool to next st., then work in pattern to end of row.

Next row.—Work in pattern to centre.
Next row.—K1, SKPO, work in pattern to end of row.
Repeat these two rows until 36 sts. remain.
Now work as first side from *** to end.

NECKBAND

Join right shoulder seam. With right side facing and commencing at left front shoulder, rejoin wool and using No. 11 needles, pick up and knit 48 sts. evenly down to 23 sts. on safety pin; work across these 23 sts. as follows: (k1, p1) eleven times, k1; then pick up and knit 48 sts. to shoulder, and work across 41 sts. of Back as follows: (p1, k1) twenty times, p1. (160 sts.)
Work on these sts. in k1, p1 rib for 7 rows.
Cast off loosely in rib.

ARMBANDS

Join Left Shoulder seam. With right side facing, using No. 11 needles, rejoin wool and pick up and knit 152 sts. evenly round armhole.
Next row.—K2tog., rib to end of row.
Repeat this row six times.
Cast off loosely in rib.
Work round second armhole in same way.

Pullover with Sleeves

Work exactly as Sleeveless Pullover, omitting armbands.

SLEEVES

Using No. 11 needles, cast on 71 sts. and work in rib as Back for 3 ins., finishing after a 1st row.

Increase row.—P10, * p4, P2IN. Repeat from * ending p6. (82 sts.)
Change to No. 9 needles and work in pattern as Back (always moving one st. to the left every 4th row) and increasing one st. at each end of every 6th row, until there are 126 sts. on the needle.
Continue in pattern on these sts. until work measures 19 ins.

SHAPE HEAD

K2tog. at the beginning of every following row until work measures 24½ ins.
Cast off.

TO MAKE UP

Pin out and press each piece on wrong side under a damp cloth, avoiding ribbed welts.
Sleeveless Pullover.—Join side seams. Press seams.
Pullover with Sleeves.—Join side, left shoulder and sleeve seams. Sew in Sleeves, placing centre of head of sleeve to shoulder seam. Press seams.

See colour plate on page 135

Hand Knitwear in Lavenda

Nº 1094

4d

BESTWAY 2005 3d.

MAN'S FAIR ISLE SLIPOVER
38 INCH CHEST
5 ozs., 1½ ozs., 1 oz., and Oddments of 3-ply

MAN'S FAIR ISLE SLIPOVER

MATERIALS

The original model was knitted in W.B. Melody Knitting Wool 3-ply in 9 different shades. Dark Blue, 5 ozs. ; Yellow, 1½ ozs. ; Fawn, 1 oz. . Light Blue, ½ oz. ; Grey, ½ oz. ; and less than ¼ oz. each of Red, Light Green, Maroon, and Brown. Two pairs of knitting needles Nos. 9 and 11.

MEASUREMENTS

Shoulder to lower edge, 21 ins. ; chest measurement, 38 ins.

TENSION

Using No. 9 needles, about 8½ sts. and 9 rows to 1 in.

ABBREVIATIONS

K., knit ; P., purl ; st., stitch ; sts.. stitches ; tog., together ; dec., decrease (take 2 tog.) ; inc., increase (work into front and back of same st.) ; in., inch ; ins., inches ; rep., repeat , DB, dark blue ; Y, yellow ; F, fawn, LB, light blue ; G, grey , R, red ; LG, light green ; M, maroon ; B, brown.

THE BACK

Using DB, and No. 11 needles, cast on 126 sts. Work 3½ ins. in ribbing of K. 1. P. 1. Change to No. 9 needles.
Next row : Rib 10, inc., (rib 3, inc.) 26 times, rib 11. (153 sts.)
1st row : K. in DB. **2nd row :** P. in DB.
3rd row : K. thus : 3 DB, (1 F, 3 DB, 1 F, 3 DB, 2 F, 3 DB) 11 times, 1 F, 3 DB. 1 F, 2 DB.
4th row : P. thus : 3 DB, 1 F, 1 DB, 1 F, 1 DB, (3 DB, 2 F, 4 DB, 1 F, 1 DB, 1 F, 1 DB) 11 times, 3 DB.
5th row : K. thus : 3 DB, (2 DB, 1 F, 3 DB, 2 F, 2 DB, 2 F, 1 DB) 11 times, 2 DB, 1 F, 4 DB.
6th row : P. thus : 4 DB, 1 F, 2 DB, (1 DB, 2 F, 2 DB, 2 F, 3 DB, 1 F, 2 DB) 11 times, 3 DB.
7th row : K. thus : 3 DB, (1 DB, 1 F, 1 DB, 1 F, 4 DB, 2 F, 3 DB) 11 times, 1 DB, 1 F, 1 DB, 1 F, 3 DB.
8th row : P. thus : 2 DB, 1 F, 3 DB, 1 F, (3 DB, 2 F, 3 DB, 1 F, 3 DB, 1 F)

11 times. 3 DB. **9th row :** K. in DB.
10th row : P. in DB. Cut DB and F. Join on G and Y. **11th row :** K. thus : (1 Y, 7 G, 1 Y) 17 times. **12th row :** P. thus : (2 Y, 5 G, 2 Y) 17 times. **13th row :** K. thus : (3 Y, 3 G, 3 Y) 17 times.
14th row : P. thus : (4 Y, 1 G, 4 Y) 17 times. Join on M **15th row :** K. thus : (1 M, 7 Y, 1 M (17 times **16th row :** P. thus : (2 M, 5 Y, 2 M) 17 times.
17th row : K. thus : (2 M, 5 Y, 2 M) 17 times. **18th row :** P. thus : (1 M, 7 Y, 1 M) 17 times. Cut M. **19th row :** K. thus : (4 Y, 1 G, 4 Y) 17 times.
20th row : P. thus : (3 Y, 3 G, 3 Y) 17 times. **21st row :** K. thus : (2 Y, 5 G, 2 Y) 17 times. **22nd row :** P. thus : (1 Y, 7 G, 1 Y) 17 times. Cut G and Y. Join on DB and F.

Rep. 1st to 10th rows again. Cut DB and F. Join on LB and Y.

33rd row : K. thus : (1 Y, 7 LB, 1 Y) 17 times. **34th row :** P. thus : (2 Y, 5 LB, 2 Y) 17 times. **35th row :** K. thus :

(3 Y, 3 LB, 3 Y) 17 times. **36th row :** P. thus : (4 Y, 1 LB, 4 Y) 17 times. Join on LG. **37th row :** K. thus : (1 LG, 7 Y, 1 LG) 17 times. **38th row :** P. thus : (2 LG, 5 Y, 2 LG) 17 times. **39th row :** K. thus : (2 LG, 5 Y, 2 LG) 17 times.
40th row : P. thus : (1 LG, 7 Y, 1 LG) 17 times. Cut LG. **41st row :** K. thus : (4 Y, 1 LB, 4 Y) 17 times. **42nd row :** P. thus : (3 Y, 3 LB, 3 Y) 17 times. **43rd row :** K. thus : (2 Y, 5 LB, 2 Y) 17 times.
44th row : P. thus : (1 Y, 7 LB, 1 Y) 17 times.
Cut LB and Y. Join on DB and F.

Work 1st to 10th rows. Cut DB and F. Join on G and Y.

55th to 58th rows : Same as 11th to 14th rows. Join on R.

59th row : K. thus : (1 R, 7 Y, 1 R) 17 times. **60th row :** P. thus : (2 R, 5 Y, 2 R) 17 times. **61st row :** K. thus : (2 R, 5 Y, 2 R) 17 times. **62nd row :** P. thus : (1 R, 7 Y, 1 R) 17 times. Cut R.

63rd to 66th rows : Same as 19th to 22nd rows.
Cut G and Y. Join on DB and F.
Rep. 1st to 10th rows. Cut DB and F. Join on LB and Y.

Rep. the 33rd to 36th rows. Join on B.
81st row : K. thus : (1 B, 7 Y, 1 B) 17 times. **82nd row :** P. thus : (2 B, 5 Y, 2 B) 17 times.
83rd row : K. thus : Cast off 5 sts. in Y, leaving 6th st. on right-hand needle in Y, then 1 Y, 2 B, (2 B, 5 Y, 2 B) 16 times.
84th row : P. thus : Cast off 5 sts. in Y, leaving 6th st. on right-hand needle in Y, then 2 Y, 1 B, (1 B, 7 Y, 1 B) 15 times, 1 B, 3 Y. Cut B.
85th row : K. thus : Cast off 5 sts. in Y, leaving 6th st. on right-hand needle in Y, then 2 Y, 1 LB, 4 Y, (4 Y, 1 LB, 4 Y) 14 times, 4 Y.
86th row : P. thus : Cast off 5 sts. in Y, leaving 6th st. on right-hand needle in Y, then 1 Y, 3 LB, 3 Y, (3 Y, 3 LB, 3 Y) 13 times, 3 Y, 3 LB, 2 Y. (133 sts.)

See colour plate on page 97

(continued on page 122)

MAN'S SLIPOVER IN FAIR ISLE PATTERNING

BESTWAY 1837 3D

5 oz. of FAIR ISLE FINGERING

1 oz. EACH IN 4 CONTRASTING SHADES

MATERIALS

The slipover took 5 ozs. of Patons Fair Isle Fingering in the main shade, and 1 oz. each in 4 contrasting shades of the same make of fingering. Also two pairs of knitting needles Nos. 9 and 11.

MEASUREMENTS

From shoulder to lower edge 21½ ins. chest measurement 40 ins.

TENSION

Using No. 9 needles, about 7½ sts. and 8 rows to 1 in.

ABBREVIATIONS

K., knit ; p., purl ; st. or sts., stitch or stitches ; in. or ins., inch or inches ; dec., decrease (take 2 sts. tog.) ; inc., increase (k. into the front and then into the back of the same stitch) ; tog., together ; rep., repeat ; M, main shade ; B, brown ; G, green ; R, rust ; L, lemon.

THE FRONT

Using the No. 11 needles and the M shade, cast on 124 sts., work in ribbing of k. 1, p. 1 for 4 ins. In last row of ribbing inc. 1 st. in every 4th st. until 4 sts. remain, rib 4. (154). Change to No. 9 needles, work either from the chart or from the directions as follows :

1st row : K. row in M.

2nd row : P. row * 9 M, 1 B, 1 M, 1 B, 10 M ; rep. from * to end.

3rd row : K. row, * 11 M, 1 B, 10 M ; rep. from * to end.

4th row : Same as 2nd row.

5th row : K. row, * 3 M, (1 B, 1 M) 3 times, 1 B, 3 M, (1 B, 1 M)

4 times, 1 M ; rep. from * to end.

6th row : P. row, * (3 M, 1 B) twice, 5 M, (1 B, 3 M) twice, 1 M ; rep. from * to end.

7th row : K. row, * 3 M, (1 B, 1 M) 3 times, 1 B, 3 M, (1 B, 1 M) 4 times, 1 M ; rep. from * to end.

8th row : P. row, * (3 M, 3 G) 3 times, 4 M ; rep. from * to end.

9th row : K. row, * 4 M, (1 G, 1 M, 1 G, 3 M) 3 times ; rep. from * to end.

10th row : Same as 8th row.

11th row : K. row, * 1 M, 1 R ; rep. from * to end.

12th row : P. row, * 1 M, (1 R, 2 M) 7 times ; rep. from * to end.

13th row : Same as 11th row.

14th row : Same as 8th row.

15th row : Same as 9th row.

16th row : Same as 8th row.

17th row : Same as 7th row.

18th row : Same as 6th row.

19th row : Same as 5th row.

20th row : Same as 2nd row.

21st row : Same as 3rd row.

22nd row : Same as 2nd row.

23rd row : Same as 1st row.

24th row : P. row, * 1 B, 19 M, 1 B, 1 M ; rep. from * to end.

25th row : K. row, * 1 B, 21 M ; rep. from * to end.

26th row : Same as 24th row.

27th row : K. row, * 2 M, (1 B, 1 M) 3 times, 1 B, 5 M, (1 B, 1 M) 4 times ; rep. from * to end.

28th row : P. row, * 2 M, 1 B, 3 M, 1 B, 7 M, 1 B, 3 M, 1 B, 3 M ; rep. from * to end.

29th row : Same as 27th row.

30th row : P. row, * 1 G, 3 M, 3 G, 7 M, 3 G, 3 M, 2 G ; rep. from * to end.

31st row : K. row, * 1 M, 1 G, 3 M, 1 G, 1 M, 1 G, 7 M, 1 G, 1 M, 1 G, 3 M, 1 G ; rep. from * to end.

32nd row : Same as 30th row.

33rd row : K. row, * 1 L, 1 M ; rep. from * to end.

34th row : P. row, * (2 M, 1 L) 3 times, 3 M, (1 L, 2 M) 3 times, 1 L ; rep. from * to end.

35th row : Same as 33rd row.

36th row : Same as 30th row.

37th row : Same as 31st row.

38th row : Same as 30th row.

39th row : Same as 27th row.

40th row : Same as 28th row.

41st row : Same as 27th row.

42nd row : Same as 24th row.

43rd row : Same as 25th row.

44th row : Same as 24th row.

These 44 rows complete the Fair Isle pattern. Now rep. from the 1st to the 34th rows inclusive. Then, still keeping the continuity of the pattern, shape the armholes by casting off 14 sts. at the beginning of the next 2 rows. Still in pattern, dec. 1 st. at both ends of next and every following alternate row until you have worked the 44th pattern row and 118 sts. remain.

Next row : K. 1, k. 2 tog., k. 56, turn. Slip the remaining 59 sts. on to a stitch-holder for the time being. Continue in pattern, dec. 1 st. at the armhole edge in alternate rows, at the same time dec. 1 st. at the neck edge in every 3rd row until the 7th row of the 3rd rep. of the pattern has been worked. Continue shaping at the neck edge only in every 3rd row until 39 sts. remain, finishing at the armhole edge. Shape the shoulder

by casting off 13 sts. at the beginning of the next and every alternate row until no sts. remain, fasten off.

Slip the 59 sts. from stitch-holder on to a No. 9 needle and rejoin the wools to the neck edge of the 59 sts. and work to correspond.

THE BACK

Work as directed for the front until you have cast off the sts. for the armholes. (126). Then dec. 1 st. at both ends of the next and every following alternate row until the 7th row of the 3rd rep. of the pattern. (110). Now continue in pattern without shaping until the armholes are the same depth as the front armholes. Then cast off 13 sts. at the beginning of the next 6 rows, cast off remaining sts.

THE NECK RIBBING

Sew up the left shoulder seam. Now, using the No. 11 needles and the M wool and with right side of work facing, pick up and k. 32 sts. across back, then pick up and k. 45 sts. down left side of

front and 1 st. in the centre of V-point and pick up and k. 44 sts. up the other side of front. (122).

Next row : K. 2, (p. 1, k. 1) 20 times, p. 2 tog., p. 1, p. 2 tog ; (k. 1, p. 1) 37 times, k. 1.

Next row : K. 2, (p. 1, k. 1) 36 times, p. 2 tog., k. 1, p. 2 tog., (k. 1, p. 1) 20 times, k. 1.

Continue in ribbing, dec. 1 st. both sides of the centre st. in every row until 104 sts. remain, cast off rather loosely in ribbing. Sew up right shoulder seam.

ARMHOLE RIBBING (both alike)

Using the No. 11 needles and the M wool, and with right side facing, pick up and k. 124 sts. along the armhole edge. Work 10 rows in ribbing of k. 1, p. 1, then cast off in ribbing.

MAKING UP

Press the work on the wrong side with a hot iron over a damp cloth. Sew up the side seams, matching the patterns. Press seams on wrong side.

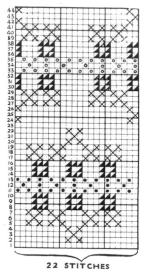

22 STITCHES

KEY
X BROWN
Z GREEN
I RUST
O LEMON
□ MAIN

MAN'S FAIR ISLE SLIPOVER

87th row : K. thus : Take 2 tog. in LB, 4 LB, 2 Y, (2 Y, 5 LB, 2 Y) 13 times, 2 Y, 4 LB, take 2 tog. in LB.

88th row : P. thus ; 6 LB, 1 Y, (1 Y 7 LB, 1 Y) 13 times, 1 Y, 6 LB. Cut LB and Y. Join on DB and F.

89th row : K. in DB, dec. 1 st. at each end of row. **90th row :** P. in DB.

91st row : K. thus : Take 2 tog. in DB, 2 DB, (1 F, 3 DB, 1 F, 3 DB, 2 F, 3 DB) 9 times, 1 F, 3 DB, 1 F, 1 DB, take 2 tog. DB. **92nd row :** P. thus : 3 DB, 1 F, 1 DB, 1 F, 1 DB, (3 DB, 2 F, 4 DB, 1 F, 1 DB, 1 F, 1 DB) 9 times, 3 DB.

93rd row : K. thus : Take 2 tog. DB, 1 DB, (2 DB, 1 F, 3 DB, 2 F, 1 DB) 9 times, 2 DB, 1 F, 2 DB, take 2 tog. DB. **94th row :** P. thus : 3 DB, 1 F, 2 DB, (1 DB, 2 F, 2 DB, 3 DB, 1 F, 2 DB) 9 times, 2 DB.

95th row : K. thus : Take 2 tog. DB, (1 DB, 1 F, 1 DB, 1 F, 4 DB, 2 F, 3 DB) 9 times, 1 DB, 1 F, 1 DB, 1 F, take 2 tog. DB. **96th row :** P. thus : 3 DB, 1 F, (3 DB, 2 F, 3 DB, 1 F, 3 DB, 1 F) 9 times, 1 DB. **97th row :** K. in DB and dec. 1 st. at both ends of row. (121.) **98th row :** P. in DB. Cut DB and F. Join on Y and G.

99th row : K. thus : 1 G, 1 Y, (1 Y, 7 G, 1 Y) 13 times, 1 Y, 1 G.

100th row : P. thus : 2 Y, (2 Y, 5 G, 2 Y) 13 times, 2 Y.

101st row : K. thus : Take 2 tog. Y, (3 Y, 3 G, 3 Y) 13 times, take 2 tog. Y.

102nd row : P. thus : 1 Y, (4 Y, 1 G, 4 Y) 13 times, 1 Y. Join on M.

103rd row : K. thus : 1 M, (1 M, 7 Y, 1 M) 13 times, 1 M. **104th row :** P. thus : 1 M, (2 M, 5 Y, 2 M) 13 times, 1 M.

105th row : K. thus : Take 2 tog. M, 1 M, 5 Y, 2 M, (2 M, 5 Y, 2 M) 11 times, 2 M, 5 Y, 1 M, take 2 tog. M. (117 sts.) This completes armhole shapings.

106th row : P. thus : (1 M, 7 Y, 1 M) 13 times, Cut M.

107th to 110th rows : As 19th to 22nd rows, but rep. pattern only 13 times in each row. Cut Y and G. Join on DB and F. **111th row :** K. in DB.

112th row : P. in DB.

113th row : K. thus : 2 DB, 1 F, 3 DB, 2 F, 3 DB (1 F, 3 DB, 1 F, 3 DB, 2 F, 3 DB) 8 times, 2 DB.

114th row : P. thus : 2 DB, (3 DB, 2 F, 4 DB, 1 F, 1 DB, 1 F, 1 DB) 8 times, 3 DB, 2 F, 4 DB, 1 F, 1 DB.

115th row : K. thus : 1 F, 3 DB, 2 F, 2 DB, 2 F, 1 DB, (2 DB, 1 F, 3 DB, 2 F, 2 DB, 2 F, 1 DB) 8 times, 2 DB.

116th row : P. thus : 2 DB, (1 DB 1 DB, 2 F, 2 DB, 3 DB, 1 F 2 DB) 8 times 1 DB, 1 F, 2 DB, 2 DB, 3 DB, 1 F.

117th row : K. thus : 1 DB, 1 F, 4 DB, 2 F, 3 DB, (1 DB, 1 F, 1 DB, 1 F, 4 DB 2 F, 3 DB) 8 times, 2 DB.

118th row : P. thus : 2 DB, (3 DB, 2 F, 3 DB, 1 F, 3 DB, 1 F) 8 times, 3 DB, 2 F, 3 DB, 1 F, 2 DB. **119th row :** K. in DB.

120th row : P. in DB. Cut DB and F wools. Join on LB, Y, and LG.

Work 33rd to 44th rows inclusive, but rep. pattern 13 times in each row. Cut LB, Y, and LG. Join on DB and F. Work 111th to 120th rows inclusive. Cut DB and F. Join on G, Y, and R. Now work the 55th to 66th rows inclusive, but rep. pattern 13 times in each row.

Cut G, Y, and R wools. Join on DB only and shape shoulders. Cast off 8 sts. at beginning of next 8 rows. Change to No. 11 needles. Using DB work 10 rows in ribbing of K. 1, P. 1 on remaining 53 sts. Cast off in ribbing.

THE FRONT

Work as for the back until the 118th row has been worked.

119th row : K. 42 in DB, cast off next 33 sts., K. to end. Work on last 42 sts.

120th row : P. 40 in DB, dec. Cut DB and F. Join on LB and Y.

121st row : K. thus : Dec. in LB, 2 LB, 1 Y, (1 Y, 7 LB, 1 Y) 4 times.

122nd row : P. thus : (2 Y, 5 LB, 2 Y) 4 times, 2 Y, dec. in LB.

123rd row : K. thus : Dec. in Y, 1 Y, (3 Y, 3 LB, 3 Y) 4 times.

124th row : P. thus : (4 Y, 1 LB, 4 Y) 4 times, dec. in Y. Join on LG.

125th row : K. thus : Dec. in Y, 7 Y, 1 LG, (1 LG, 7 Y, 1 LG) 3 times.

126th row : P. thus : (2 LG, 5 Y, 2 LG) 3 times, 2 LG, 7 Y.

127th row : K. thus : Dec. in Y, 5 Y, 2 LG, (2 LG, 5 Y, 2 LG) 3 times.

128th row : P. thus : (1 LG, 7 Y, 1 LG) 3 times, 1 LG, 7 Y. Cut LG wool.

129th row : K. thus : Dec. in Y, 1 Y, 1 LB, 4 Y, (4 Y, 1 LB, 4 Y) 3 times.

130th row : P. thus : (3 Y, 3 LB, 3 Y) 3 times, 3 Y, 3 LB, 1 Y.

131st row : K. thus : Dec. in LB, 3 LB, 2 Y, (2 Y, 5 LB 2 Y) 3 times.

132nd row : P. thus : (1 Y, 7 LB, 1 Y) 3 times, 1 Y, 5 LB. Cut LB and Y. Join on DB and F.

133rd row : Dec. in DB, K. to end in DB. (32.) **134th row :** P. in DB.

135th row : K. thus : 4 DB, (1 F, 3 DB, 1 F, 3 DB, 2 F, 3 DB) twice, 2 DB.

136th row : P. thus : 2 DB, (3 DB, 2 F, 4 DB, 1 F, 1 DB, 1 F, 1 DB) twice, 4 DB.

137th row : K. thus : 4 DB, (2 DB, 1 F, 3 DB, 2 F, 2 DB, 2 F, 1 DB) twice, 2 DB.

138th row : P. thus : 2 DB, (1 DB, 2 F, 2 DB, 2 F, 3 DB, 1 F, 2 DB) twice, 4 DB.

139th row : K. thus : 4 DB, (1 DB, 1 F, 1 DB, 1 F, 4 DB, 2 F, 3 DB) twice, 2 DB.

140th row : P. thus : 2 DB, (3 DB, 2 F, 3 DB, 1 F, 3 DB, 1 F) twice, 4 DB.

141st row : K. in DB.

142nd row : P. in DB. Cut DB and F. Join on G and Y. **143rd row :** K. thus : 4 G, 1 Y, (1 Y, 7 G, 1 Y) 3 times.

144th row : P. thus : (2 Y, 5 G, 2 Y) 3 times, 2 Y, 3 G. **145th row :** K. thus : 2 G, 3 Y, (3 Y, 3 G, 3 Y) 3 times.

146th row : P. thus : (4 Y, 1 G, 4 Y) 3 times, 4 Y, 1 G. Join on R.

147th row : K. thus : 4 Y, 1 R, (1 R, 7 Y, 1 R) 3 times. **148th row :** P. thus : (2 R, 5 Y, 2 R) 3 times, 2 R, 3 Y.

149th row : K. thus : 3 Y, 2 R, (2 R, 5 Y, 2 R) 3 times. **150th row :** P. thus : (1 R, 7 Y, 1 R) 3 times, 1 R, 4 Y. Cut R.

151st row : K. thus : 1 G, 4 Y, (4 Y, 1 G, 4 Y) 3 times. **152nd row :** P. thus : (3 Y, 3 G, 3 Y) 3 times, 3 Y, 2 G.

153rd row : K. thus : 3 G, 2 Y, (2 Y, 5 G, 2 Y) 3 times. **154th row :** P. thus : (1 Y, 7 G, 1 Y) 3 times, 1 Y, 4 G. Cut G and Y.

Join on DB only. K. 1 row, cast off 8 sts. at beginning of next and following alternate rows, until no sts. remain. Fasten off.

With wrong side facing, rejoin DB to inner (neck) edge of remaining 42 sts., then take 2 tog. in DB and P. to end. Cut DB wool. Join on LB and Y.

121st row : K. thus : (1 Y, 7 LB, 1 Y) 4 times, 3 Y, dec. in Y.

122nd row : P. thus : Dec. in Y, 2 Y, (2 Y, 5 LB, 2 Y) 4 times.

123rd row : K. thus : (3 Y, 3 LB, 3 Y) 4 times, 1 Y, dec. in Y.

124th row : P. thus : Dec. in Y, (4 Y, 1 LB, 4 Y) 4 times. Join on LG.

125th row : K. thus : (1 LG, 7 Y, 1 LG) 3 times, 1 LG, 7 Y, dec. in Y.

126th row : P. thus : 7 Y, 2 LG, (2 LG, 5 Y, 2 LG) 3 times.

127th row : K. thus : (2 LG, 5 Y, 2 LG) 3 times, 2 LG, 5 Y, dec. in Y.

128th row : P. thus : 7 Y, 1 LG, (1 LG, 7 Y, 1 LG) 3 times. Cut LG.

129th row : K. thus : (4 Y, 1 LB, 4 Y) 3 times, 4 Y, 1 LB, 1 Y, dec. in Y.

130th row : P. thus : 1 Y, 3 LB, 3 Y, (3 Y, 3 LB, 3 Y) 3 times.

131st row : K. thus : (2 Y, 5 LB, 2 Y) 3 times, 2 Y, 3 LB, dec. in LB.

132nd row : P. thus : 5 LB, 1 Y, (1 Y, 7 LB, 1 Y) 3 times.

Cut LB and Y. Join on DB and F.

133rd row : K. in DB, and dec. 1 st. at end of row. (32 sts.)

134th row : P. in DB.

135th row : K. thus : 2 DB, 1 F, 1 DB, (2 DB, 2 F, 3 DB, 1 F, 3 DB, 1 F, 1 DB) twice, 2 DB.

136th row : P. thus : 2 DB, (2 DB, 1 F, 1 DB, 1 F, 4 DB, 2 F, 2 DB) twice, 2 DB, 1 F, 1 DB. **137th row :** K. thus : 1 DB, 3 DB, (2 F, 2 DB, 2 F, 3 DB, 1 F, 3 DB) twice, 2 DB.

138th row : P. thus : 2 DB, (3 DB, 1 F, 3 DB, 2 F, 2 DB, 2 F) twice, 3 DB, 1 F.

139th row : K. thus : 1 DB, 1 F, 2 DB, (2 DB, 2 F, 4 DB, 1 DB, 1 F, 1 F) twice, 2 DB.

140th row : P. thus : 2 DB, (1 DB, 1 F, 3 DB, 1 F, 3 DB, 2 F) twice, 1 DB, 1 F, 2 DB. **141st row :** K. in DB.

142nd row : P. in DB. Cut DB and F. Join on G and Y.

143rd row : K. thus : (1 Y, 7 G, 1 Y) 3 times, 1 Y, 4 G. **144th row :** P. thus : 3 G, 2 Y, (2 Y, 5 G, 2 Y) 3 times.

145th row : K. thus : (3 Y, 3 G, 3 Y) 3 times, 3 Y, 2 G.

146th row : P. thus : 1 G, 4 Y, (4 Y, 1 G, 4 Y) 3 times. Join on R.

147th row : K. thus : (1 R, 7 Y, 1 R) 3 times, 1 R, 4 Y. **148th row :** P. thus : 3 Y, 2 R, (2 R, 5 Y, 2 R) 3 times.

149th row : K. thus : (2 R, 5 Y, 2 R) 3 times, 2 R, 3 Y.

150th row : P. thus : 4 Y, 1 R, (1 R, 7 Y, 1 R) 3 times. Cut R.

151st row : K. thus : (4 Y, 1 G, 4 Y) 3 times, 4 Y, 1 G. **152nd row :** P. thus : 2 G, 3 Y, (3 Y, 3 G, 3 Y) 3 times.

153rd row : K. thus : (2 Y, 5 G, 2 Y) 3 times, 2 Y, 3 G. **154th row :** P. thus : 4 G, 1 Y, (1 Y, 7 G, 1 Y) 3 times.

Cut G and Y. Join on DB only. Cast off 8 sts. at beginning of next and following alternate rows, until no sts. remain. Fasten off.

MAKING UP, AND NECK AND ARMHOLE RIBBING

With right side of front facing, and using DB and No. 11 needles, pick up and K. 110 sts. evenly round neck edge. Work 10 rows in ribbing of K. 1, P. 1. Cast off in ribbing.

Sew up shoulder seams, and press seams. With right side facing, and using DB wool and No. 11 needles, pick up and K. 138 sts. round one armhole edge. Work 10 rows in ribbing of K. 1, P. 1. Cast off in ribbing.

Work round other armhole in same way. Press work, avoiding ribbing. Sew up side seams, and press seams.

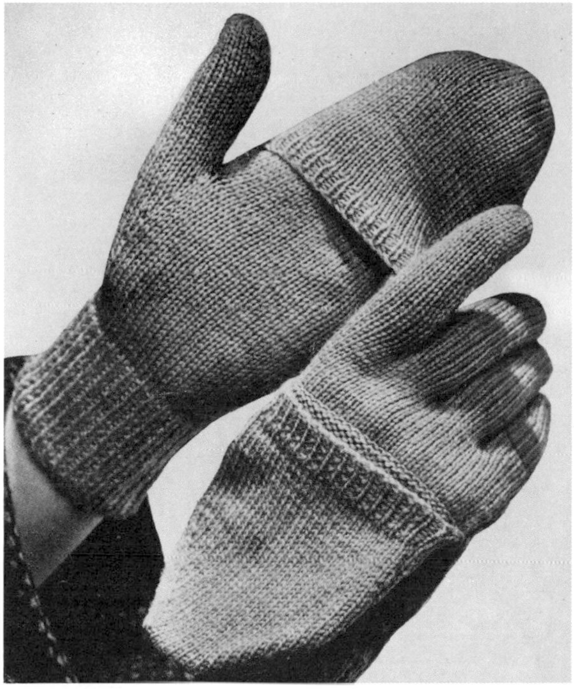

THE LADY'S GLOVES WITH MITT MUFFS

MATERIALS : *2 ozs. of Penelope's W.B. Melody Knitting Wool 3 ply, and a pair of No. 12 knitting needles.*

TENSION : *Over the stocking-stitch, 9 sts. and 12 rows to 1 inch.*

MEASUREMENTS : *Width all round hand, above thumb division, 6¾ inches; overall length, 9½ inches.*

ABBREVIATIONS : *K., knit; p., purl; st., stitch; sts., stitches; rep., repeat; tog., together; inc., increase (by working twice into same st.); dec., decrease (by taking 2 sts. tog.); st.-st., stocking-stitch (1 row k. and 1 row p., alternately); sl., slip; p.s.s.o., pass slipped st. over.*

Sts. in brackets must be worked along row to the extent stated after 2nd bracket.

THE LEFT GLOVE

* Cast on 60 sts. and work in k. 1, p. 1 ribs for 2½ inches, then work 2 rows st.-st. Now commence thumb gusset increases.*

1st gusset row : K. 26 sts. for palm, inc. in next st., k. 1, inc. in next st., k. 31 sts. for back of hand. Work 3 rows st.-st.

5th row : K. 26, inc. in next st., k. 3, inc. in next st., k. 31. Work 3 rows st.-st. Continue in this way, increasing 2 sts. in every 4th row and noting that you should k. 2 more sts. between each inc. than in preceding inc. row, until you reach the **25th row,** which is worked thus : K. 26, inc. in next st., k. 13, inc. in next st., k. 31.

26th row : P. Now divide for thumb.

27th row : K. 43 sts. ; turn, slipping remaining 31 sts. on to a piece of thread.

** **The thumb—1st row :** Cast on 2 sts., then p. 19 ; turn, slipping remaining sts. on to another piece of thread.

2nd row : Cast on 2, then k. 21 sts. Starting with a p. row, work 23 rows more on these 21 sts. Now shape top.

1st top shaping row : (K. 1, k. 2 tog.) to end. **2nd row :** P. 2 tog., (p. 1, p 2 tog.) to end.

Break off wool, leaving a longish end, run it through remaining sts., draw up and fasten off, then join thumb seam.**

With right side of work facing you, join on wool and pick up and k. 4 sts. from those cast on at base of thumb, then k. the sts. from 1st thread, thus completing the 27th row of hand.

28th row : Using a coloured thread together with wool to mark this row, p. 31, then using wool only, p. remaining 4 sts., also p. the 26 sts. from other thread.

Continue in st.-st. for 16 rows, then commence fingers.

1st finger—1st row : K. 38 sts. ; turn, slipping remaining sts. on to a piece of thread. **2nd row :** Cast on 1, p. 18 ; turn, slipping remaining sts. on to another piece of thread. **3rd row :** Cast on 1, k. 19. Starting with a p. row, work 27 rows on these 19 sts.

1st top shaping row : K. 1, (k. 2 tog., k. 1) to end.

2nd row : P. 1, (p. 2 tog., p. 1) to end.

Break wool, draw up top and join seam of finger as explained for thumb.

2nd finger—1st row : With right side of work facing you, join on wool and pick up and k. 2 sts. from those cast on at base of preceding finger, then k. 8 sts. from left-hand thread ; turn. **2nd row :** Cast on 1, p. 11, then p. 7 sts. from other thread ; turn. **3rd row :** Cast on 1, k. 19. Starting with a p. row, work 31 rows on these 19 sts., then shape top, draw up and join seam as for 1st finger.

3rd finger : Work as 2nd finger, but only work 27 rows instead of 31 on the 19 sts., before shaping top.

4th finger—1st row : With right side of work facing you, join on wool and pick up and k. 2 sts. from base of preceding finger, then k. remaining sts. from left-hand thread.

2nd row : P. these 9 sts., then p. remaining sts. from other thread.

3rd row : K. 16. Starting with a p. row, work 23 rows more. Now shape top.

1st top shaping row : K. 1, (k. 2 tog., k. 1) to end.

2nd row : P. 2 tog., (p. 1, p. 2 tog.) to end.

Break wool and draw up top, then join seam down to wrist. Press lightly.

THE RIGHT GLOVE

Work as left glove from * to *

1st gusset row : K. 31 sts. for back of hand, inc. in next st., k. 1, inc. in next st., k. 26 sts. for palm. Work 3 rows st.-st.

5th row : K. 31, inc. in next st., k. 3, inc. in next st., k. 26. Work 3 rows st.-st. Continue in this way, increasing 2 sts. in every 4th row and noting that you should k. 2 more sts. between each inc. than in preceding inc. row, until you reach the **25th row,** which is worked thus : K. 31, inc. in next st., k. 13, inc. in next st., k. 26.

26th row : P. Now divide for thumb.

27th row : K. 48 sts. ; turn, slipping remaining 26 sts. on to a piece of thread. To complete thumb, work as left glove from ** to **.

Now continue as follows :

With right side of work facing you, join on wool and pick up and k. 4 sts. from those cast on at base of thumb, then k. the sts. from left-hand thread, thus completing 27th row of hand.

28th row : P. 30, then using a coloured thread and the wool together to mark the row, p. the 31 sts. from other thread. Work 16 rows st.-st., then begin fingers.

1st finger—1st row : K. 40 sts. ; turn, slipping remaining sts. on to a piece of thread. Now proceed as for 1st finger of left glove, commencing with its 2nd row.

2nd finger—1st row : With right side of work facing you, join on wool and pick up and k. 2 sts. from base of preceding finger, then k. 7 sts. from left-hand thread ; turn. **2nd row :** Cast on 1, p. 10, then p. 8 sts. from other thread ; turn.

3rd row : Cast on 1, k. 19. Work 31 more rows on these sts., then shape top, draw up and join seam as for preceding finger.

3rd finger : Work as for 2nd finger, but only work 27 rows on the 19 sts. instead of 31 rows, before you shape the top.

4th finger : Work this and complete glove as for left hand.

THE MITT MUFFS

Left Muff : Cast on 31 sts., then on to the needle holding these sts., pick up and k. 31 sts. along the marked row of left glove, starting at thumb end and picking up 1 st. from each of the marked sts.

1st row : P. 31, then k. 1, (p. 1, k. 1) to end. **2nd row :** P. 1, (k. 1, p. 1) 15 times, k. 31.

Rep. these 2 rows twice more, then work 1st of these rows again.

Now work 26 rows st.-st. over all sts.

1st top shaping row : K. 1, sl. 1, k. 1, p.s.s.o., k. 25, k. 2 tog., k. 2, sl. 1, k. 1, p.s.s.o., k. 25, k. 2 tog., k. 1.

2nd and every alternate row : P.

3rd row : K. 1, sl. 1, k. 1, p.s.s.o., k. 23, k. 2 tog., k. 2, sl. 1, k. 1, p.s.s.o., k. 23, k. 2 tog., k. 1.

5th row : K. 1, sl. 1, k. 1, p.s.s.o., k. 21, k. 2 tog., k. 2, sl. 1, k. 1, p.s.s.o., k. 21, k. 2 tog., k. 1.

Continue in this way, decreasing 4 sts. in every alternate row and noting that you should k. 2 sts. less between each dec. than in preceding dec. row until you reach the **19th row,** which is worked thus : K. 1, sl. 1, k. 1, p.s.s.o., k. 7, k. 2 tog., k. 2, sl. 1, k. 1, p.s.s.o., k. 7, k. 2 tog., k. 1. **20th row :** P. Cast off, join seam and press.

Right Muff : With right side of right glove facing you, pick up and k. 31 sts. along the marked row, commencing at side edge and picking up 1 st. from each of the marked sts. ; turn.

Next row : Cast on 31 sts., k. 1, (p. 1, k. 1) 15 times, p. 31.

Next row : K. 31, (p. 1, k. 1) to last st., p. 1.

Next row : K. 1, (p. 1, k. 1) 15 times, p. 31. Rep. the last 2 rows twice more. Work 26 rows st.-st. over all sts., then shape top and complete as given for left muff.

MEN'S GLOVES WITH MITT MUFFS

MATERIALS : *3 ozs. of Penelope's W.B. Melody Knitting Wool 4 ply, and a pair of No. 12 knitting needles.*

TENSION : *Over the stocking-stitch, 17 sts. to 2 inches and 11 rows to 1 inch.*

MEASUREMENTS : *All round hand, above thumb division, 7¾ inches; overall length, about 10½ inches.*

ABBREVIATIONS : *As for Lady's Gloves.*

THE LEFT GLOVE

Cast on 64 sts. Work in k. 1, p. 1 ribs for 2½ inches, then 8 rows st.-st. Now commence thumb gusset increases.

9th row : K. 29, inc. in each of next 2 sts., k. 33.

10th and every alternate row : P.

11th row : K. 29, inc. in next st., k. 2, inc. in next st., k. 33.

13th row : K. 29, inc. in next st., k. 4, inc. in next st., k. 33.

15th row : K. 29, inc. in next st., k. 6, inc. in next st., k. 33.

17th row : K. 29, inc. in next st., k. 8, inc. in next st., k. 33.

19th row : K. 29, inc. in next st., k. 10, inc. in next st., k. 33.

21st row : K. 29, inc. in next st., k. 12, inc. in next st., k. 33.

23rd row : K. 29, inc. in next st., k. 14, inc. in next st., k. 33.

25th row : K. 29, inc. in next st. k. 16, inc. in next st., k. 33. Work 3 rows st.-st. Now divide for thumb.

29th row : K. 49 sts. ; turn, slipping remaining sts. on to a piece of thread.

The thumb—1st row : Cast on 2, p. 22 ; turn, slipping remaining sts. on to another piece of thread. **2nd row :** Cast on 2, k. 24. Work 23 rows st.-st. on these 24 sts., then shape top.

1st top shaping row : (K. 2 tog.) to end. **2nd row :** (P. 2 tog.) to end. Break wool, run end through remaining sts., draw up and fasten off securely, then join seam.

With right side of work facing you, join on wool and pick up and k. 4 sts. from those cast on at base of thumb, then k. the sts. from left-hand thread, thus completing 29th row of hand.

30th row : Using coloured thread together with the wool to mark these sts., p. 33, then using wool only, p. remaining 4 sts., also p. the sts. from other thread. Work 22 rows st.-st., then commence fingers.

1st finger—1st row : K. 42 sts. ; turn, slipping remaining sts. on to a piece of thread. **2nd row :** Cast on 1, p. 19 ; turn, slipping remaining sts. on to another piece of thread. **3rd row :** Cast on 1, k. 20.

Work 27 rows st.-st. on these 20 sts., then shape top, draw up and join seam as for thumb.

2nd finger—1st row : Join on wool and pick up and k. 2 sts. from those cast on at base of preceding finger, then k. 8 sts. from left-hand thread ; turn. **2nd row :** Cast on 1, p. 11, then p. 8 sts. from other thread. **3rd row :** Cast on 1, k. 20. Work 31 rows st.-st. on these 20 sts., then shape top and complete as for thumb.

3rd finger : Work as for 2nd finger, but work only 27 rows st.-st. instead of 31 rows before shaping top.

4th finger—1st row : Join on wool and pick up and k. 2 sts. from base of preceding finger, then k. 8 sts. from left-hand thread. **2nd row :** P. 10, then p. remaining sts. from other thread.

Work 24 rows st.-st. on these 18 sts.

1st top shaping row : (K. 2 tog.) to end. **2nd row :** P. 1, (p. 2 tog.) to end. Break wool, run end through remaining sts., draw up and fasten off, then join seam down to wrist. Press glove.

THE RIGHT GLOVE

Cast on 64 sts. and work in k. 1, p. 1 ribbing for 2½ inches.

Work 8 rows st.-st., then work 9th to 25th rows of left glove, but read each of these rows backwards. Thus 9th row would read, "K. 33, inc. in each of the next 2 sts., k. 29." After completing 25th row, work 3 rows st.-st., then divide for thumb. **29th row :** K. 53 sts. ; turn, slipping remaining sts. on to a piece of thread. Now work thumb as given for left glove, starting with its 1st row. With right side of work facing you, join on wool and pick up and k. 4 sts. from those cast on at base of thumb, then k. the sts. from left-hand thread.

30th row : P. 33 sts., then using coloured thread together with the wool to mark this row, p. the 33 sts. from other thread. Work 22 rows st.-st., then work fingers as for left glove.

THE MITT MUFFS

Left Muff : Cast on 33 sts., then on to the needle holding these sts., pick up and k. 33 sts. along the marked row of left glove, commencing at thumb and picking up 1 st. from each of the marked sts.

1st row : P. 33, k. 1, (p. 1, k. 1) to end. **2nd row :** P. 1, (k. 1, p. 1) 16 times, k. 33.

Rep. these 2 rows twice more, then work 1st of these rows again. Work 30 rows st.-st. over all sts. Shape top.

Next row : K. 1, sl. 1, k. 1, p.s.s.o., k. 27, k. 2 tog., k. 2, sl. 1, k. 1, p.s.s.o., k. 27, k. 2 tog., k. 1. **Next row :** P.

Now work 1st to 20th top shaping rows of lady's left mitt muff. Join seam and press.

Right Muff : With right glove facing you, pick up and k. 33 sts. along the marked row, commencing at side edge and picking up 1 st. from each of the marked sts. ; turn.

Next row : Cast on 33 sts., k. 1, (p. 1, k. 1) 16 times, p. 33.

Next row : K. 33, (p. 1, k. 1) to last st., p. 1. **Next row :** K. 1, (p. 1, k. 1) 16 times, p. 33.

Rep. last 2 rows twice more. Work 30 rows st.-st. over all sts., then shape top and complete as for left muff.

GENT'S LONG SLEEVE PULLOVER

in Wendy Family Wool 4 ply to fit 38"/40" chest

MATERIALS REQUIRED.
15 OZS. WENDY FAMILY WOOL 4 PLY, WHITE.
1 OZ. WENDY FAMILY WOOL 4 PLY, NAVY.
1 OZ. WENDY FAMILY WOOL 4 PLY, LIGHT BLUE.
2 No. 9 Needles. 2 No. 11 Needles. 1 Cable Needle. 1 Stitch-holder.

MEASUREMENTS. Chest 38/40 ins. Length from top of shoulder 26 ins. Length of sleeve seam 22 ins.

TENSION. 8 sts. to 1 in. on No. 9 needles.

ABBREVIATIONS.

K. = Knit.	P. = Purl.	Sts. = stitches.
Tog. = together.	Ins. = inches.	Beg. = beginning.
Inc. = increase.	Dec. = decrease.	Rept. = repeat.
T.B.L. = Through back of loop.	Alt. = alternate.	

THE FRONT

Using No. 11 needles and White wool, cast on 130 sts. Work 2 ins. in K.1, P.1 rib. Break off White wool and join in Navy.

Work 4 rows in K.1, P.1 rib, break off Navy, join in Light Blue.

Work 2 rows in rib, break off Light Blue, join in Navy.

Work another 2 rows in rib, break off Navy wool and join in Light Blue.

Work 3 rows in rib.

Next Row. Inc. in first st., P.1, K.1, P.1, K.1, (inc. in next st., K.1, P.1, K.1, P.1, K.1, P.1, inc. in next st., P.1, K.1, P.1, K.1, P.1, K.1) 8 times, inc. in next st., K.1, P.1, K.1, P.1, K.1, P.1, inc. in next st., P.1, K.1, P.1, K.1, inc. in next st. (150 sts.).

Break off Light Blue wool and join in White wool. Change to No. 9 needles and commence pattern.

1st Row. K.8, (P.1, K.12, P.1, K.6) 7 times, K.2.

2nd Row. P.2, (P.6, K.1, P.12, K.1) 7 times, P.8.

Rept. the 1st and 2nd rows twice more.

7th Row. K.8, P.1, (slip the next 3 sts. on to the cable needle and put to back of work. Knit the next 3 sts. from left-hand needle, then knit the 3 sts. from cable needle. Slip the next 3 sts. from left-hand needle on to cable needle and put to front of work. Knit the next 3 sts. on left-hand needle. Knit the 3 sts. from cable needle). This will be called—Twist 3 back, Twist 3 front. P.1, K.6, (P.1, Twist 3 back, Twist 3 front, P.1, K.6) 6 times, K.2.

8th Row. P.2, (P.6, K.1, P.12, K.1) 7 times, P.8.

These 8 rows form the pattern and are used throughout the pullover.

Continue in pattern until work measures 17 ins. from commencement, ending on the 8th row of pattern.

Shape Armholes

1st Row. Cast off 8 sts., (K.12, P.1, K.6, P.1) 6 times, K.12, K.8.

2nd Row. Cast off 8 sts., (P.12, K.1, P.6, K.1) 6 times, P.12, K.1.

3rd Row. K.2 tog., K.11, (P.1, K.6, P.1, K.12) 5 times, P.1, K.6, P.1, K.11, K.2 tog.

4th Row. K.2 tog., P.10, K.1, P.6, K.1, (P.12, K.1, P.6, K.1) 5 times, P.10, K.2 tog.

5th Row. K.2 tog., K.9 (P.1, K.6, P.1, K.12) 5 times, P.1, K.6, P.1, K.9, K.2 tog.

6th Row. K.2 tog., P.8, K.1, P.6, K.1, (P.12, K.1, P.6, K.1) 5 times, P.8, K.2 tog.

7th Row. K.2 tog., K.7, P.1, K.6, (P.1, Twist 3 back, Twist 3 front, P.1, K.6) twice, P.1, K.6, turn, slip the remaining 63 sts. on to a stitch-holder.

8th Row. K.2 tog., P.4, K.1, (P.6, K.1, P.12, K.1) twice, P.6, K.1, P.6, K.2 tog.

9th Row. K.2 tog., K.5 (P.1, K.6, P.1, K.12) twice, P.1, K.6, P.1, K.3, K.2 tog.

10th Row. K.2 tog., P.2, K.1, P.6, K.1, (P.12, K.1, P.6, K.1) twice, P.4, K.2 tog.

11th Row. K.2 tog., K.3, (P.1, K.6, P.1, K.12) twice, P.1, K.6, P.1, K.1, K.2 tog.

12th Row. K.2 tog., K.1, P.6, K.1, (P.12, K.1, P.6, K.1) twice, P.4.

13th Row. K.2 tog., K.2, (P.1, K.6, P.1, K.12) twice, P.1, K.6, K.2 tog.

14th Row. P.7, K.1, (P.12, K.1, P.6, K.1) twice, P.3.

15th Row. K.2 tog., K.1, P.1, K.6, P.1, Twist 3 back, Twist 3 front, P.1, K.6, P.1, Twist 3 back, Twist 3 front, P.1, K.5, K.2 tog.

16th Row. P.6, K.1, (P.12, K.1, P.6, K.1) twice, P.2.

Keeping the pattern correct, continue dec. at neck edge only by K.2 tog. at neck edge on every 3rd row until 32 sts. remain. Continue without further dec. until armhole measures 9½ ins. from commencement, finishing at armhole edge.

Shape Shoulder

1st, 3rd and 5th Rows. Cast off 8 sts., work to end.

2nd, 4th and 6th Rows. Work all across.

Cast off.

With right side of work facing, rejoin wool at neck centre and slip sts. from stitch-holder on to No. 9 needles.

1st Row. K.6, P.1, K.6, (P.1, Twist 3 back, Twist 3 front, P.1, K.6) twice, P.1, K.7, K.2 tog.

Continue in pattern and work to correspond with other side, commencing on 8th row of armhole shaping and reading the rows from end to beg.

THE BACK

Using No. 11 needles and White wool, cast on 130 sts. and work exactly as instructions given for the Front until the armhole shaping is reached.

Shape Armhole

1st Row. Cast off 8 sts., (K.12, P.1, K.6, P.1) 6 times, K.12, P.1, K.8.

2nd Row. Cast off 8 sts., (P.12, K.1, P.6, K.1) 6 times, P.12, K.1.

3rd Row. K.2 tog., K.11, (P.1, K.6, P.1, K.12) 5 times, P.1, K.6, P.1, K.11, K.2 tog.

4th Row. K.2 tog., P.10, K.1, P.6, K.1, (P.12, K.1, P.6, K.1) 5 times, P.10, K.2 tog.

5th Row. K.2 tog., K.9, (P.1, K.6, P.1, K.12) 5 times, P.1, K.6, P.1, K.9, K.2 tog.

6th Row. K.2 tog., P.8, K.1, P.6, K.1, (P.12, K.1, P.6, K.1) 5 times, P.8, K.2 tog.

7th Row. K.2 tog., K.7, P.1, K.6, (P.1, Twist 3 back, Twist 3 front, P.1, K.6) 5 times, P.1, K.7, K.2 tog.

8th Row. K.2 tog., P.6, K.1, (P.6, K.1, P.12, K.1) 5 times, P.6, K.1, P.6, K.2 tog.

9th Row. K.2 tog., K.5, (P.1, K.6, P.1, K.12) 5 times, P.1, K.6, P.1, K.5, K.2 tog.

10th Row. K.2 tog., P.4, K.1, P.6, (P.12, K.1, P.6, K.1) 5 times, P.4, K.2 tog.

11th Row. K.2 tog., K.3, (P.1, K.6, P.1, K.12) 5 times, P.1, K.6, P.1, K.3, K.2 tog.

12th Row. P.4, K.1, P.6, K.1 (P.12, K.1, P.6, K.1) 5 times, P.4.

13th Row. K.2 tog., K.2 (P.1, K.6, P.1, K.12) 5 times, P.1, K.6, P.1, K.2, K.2 tog.

14th Row. P.3, K.1, P.6, K.1, (P.12, K.1, P.6, K.1) 5 times, P.3.

15th Row. K.2 tog., K.1, P.1, K.6, P.1, (Twist 3 back, Twist 3 front, P.1, K.6, P.1) 5 times, K.1, K.2 tog.

Keeping the pattern correct, continue without further dec. until armhole measures 10 ins. from commencement. Cast off.

THE SLEEVES (Both Alike)

Using White wool and No. 11 needles, cast on 70 sts. and work 2 ins. in K.1, P.1 rib.

Continue in rib, working 4 rows in Navy, 2 rows in Light Blue, 2 rows in Navy, 4 rows in Light Blue. Break off Light Blue, join in White wool.

Change to No. 9 needles and commence pattern.

1st Row. K.1, P.1, K.6, (P.1, K.12, P.1, K.6) 3 times, P.1, K.1.

2nd Row. P.1, K.1, (P.6, K.1, P.12, K.1) 3 times, P.6, K.1, P.1.

Rept. the 1st and 2nd rows twice more.

7th Row. K.1, P.1, K.6, (P.1, Twist 3 back, Twist 3 front, P.1, K.6) 3 times, P.1, K.1.

8th Row. P.1, K.1, (P.6, K.1, P.12, K.1) 3 times, P.6, K.1, P.1.

Keeping the pattern correct, rept. the 8 pattern rows, inc. one st. each end of the needle on the next and every following 6th row until 110 sts. are on the needle. Working all inc. sts. into pattern, continue until sleeve measures 22 ins. from commencement, ending on the 8th row of pattern.

Shape Top

1st Row. Cast off 8 sts., (K.12, P.1, K.6, P.1) 5 times, K.1.

2nd Row. Cast off 8 sts., (P.12, K.1, P.6, K.1) 4 times, P.12, K.1.

3rd Row. K.2 tog., pattern to last 2 sts., K.2 tog.

4th Row. K.2 tog., pattern to last 2 sts., K.2 tog.

5th Row. Pattern all across.

Keeping the pattern correct, rept. rows 3 to 5 incl. until 44 sts. are on the needle.

Work 3 rows without dec.

Cast off 2 sts. at beg. of next 12 rows, then cast off 4 sts. at beg. of next 2 rows.

Cast off.

Work another sleeve in the same manner.

See colour plate on page 135

THE NECK BAND

Join right shoulder seam by back-stitching and with right side of work facing and using a No. 11 needle and Navy wool, pick up and knit 96 sts. down left side of neck, 97 sts. up right side of neck, 50 sts. across back.

1st Row. Work in P.1, K.1 rib to last st., P.1.

2nd Row. (K.1, P.1) 47 times, K.2 tog.T.B.L., K.1, K.2 tog., rib to end of row, break off Navy wool.

3rd Row. Using Light Blue wool, work in rib all across, keeping the centre st. in knit and dec. either side as given for the 2nd row in every other row.

Work one more row in Light Blue, two rows in Navy, two rows in Light Blue.

Cast off in Light Blue.

TO MAKE UP

To obtain the perfect fitting garment, it is *important* to follow these instructions when making up the garment.

With wrong side of work facing, pin out all pieces to measurements given. Using a hot iron and damp cloth, press carefully all work.

Join shoulder seam by placing together and back-stitching. Join side and sleeve seams by back-stitching, omitting the rib. Join rib by top sewing. Pin sleeves into position, placing sleeve seam to side seam, and back-stitch.

Press all seams flat.

A very practical Cardigan

In Templeton's **"AYRBEAM"** Super Scotch Fingering, 4 ply

MATERIALS
11 ozs. "Ayrbeam" Super Scotch Fingering, 4-ply.
6 buttons. 1 pair No. 9 "Aero" knitting needles. A short cable needle.

MEASUREMENTS
Length from the top of the shoulder, 22 ins.; width all round, closed, 38 ins.; length of sleeve
and shoulder from neck, including cuff, 29½ ins.; length of sleeve seam, including cuff, 22 ins.

TENSION
7 sts. to 1 inch in width.

ABBREVIATIONS
K=knit ; p=purl ; sts.=stitches ; ins.=inches.

THE BACK

Begin at the lower edge by casting on 132 sts.

Work a depth of 2 ins. in K1, P1 rib, working into the backs of the sts. on the first row.

Change to the following pattern:—

1st row—P1, then * K2, P6, K2, P2, and repeat from * all across ending K2, P6, K2, P1.

2nd row—K1, then * P2, K6, P2, K2, and repeat from * all across, ending P2, K6, P2, K1.

Repeat these 2 rows 3 times more then row 1 again.

10th row—K1, * P2, pass the next 3 sts. to a spare needle, K3, then knit across the 3 sts. on the spare needle, P2, K2 and repeat from * all across, ending K2, P1.

Repeat these 10 rows for the pattern.

Continue quite straight in the pattern till the work measures a depth of 14 ins. from the beginning, finishing at the end of the first row of the pattern. Shape the armholes by casting off 4 sts. at the beginning of each of the next 4 rows, then by decreasing the edge st. at both ends of the needle on each of the next 6 alternate rows.

104 sts. remain on the needle.

Work quite straight on these sts. for a depth of 5 ins., finishing at the end of the pattern.

Cast off.

THE LEFT FRONT

Begin at the lower edge by casting on 77 sts.

Work a depth of 6 rows in P1, K1 rib, working into the backs of the sts. on the first row.

Now make a buttonhole.

For this rib across 68 sts., cast off 3 sts. and complete the row.

On the next row work along as far as the cast off sts., then cast on 3 sts. and complete the row.

Now continue quite straight in the ribbing till this is the same depth as that of the back.

On the next row—beginning at the front edge—rib across 14 sts. then * K2, P2, K2, P6, and repeat from * all across, ending K2, P2, K2, P1.

Now keep the 14 sts. at the front edge in the ribbing as a border, and work the remainder in the main pattern.

Continue quite straight, making buttonholes as before on successive 19th and 20th rows till there are 6 buttonholes in all.

Work 4 rows past 6th buttonhole.

On the next and every following 4th row decrease next to the front border till there are 18 decreases in all, and at the same time, when the side edge is the same depth as that of the back to the armhole shape the armhole by casting off 4 sts. at the beginning of each of the next 2 rows commencing at the side edge, then by decreasing the edge sts. on alternate rows till there are 6 decreases in all.

Continue quite straight till the armhole edge is 1 pattern longer than that of the back.

3'i sts. remain on the needle.

Cast off the shoulder sts. and continue over the 14 sts. of the border for a depth of 2½ ins.

Leave these sts. on a safety pin for grafting.

THE RIGHT FRONT

Work this to match the left front with the front border and all shapings at opposite edges and without buttonholes.

THE SLEEVES

Begin at the cuff edge by casting on 60 sts., work a depth of 3½ ins. in K1, P1 rib, working into the backs of the sts. on the first row.

Change to the cable pattern and work a depth of 11 rows straight.

On the next and every following 6th row increase in the edge sts. at both ends of the needle till there are 102 sts. on the needle.

Work 5 rows straight.

Shape the top by decreasing the edge sts. at both ends of the needle on every row till 36 sts. remain.

Cast off.

Make the second sleeve in the same way.

TO COMPLETE THE GARMENT

Sew the shoulders of the back and fronts together.

Graft the sts. of the neck borders.

Sew one edge of this border to the back of the neck.

Sew the tops of the sleeves into the armholes.

Press out the work on the wrong side with a hot iron over a damp cloth.

Sew up the side and sleeve seams and press these well.

Sew the buttons on the right front to meet the buttonholes.

A simple Sleeveless Pullover

MATERIALS
7 ozs. "Ayrbeam" Super Scotch Fingering, 4-ply.
A set of long No. 12 "Aero" knitting needles.
1 pair No. 9 "Aero" knitting needles.

MEASUREMENTS
Length from the top of the shoulder, 22 ins.; width all round below sleeves, 37 ins.—
stretching; round armhole—without stretching, 18 ins.

TENSION
7 sts. to 1 inch in width ; 17 rows to 2 inches in depth.

ABBREVIATIONS
K=knit ; p=purl : sts.=stitches ; ins.=inches.

THE BACK

Using a pair of No. 12 needles, begin at the lower edge by casting on 130 sts.

Work a depth of 3½ ins. in K1, P1 rib, working into the backs of the sts. on the first row.

Change to No. 9 needles and work in the following pattern:—

1st row—K1, then * P2, K4, P2, K2, and repeat from * all across, ending K1, instead of K2.

2nd row—P1, then * K2, P4, K2, P2, and repeat from * all across, ending P1, instead of P2.

3rd row—As for the first row.

4th row—P1, then * K8, P2, and repeat from * all across, ending P1, instead of P2.

Repeat these 4 rows for the pattern and continue quite straight till the work measures a depth of 14½ ins. from the beginning.

Shape the armholes by casting off 4 sts. at the beginning of each of the next 6 rows, then by decreasing the edge sts. at both ends of the needle on alternate rows till there are 6 decreases at each edge.

No. 1014
Price 6d
38" Chest
AYRBEAM, 4 Ply

Templeton

94 sts. remain on the needle.

Work quite straight on these sts. for a depth of 5½ ins. then shape the neck and shoulders.

1st row—Work to within 7 sts. of the end, turn.

2nd row—Work to within 7 sts. of the opposite end, turn.

3rd row—Work to within 14 sts. of the end, turn.

4th row—Work to within 14 sts. of the opposite end, turn.

5th row—Work over 25 sts., cast off 16 sts., then work to within 21 sts. of the end, turn.

6th row—Work to neck.

7th row—Cast off 10 sts. and work across the remainder.

8th row—Cast off.

9th row—Join the wool to the neck edge of the opposite side and work to within 21 sts. of the end, turn.

10th row—Work to neck.

11th row—Cast off 10 sts. and work across the remainder.

12th row—Cast off.

THE FRONT

Work this in the same way as for the back till the position for the armhole shaping is reached.

On the next row—the right side of the work—

cast off 4 sts., work over 60 more sts., making 61 sts. on the needle, then turn and work back to the side edge.

Continue over the sts. of this half of the garment, and on the next row cast off 4 sts. then work along to the neck, decreasing at the end of the row.

Complete the armhole shaping by casting off 4 sts. at the beginning of the next row commencing at the side edge, then by decreasing the edge st. on the same edge on alternate rows till there are 6 decreases in all, and at the same time decrease the edge sts. at the neck edge on every 3rd row till there are 18 decreases in all.

Work quite straight on the remaining 29 sts. till the armhole edge is 6 rows longer than that of the back.

Shape the Shoulder

1st row—Working from the neck edge work to within 7 sts. of the end, turn.

2nd row—Work back to neck.

3rd row—Work to within 14 sts. of the end, turn.

4th row—Work back to neck.

5th row—Work to within 21 sts. of the end, turn.

6th row—Work back to neck.

7th row—Work across all sts.

8th row—Cast off.

Join the wool to the neck edge of the opposite side and complete this side to match the first. Sew the shoulders of the back and front together.

THE ARMHOLES

Holding the right side of the work towards you and using No. 12 needles, pick up and knit through every st. and the edge of every row on the armhole shaping, then miss the edge of every 6th row along the straight part of the armhole, then work along the shaped edge as for the first part.

On the original there were 136 sts. in all.

Work a depth of 1 inch in K1, P1 rib, then cast off.

Complete the second armhole in the same way.

THE NECK

Using the set of No. 12 needles and holding the right side of the work towards you pick up and knit through every st. across the back of the neck, and the edge of every row on the sides of the neck—commencing at a shoulder seam.

Work round and round in K1, P1 rib, decreasing on each side of the V point at the front of the neck on every row.

Continue for a depth of 1 inch.

Cast off.

TO COMPLETE THE GARMENT

Press out the work lightly on the wrong side with a warm iron over a slightly damp cloth.

Sew up the side seams and press these on the wrong side.

Well-fitting Golf Hose

MATERIALS

6 ozs. "Ayrbeam" Super Scotch Fingering, 4-ply.
A set of No. 12 "Aero" knitting needles.

MEASUREMENTS

Length from fold at top, 21 ins.; length of foot, 10½ ins., or as required.

TENSION

9 sts. to 1 inch in width; 9 rows to 1 inch in depth.

ABBREVIATIONS

K=knit; p=purl; ins.=inches; sts.=stitches tog.=together.

Begin at the edge of the turn-over top by casting on 80 sts. 30 on each of 2 needles and 20 on the third.

Work a depth of 1 inch in K1, P1 rib, working into the backs of the sts. on the first row.

Change to the following pattern:—

1st row—* P2, K4, P2, K2, and repeat from * all round.

2nd row—As for the first row.

3rd row—As for the first row.

4th row—* P8, K2, and repeat from * all round.

Repeat these 4 rounds for the pattern and continue till the work measures a depth of 3¾ inches from the beginning, finishing at the end of the 3rd round of the pattern.

Change to K1, P1 rib and work a depth of 4 ins.

Turn the work inside out and work a depth of 6 ins. in the pattern.

On the next round at the beginning of the round—work 2 sts. tog., then work along as far as the last 4 sts. and here work 2 sts. tog., K2.

Continue decreasing on each side of the same K2 sts. on every following 6th round till there are 10 sets of decreases in all.

60 sts. remain in the round.

Work quite straight for a depth of 3½ ins., finishing at the end of the round.

On the third needle K1, K2 tog., through the backs of the sts. and complete the needle.

Repeat the last 2 rounds 8 times more.
60 sts. remain on the needle.

For the heel KNIT the first 14 sts. of the round, then pass the last 16 sts. of the same round to the opposite end of the needle holding the 14 sts. already knitted.

Divide the remaining 30 sts. to 2 needles for the instep.

Continue over the heel sts., working 29 more rows in s.st.

Now turn the heel.

1st row—Knit over 18 sts., K2 tog., turn.

2nd row—P7, P2 tog., turn.

3rd row—K8, K2 tog., turn.

4th row—P9, P2 tog., turn.

5th row—K10, K2 tog., turn.

Continue in this way, working an extra st. on each successive row till all sts. are in one row again.

Knit back half the sts., thus completing the heel.

Now slip all the instep sts. to one needle.

Knit the remaining half of the heel sts., then knit up 15 sts., at the side of the heel.

With a second needle work across the instep sts. in the pattern.

With a third needle knit up 15 sts. at the side of the heel and the remaining heel sts.

Work one round quite straight, keeping the instep sts. in the pattern and the remaining sts. in s.st.

On the next round work as far as the last 3 sts. of the first needle, K2 tog., K1.

Work across the second needle in the pattern without shaping.

Work quite straight on these sts. for a depth of 6 ins.—or more or less according to the length of foot required.

Now change all sts. to s.st. for the working of the toe.

1st round—Knit every 9th and 10th st. tog., all round.

Knit 2 rounds without shaping.

4th round—Knit every 8th and 9th st. tog. all round.

Knit 2 rounds without shaping.

7th round—Knit every 7th and 8th st. tog. all round.

Knit 2 rounds without shaping.

Continue decreasing in this way on every following 3rd round, always with one st. fewer before the decreases on successive decrease rounds till 18 sts. remain on the needle.

Thread the wool through these sts., draw up and fasten off.

Make the second stocking in the same way.

TO COMPLETE THE HOSE

Fold the hose correctly then press on the right side lightly with a warm iron over a slightly damp cloth.

Fold the tops down to show a little of the ribbing at the top.

SLOPPY JOES

Materials
9 [9, 9] oz. PATONS BEEHIVE Fingering 3-ply, Patonised. Two No. 13 and two No. 11 BEEHIVE or QUEEN BEE needles. One set of four No. 13 and one set of four No. 11 BEEHIVE or QUEEN BEE needles with points at both ends. Two BEEHIVE stitch-holders.

Measurements
To fit 36 [38, 40] inch chest. Length from top of shoulder, 25½ ins. Sleeve seam, 6 ins.

Tension
8 sts. and 10 rows to one square inch on No. 11 needles, measured over stocking stitch.

Front
Using **two No. 13** needles and 3-ply (2-ply), cast on 140 [146, 152] sts.

Work in stocking stitch (1 row K., 1 row P.) for 20 rows.

Next row—Make hem by knitting tog. 1 st. from needle and one loop from cast-on edge all across row. **Next row**—K., thus making ridge.

Change to No. 11 needles and continue in stocking stitch (1 row K., 1 row P.) until work measures 17 (16) ins. from beg.

Shape armholes by casting off 9 [10, 11] sts. at beg. of next 2 rows.

Dec. 1 st. at both ends of next and every alt. row until 110 [112, 114] sts. remain. Continue in stocking stitch on these sts. until work measures 6 (5) ins. from beg. of armhole shaping, finishing at end of a P. row.

Next row—K.44 [46, 48], K.22 [20, 18] sts. on to a stitch-holder and leave, K. to end.

Proceed on each group of 44 [46, 48] sts. as follows:—

Dec. 1 st. at neck edge on next and every alt. row until 36 [38, 40] sts. remain. Continue on these sts. until work measures 8½ (7½) ins. from beg. of armhole shaping, finishing at armhole edge.

Shape shoulder as follows:—
1st row—Cast off 12 [12, 12] sts., work to end. **2nd row**—Work all across. **3rd row**—Cast off 12 [13, 13] sts., work to end. **4th row**—Work all across.
Cast off remaining sts. •

Back
Work as Front until armhole shaping is completed and there are 110 [112, 114] sts. on needle.

Continue on these sts. until work measures 8½ (7½) ins. from beg. of armhole shaping, finishing at end of a P. row.

Next row—Cast off 36 [38, 40] sts., K. next 38 [36, 34] sts. on to a stitch-holder and leave. Cast off remaining sts.

Sleeves
Using **two No. 13** needles and 3-ply (2-ply), cast on 86 sts.

Work in stocking stitch for 14 rows.

Next row—Make hem by knitting tog. 1 st. from needle and one loop from cast-on edge all across row. **Next row**—K., thus forming a ridge as on Front.

Change to No. 11 needles and proceed in stocking stitch inc. 1 st. at both ends of next and every following 3rd row until there are 114 sts. on needle. Continue on these sts. until work measures 6 (5½) ins. from beg.

Shape top by casting off 3 sts. at beg. of next 6 rows; 2 sts. at beg. of following 6 rows. Dec. 1 st. at both ends of next and every alt. row until 46 sts. remain.

Cast off 6 sts. at beg. of next 6 rows. Cast off.

Work another Sleeve in same manner.

Neckband
Using a back-stitch seam, join shoulders of Back and Front.

Using set of four No. 11 needles and 3-ply (2-ply) with right side of work facing, **knit up** 110 sts. round neck.

Proceed in rounds as follows:—
1st round—P., thus making ridge as on top of hem of Front. **2nd–5th rounds**—K.
6th–12th rounds—Using No. 13 needles, K.
13th–17th rounds—Using No. 11 needles, K.
Cast off loosely.

To Make Up
Press all pieces of work on wrong side, using a warm iron and damp cloth. Using a back-stitch seam, join side and sleeve seams and stitch sleeves into position, placing sleeve seam on woman's sweater **only**, ½ inch. to front of side seam. Using a flat seam, fold neckband along centre to wrong side of work and neatly stitch down cast-off to knitted-up edge. Press all seams.

RAGLAN SHIRT

● *loose-fitting and comfortable slip it on after a bathe*

Materials: 5 ozs. dark shade and 4 ozs. light shade of PATONS FAIR ISLE FINGERING. A pair each No. 11 and No. 12 "Beehive" needles.

Measurements: To fit 36–38-inch chest; length from top of shoulders, 25 ins.; sleeve seam, 7 ins.

Tension: 8 sts. to an inch on No. 11 needles unpressed.

BACK. With No. 11 needles and dark shade, cast on 150 sts. and knit 4 rows. Change to stocking-stitch, working 2 rows light shade and 2 rows dark throughout.

When side edge measures 15½ ins. start shaping raglan armholes. With right side facing and starting with a light stripe, decrease at each end of following 5 rows, then each end of every alternate row until 50 sts. remain. Leave these sts. on a spare needle.

FRONT. Work as for back until 66 sts. remain. Shape neck:—work 24, turn, k. 2 tog. at neck edge and continue on these sts., decreasing 1 st. at neck edge on every row, and at outer edge every other row until all sts. are worked off. Put centre 18 sts. on spare needle and work remaining 24 to match first shoulder.

SLEEVES
With No. 11 needles and dark shade, cast on 114 sts. and knit 4 rows. Work in stripes until side edge measures 7 ins.

Starting with a light stripe, shape top by decreasing at each end of next 5 rows then at each end of every alternate row until 14 sts. remain.

Leave remaining sts. on a spare needle and work second sleeve.

NECK BAND
Arrange sts. thus on a No. 12 needle, with right side of work facing and dark wool:— k. 14 from one sleeve, 50 from back, 14 from second sleeve, pick up and k. 14 from left side of neck, 18 from needle at front, 14 from other side of neck; turn and work 8 rows k. 2, p. 2 rib. Cast off loosely in rib.

TO MAKE UP
Press pieces lightly on wrong side under a damp cloth, avoiding rib. Join side, sleeve and raglan seams.

Made for two

A perfect partnership for a handsome pair

woman's own KNITTING for all the Family

16 PAGE PULL-OUT SUPPLEMENT

September 18th 1957

How to fold the Supplement

Pull out the centre 4 pages of the magazine and fold them back so that this page is outside. Fold again along the yellow border on the left. Trim along top of the Supplement with scissors.

RIB and plain stitch combine to give an effective zig-zag pattern to this perfect twosome. A deep ribbed border is doubled over at the neckline for the snuggest fit.

Materials.—23(19) ozs. of Sirdar double knitting wool, one pair each of No. 9 and 11 knitting needles, one set of No. 11 needles pointed at both ends.

Measurements.—Length 25(23) ins.; chest 44; bust 34-36 ins.; sleeve seam 20(18) ins.

N.B.—Follow the first figure for man's size, and second for woman's size.

Tension.—7 sts. and 8 rows to one inch in patt. on No. 9 needles.

PATTERN.—The whole jersey is knitted in the following patt.:—

1st row.—(P. 2, k. 2, p. 8, k. 2) to end of row.
2nd row.—(P. 2, k. 8, p. 2, k. 2) to end of row.
3rd row.—(P. 2, k. 8, p. 2, k. 2) to end of row.
4th row—(P. 2, k. 2, p. 8, k. 2) to end of row.
5th row.—(P. 8, k. 2, p. 2, k. 2) to end of row.
6th row.—(P. 2, k. 2, p. 2, k. 8) to end of row.
7th row.—K. 6, (p. 2, k. 2, p. 2, k. 8) 7(6) times, p. 2, k. 2, p. 2, k. 2.
8th row.—P. 2, k. 2, p. 2, k. 2, (p. 8, k. 2, p. 2, k. 2), 7(6) times, p. 6.
9th row.—P. 4, (k. 2, p. 2, k. 2, p. 8) 7(6) times, k. 2, p. 2, k. 2, p. 4.

10th row.—K. 4, p. 2, k. 2, p. 2, (k. 8, p. 2, k. 2, p. 2) 7(6) times, k. 4.
11th row.—K. 2, (p. 2, k. 2, p. 2, k. 8) 7(6) times, p. 2, k. 2, p. 2, k. 6.
12th row.—P. 6, k. 2, p. 2, k. 2, (p. 8, k. 2, p. 2, k. 2) 7(6) times, p. 2.
13th row.—(K. 2, p. 2, k. 2, p. 8) to end of row.
14th row.—(K. 8, p. 2, k. 2, p. 2) to end of row.
15th row.—(K. 2, p. 2, k. 8, p. 2) to end of row.
16th row.—(K. 2, p. 8, k. 2, p. 2) to end of row.
17th row.—(K. 2, p. 8, k. 2, p. 2) to end of row.
18th row.—(K. 2, p. 2, k. 8, p. 2) to end of row.
19th row.—(K. 8, p. 2, k. 2, p. 2) to end of row.
20th row.—(K. 2, p. 2, k. 2, p. 8) to end of row.
21st row.—P. 6, (k. 2, p. 2, k. 2, p. 8) 7(6) times, k. 2, p. 2, k. 2, p. 2.
22nd row.—K. 2, p. 2, k. 2, p. 2, (k. 8, p. 2, k. 2, p. 2) 7(6) times, k. 6.
23rd row.—K. 4, (p. 2, k. 2, p. 2, k. 8) 7(6) times, p. 2, k. 2, p. 2, k. 4.
24th row.—P. 4, k. 2, p. 2, k. 2, (p. 8, k. 2, p. 2, k. 2) 7(6) times, p. 4.
25th row.—P. 2 (k. 2, p. 2, k. 2, p. 8) 7(6) times, k. 2, p. 2, k. 2, p. 6.
26th row.—K. 6, p. 2, k. 2, p. 2, (k. 8, p. 2, k. 2, p. 2) 7(6) times, k. 2.
27th row.—(P. 2, k. 2, p. 2, k. 8) to end of row.
28th row.—(P. 8, k. 2, p. 2, k. 2) to end. These 28 rows complete patt. throughout.

FRONT.—Cast on 112(98) on No. 11 needles and work p. 2, k. 2 in rib for 3 ins. Change to No. 9 needles and begin patt. inc. at both ends of 9th and every foll. 4th row 20 times in all, working inc. sts. into patt. (152, 138). Cont. until work measures 14½(14) ins.

Cast off 8(6) at beg. of next 2 rows, 3 at beg. of next 2 rows. Then take 2 tog. at both ends of next 9(11) rows (112, 98). Cont. until work measures 22 (20½) ins.

Next row — Patt. 50(44), cast off 12(10), patt. 50(44). Cast off 5 at beg. of next 3 right side rows and cast off 2(1) at beg. of next 3(2) right side rows. Cast off 1 at beg. of next right side row and 9(8) at beg. of foll. wrong side row.

Rep. these last 2 rows twice.

Work second shoulder to match, reverse shapings.

BACK.—Work as for front until work measures 22(20½) ins., then cont. straight until back measures 24(22) ins.

Next row.—Patt. 47(44), cast off 18(10), patt. 47(44). Work back.

Next row.—Cast off 8 at beg. of next row and 9(8) at beg. of foll. row. Cast off 7 at beg. of next row and 9(8) at beg. of next row. Cast off 5 at beg. of next row and 9(8) at beg. of last row.

Work second shoulder to match, reversing shapings.

SLEEVE.—Cast on 70(56) on No. 11 needles and rib for 3 ins. Change to No. 9 needles and patt. and work 6 rows.

Inc. at both ends of next and every foll. 8th(6th) row 10(16) times, then on every 6th(4th) row 8(4) times (106, 96). When work measures 20(18) ins. cast off 8(6) at beg. of next 2 rows, then k. 2 tog. at both ends of next 10(5) right side rows, then at both ends of every row 25(27) times. Cast off 5 at beg. of last 4 rows.

TO MAKE UP.—Press all pieces very lightly under damp cloth, really only steaming work. Join shoulder seams. Set in sleeves. Join sleeve and side seams. With set of No. 11 needles pick up 70(60) from back and 82(68) from front and rib in k. 2, p. 2 for 3 ins.

Cast off fairly loosely in rib. Press seams. Fold over ribbed neckband and sew down neatly.

See colour plate on page 26

MAN'S PULLOVER

Chest Size: 39-41 inches

MATERIALS: 21 ozs. of Patons Moorland Double Knitting wool; 1 pair each No. 8 and No. 10 knitting needles; 2 buttons.

TENSION: Over the 6 and 1 rib, 11 sts. to 2 inches and 22 rows to 3 inches.

MEASUREMENTS: To suit a 39 to 41 inch chest size; length from shoulder, about 27 inches; sleeve seam (including turn back cuff), 22 inches.

ABBREVIATIONS: K., knit; p., purl; st., stitch; sts., stitches; rep., repeat; tog., together; inc., increase (by working twice into same st. before slipping it off left-hand needle); dec., decrease (by taking 2 sts. tog.); g.-st., garter-stitch (every row k.). Sts. in brackets must be worked along row to the extent stated after 2nd bracket.

THE BACK

* With No. 10 needles, cast on 98 sts., and work in k. 1, p. 1 ribs for 4 inches, but inc. 1 st. at end of last rib row.

Changing to No. 8 needles, proceed in pattern as follows :

1st pattern row: P. 1, (k. 6, p. 1) to end. **2nd pattern row:** K. 1, (p. 6, k. 1) to end. These 2 rows form the pattern. Rep. them 4 times more, then keeping continuity of the pattern, Inc. 1 st. at each end of the next row and every following 14th row until there are 107 sts. Work 39 rows straight after last inc. row. To shape armholes, dec. 1 st. at each end of the next 10 rows.*

Work 64 rows straight on the remaining 87 sts. Now shape neck.

Next row: Pattern 31 sts.; turn. Leaving remaining sts. on a spare needle, continue only on 1st set of sts. as follows: Dec. 1 st. at neck edge on each of the next 3 rows. Cast off.

With right side of work facing you, join wool to inner end of sts. on spare needle, cast off the next 25 sts., then pattern to end of row. Dec. 1 st. at neck edge on each of the next 3 rows. Work 1 row straight, then cast off.

THE FRONT

Work as given for back from * to *. Now commence shapings for neck.

Next row: Pattern 42 sts., k. 2 tog.; turn. Leaving remaining sts. on a spare needle, continue only on 1st set of sts. as follows :

** Dec. 1 st. at neck edge on next row and every following 4th row until 28 sts. remain. Work 15 rows straight.

Cast off **.

With right side of work facing you, join wool to inner end of sts. on spare needle and pattern to end of row. Now work as 1st side from ** to **.

THE SLEEVES (both alike)

With No. 10 needles, cast on 50 sts. and work in k. 1, p. 1 ribs for 4 inches.

Changing to No. 8 needles, work the 2 pattern rows as given for back 3 times, then keeping the continuity of the pattern, inc. 1 st. at each end of next row and every following 6th row until there are 92 sts. Work 5 rows after last inc.

MAN'S DOUBLE KNITTING
PULLOVER
39-41 inch Chest Size
21 ozs. Double Knitting Wool

WELDONS
KNITWEAR 4ᴅ.
A1027

row. To shape top, dec. 1 st. at each end of the next 4 rows, then dec. 1 st. at start only of the following 20 rows. Cast off remainder.

THE COLLAR

Front Sections (2 alike): With No. 8 needles, cast on 3 sts. and k. 1 row. Now working in g.-st., inc. 1 st. at end of next row and every following alternate row until there are 17 sts., then inc. 1 st. at end of every 4th row from preceding inc. until there are 32 sts. Work 17 rows straight. Cast off. (The long straight edge of each of these sections is the neck edge.)

Back Section: With No. 8 needles, cast on 39 sts. and work 18 rows g.-st. Now dec. 1 st. at each end of next row and every following 10th row until 33 sts. remain. Work 17 rows straight, then cast off. (The cast-off edge of this section is the neck edge.)

TO COMPLETE

Press work lightly on the wrong side with a warm iron over a damp cloth, avoiding the ribbing. Join shoulder seams, taking ¼ inch seam turnings. Sew sleeves into the armholes, then join side and sleeve seams. Oversew the *cast off* edges of the two front sections of collar to the *side* edges of back piece. Stitch collar to neck, arranging the narrow pointed ends to the centre front and taking ⅜ inch seam turnings on the wrong side. Fold the seam turning flat over to the inside of neck and catch-stitch down the edge. Press seam flat. Add a loop to the left edge of collar, about 2½ inches above base of centre front and another 2½ inches higher. Add buttons to opposite edge to correspond with the loops. Roll over collar.

GARDENING SWEATER

*sturdy pullover
in basket-stitch
for gardening
and golf—in
2 popular sizes*

MATERIALS: 13 (12) ozs. Patons Purple Heather Fingering 4-ply. A pair each No. 11 and No. 9 "Beehive" needles.

MEASUREMENTS: To fit 38–40 (36–38) inch chest; length from top of shoulders, 22½ inches; sleeve seam, 18½ inches.

TENSION: 6½ sts. and 8½ rows to an inch.

N.B.—Small size in brackets thus ( ). Where one set of figures is given this applies to both sizes.

BACK

With No. 11 needles cast on 132 (124) sts. and work 3½ inches k. 1, p. 1 rib.

Change to No. 9 needles and pattern. 1ST ROW: Right side facing, * k. 4, p. 4; repeat from * to last 4 sts., k. 4. 2ND ROW: p. 4, * k. 4, p. 4; repeat from * to end. 3RD ROW: As 1st. 4TH ROW: As 2nd. 5TH row: Knit. 6TH ROW: Purl. 7TH–8TH ROWS: As 5th and 6th. These 8 rows form pattern.

Continue straight in pattern until back measures 13½ inches at centre. With right side facing, shape armholes by casting off 11 (10) sts. at beginning of next 2 rows, then k. 2 tog. at each end of next and every following alternate row until 98 (92) sts. remain. Work straight until back measures 22 inches.

With right side facing, shape shoulders by casting off 10 (10) sts. at beginning of next 6 rows; slip remaining sts. on a spare needle.

FRONT

Work exactly as for back to end of armhole shapings, 98 (92) sts. remain. Work straight over all sts. in pattern until front measures 18 inches at centre.

With right side facing, divide for neck:—NEXT ROW: Pattern 38 (37) sts., turn and leave remaining sts. on a spare needle. Continue on first 38 (37) sts., decreasing 1 stitch at neck edge on next and every following 3rd row until 30 (30) sts. remain. Work straight until front matches back.

With right side facing, shape shoulder by casting off 10 (10) sts. at beg. of next and following 2 alternate rows, armhole edge.

Return to remaining sts. and slip centre 22 (18) sts. on a spare needle. Rejoin wool to last 38 (37) sts., neck edge, and work to correspond with first shoulder.

SLEEVES

With No. 11 needles cast on 60 sts. and work 3 inches k. 1, p. 1 rib. Change to No. 9 needles and pattern as for back, shaping sides by increasing 1 stitch at each end of 7th and every following 6th row until there are 96 sts., taking extra sts. into pattern as they are made. Work straight until sleeve measures 18½ inches or required length.

With right side facing, shape top by casting off 4 sts. at beginning of next 2 rows, then k. 2 tog. at beginning of every row until 56 sts. remain, then at each end of every row until 26 sts. remain. Cast off.

TO MAKE UP

Press parts lightly on wrong side under a damp cloth, taking care not to flatten the pattern. Join right shoulder seam. *Neck:* With right side facing and No. 11 needles, pick up and k. 116 (110) sts. all round neck, including those on spare needles at back and front. Work 1 inch k. 1, p. 1 rib; cast off in rib. Join left shoulder, side and sleeve seams; insert sleeves. Press all seams.

Fine-textured 3-ply · For pattern see page 115

Fair Isle set · For pattern see page 79

Fine for the courts · For patterns see page 118 (left) and page 124 (right)

Jazz Age jerseys · For patterns see page 22 (left) and page 10 (right)

MEASUREMENTS AND QUANTITIES

Chest Sizes	42 ins.	44 ins.	46 ins.
Length	21½ ins.	22 ins.	22 ins.
Sleeve	17 ins.	17 ins.	17 ins.

Emu SCOTCH 3-PLY FINGERING

	42	44	46
No. of ozs. for Sleeveless Pull-over ..	7	8	8
No. of ozs. with Sleeves	11	12	12

Emu BOTANY 3-PLY FINGERING

	42	44	46
No. of ozs. for Sleeveless Pull-over ..	7	7	7
No. of ozs. with Sleeves	11	11	12

One pair each Emu Jouvenia Knitting Needles Nos. 11 and 12.

THE WOOL CENTRE
10 THE WALK
IPSWICH

291

TENSION. 8½ sts. to 1 inch.

ABBREVIATIONS. K., knit : p., purl : st(s)., stitch(es) ; ins., inches.

THE BACK. Using No. 12 needles cast on 162 (170) (178) sts. Work in k. 1, p. 1 ribbing for 3½ ins., working last 2 sts. of last row together. Change to No. 11 needles.

1st row. * P. 1, k. 7. repeat from * to last st., p. 1.

2nd row. * K. 1, p. 7, repeat from * to last st., k. 1.

These 2 rows establish wider ribbing. Continue in wider ribbing, increasing at each end of 9th and every following 10th row until 179 (187) (195) sts. are on needle, working all extra sts. into pattern as they are made.

Continue without further shaping until back measures 12¾ (13) (13) ins. Cast off 8 sts. at beginning of next 2 rows, then decrease at each end of next 10 rows, and at beginning of following 6 rows. Continue on remaining 137 (145) (153) sts. until back measures 21½ (22) (22) ins. Cast off 15 sts. at beginning of next 4 rows, and 13 (15) (17) sts. at beginning of following 2 rows. Cast off remaining 51 (55) (59) sts.

THE FRONT. Work as for back until front measures 12 (12¼) (12¼) ins., (when 179 (187) (195) sts. will be on needle) ending on a wrong-side row.

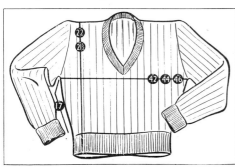

Next row. Work 89 (93) (97) sts. in pattern, cast off 1 st., work 89 (93) (97) sts. in pattern.

Leave sts. for left shoulder on a spare needle and continue on sts. for right shoulder, decreasing at neck on next and every following 4th row. Whilst neck shaping continues, commence armhole when front measures 12¾ (13) (13) ins. by casting off 8 sts. at beginning of next row to commence at side seam, afterwards decreasing at this edge on next 10 rows and on following 6 alternate rows.

When armhole shaping is completed, continue decreasing at neck edge every 4th row until only 43 (45) (47) sts. remain. afterwards working on these sts. until front measures 21½ (22) (22) ins. Cast off 15 sts. at beginning of next 2 rows to commence at side seam, then work 1 row. Cast off remaining 13 (15) (17) sts.

Return to sts. left on spare needle, and joining wool at neck edge work to match first shoulder.

THE SLEEVES. Using No. 12 needles cast on 97 (105) (113) sts. Work in k. 1, p. 1 ribbing for 3 ins., increasing 1 st. at end of last row. Change to No. 11 needles and work in wider ribbing given for back, increasing at each end of 4th and every following 5th row, working these extra sts. into pattern as they are made. When

147 (155) (163) sts. are on needle continue without further shaping until sleeve measures 17 ins. Cast off 8 sts. at beginning of next 2 rows, then decrease at each end of next 12 rows. Decrease at beginning of each row until 61 (69) (77) sts. remain, and then at each end of next 12 rows. Cast off remaining 37 (45) (53) sts.

NECK BAND. Join right shoulder seam. Using No. 12 needles and with right side of work toward you, pick up 84 (88) (88) sts. down left front neck edge, 1 st. at centre front, 84 (88) (88) sts. up right front neck edge, and 51 (55) (59) sts. across back neck.

Work in k. 1, p. 1 ribbing, decreasing either side of single st. exactly at centre front every right side row until neck band measures 1¼ ins. Cast off loosely ribwise. Join second shoulder seam.

ARMHOLE BANDS. (For sleeveless version.) Join second shoulder seam. Using No. 12 needles and with right side of work towards you pick up 160 (168) (168) sts. along armhole edge. Work in k. 1, p. 1 ribbing for 1¼ ins. Cast off loosely ribwise. Work second band to correspond.

TO COMPLETE GARMENT. Press with hot iron over damp cloth. Join side and —if necessary—sleeve seams, then set sleeves into armholes. Press again for final fabric finish.

See colour plate on page 98

3287

6^{D.}

In 2 sizes
To fit 38 to 39 inch and
40 to 41 inch Chest
28 or 29 ozs.
CHUBBY DOUBLE TWIST
or DOUBLE KNITTING

Ladyship
WOOLS

A LADYSHIP DESIGN

Man's Sweater (with Crew Neck)

(In two sizes, to fit 38-39 and 40-41 inch Chest)

MATERIALS REQUIRED:

28 [29] ozs. BALDWIN & WALKER'S LADYSHIP CHUBBY DOUBLE TWIST or DOUBLE KNITTING.

1 Pair each Knitting Needles Nos. 9 and 11. 1 4 4

A No. 9 Cable Needle.

Measurements:

Length from shoulder to lower edge, 25 ins.

Length of sleeve seam, 19½ ins.

Details for larger size are given in square brackets.

Where only one set of figures is given, this applies to both sizes.

Tension: 1 pattern (12 sts.) to 1½ ins. in width; 1 pattern (20 rows) to 2⅜ ins. in depth when pressed.

Note.—If the needles stated do not produce this tension, try different sizes until you get it correct.

Abbreviations: K, knit; P, purl; st., stitch; inc., increase by working into front and back of same st.; sl. st., slip stitch; beg., beginning; rep., repeat; ins., inches.

BACK

Using No. 11 needles, cast on 144 [154] sts.

1st row. K 2, * P 1, K 1, rep. from * to end. Rep. this row 16 times.

18th row. Small size. K 2, (P 1, K 1) twice, * inc. once in next st. purlways, (K 1, P 1) 4 times, K 1, rep. from * to last 8 sts., inc. once in next st. purlways, (K 1, P 1) 3 times, K 1. (158 sts.).
[Large size: K 2, (P 1, K 1) 3 times, * inc. once in next st. purlways, (K 1, P 1) 4 times, inc. once in next st. knitways, (P 1, K 1) 4 times, rep. from * to last 2 sts., P 1, K 1. (170 sts.).]

Change to No. 9 needles and proceed as follows:—

1st row. K 4, * P 6, K 6, rep. from * to last 10 sts., P 6, K 4.

2nd row. K 1, P 3, * K 6, P 6, rep. from * to last 10 sts., K 6, P 3, K 1.

3rd row. K 3, * sl. next st. on to a cable needle and let it fall to front of work, P 3, K st. from cable needle, sl. next 3 sts. on to a cable needle, let it fall to back of work, K 1, P 3 from cable needle, K 4, rep. from * ending with K 3 instead of K 4.

4th row. K 1, P 2, * K 3, P 2, K 3, P 4, rep. from * to last 11 sts., (K 3, P 2) twice, K 1.

5th row. K 2, * sl. next st. on to cable needle and let it fall to front of work, P 3, K st. from cable needle, K 2, sl. next 3 sts. on to cable needle, let it fall to back of work, K 1, P 3, from cable needle, K 2, rep. from * to end.

6th row. K 1, P 1, * K 3, P 4, K 3, P 2, rep. from * to last 12 sts., K 3, P 4, K 3, P 1, K 1.

7th row. K 1, * sl. next st. on to cable needle and let it fall to front of work, P 3, K st. from cable needle, K 4, sl. next 3 sts. on to cable needle and let it fall to back of work, K 1, P 3 from cable needle, rep. from * to last st., K 1.

Rep. 1st and 2nd rows twice, then 1st row once.

13th row. K 1, * sl. next 3 sts. on to cable needle, let it fall to back of work, K 1, P 3 from cable needle, K 4, sl. next st. on to cable needle, let it fall to front of work, P 3, K st. from cable needle, rep. from * to last st., K 1.

14th row. K 1, P 1, * K 3, P 4, K 3, P 2, rep. from * to last 12 sts., K 3, P 4, K 3, P 1, K 1.

15th row. K 2, * sl. next 3 sts. on to cable needle, let it fall to back of work, K 1, P 3, from cable needle, K 2, sl. next st. on to cable needle, let it fall to front of work, P 3, K. st. from cable needle, K 2, rep. from * to end.

16th row. K 1, P 2, * K 3, P 2, K 3, P 4, rep. from * to last 11 sts., (K 3, P 2) twice, K 1.

17th row. K 3, * sl. next 3 sts. on to cable needle, let it fall to back of work, K 1, P 3 from cable needle, sl. next st. on to cable needle, let it fall to front of work, P 3, K st. from cable needle, K 4, rep. from * ending with K 3 instead of K 4.

18th row. K 1, P 3, * K 6, P 6, rep. from * to last 10 sts., K 6, P 3, K 1.

19th row. K 4, * P 6, K 6, rep. from * to last 10 sts., P 6, K 4.

20th row. K 1, P 3, * K 6, P 6, rep. from * to last 10 sts., K 6, P 3, K 1.

These 20 rows form pattern.

Rep. from 1st to 20th row 5 times, from 1st to 7th row once, then 1st row once.

In next row. Cast off 12 sts. in pattern, P 4, * K 6, P 6, rep. from * to last 10 sts., K 6, P 3, K 1.

In following row. Cast off 12 sts. in pattern, K 4, * P 6, K 6, rep. from * to last 10 sts., P 6, K 4. **

Rep. 2nd row once, 1st row once, from 13th to 20th row once, then from 1st to 20th row 3 times.

Shape for Shoulder and Neck as follows:—

In next row. Cast off 10 [11] sts., in pattern, K 6 [5], P 6, K 6, P 6, K 5 [K 6, P 2, K 1] turn.

Work on these 29 [32] sts. as follows:—

1st row. Work in pattern to end.

2nd row. Cast off 10 [11] sts. in pattern, work in pattern to end.

Rep. 1st and 2nd rows once, then 1st row once. Cast off 9 [10] sts. in pattern, slip next 56 [60] sts. on to a length of wool, join in wool and K 5 [K 1, P 2, K 6], (P 6, K 6) twice, P 6, K 4 across remaining 39 [43] sts.

Shape for Shoulder as follows:—

1st row. Cast off 10 [11] sts. in pattern, work in pattern to end.

2nd row. Work in pattern to end. Rep. 1st and 2nd rows twice. Cast off 9 [10] sts. in pattern.

FRONT

Using No. 11 needles, cast on 144 [154] sts.

Work exactly as given for Back until ** are reached.

Rep. 2nd row once, 1st row once from 13th to 20th row once, then from 1st to 20th row twice.

In next row. K 4, (P 6, K 6) 4 [5] times, P 6, K 4 [P 1, K 1], turn.

Work in pattern on these 62 [66] sts. as follows:—

****1st row.* Cast off 3 sts. in pattern, work in pattern to end.

2nd row. Work in pattern to end. Rep. 1st and 2nd rows 4 times.

11th row. Cast off 2 sts. in pattern, work in pattern to end.

12th row. Work in pattern to end. Rep. 11th and 12th rows 3 times. (39 [43] sts.).

Work 1 row in pattern without shaping.

Shape for Shoulder as follows:—

1st row. Cast off 10 [11] sts. in pattern, work in pattern to end.

2nd row. Work in pattern to end.

Rep. 1st and 2nd rows twice. Cast off remaining 9 [10] sts. in pattern. ***

Slip next 10 [14] sts. on to a length of wool.

Join in wool and K 4 [K 1, P 1, K 6], (P 6, K 6) 4 times, P 6, K 4 across remaining 62 [66] sts.

In next row. K 1, P 3, (K 6, P 6) 4 times, K 6, P 3, K 1 [K 1, P 3, (K 6, P 6) 5 times, K 2].

In following row. Work in pattern to end.

Rep. from *** to *** as given for other side. Sew up Right Shoulder Seam.

NECK BAND

With right side of work facing, using No. 11 needles, commencing at Left Front Shoulder, knit up 30 sts. evenly down Left side of Neck; work in pattern across 10 [14] sts. at front of Neck; knit up 34 sts. evenly along other side of Neck; work in pattern across 56 [60] sts. at back of Neck; knit up 4 sts. along side of back Neck. (134 [142] sts.).

In next row. K 2, * P 1, K 1, rep. from * to end.

Rep. this row 16 times. Cast off in rib fairly loosely.

SLEEVE

Using No. 11 needles, cast on 66 sts.

1st row. K 2, * P 1, K 1, rep. from * to end. Rep. this row 26 times.

28th row. K 2, P 1, K 1, * inc. once in next st., purlways, K 1, P 1, inc. once in next st., knitways, P 1, K 1, rep. from * to last 2 sts., P 1, K 1. (86 sts.)

Change to No. 9 needles and rep. from 1st to 7th row once, as given for Back.

Proceed as follows:—

1st row. Inc. once in first st., K 3, * P 6, K 6, rep. from * to last 10 sts., P 6, K 2, inc. once in next st., K 1.

2nd row. K 1, P 4, * K 6, P 6, rep. from * to last 11 sts., K 6, P 4, K 1.

3rd row. K 5, * P 6, K 6, rep. from * to last 11 sts., P 6, K 5. Rep. 2nd and 3rd rows once.

6th row. K 2, * sl. next 3 sts. on to cable needle and let it fall to back of work, K 1, P 3 from cable needle, K 4, sl. next st. on to cable needle and let it fall to front of work, P 3, K st. from cable needle, rep. from * to last 2 sts., K 2.

7th row. Inc. once in first st., P 2, * K 3, P 4, K 3, P 2, rep. from * to last 13 sts., K 3, P 4, K 3, P 1, inc. once in next st., purlways, K 1.

8th row. K 4, * sl. next 3 sts. on to cable needle and let it fall to back of work, K 1, P 3, from cable needle, K 2, sl. next st. on to cable needle and let it fall to front of work, P 3, K st. from cable needle, K 2, rep. from * to last 2 sts., K 2.

9th row. K 1, P 4, * K 3, P 2, K 3, P 4, rep. from * to last st., K 1.

10th row. K 5, * sl. next 3 sts. on to cable needle and let it fall to back of work, K 1, P 3 from cable needle, sl. next st. on to cable needle and let it fall to front of work, P 3, K st. from cable needle, K 4, rep. from * to last st., K 1.

11th row. K 1, P 5, * K 6, P 6, rep. from * to last 12 sts., K 6, P 5, K 1.

12th row. * K 6, P 6, rep. from * to last 6 sts., K 6.

13th row. Inc. once in first st., P 5, * K 6, P 6, rep. from * to last 12 sts., K 6, P 4, inc. once in next st., purlways, K 1.

14th row. K 7, * P 6, K 6, rep. from * to last st., K 1.

15th row. K 1, * P 6, K 6, rep. from * to last 7 sts., P 6, K 1.

16th row. K 1, P 1, K 4, * sl. next st. on to cable needle and let it fall to front of work, P 3, K st. from cable needle, sl. next 3 sts. on to cable needle and let it fall to back of work, K 1, P 3 from cable needle, K 4, rep. from * to last 2 sts., P 1, K 1.

17th row. K 2, P 4, * K 3, P 2, K 3, P 4, rep. from * to last 2 sts., K 2.

18th row. K 1, P 2, K 2, * sl. next st. on to cable needle and let it fall to front of work, P 3, K st. from cable needle, K 2, sl. next 3 sts. on to cable needle and let it fall to back of work, K 1, P 3 from cable needle, K 2, rep. from * to last 3 sts., P 2, K 1.

19th row. Inc. once in first st., K 2, P 2, * K 3, P 4, K 3, P 2, rep. from * to last 3 sts., K 1, inc. once in next st., K 1.

20th row. K 2, P 3, * sl. next st. on to cable needle and let it fall to front of work, P 3, K st. from cable needle, K 4, sl. next 3 sts. on to cable needle and let it fall to back of work, K 1, P 3 from cable needle, rep. from * to last 5 sts., P 3, K 2.

21st row. K 1, P 1, * K 6, P 6, rep. from * to last 8 sts., K 6, P 1, K 1.

22nd row. K 2, * P 6, K 6, rep. from * to last 8 sts., P 6, K 2. Rep. 21st and 22nd rows once.

25th row. Inc. once in first st., P 1, * K 6, P 6, rep. from * to last 8 sts., K 6, inc. once in next st., purlways, K 1.

26th row. K 2, * sl. next st. on to cable needle and let it fall to front of work, P 3, K st. from cable needle, sl. next 3 sts. on to a cable needle and let it fall to back of work, K 1, P 3 from cable needle, K 4, rep. from * ending K 2 instead of K 4.

27th row. K 1, P 1, * K 3, P 2, K 3, P 4, rep. from * to last 10 sts., K 3, P 2, K 3, P 1, K 1.

28th row. K 1, * sl. next st. on to cable needle and let it fall to front of work, P 3, K st. from cable needle, K 2, sl. next 3 sts. on to cable needle and let it fall to back of work, K 1, P 3 from cable needle, K 2, rep. from * ending with K 1, instead of K 2.

29th row. K 4, * P 4, K 3, P 2, K 3, rep. from * to last 8 sts., P 4, K 4.

30th row. Sl. 1st st. on to cable needle and let it fall to front of work, K 1, P 2, K st. from cable needle, * K 4, sl. next 3 sts. on to cable needle and let it fall to back of work, K 1, P 3, from cable needle, sl. next st. on to cable needle and let it fall to front of work, P 3, K st. from cable needle, rep. from * to last 8 sts., K 4, sl. next 3 sts. on to cable needle and let it fall to back of work, K 1, then P 2, K 1 from cable needle.

31st row. Inc. once in 1st st., K 2, * P 6, K 6, rep. from * to last 9 sts., P 6, K 1, inc. once in next st., K 1.

32nd row. K 1, P 3, * K 6, P 6, rep. from * to last 10 sts., K 6, P 3, K 1.

33rd row. K 4, * P 6, K 6, rep. from * to last 10 sts., P 6, K 4. Rep. 32nd and 33rd rows once.

36th row. K 1, * sl. next 3 sts. on to cable needle and let it fall to back of work, K 1, P 3 from cable needle, K 4, sl. next st. on to cable needle and let it fall to front of work, P 3, K st. from cable needle, rep. from * to last st., K 1.

37th row. Inc. once in first st., P 1, * K 3, P 4, K 3, P 2, rep. from * to last 12 sts., K 3, P 4, K 3, inc. once in next st., purlways, K 1.

Continue in pattern, inc. once at each end of needle in every following 6th row (working all inc. sts. into pattern) until there are 112 sts. on needle, then in every following 4th row until there are 132 [134] sts. on needle.

Work 28 [24] rows in pattern without shaping.

Cast off 10 sts. in pattern at beg. of each of next 2 rows.

Cast off 10 [11] sts. in pattern at beg. of each of next 2 rows.

Cast off 11 sts. in pattern at beg. of each of next 6 rows.

Cast off remaining 26 sts. in pattern. Work another Sleeve in same manner.

TO MAKE UP

Using damp cloth and hot iron, press carefully on wrong side of work. Sew up side, left shoulder and neck band seam. Sew up sleeve seams to within 12 rows from top. Sew in sleeves, placing seam to seam, sewing the 12 rows to 12 cast-off sts. at back and front.

See colour plate on page 26

SOCKS AND SLIPOVER TO MATCH

SOCKS

MATERIALS: Of Patons Purple Heather Fingering 3-ply, 3 ozs. dark shade and 1 oz. light shade. A set each of four No. 11 and No. 12 "Beehive" needles, pointed both ends.

MEASUREMENTS: Length from top to bottom of heel, 12½ inches; length of foot 11 inches (adjustable).

TENSION: 8 stitches to an inch on No. 11 needles.

With dark shade and No. 12 needles cast on 72 sts. (24 on each needle) and work 3½ inches in rounds of k. 1, p. 1 rib. Change to pattern and No. 11 needles and work as follows:—

1ST ROUND: Knit in light. 2ND ROUND: In dark, * slip 1, k. 3; repeat from * to end. 3RD ROUND: As 2nd. 4TH ROUND: As 1st. 5TH ROUND: In dark, * slip 1, k. 5; repeat from * to end. 6TH ROUND: As 5th. These 6 rounds form pattern.

Continue in pattern until work measures about 10 inches, ending with 6th pattern round. Here divide for heel:—Slip 18 sts. from beginning of first needle and 18 from end of 3rd needle on to one needle (36 sts. for heel); divide remaining 36 sts. on 2 needles and leave for instep.

Heel: Change to No. 12 needles and join in dark. 1ST ROW: Wrong side facing, purl. 2ND ROW: * slip 1, k. 1; repeat from * to end. Repeat these 2 rows until piece measures 2¼ inches, ending with a purl row.

Turn heel:—1ST ROW: k. 21, k. 2 tog., k. 1, turn. 2ND ROW: sl. 1, p. 7, p. 2 tog., p. 1, turn. 3RD ROW: sl. 1, k. 8, k. 2 tog., k. 1, turn. 4TH ROW: sl. 1, p. 9, p. 2 tog., p. 1, turn. 5TH ROW: sl. 1, k. 10, k. 2 tog., k. 1, turn. 6TH ROW: sl. 1, p. 11, p. 2 tog., p. 1, turn.

7TH ROW: sl. 1, k. 12, k. 2 tog., k. 1, turn. 8TH ROW: sl. 1, p. 13, p. 2 tog., p. 1, turn. 9TH ROW: sl. 1, k. 14, k. 2 tog., k. 1, turn. 10TH ROW: sl. 1, p. 15, p. 2 tog., p. 1, turn. 11TH ROW: sl. 1, k. 16, k. 2 tog., k. 1, turn. 12TH ROW: sl. 1, p. 17, p. 2 tog., p. 1, turn. 13TH ROW: sl. 1, k. 18, k. 2 tog., k. 1, turn. 14TH ROW: sl. 1, p. 19, p. 2 tog., p. 1, turn. 15TH ROW: k. 22.

Now pick up and k. 15 sts. down side of heel piece, turn and p. 37, then pick up and p. 15 sts. down other side of heel, turn (52 sts.).

Shape instep by working backwards and forwards over these 52 sts. as follows:—1ST ROW: k. 1, sl. 1, k. 1, pass slipped stitch over, knit to last 3 sts., k. 2 tog., k. 1. 2ND ROW: Purl. Repeat last 2 rows until 34 sts. remain. Work straight in stocking-stitch in dark shade until foot measures 8¾ inches or required length (toe takes about 2¼ inches). Leave these stitches on a spare needle.

Return to instep stitches and continue on No. 11 needles as follows:—1ST ROW: Right side facing, in light, k. 2 tog., knit to end. 2ND ROW: In dark, p. 1, * slip 1, p. 3; repeat from * to last 2 sts., sl. 1, p. 1. 3RD ROW: In dark, k. 1, * sl. 1, k. 3; repeat from * to last 2 sts., sl. 1, k. 1. 4TH ROW: Purl in light. 5TH ROW: In dark, * k. 5, sl. 1; repeat from * to last 5 sts., k. 5. 6TH ROW: In dark, * p. 5, sl. 1; repeat from * to last 5 sts., p. 5. 7TH ROW: In light, knit.

Continue repeating rows 2–7 inclusive until piece measures same length as foot, ending with a row on wrong side and decreasing 1 stitch at end of last row (34 sts.).

Change to No. 12 needles and arrange two lots of 34 sts. on 3 needles thus: 34 on instep needle, 17 on 1st and 3rd needles. Work 2 knit rounds in dark then shape toe as follows:—

1ST ROUND: 1st needle: Knit to last 3 sts., k. 2 tog., k. 1. 2nd needle: k. 1, sl. 1, k. 1, p.s.s.o., knit to last 3 sts., k. 2 tog., k. 1. 3rd needle: k. 1, sl. 1, k. 1, p.s.s.o., knit to end. 2ND ROUND: Knit. Repeat these 2 rounds until 28 sts. remain. Divide stitches evenly on 2 needles and graft together.

Sew up foot seams; press socks under a damp cloth.

See colour plate on page 62

PULLOVER TO MATCH

MATERIALS: Of Patons Purple Heather Fingering 4-ply, 6 ozs. dark shade and 3 ozs. light shade both sizes. A pair each No. 12 and No. 9 "Beehive" needles.

MEASUREMENTS: To fit 36–38 (38–40)-inch chest; length from top of shoulders, 22 inches.

TENSION: See life-size close-up.

N.B.—Large size in brackets thus ( ). Where one set of figures is given this applies to both sizes.

BACK

Begin by winding dark shade into 2 balls; keep 1 ball at each end of needle to prevent rejoining on every third row.

With No. 12 needles and dark shade, cast on 130 (136) sts. and work 3½ inches k. 1, p. 1 rib, increasing on last row thus:—On small size increase 1 stitch; on large size 7 sts. evenly across [131 (143) sts.]. Leave dark shade hanging.

Change to No. 9 needles and pattern. 1ST ROW: Right side facing, knit in light (do not break off light—carry it up the edge until the next row in light). 2ND ROW: Join in 2nd ball of dark, * p. 3 dark, slip 1 purlways; repeat from * to last 3 sts., p. 3.

3RD ROW: In dark, * k. 3, slip 1; repeat from * to last 3 sts., k. 3. 4TH ROW: Purl in light. 5TH ROW: In dark, * k. 5, sl. 1; repeat from * to last 5 sts., k. 5. 6TH ROW: In dark, * p. 5, sl. 1 purlways; repeat from * to last 5 sts., p. 5. These 6 rows form pattern.

Continue straight in pattern until back measures 13 inches. With right side facing, shape armholes by casting off 12 (14) sts. at beginning of next 2 rows, then k. 2 tog. at each end of next and every following alternate row until 95 (103) sts. remain. Work straight until back measures 21½ ins.

With right side facing, shape shoulders by casting off 10 sts. at beginning of next 6 rows; cast off remainder.

FRONT

Work exactly as for back until first 2 rows of armhole shaping have been done; 107 (115) sts. remain. Here divide for neck:—

NEXT ROW: Right side facing, k. 2 tog., pattern 51 (55), turn and leave remaining stitches on a spare needle. Continue on first 52 (56) sts. decreasing 1 stitch at armhole edge on following 5 alternate rows, afterwards keep armhole edge straight, and at neck edge on next and every following 3rd row until 30 sts. remain.

Work straight until front matches back, then with right side facing, shape shoulder by casting off 10 sts. at beginning of next and following 2 alternate rows, armhole edge.

Join wool to remaining stitches neck edge, cast off 1, then work to correspond with left shoulder.

NECK & SLEEVE RIBBING

Join right shoulder seam. *Neck:* With right side facing, No. 12 needles and dark shade, pick up and k. 77 (81) sts. down left side of neck, 1 from centre front, 77 (81) up right side and 41 (43) across back of neck. Work 1¼ inches k. 1, p. 1 rib, decreasing 1 stitch either side of centre stitch on every row; cast off in rib.

Join left shoulder seam. *Armholes:* With right side facing, No. 12 needles and dark shade, pick up and k. 163 sts. round each armhole. Work 1¼ inches rib; cast off in rib.

TO MAKE UP

Press parts on wrong side under a damp cloth. Join side seams; press all seams.

MAN'S LUMBER JACKET

in **Wendy** Family Wool 4 ply to fit 38"/40" Chest

MATERIALS REQUIRED
14 ozs. WENDY FAMILY WOOL, 4 ply.
2 No. 8 and 2 No. 10 needles. 1 stitch-holder.
1 zip, 20 ins., open end. 2 4" zips.

MEASUREMENTS Length from top of shoulder, 21½ ins.
Chest 38/40 ins.
Sleeve seam 21 ins.

TENSION 6 sts. to 1 inch on No. 8 needles.

ABBREVIATIONS

K.—knit.	P.—purl.	sts.—stitches.
tog.—together.	beg.—beginning.	alt.—alternate.
ins.—inches.	inc.—increase.	dec.—decrease.
rept.—repeat.	st.st.—stocking stitch.	

THE RIGHT FRONT

Using No. 10 needles, cast on 50 sts. and work 4 ins. in K.1, P.1 rib.

Next Row. K.1, P.1 (inc. in next st., rib 4) 9 times, inc. in next st., K.1, P.1. (60 sts.).

Change to No. 8 needles and commence pattern.

1st Row. * K.10, P.10, rept. from * to the end of the row.

Rept. the 1st row 11 times more.

13th Row. * P.10, K.10, rept. from * to end of row.

Rept. the 13th row 11 times more.

These 24 rows form the pattern.

Next Row. K.10, P.4, cast off 26 sts., K.9, P.10.

Next Row. K.10, P.10, cast on 26 sts., K.4, P.10.

Keeping the pattern correct, continue until work measures 13 ins. from commencement.

Shape Armhole

Keeping the pattern correct, cast off 8 sts. at beg. of the next row, then K.2 tog. on the next and every alt. row 6 times.

Continue without further dec. until armhole measures 6 ins. from commencement, finishing at front edge.

Shape Neck

Next Row. Cast off 8 sts., pattern to end.

Next Row. Pattern to end.

Cast off 2 sts. at neck edge on every other row 3 times.

Continue in pattern without further dec. until armhole measures 8½ ins. from commencement, finishing at armhole edge.

Shape Shoulder

1st & 3rd Rows. Cast off 10 sts., pattern to end.

2nd & 4th Rows. Pattern to end.
Cast off.

THE LEFT FRONT

Using No. 10 needles, cast on 50 sts. and work to correspond with Right Front, reading the rows from end to beginning.

THE BACK

Using No. 10 needles, cast on 110 sts. and work 4 ins. in K.1, P.1 rib.

Next Row. Rib 7 (inc. in next st., rib 4) 19 times, inc. in next st., rib 7. (130 sts.).

Change to No. 8 needles and commence pattern.

1st Row. * K.10, P.10, rept. from * to last 10 sts., K.10.

2nd Row. * P.10, K.10, rept. from * to last 10 sts., P.10.

Rept. the 1st and 2nd rows 5 times more.

13th Row. * P.10, K.10, rept. from * to last 10 sts., P.10.

14th Row. * K.10, P.10, rept. from * to last 10 sts., K.10.

Rept. 13th and 14th rows 5 times more.

Keeping pattern correct, continue until work measures 13 ins. from commencement.

Shape Armhole

Cast off 8 sts. at beg. of next 2 rows, then K.2 tog. at beg. and end of the needle on the next and every alt. row 6 times. (102 sts.).

Continue without further dec. until armhole measures 9 ins. from commencement.
Cast off.

SLEEVES (Both Alike)

Using No. 10 needles, cast on 70 sts. and work 4 ins. in K.1, P.1 rib.

Change to No. 8 needles and commence pattern.

1st Row. * K.10, P.10, rept. from * to last 10 sts., K.10.

2nd Row. * P.10, K.10, rept. from * to last 10 sts., P.10.

Rept. these 2 rows 5 times more.

13th Row. * P.10, K.10, rept. from * to last 10 sts., P.10.

14th Row. * K.10, P.10, rept. from * to last 10 sts., K.10.

Keeping the pattern correct, inc. 1 st. each end of the needle on the next and every 6th row from previous inc. until 108 sts. are on the needle, working all inc. sts. into pattern. Continue without further inc. until work measures 21 ins. from commencement.

Shape Top

Cast off 8 sts. at beg. of next 2 rows.

K.2 tog. each end of the needle on the next and every 3rd row 6 times, then K.2 tog. each end of

the needle on every alt. row 10 times. Cast off 3 sts. at beg. of the next 6 rows.
Cast off.
Work another sleeve in the same manner.

THE COLLAR

Using No. 10 needles, cast on 140 sts. and work 3¼ ins. in K.1, P.1 rib.

Next Row. Rib to last 30 sts., turn.

Next Row. Rib to last 30 sts., turn.

Next Row. Rib 70, turn.

Next Row. Rib 60, turn.

Next Row. Rib 50, turn.

Continue in this manner, working 10 less sts. every row until the row Rib 20, turn, rib to end of row, has been worked.

Work 2 rows in K.1, P.1 rib.
Cast off in rib.

THE POCKETS (Both Alike)

Using No. 10 needles, cast on 26 sts. and work 2½ ins. in st.st. (1 row plain, 1 row purl). Cast on 5 sts. at beg. of the next two rows, and continue in st.st. until work measures 3½ ins. from commencement.

Cast off.
Work another pocket in the same manner.

TO MAKE UP

To obtain the perfect fitting garment, it is *important* to follow these instructions when making up the garment.

With wrong side of work facing, pin out all pieces to measurements given. Using a hot iron and damp cloth, press carefully.

Join shoulder seams by placing together and neatly back-stitching. Join side and sleeve seams in the same manner, omitting all ribbing. Join rib by top sewing. Pin sleeves into position, **placing sleeve seam ½ in. to front of side seam, and back-stitch.**

Pin zip to fronts and neatly back-stitch. Pin pocket zips into position, placing the open end of zip to front edge of pocket, and slip-stitch. Pin collar into position, placing cast-off edge to neck edge and side edges either side of the zip. Sew on by top sewing.

Pin pocket linings into position with the wrong side of work facing, and the 5 cast-on sts. at the top over the zip. Neatly slip-stitch all round. Press all seams flat.

See colour plate on page 28

Wendywear
NUMBER **487**
38"/40" CHEST
SIXPENCE

Collegian   *Argyle Slipover*

The Argyle design for men's Sweaters is a National favorite. It's a Sweater for young men and men who are always young. The colors are Gray, Medium and Dark Blue, with just a dash of Red. Made of Minerva Sports Yarn.

Sizes: 38 to 40 and 42 to 44

MATERIALS REQUIRED:

Minerva Sports Yarn (2 ounce ball)

	Size 38 to 40	Size 42 to 44
Navy	1 Ball	1 Ball
Medium Blue	1 Ball	1 Ball
Scarlet	1 Ball	1 Ball
Gray	5 Balls	6 Balls

Knitting Needles: 1 Pair Standard Size 2—14 inch
1 Pair Standard Size 3—14 inch
Gauge: 8 Sts. to 1 inch
1 Blunt End Tapestry Needle (Size 3 Needle)

Symbols for Argyle Pattern Chart
A—Medium Blue   X—Scarlet
N—Navy   O—Navy   } For Duplicate St.
        M—Gray (Background)

The sweater is worked in Stockinette St. with the diagonal stripes, (O and X) worked in Duplicate St. after the Front is completed.
1 Row on the Chart—means 2 rows (K. across and P. back same colors).

FRONT: With Size 2 Needles and Gray cast on

128 Sts.	148 Sts.

Work in Ribbing of K. 2, P. 2, for

	1¼″	2″
increasing	8 Sts.	22 Sts.
across last row.	(increase 1 St. in every 15th St.)	(increase 1 St. in every 6th St.)
Sts. on needle:	136 Sts.	170 Sts.

Change to Size 3 Needles and work from Chart, working Pattern

2 times	2½ times

across row.
Do not carry yarn across back of work but wind Color A, N and M in small balls, using 1 ball for each diamond across.
Work first 2 rows as follows:

Row 1—1 A, 32 M, 2 N (tie on 2nd ball of M) 32 M, (tie on 2nd ball of A) 2A, (tie on 3rd ball of M) 32 M, (tie on 2nd ball of N) 2 N, (tie on 4th ball of M) 32 M, (tie on 3rd ball of A). On Size 38 to 40 end 1A; on Size 42 to 44, 2A, (tie on 5th ball of M, 32 M, (tie on 3rd ball of N) end 1 N.
Row 2—P. back in same manner (always being careful to pick up new color from underneath the dropped color).

Continue from Chart (66 rows to complete 1 diamond), for

2¼ diamonds	2½ diamonds

to underarm

To Shape Armholes: Bind off

8 Sts.	14 Sts.

at beginning of each of the next 2 rows then decrease 1 St. each side every other row

10 times	12 times

When Armhole measures

5½″	6″

(measure straight up from bound off Sts. at underarm).
To Shape Neck: Work across

40 Sts.	46 Sts.
(Slip remaining 60 Sts.	72 Sts.

on St. holder), work Left Shoulder. Decrease 1 St. at neck edge every other row 10 times.

When armhole measures

7½″	8″

To Shape Shoulder: Bind off

10 Sts.	12 Sts.

every other row 3 times.
Leaving

20 Sts.	26 Sts.

at center front on St. Holder, work Right Shoulder to correspond. With Tapestry Needle and strand of Navy or Scarlet yarn work Duplicate St. from chart.
With Size 2 Needles and Gray pick up and K.

92 Sts.	96 Sts.

at Neck Edge (including the Sts. on the St. Holder).

Duplicate Stitch

Work in Ribbing of K. 2, P. 2, for ¾ inch, bind off loosely in Ribbing.

BACK: With Size 2 Needles and Gray cast on

| 128 Sts. | 132 Sts. |

Work Ribbing same as Front increasing

| 8 Sts. | 12 Sts. |

across last row.

Sts. on Needle: 136 Sts.   144 Sts.

Change to Size 3 Needles and work in Stockinette St. same length as Front to underarm.

To Shape Armholes: Bind off

| 8 Sts. | 6 Sts. |

at beginning of each of the next 2 rows, then decrease 1 St. each side every other row 10 times.

When Armhole measures

| 7½" | 8" |

bind off   10 Sts.   12 Sts.

at beginning of each of the next 6 rows. Slip remaining Sts. on Size 2 Needles and work in Ribbing of K. 2, P. 2, for ¾ inch, bind off loosely in Ribbing.

SLEEVES: With Size 2 needles and Gray cast on

| 56 Sts. | 62 Sts. |

Work in Ribbing of K. 2, P. 2, for

| 2" | 3" |

increasing 16 Sts. across last row.

Change to Size 3 needles and work in Stockinette St.

Work even for 3 inches, then increase 1 St. each side, then increase 1 St. each side every inch

| 11 times | 12 times |

When Sleeve measures

| 19" | 20" |

(or desired length to underarm), bind off 8 Sts. at beginning of each of the next 2 rows then decrease 1 St. each side every other row   12 times   16 times

then 1 St. each side every row

| 12 times | 14 times |

bind off remaining Sts.

Sew shoulder seams, sew sleeves in place, sew underarm and sleeve seams.

Fishing Story

The patterns on this 4-ply sweater are based on the elaborate stitches traditionally used on fisherman's sweaters —or bridal shirts

MATERIALS

15 oz. PATONS BEEHIVE Fingering 4-ply, Patonised, or 18 oz. PATONS PURPLE HEATHER Fingering 4-ply. Two No. 13 and two No. 11 BEEHIVE or QUEEN BEE needles, set of four No. 13 QUEEN BEE needles with points at both ends, measured by BEEHIVE gauge. Two BEEHIVE stitch-holders.

 # 1 + 2

MEASUREMENTS

To fit 40–42 inch chest. Length from shoulder to lower edge, 25½ ins. Sleeve seam, 18½ ins.

TENSION

7½ sts. and 9½ rows to one square inch on No. 11 needles, measured over stocking stitch.

ABBREVIATIONS

K.=knit; P.=purl; K.B.=knit into back of stitch; P.B.=purl into back of stitch; st.=stitch; inc.=increase by working into front and back of stitch; dec.=decrease by working 2 sts. together; beg.=beginning; alt. =alternate; rep.=repeat; patt.= pattern; incl.=inclusive; ins.=inches; D.=Dark; L.=Light.

BRACKETS

The figures in square brackets [ ] refer to the medium and large sizes respectively.

Instructions in the round brackets to be repeated the number of times stated after the round brackets and all instructions in square brackets to be repeated the number of times stated after the square brackets.

BACK

Using No. 13 needles, cast on 150 sts.

Work in K.1, P.1 rib for 3 ins., inc. 1 st. at both ends of last row (152 sts.).

Change to No. 11 needles and work **ridge patt. band** as follows:—

1st and 2nd rows—K.
3rd to 5th rows—P.
6th row—K.
Proceed for **first panel** as follows:—

1st row—[K.B.2, P.1, (K.2, P.2) 6 times, K.2, P.1] 5 times, K.B.2.
2nd row—[P.B.2, K.1, (P.2, K.2) 6 times, P.2, K.1] 5 times, P.B.2.
3rd row—[K.B.2, K.28] 5 times, K.B.2.
4th row—[P.B.2, P.28] 5 times, P.B.2.
5th to 24th rows— Rep. 1st to 4th rows 5 times.
Work rows 1 to 6 ridge patt.
Proceed for **second panel** as follows:—
1st row—[K.B.2, P.1, K.26, P.1] 5 times, K.B.2.
2nd row—[P.B.2, P.28] 5 times, P.B.2.
3rd row—[K.B.2, P.1, K.12, P.2, K.12, P.1] 5 times, K.B.2.
4th row—[P.B.2, P.12, K.4, P.12] 5 times, P.B.2.
5th row—[K.B.2, P.1, K.10, P.2, K.2, P.2, K.10, P.1] 5 times, K.B.2.
6th row—[P.B.2, P.10, K.2, P.4, K.2, P.10] 5 times, P.B.2.
7th row—[K.B.2, P.1, K.8, P.2, K.6, P.2, K.8, P.1] 5 times, K.B.2.
8th row—[P.B.2, P.8, K.2, P.8, K.2, P.8] 5 times, P.B.2.

9th to 11th rows—Continue movement of diamond in this manner until:—
12th row—[P.B.2, P.4, K.2, P.16, K.2, P.4] 5 times, P.B.2.
13th row—[K.B.2, P.1, K.3, P.2, K.16, P.2, K.3, P.1] 5 times, K.B.2.
14th row—[P.B.2, P.5, K.2, P.14, K.2, P.5] 5 times, P.B.2.
15th row—[K.B.2, P.1, K.5, P.2,

K.12, P.2, K.5, P.1] 5 times, K.B.2.
16th to 21st rows—Continue movement of diamond in this manner until:—
22nd row—[P.B.2, P.13, K.2, P.13] 5 times, P.B.2.
23rd and 24th rows—As 1st and 2nd.
Work rows 1 to 6 ridge patt.
Proceed for **third panel** as follows:—
1st row—[K.B.2, (K.3, P.2) 5 times, K.3] 5 times, K.B.2.
2nd row—[P.B.2, K.1, (P.3, K.2) 5 times, P.2] 5 times, P.B.2.
3rd row—[K.B.2, K.1, (P.2, K.3) 5 times, P.2] 5 times, K.B.2.
4th row—[P.B.2, P.1, (K.2, P.3) 5 times, K.2] 5 times, P.B.2.
5th row—[K.B.2, P.1, (K.3, P.2) 5 times, K.2] 5 times, K.B.2.
6th to 24th rows—Keeping diagonal movement correct, work 19 rows.

Work rows 1 to 6 ridge patt.
Proceed for **fourth panel** as follows:—

1st row—[K.B.2, (P.1, K.1) 14 times] 5 times, K.B.2.
2nd row—[P.B.2, (K.1, P.1) 14 times] 5 times, P.B.2.
3rd to 24th rows—Rep. 1st and 2nd rows 11 times.
Work rows 1 to 6 ridge patt.

Proceed for **fifth panel** as follows:—
1st row—[K.B.2, K.28] 5 times, K.B.2.
2nd row—[P.B.2, P.28] 5 times, P.B.2.
3rd row—[K.B.2, K.2, (P.2, K.4) 4 times, P.2] 5 times, K.B.2.
4th row—[P.B.2, P.1, (K.2, P.4) 4 times, K.2, P.1] 5 times, P.B.2.
5th row—[K.B.2, (P.2, K.4) 4 times, P.2, K.2] 5 times, K.B.2.
6th row—[P.B.2, P.3, (K.2, P.4) 4 times, K.1] 5 times, P.B.2.
7th row—[K.B.2, (K.4, P.2) 4 times, K.4] 5 times, K.B.2.
8th row—[P.B.2, K.1, (P.4, K.2) 4 times, P.3] 5 times, P.B.2.
9th to 11th rows—As 3rd to 5th.
12th row—K.
13th row—P.
14th row—[P.B.2, P.2, (K.2, P.4) 4 times, K.2] 5 times, P.B.2.
15th row—[K.B.2, K.1, (P.2, K.4) 4 times, P.2, K.1] 5 times, K.B.2.
16th row—[P.B.2, (K.2, P.4) 4 times, K.2, P.2] 5 times, P.B.2.
17th row—[K.B.2, K.3, (P.2, K.4) 4 times, P.1] 5 times, K.B.2.
18th row—[P.B.2, (P.4, K.2) 4 times, P.4] 5 times, P.B.2.
19th row—[K.B.2, P.1, (K.4, P.2) 4 times, K.3] 5 times, K.B.2.
20th to 22nd rows—As 14th to 16th.
23rd and 24th rows—As 1st and 2nd.
Work rows 1 to 6 ridge patt.
Proceed for **sixth panel** as follows:—
1st row—[K.B.2, (P.2, K.2) 7 times,] 5 times, K.B.2.
2nd row—[P.B.2, (K.2, P.2) 7 times,] 5 times, P.B.2.
3rd to 24th rows—Rep. 1st and 2nd rows 11 times.
Work rows 1 to 6 ridge patt.
Keeping sequence of panel patt. and ridge patt. correct throughout, continue on these sts. until work measures 23¼ ins. (slightly stretched) from beg.

Shape back of neck as follows:—
Next row—Patt. 65, patt. next 22 sts. on to a stitch-holder, patt. 65.
Proceed on **each** group of 65 sts. as follows:—
Dec. 1 st. at neck edge on every row until 57 sts. remain.

Continue on these sts. until work measures 25 ins. (slightly stretched) from beg., finishing at side edge.
Shape shoulder by casting off 19 sts. at beg. of next and every alt. row until all sts. are cast off.

FRONT

Proceed as on Back until work measures 22¾ ins. from beg.
Shape neck and complete as on Back, **noting** that neck dec. are worked on every **alt.** row in place of every row.

SLEEVES

Using No. 13 needles, cast on 70 sts. Work in K.1, P.1 rib for 3 ins.
Next row—Rib 7, (inc. in next st., rib 10) 5 times, inc. in next st., rib to end (76 sts.).
Change to No. 11 needles and proceed in stocking stitch, inc. 1 st. at both ends of 6th and every following 7th row until there are 92 sts., every following 6th row until there are 112 sts. Work 5 rows.
Shape gusset by inc. 1 st. at both ends of next and every alt. row until there are 140 sts.
Shape top by casting off 8 sts. at beg. of next 12 rows. Cast off.

NECKBAND

Using a back-stitch seam join shoulders of Back and Front.
Using set of No. 13 needles with right side of work facing, **knit up** 136 sts. round neck including sts. from stitch-holders.
Work in rounds of K.1, P.1 rib for 2¼ ins. Cast off **loosely** in rib.

TO MAKE UP

Omitting ribbing, with wrong side of work facing block each piece by pinning out round edges. Omitting ribbing, press each piece **very lightly** using a warm iron and damp cloth. Using a flat seam for ribbing and a back-stitch seam for remainder join sleeve seams and side seams to 9½ ins. from shoulder. Stitch Sleeves into position. Fold Neckband at centre and flat stitch on wrong side to form hem. Press seams.

Figured in 4-ply

rib, cable and all-over pattern

combine to make a richly surfaced fabric

MATERIALS

14 oz. PATONS BEEHIVE Fingering 4-ply, Patonised, or 17 oz. PATONS PURPLE HEATHER Fingering 4-ply. Two No. 12 and two No. 10 BEEHIVE or QUEEN BEE needles, measured by BEEHIVE gauge. A BEEHIVE cable needle.

#2 + 3 needles

MEASUREMENTS

To fit 40–42 inch chest. Length from top of shoulder, 24 ins. Sleeve seam, 18½ ins.

These instructions apply to the above measurements only; adaptations to other sizes are not available.

TENSION

7 sts. and 9 rows to one square <u>inch</u> on No. 10 needles, measured over stocking stitch.

ABBREVIATIONS

K.=knit; P.=purl; st.=stitch; tog. =together; inc.=increase by working into front and back of stitch; dec. =decrease by working 2 sts. together; beg.=beginning; alt.=alternate; rep. =repeat; patt.=pattern; incl.=inclusive; ins.=inches; C.3=Cable 3 by working across next 6 sts. as follows:—Slip next 3 sts. on to cable needle and leave at front of work, knit next 3 sts. then knit 3 sts. from cable needle.

BRACKETS

Instructions in the round brackets to be repeated the number of times stated after the round brackets and all instructions in square brackets to be repeated the number of times stated after the square brackets.

FRONT AND BACK
(Both alike)

Using No. 12 needles, cast on 140 sts. Work in K.1, P.1 rib for 3 ins.

Next row—Rib 9, (inc. in next st., rib 14) 8 times, inc. in next st., rib to end (149 sts.).

Change to No. 10 needles and proceed in patt. as follows:—

1st row—(K.2, P.2) twice, K.2, [P.2, K.6, P.2, (K.1, P.1) 5 times, K.1, P.2, K.6, P.2, (K.2, P.2) 4 times, K.2] twice, P.2, K.6, P.2, (K.1, P.1) 5 times, K.1, P.2, K.6, P.2, (K.2, P.2) twice, K.2.

2nd row—(P.2, K.2) twice, P.2, K.2, P.6, K.2, (P.1, K.1) 5 times, P.1, [K.2, P.6, K.2, (P.2, K.2) 4 times, P.2, K.2, P.6, K.2, (P.1, K.1) 5 times, P.1] twice, K.2, P.6, K.2, (P.2, K.2) twice, P.2.

3rd row—(P.2, K.2) twice, P.2, [P.2, K.6, P.2, (K.1, P.1) 5 times, K.1, P.2, K.6, P.2, (P.2, K.2) 4 times, P.2] twice, P.2, K.6, P.2, (K.1, P.1) 5 times, K.1, P.2, K.6, P.2, (P.2, K.2) twice, P.2.

4th row—(K.2, P.2) twice, K.4, P.6, K.2, (P.1, K.1) 5 times, P.1, [K.2, P.6, K.2, (K.2, P.2) 4 times, K.4, P.6, K.2, (P.1, K.1) 5 times, P.1] twice, K.2, P.6, K.2, (K.2, P.2) twice, K.2.

5th row—As 1st row, reading "C.3" in place of "K.6" all across row.

6th row—As 2nd row.

7th and 8th rows—As 3rd and 4th. These 8 rows form the patt.

Continue in patt. until work measures 15½ ins. from beg., finishing so that right side of work will be facing when working next row.

Shape armholes by casting off 2 sts. at beg. of next 14 rows (121 sts.).

Change to No. 12 needles and K. 11 rows.

Next row—K.2 tog., K.59, K.2 tog., K. to last 2 sts., K.2 tog. (118 sts.).

Change to No. 10 needles and proceed for **Yoke patt.** as follows:—

1st row—* K.2, P.2, rep. from * to last 2 sts., K.2.

2nd row—* P.2, K.2, rep. from * to last 2 sts:, P.2.

3rd row—* P.2, K.2, rep. from * to last 2 sts., P.2.

4th row—* K.2, P.2, rep. from * to last 2 sts., K.2.
These 4 rows form the patt.

Continue in patt. until work measures 8½ ins. from beg. of armhole shaping, finishing so that right side of work will be facing when working next row.

Shape shoulders by casting off 9 sts. at beg. of next 6 rows (64 sts.).

Work 8 rows in K.1, P.1 rib.

Cast off in rib.

SLEEVES

Using No. 12 needles, cast on 64 sts. Work in K.1, P.1 rib for 3 ins.

Next row—Rib 6, (inc. in next st., rib 3) 13 times, inc. in next st., rib to end (78 sts.).

Change to No. 10 needles and proceed in yoke patt., inc. 1 st. at both ends of 5th and every following 8th row until there are 100 sts., every following 6th row until there are 112 sts.

Continue on these sts. until work measures 18½ ins. from beg.

Shape top by casting off 2 sts. at beg.

of next 14 rows. Dec. 1 st. at both ends of every row until 74 sts. remain, every alt. row until 64 sts. remain, then every following 3rd row until 48 sts. remain. Cast off 6 sts. at beg. of next 6 rows. Cast off.

TO MAKE UP

Omitting K.1, P.1 rib, with wrong side of work facing block each piece by pinning out round edges. Omitting K.1, P.1 rib, press each piece **very lightly** using a warm iron and damp cloth. Using a flat seam for ribbing and a back-stitch seam for remainder join shoulder, side and sleeve seams and stitch Sleeves into position. Fold over 8 rows of rib at neck and flat stitch on wrong side to form hem. Press seams.

MAN'S NORWEGIAN SWEATER (3 sizes)

MATERIALS

15 [16] [17] ozs. Sirdar Double Knitting Wool. Main Colour.
4 [4] [4] ozs. Sirdar Double Knitting Wool. Dark.
1 pair No. 10 and No. 8 Knitting Needles.

MEASUREMENTS

Width all round at underarm—34 [36] [38] inches.
Length from top of shoulder—24 [24] [24] inches.
Length of sleeve seam—19½ [19½] [19½] inches.
N.B. The colour not in use should be woven loosely across the back of the work to retain the elasticity of the fabric.

THE BACK

Using the No. 10 needles and M.C. wool cast on 101 [107] [113] sts.
1st ROW. Sl.1, k.1, * p.1, k.1, repeat from * to the last st., k.1.
2nd ROW. Sl.1, * p.1, k.1, repeat from * to end of row.
Repeat the 1st and 2nd rows 15 times increasing once at the end of the last row. 102 [108] [114] sts.
Change to No. 8 needles and proceed as follows:
1st ROW. Sl.1, knit to end of row.
2nd ROW. Sl.1, purl to the last st., k.1.
Repeat the 1st and 2nd rows once.
Join in the D. wool and working the 1st and 2nd rows of stitch diagram "A" proceed as follows:
1st ROW. * K.3 D., 3 M.C., repeat from * to end of row.
2nd ROW. * P.1 D., 1 M.C., 3 D., 1 M.C., repeat from * to end of row.
Commencing with the 3rd row, proceed as shown on stitch diagram "A" changing the colours when necessary until the 28th row has been worked.

STITCH DIAGRAM "A"

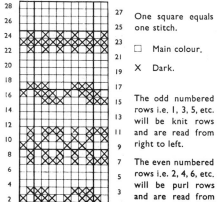

27 One square equals one stitch.

☐ Main colour.

X Dark.

The odd numbered rows i.e. 1, 3, 5, etc. will be knit rows and are read from right to left.

The even numbered rows i.e. 2, 4, 6, etc. will be purl rows and are read from left to right.

Join in the D. wool and repeat from the 1st to the 28th row (inclusive) of stitch diagram "A" once then from the 1st to the 20th row (inclusive) once.
Join in the D. wool and proceed as follows:
1st ROW. * K.1 D., 1 M.C., repeat from * to end of row.
Break off the M.C. wool.
2nd ROW. K.1, purl to the last st., k.1.
Join in the M.C. wool and repeat the 1st row once.
4th ROW. * P.1 D., 1 M.C., repeat from * to end of row.
Break off the D. wool.
Work 2 rows in st.st.
Break off the M.C. wool.

The Armhole

Slip the first 10 [10] [10] sts. on to a safety pin, rejoin the M.C. wool to the remaining 92 [98] [104] sts. and knit to the last 10 [10] [10] sts. slip these sts. on to a safety pin. 82 [88] [94] sts.
Proceed as follows for all 3 sizes:
NEXT ROW. Sl.1, purl to the last st., k.1.
If the stags are to be worked in Continental Embroidery work the following 39 rows in st.st.
If the stags are to be worked in Fair Isle proceed as follows:
Join in a ball of D. wool and proceed as follows:
1st ROW. Sl.1, k.6 [9] [12], working across the 1st row of stitch diagram "B" k.5 M.C., 2 D., 10 M.C., 2 D., 1 M.C., 2 D., 24 M.C., join in a second ball of D. wool, 2 D., 1 M.C., 2 D., 10 M.C., 2 D., 5 M.C. 7 [10] [13] M.C.
2nd ROW. Sl.1, p.6 [9] [12] M.C. working across the 2nd row of stitch diagram "B" p.5 M.C., 2 D., 4 M.C., 2 D., 4 M.C., 1 D., 2 M.C., 1 D., 26 M.C., 1 D., 2 M.C., 1 D., 4 M.C., 2 D., 4 M.C., 2 D., 5 M.C., 6 [9] [12] M.C., k.1 M.C.
Keeping the 7 [10] [13] sts. in M.C. at each end of every row and commencing with the 3rd row, proceed as shown on stitch diagram "B" until the 39th row has been worked.
Break off the D. wools. * *

Shape the Shoulders

Cast off 8 [9] [10] sts. at the beginning of each of the next 2 rows.
Cast off 9 [10] [11] sts. at the beginning of each of the next 4 rows.
Cast off the remaining 30 [30] [30] sts.

THE FRONT

Using the No. 10 needles and M.C. wool cast on 101 [107] [113] sts.
Work exactly as given for the Back until * * is reached.
NEXT ROW. Sl.1, purl to the last st., k.1.

Shape the Neck

NEXT ROW. Sl.1, k.35 [38] [41] sts., cast off 10 [10] [10] sts., k.35 [38] [41].
Working on the first 36 [39] [42] sts. only, proceed as follows:
NEXT ROW. Sl.1, purl to the last st., k.1.
Decrease once at the neck edge in each of the next 10 rows. 26 [29] [32] sts.
Work 11 rows without shaping.

Shape the Shoulder

1st ROW. Cast off 8 [9] [10] sts. purlways, purl to last st., k.1.
2nd AND 4th ROWS. Sl.1, knit to end of row.
3rd ROW. Cast off 9 [10] [11] sts. purlways, purl to last st., k.1.
Cast off the remaining 9 [10] [11] sts. purlways.
With the wrong side of the work facing, rejoin the wool to the remaining 36 [39] [42] sts. and proceed as follows:
NEXT ROW. K.1, purl to the last st., k.1.
Decrease once at the neck edge in each of the next 10 rows. 26 [29] [32] sts.
Work 10 rows without shaping.

Shape the Shoulder

1st ROW. Cast off 8 [9] [10] sts., knit to end of row.
2nd AND 4th ROWS. Sl.1, purl to end of row.
3rd ROW. Cast off 9 [10] [11] sts. knit to end of row.
Cast off the remaining 9 [10] [11] sts.
Sew up the right shoulder seam.

THE NECKBAND (For all 3 sizes)

With the right side of the work facing and using the No. 10 needles, pick up and knit 29 sts. evenly along the left side of the front of the neck, 10 sts. from the 10 cast off sts., 30 sts. evenly along the right side of the neck and 30 sts. from the 30 cast off sts. at the back of the neck. (99 sts.).
1st ROW. Sl.1, * p.1, k.1, repeat from * to end of row.
2nd ROW. Sl.1, k.1, * p.1, k.1, repeat from * to the last st., k.1.
Repeat the 1st and 2nd rows 3 times then the 1st row once.
Cast off loosely in rib.
Sew up the left shoulder seam.

THE SLEEVES (Both alike for all 3 sizes)

Using the No. 8 needles and M.C. wool and with the right side of the work facing, knit across the 10 sts. left on a safety pin at the commencement of the armhole, pick up and knit 96 sts. evenly round the armhole edge then knit across the 10 sts. left on the other safety pin. (116 sts.).
1st ROW. Sl.1, purl to the last st., k.1.
2nd ROW. Sl.1, k.8, k.2 tog., knit to the last 11 sts., k.2 tog. t.b.l., k.9.
3rd ROW. Sl.1, p.7, p.2 tog. t.b.l., purl to the last 10 sts., p.2 tog., p.7, k.1.
4th ROW. Sl.1, k.6, k.2 tog., knit to the last 9 sts., k.2 tog. t.b.l., k.7.
5th ROW. Sl.1, p.5, p.2 tog. t.b.l., purl to the last 8 sts., p.2 tog., p.5, k.1.
6th ROW. Sl.1, k.4, k.2 tog., knit to the last 7 sts., k.2 tog. t.b.l., k.5.
7th ROW. Sl.1, p.3, p.2 tog. t.b.l., purl to the last 6 sts., p.2 tog., p.3, k.1.
8th ROW. Sl.1, k.2, k.2 tog., knit to the last 5 sts., k.2 tog. t.b.l., k.3.
9th ROW. Sl.1, p.1, p.2 tog. t.b.l., purl to the last 4 sts., p.2 tog., p.1, k.1.

THE TENSION FOR THIS GARMENT IS 6 stitches to one inch (pressed and unpressed).

ABBREVIATIONS

K. knit; p. purl; sts. stitches; tog. together; sl.1 slip one stitch knitways; t.b.l. through back of loops; M.C. Main Colour; D. Dark.
After casting off stitches for shaping, one stitch will remain on the right hand needle which is not included in the instructions that follow.

STITCH DIAGRAM "B"

One square equals one stitch. ☐ Main Colour. X Dark.
The odd numbered rows i.e. 1, 3, 5, etc. will be knit rows and are read from right to left.
The even numbered rows i.e. 2, 4, 6, etc. will be purl rows and are read from left to right.

Sirdar
No 1661
DOUBLE KNITTING WOOL
THREE SIZES
Chest 34/36/38 inches
6.ᴰ

10th ROW. Sl.1, k.2 tog., knit to the last 3 sts., k.2 tog. t.b.l., k.1.

11th ROW. K.2 tog., purl to the last 2 sts., k.2 tog. (96 sts.).

Proceed as follows:

1st ROW. Sl.1, knit to end of row.

Join in the D. wool.

2nd ROW. * P.1 D., 1 M.C., repeat from * to end of row.

3rd ROW. * K.1 D., 1 M.C., repeat from * to end of row.

Break off the M.C. wool.

4th ROW. K.1, purl to the last st., k.1.

Join in the M.C. wool and repeat the 3rd row once. Break off the D. wool.

Commencing with a purl row work 3 rows in st.st.

Join in the D. wool and working the 1st and 2nd rows of stitch diagram "A" proceed as follows:

1st ROW. * K.3 D., 3 M.C., repeat from * to end of row.

2nd ROW. * P.1 D., 1 M.C., 3 D., 1 M.C., repeat from * to end of row.

Commencing with the 3rd row, proceed as shown on stitch diagram "A" changing the colours when necessary until the 17th row has been worked.

Break off the D. wool.

NEXT ROW. Sl.1, purl to the last st., k.1.

Continue in st.st. decreasing once at each end of the next and every following 6th row until 72 sts. remain.

Commencing with a purl row work 3 rows in st.st. without shaping

Join in the D. wool and working the 15th and 16th rows of stitch diagram "A" proceed as follows:

NEXT ROW. * K.3 D., 3 M.C., repeat from * to end of row.

NEXT ROW. * P.1 D., 1 M.C., 3 D., 1 M.C., repeat from * to end of row.

Commencing with the 17th row, proceed as shown on the stitch diagram "A" changing the colours when necessary until the 28th row has been worked.

Join in the D. wool and repeat from the 1st to the 5th row (inclusive) of stitch diagram "A" once.

NEXT ROW. K.2 tog., * p.5, p.2 tog., repeat from * to the last 7 sts., p.5, k.2 tog. (61 sts.).

Change to No. 10 needles and proceed as follows:

1st ROW. Sl.1, k.1, * p.1, k.1, repeat from * to the last st., k.1.

2nd ROW. Sl.1, * p.1, k.1, repeat from * to end of row.

Repeat the 1st and 2nd rows 14 times.

Cast off loosely in rib.

Press carefully on the wrong side under a damp cloth with a hot iron.

CONTINENTAL EMBROIDERY

Following stitch diagram "B" embroider the motif on the centre 68 sts. commencing 4 rows up from the last dark row under the armholes, using the Continental or Swiss darning method.

TO MAKE UP THE SWEATER

Sew up the side and sleeve seams.

Press all seams.

MAN'S CARDIGAN

To fit 38 — 42 inch chest.

Materials : 19 (20) (21) ozs. ROBIN Ny-lona Sportswear, Sportsfleck or Tobie 4-Ply Fingering ; 1 pair each " ROBINOID " Knitting Needles, Nos. 10 and 12 ; 3 Buttons.

Measurements : To fit 38 (40) (42) inch chest. Length from shoulder to lower edge, 24 inches. Sleeve length, including turned back cuff, 20 inches.

Tension : 7 stitches and 9 rows = 1 inch, worked in Zig-zag pattern on No. 10 needles.
7 stitches and 11 rows = 1 inch, worked in Ridge pattern on No. 10 needles.

Abbreviations : K.—knit ; P.—purl ; sts.—stitches ; tog.—together ; inc.—increase ; dec.—decrease ; ins.—inches ; rep.—repeat.

Note.—The **first set** of stitches and measurements given are for the 38 inch chest, the **second set** in brackets ( ) for the 40 inch and the **third set** for the 42 inch chest. Where one set of stitches and measurements only are given, this applies to all sizes.

THE BACK

Using the No. 12 needles, commence at the lower edge by casting on 132 (140) (148) sts.
Work 2 ins. in K.1, P.1 rib.
Change to No. 10 needles.
1st—3rd Row.—Knit.
4th Row.—Purl.
These 4 rows form the Ridge pattern.
Proceed until the work measures 15 ins. from the commencement, ending with a rep. of the 4th row.

Shape Armholes

Cast off 6 (8) (10) sts. at the beginning of the next 2 rows.
K.2 tog. at both ends of the next and each alternate row, until 104 (108) (112) sts. remain.
Proceed in the pattern without shaping until the armholes measure 9 ins. from the cast off sts. (measured on the straight), ending on the wrong side of the work.

Shape Shoulders

Cast off 12 (12) (13) sts. at the beginning of the next 2 rows.
Cast off 11 (12) (13) sts. at the beginning of the next 2 rows.
Cast off 11 (12) (12) sts. at the beginning of the next 2 rows.
Cast off the 36 remaining sts. for back of neck.

THE RIGHT FRONT

Using the No. 12 needles, commence at the lower edge by casting on 64 (68) (72) sts.
Work 2 ins. in K.1, P.1 rib, inc. one st. at the **beginning** of the last row worked.   (65) (69) (73) sts. on needle).
Change to No. 10 needles.
1st—3rd Row.—Knit.
4th Row.—Purl.
Rep. these 4 rows 14 times more.
The work should now measure 7½ ins. from commencement.

Shape Front

1st Row.—K.2 tog., knit to end of row.
2nd Row.—Purl.
Now commence the Zig-zag pattern.
1st Row.—K.15 (K.19) (K.23), P.1, * K.23, P.1, rep. from * to end of row.
2nd Row.—P.1, K.1, * P.21, K.1, P.1, K.1, rep. from * once, P.14 (P.18) (P.21, K.1).
3rd Row.—K.13 (K.17) (K.1, P.1, K.19), * P.1, K.3, P.1, K.19, rep. from * once, P.1, K.2.
4th Row.—P.3, K.1, * P.17, K.1, P.5, K.1, rep. from * once, P.12 (P.16) (P.17, K.1, P.2).
5th Row.—K.11 (K.15) (K.3, P.1, K.15), * P.1, K.7, P.1, K.15, rep. from * once, P.1, K.4.
6th Row.—P.5, K.1, * P.13, K.1, P.9, K.1, rep. from * once, P.10 (P.13, K.1) (P.13, K.1, P.4).
7th Row.—K.2 tog., K.7 (K.11) (K.3, P.1, K.11), * P.1, K.11, rep. from * 3 times, P.1, K.6.
8th Row.—P.7, K.1, * P.9, K.1, P.13, K.1, rep. from * once, P.7 (P.9, K.1, P.1) (P.9, K.1, P.5).
9th Row.—K.6, P.1 (K.2, P.1, K.7, P.1), * K.15, P.1, K.7, P.1, rep. from * once, K.8.
10th Row.—P.9, K.1, * P.5, K.1, P.17, K.1, rep. from * once, P.5 (P.5, K.1, P.3) (P.5, K.1, P.7).
11th Row.—P.1, K.3 (K.4, P.1, K.3) (K.8, P.1, K.3), * P.1, K.19, P.1, K.3, rep. from * once, P.1, K.10.
12th Row.—P.11, K.1, P.1, K.1, * P 21, K.1, P.1, K.1, rep. from * once, P.1 (P.5) (P.9).
13th Row.—K.2 (K.6) (K.10), * P.1, K.23, rep. from * once, P.1, K.12.
14th Row.—Purl.

15th Row.—K.2 tog., knit to end of row.
16th Row.—Purl.
17th Row.—Knit.
Rep. the 16th and 17th rows twice more, then the 16th row again.
23rd Row.—K.2 tog. (K.2 tog., K.3, P.1) (K.2 tog., K.7, P.1), K.23, P.1, rep. from * once, K.12.
24th Row.—P.11, * K.1, P.1, K.1, P.21, rep. from * once, K.1, P.1 (K.1, P.1, K.1, P.3) (K.1, P.1, K.1, P.7).
25th Row.—K.2, P.1 (K.2, P.1, K.3, P.1) (K.6, P.1, K.3, P.1), * K.19, P.1, K.3, P.1, rep. from * once, K.10.
26th Row.—P.9, * K1, P.5, K.1, P.17, rep. from * once, K.1, P.3 (K.1, P.5, K.1, P.1,) (K.1, P.5, K.1. P.5).
27th Row.—K.4, P.1 (P.1, K.7, P.1) (K.4, P.1, K.7, P.1), * K.15, P.1, K.7, P.1, rep. from * once, K.8.
28th Row.—P.7, * K.1, P.9, K.1, P.13, rep. from * once, K.1, P.5 (K.1, P.9) (K.1, P.9, K.1, P.3).
29th Row.—K.6, P.1 (K.10, P.1) (K.2, P.1, K.11, P.1), * K.11, P.1, rep. from * 3 times, K.6.
30th Row.—P.5, K.1, * P.13, K.1, P.9, K.1, rep. from * once, P.7 (P.11) (P.13, K.1, P.1).
31st Row.—K.2 tog., K.6 (K.10, P.1) (K.14, P.1), * K.7, P.1, K.15, P.1, rep. from * once, K.4.
32nd Row.—P.3, K.1, * P.17, K.1, P.5, K.1, rep. from * once, P.8 (P.12) (P.16).
33rd Row.—K.9 (K.13) (K.17), * P.1, K.3, P.1, K.19, rep. from * once, P.1, K.2.
34th Row.—P.1, K.1, * P.21, K.1, P.1, K.1, rep. from * once, P.10 (P.14) (P.18).
35th Row.—K.11 (K.15) (K.19), * P.1, K.23, rep. from * once, P.1.
36th Row.—Purl.
37th Row.—Knit.
38th Row.—Purl.
Work 33 rows in Ridge pattern, dec. one st. at the beginning of the next and at this edge in every following 8th row.
There will now be 55 (59) (63) sts. on the needle.

Shape Armhole

Continue in the Ridge pattern.
1st Row.—Cast off 6 (8) (10) sts., knit to end of row.
K.2 tog. at the armhole in the next and each alternate row, until 8 decreasings are made at this edge, at the same time, continue to dec. one st. at the front edge in every 8th row as before.
There will now be 39 (41) (43) sts. on the needle.
Keeping the armhole edge straight, continue in the Ridge pattern until 15 complete patterns are worked from the end of the Zig-zag pattern, continuing to dec. at the front edge in every 8th row as before.
There will now be 38 (40) (42) sts. on the needle.
Next Row.—Knit.
Next Row.—Purl.
Change to Zig-zag pattern and proceed as follows :—
1st Row.—K.17 (K.19) (K.21), P.1, K.20.
2nd Row.—P.19, K.1, P.1, K.1, P.16 (P.18) (P.20).
3rd Row.—K.2 tog., K.13 (K.15) (K.17), P.1, K.3, P.1, K.18.
4th Row.—P.17, K.1, P.5, K.1, P.13 (P.15) (P.17).
5th Row.—K.12 (K.14) (P.1, K.15), P.1, K.7, P.1, K.15, P.1.
6th Row.—P.1, K.1, P.13, K.1, P.9, K.1, P.11 (P.13) (P.13, K.1, P.1).
7th Row.—K.10 (P.1, K.11) (K.2, P.1, K.11), P.1, * K.11, P.1, rep. from * once, K.2.
8th Row.—P.3, K.1, P.9, K.1, P.13, K.1, P.9 (P.9, K.1, P.1) (P.9, K.1, P.3).
9th Row.—K.1, K.7 (K.2, P.1, K.7) (K.4, P.1, K.7), P.1, K.15, P.1, K.7, P.1, K.4
10th Row.—P.5, K.1, P.5, K.1, P.17, K.1, P.5, K.1, P.1 (P.3) (P.5).
11th Row.—K.2 tog., P.1 (K.2, P.1) (K.4, P.1), K.3, P.1, K.19, P.1, K.3, P.1, K.6.
12th Row.—P.7, K.1, P.1, K.1, P.21, K.1, P.1, K.1, P.2 (P.4) (P.6).
13th Row.—K.3 (K.5) (K.7), P.1, K.23, P.1, K.8.

14th Row.—Purl.
15th Row.—Knit.
Rep. the 14th and 15th rows once, then the 14th row again.
19th Row.—K.2 tog., knit to end of row.
Rep. the 14th and 15th rows once, then the 14th row again.
23rd Row.—K.2 (K.4) (K.6), P.1, K.23, P.1, K.8.
24th Row.—P.7, K.1, P.1, K.1, P.21, K.1, P.1, K.1, P.1 (P.3) (P.5).
25th Row.—P.1 (K.2, P.1) (K.4, P.1), K.3, P.1, K.19, P.1, K.3, P.1, K.6.
26th Row.—P.5, K.1, P.5, K.1, P.17, K.1, P.5 (P.5, K.1, P.1) (P.5, K.1, P.3).
27th Row.—K.2 tog., K.4 (K.6) (P.1, K.7), P.1, K.15, P.1, K.7, P.1, K.4.
This completes the front shaping and there will now be 34 (36) (38) sts. on the needle.
28th Row.—P.3, K.1, P.9, K.1, P.13, K.1, P.6 (P.8) (P.9, K.1).
29th Row.—K.7, P.1 (K.9, P.1) (K.11, P.1), K.11, P.1, rep. from * once, K.2.
30th Row.—P.1, K.1, P.13, K.1, P.9, K.1, P.8 (P.10) (P.12).
31st Row.—K.9 (K.11) (K.13), P.1, K.7, P.1, K.15, P.1.
32nd Row.—P.17, K.1, P.5, K.1, P.10 (P.12) (P.14).
33rd Row.—K.11 (K.13) (K.15), P.1, K.3, P.1, K.18.
34th Row.—P.19, K.1, P.1, K.1, P.12 (P.14) (P.16).
35th Row.—K.13 (K.15) (K.17), P.1, K.20.
36th Row.—Purl.
37th Row.—Knit.
38th Row.—Purl.
Change to Ridge pattern and proceed without shaping until the armhole measures 9 ins. from the commencement (measured on the straight), ending at the armhole edge.

Shape Shoulder

1st Row.—Cast off 12 (12) (13) sts., work to neck.
2nd Row.—Work to end of row.
3rd Row.—Cast off 11 (12) (13) sts., work to neck.
4th Row.—Work to end of row.
Cast off the 11 (12) (12) remaining sts.

THE LEFT FRONT

Work as given for the Right Front until the first 15 Ridge patterns are completed, inc. one st. at the **end** of the last row of the welt.

Shape Front

1st Row.—Knit to the last 2 sts., K.2 tog.
2nd Row.—Purl.
Now commence the Zig-zag pattern.
1st Row.—P.1, * K.23, P.1, rep. from * once, K.15 (K.19) (K.23).
2nd Row.—P.14 (P.18) (K.1, P.21), * K.1, P.1, K.1, P.21, rep. from * once, K.1, P.1.
3rd Row.—K.2, P.1, * K.19, P.1, K.3, P.1, rep. from * once, K.13 (K.17) (K.19, P.1, K.1).
4th Row.—P.12 (P.16) (P.2, K.1, P.17), * K.1, P.5, K.1, P.17, rep. from * once, K.1, P.3.
5th Row.—K.4, P.1, * K.15, P.1, K.7, P.1, rep. from * once, K.11 (K.15) (K.15, P.1, K.3).
6th Row.—P.10 (K.1, P.13) (P.4, K.1, P.13), * K.1, P.9, K.1, P.13, rep. from * once, K.1, P.5.
7th Row.—K.6, P.1, * K.11, P.1, rep. from * 3 times, K.7 (K.11) (K.11, P.1, K.3), K.2 tog.
Proceed as given for Right Front until the 38th row of the first Zig-zag pattern is completed, reading the rows backwards.
Work 32 rows in Ridge pattern, dec. one st. at the **end** of the next and at this edge in every following 8th row.
There will now be 56 (60) (64) sts. on the needle.

Shape Armhole

Continue in the Ridge pattern.
1st Row.—Cast off 6 (8) (10) sts., knit to the last 2 sts., K.2 tog.

See colour plate on page 27

A **Robin** LEAFLET

IN

Ny-lona Sportswear

OR

Sportsfleck

No 210
PRICE 4ᴰ
TO FIT
38" – 42" CHEST

AN ORIGINAL ROBIN

K.2 tog. at the armhole edge in each alternate row until 8 decreasings are made at this edge, at the same time, continue to dec. one st. at the front edge in every 8th row as before.

Proceed to match the Right Front, reading the rows backwards until the shoulder is reached, then follow the instructions given for shaping the shoulder.

THE SLEEVES (both alike)

Using the No. 10 needles, commence at the top of side seam by casting on 12 (4) (5) sts.

Work in the Ridge pattern, casting on 6 (6) (5) sts. at the beginning of the 3rd row and at this edge in each alternate row, 2 (4) (6) times more.

There will now be 30 (34) (40) sts. on the needle.

Work 1 row more.

Shape the Top

1st Row.—Cast on 6 (6) (5) sts., work to end of row.
2nd Row.—Cast on 1 st., work to end of row.
Rep. these 2 rows 11 times more.
Next Row.—Cast on 10 (6) (12) sts., work to end of row.
There will now be 124 sts. on the needle.

Keeping the cuff edge straight, continue to cast on 1 st. at the top edge in the next and each alternate row until there are 144 sts. on the needle.

Work 19 rows without shaping, thus ending at the top edge.

Cast off 1 st. at the beginning of the next and at this edge in each alternate row, until 124 sts., remain, thus ending at the cuff edge.

Next Row.—Cast off 10 (6) (12) sts., work to end of row.
Next Row.—Cast off 1 st., work to end of row.
Next Row.—Cast off 6 (6) (5) sts., work to end of row.
Rep. the last 2 rows 11 times more.
There will now be 30 (34) (40) sts. on the needle.
Next Row.—Work to end of row.
Next Row.—Cast off 6 (6) (5) sts., work to end of row.
Rep. the last 2 rows 2 (4) (6) times more, then the 1st row again.
Cast off the 12 (4) (5) remaining sts.

THE CUFF

Using the No. 12 needles and with the right side of work facing, pick up and knit 66 sts. evenly along the lower edge of sleeve.

Work 4 ins. in K.1, P.1 rib.

Cast off **fairly loosely**, working in the rib.

THE FRONT AND NECK BORDER

Join the shoulders.

Using the No. 10 needles, cast on 18 sts.

Work 4 rows in stocking stitch.

5th Row.—K.3, cast off the next 3 sts. for a buttonhole, knit the next 5 sts., making 6 sts. on the needle after the cast off sts., cast off the next 3 sts., knit the 2 remaining sts.

6th Row.—P.3, cast on 3 sts., P.6, cast on 3 sts., P.3.

Proceed in stocking stitch until sufficient length to go up the fronts and across the back of neck, making 2 more sets of buttonholes, working 28 rows between each set.

Cast off.

TO MAKE UP

Pin out to correct measurements and press on the wrong side under a damp cloth with a warm iron. Sew in the sleeves, join the side and sleeve seams. Sew one edge of the border neatly to the fronts and neck of cardigan, placing the buttonholes to the left front, then fold in half and stitch down on the wrong side. Join the ends of border neatly. Work buttonhole stitch around the buttonholes, taking through both fabrics. Sew the buttons to the right front to correspond with the buttonholes. Press the seams.

	Sizes	34	36	38	40
MATERIALS — BEAR BRAND OR FLEISHER'S MANNIKIN *Bulky (OR) heavy Worsted* ozs.		18	18	20	22

"Boye" Non-Inflammable Needles, 1 pair Size 10 — OR SIZE YOU REQUIRE TO KNIT TO GAUGE GIVEN BELOW.

"Boye" Non-Inflammable Needles, 1 pair Size 5 for ribbing.

GAUGE: Size 10 Needles — 9 sts = 2 inches   13 rows = 2 inches

Regular worsted = 11 needles to get 3½ sts per inch on blue ambré for extra big size

		34	36	38	40
MEASUREMENTS FOR BLOCKING — Chest	ins.	36	38	40	42
Width of back at underarm	ins.	18	19	20	21
Width of sleeve at underarm	ins.	14½	15¼	16	17
BACK — With size 5 needles, cast on	sts	81	85	91	95

Ribbing — Row 1 — K 1, * p 1, k 1; repeat from * to end.
Row 2 — wrong side — P 1, * k 1, p 1; repeat from * to end.

		34	36	38	40
Repeat these 2 rows until ribbing measures	ins.	3	3	3¼	3½

end with row 2. Begin pattern.

Pattern — Row 1 — right side — With size 10 needles, k.
Row 2 — P 1, * k 1, p 1; repeat from * to end.
Repeat these 2 rows for pat.

		34	36	38	40
Work in pat. until measurement above ribbing is	ins.	9¼	9½	10	~~10½~~ 15

or desired length (end on wrong side with pat. row 2).

Raglan Yoke Shaping — First dec. row — K 1, k 2 tog., k to within 3 sts of end, slip,

		34	36	38	40
k and pass, k 1	sts	79	83	89	93

Next row — P 2, * k 1, p 1; repeat from *, end last repeat p 2.

		34	36	38	40
2nd dec. row — Same as first dec. row	sts	77	81	87	91

Next row — P 1, * k 1, p 1; repeat from * across row.

		34	36	38	40
Dec. 1 st each side of next row and repeat decs. every 2nd row	times	25	27	29	31
working pat. as in first 4 rows of raglan shaping	sts	25	25	27	27

Back Neck Ribbing — Wide Turtle Neck — With size 10 needles, work ribbing as

		34	36	38	40
for back for	ins.	3½	3½	4	4

Bind off loosely in ribbing.

Tight Turtle Neck — Work same as for wide turtle neck using size 5 needles.

		34	36	38	40
Round Neck — With size 5 needles, work ribbing for	ins.	1¼	1¼	1½	1½

Bind off loosely in ribbing.

FRONT — Work same as back until there are remaining on needle (end on right

		34	36	38	40
side with pat. row 1)	sts	35	35	39	39
Measurement above beg. of raglan yoke should be about	ins.	7	7½	8	8½

Divide for neck as follows:

		34	36	38	40
Next row — wrong side — Work	sts	12	12	14	14

place these sts on holder for right side, work next 11 sts and place on holder for neck, finish row.

		34	36	38	40
Continue to dec. at armhole edge as before	times	5	5	6	6
at the same time, dec. 1 st at neck edge every row twice; every 2nd row	times	3	3	4	4

Bind off remaining 2 sts.
Take up sts of right side from holder and work to correspond.

		34	36	38	40
SLEEVES — With size 5 needles, cast on	sts	41	41	45	45
Work ribbing as on back for	ins.	3½	3½	4	4

With size 10 needles, work pat. as on back, increasing 1 st each side (keeping

		34	36	38	40
pat.) every ¾ in.	times	3	7	7	11
every 1¼ ins.	times	9	7	7	5
Work even on	sts	65	69	73	77
until length above ribbing is	ins.	14½	15	15	15¾

or desired length (end with pat. row 2).
Working as for raglan yoke shaping on back, dec. 1 st each side of next row and

		34	36	38	40
repeat decs. every 2nd row	times	27	29	31	33

Work 1 row even after last dec. row, end on wrong side. Break yarn. Place sts on holder. Make second sleeve in same way; do not break yarn, leave sts on needle.

FRONT NECK RIBBING — Using same size needles as on back neck ribbing, k across

		34	36	38	40
9 sts of 2nd sleeve; from right side, pick up and k	sts	10	10	13	13
on left neck edge of front; take up and k 11 sts from holder; pick up and k	sts	10	10	13	13
on right neck edge, k across 9 sts of first sleeve	sts	49	49	55	55

Work ribbing as on back for same length as back neck. Bind off in ribbing.

FINISHING — Sew raglan seams joining sleeves to back and front. Sew underarm and sleeve seams. Steam.

The Continental Line for men

Materials: Of Patons Moorland Double Knitting, 14 (15) ozs. Black, 4 (5) ozs. White, and 5 (6) ozs. Light Steel Grey 68. A pair each No. 10 and No. 6 "Beehive" needles.

Measurements: To fit 36–38 (39–41) inch chest; length from top of shoulders, 22 (22½) ins.; sleeve seam, 19 (19) ins.

Tension: Equivalent to a basic tension of 5 sts. and 6½ rows to an inch in stocking-stitch on No. 6 needles, or 8 sts. and 7 rows to an inch over pattern.

N.B.—Instructions for large size given in brackets thus ( ). Square brackets and where one set of figures is given this applies to both sizes.

Striped Pattern: 1ST ROW: In grey, k. 1, * slip 1 purlways, k. 1, pass slipped stitch over; repeat from * to last st., k. 1. 2ND ROW: k. 1, * [k. 1, p. 1 into next stitch]; repeat from * to last stitch, k. 1. Leave grey hanging, join in white and repeat 1st and 2nd rows. Leave white hanging, join in black and repeat 1st and 2nd rows. These 6 rows form pattern.

Back: With No. 10 needles and black wool, cast on 110 (118) sts. and work 3½ ins. k. 1, p. 1 rib, increasing 6 (16) sts. evenly across on last row: 116 (134) sts.

Change to No. 6 needles and pattern, dividing for panels thus:—Join in grey. 1ST ROW: right side facing, k. 1, [slip 1 purlways, k. 1, p.s.s.o.] 18 (21) times, k. 1, turn and leave remaining sts. on a spare needle. 2ND ROW: k. 1, [k. 1, p. 1 into next st.] 18 (21) times, k. 1. Leave grey hanging, join in white and repeat last 2 rows. Leave white hanging, join in black and repeat last 2 rows again. Now repeat these 6 rows once more.

Continue in striped pattern exactly as given starting with 1st row and shape side edge by casting on 2 sts. at beginning of next and every following alternate row, 17 (17) times: [72 (78) sts.]. Pattern back.

Continue in pattern, still shaping side edge by casting on 6 (6) sts. at beginning of next and following 5 alternate rows, 108 (114) sts., then cast on 12 sts. at beginning of following 5 alternate rows: [168 (174) sts.] Pattern back. Work 30 (36) rows straight in striped pattern.

With right side facing, continue in pattern *but in black only* and shape shoulder by casting off 16 (16) sts. at beginning of next row, then 12 (12) sts. at beginning of following 12 (12) alternate rows; cast off remaining 8 (14) sts.

Return to remaining sts., slip centre 40 (46) sts. on a spare needle. Rejoin wool to last 38 (44) sts. and work to correspond with first 38 (44) sts. Remember that you will be casting on with wrong side facing, therefore you must always purl the stitches you cast on, then work the remainder in pattern exactly as given in the pattern rows. Your first row of increasings will therefore read:—cast on 2, p. 2, k. 1, * [k. 1, p. 1 in next stitch]; repeat from * to last stitch, k. 1. When this side of back is done, with right side facing, join black wool to centre 40 (46) sts. Work straight in pattern in black only on centre 40 (46) sts. until piece fits up straight edges of striped pieces to top of shoulders; leave stitches on a spare needle; sew panel neatly in position with a flat seam.

Front: Work striped pieces exactly as given for back. Join black wool to centre 40 (46) sts. and continue in pattern in black only until piece fits up sides of striped pieces to within 16 rows of top of shoulder. Here divide for neck:—

NEXT ROW: right side facing, pattern 8 (8), k. 2 tog.; turn and leave remaining stitches on a spare needle. Continue in pattern on these 9 (9) sts.; decreasing 1 stitch at neck edge on alternate rows until all stitches are gone; fasten off.

With right side facing, slip centre 20 (26) sts. on a spare needle, rejoin wool to last 10 (10) sts., k. 2 tog., pattern to end. Work to correspond with first half. Sew panel in position as on back.

To Make Up: Press parts carefully on wrong side under a damp cloth. Join shoulder seams. *Neckband:* with right side facing, No. 10 needles and black wool, pick up and k. 94 (106) sts. all round neck, including those on spare needles at back and front. Work 1¾ inches k. 1, p. 1 rib; cast off loosely in rib. *Cuffs:* with right side facing, No. 10 needles and black wool, pick up and k. 58 (66) sts, along each sleeve edge; work 3½ inches k. 1, p. 1 rib; cast off loosely in rib. Join side and underarm seams with tailored seams.

Press all seams.

Men abroad wear striking sweaters like this, with wide dolman sleeves in a loose-fit casual style

Lumber Jackets for Him and Her

MATERIALS

23 ozs. Templeton's Fisherknit for Woman's Jacket.
31 ozs. Templeton's Fisherknit for Man's Jacket.
2 No. 5 and 2 No. 9 " Aero " knitting needles.
A 22 inch open end " Lightning " fastener for Woman's Jacket.
A 24 inch open end " Lightning " fastener for Man's Jacket.

MEASUREMENTS

Woman's Jacket. To fit a 34 to 36 inch bust.
Length: 22½ inches.
Sleeve: 17 inches.

Man's Jacket. To fit a 40-42 inch chest.
Length: 25½ inches.
Sleeve: 20½ inches.

TENSION

4 stitches to 1 inch.

ABBREVIATIONS

K=knit; P=purl; sts.=stitches; st.st.=stocking stitch; sl.=slip; p.s.s.o.=pass slipped stitch over; tog.=together; cont.=continue; rep.=repeat; ins.=inches; inc.=increase; fin.=finishing; beg.=beginning; dec.=decrease; rem.=remain(ing).

N.B.—For Back, Pocket Linings, Pocket Tops, Neckband, and Yoke follow the first figures given for the Woman's Jacket and the figures in brackets for the Man's Jacket, unless otherwise stated. For Fronts to armholes, separate instructions are given for both jackets. When working the first part of the yoke it will be found easier to use extra No. 5 needles than to assemble the full number of sts. on one needle.

There are two ways of outlining the raglan shaping: (1) As given in the instructions and as shown on the girl on the cover, or (2) By working the two shaping stitches together in pattern, as shown on the man's garment.

THE BACK

Using No. 9 needles cast on 66 (76) sts. and work in K1, P1 rib for 4 (3½) ins.
Next row—Rib 3 * inc. in next st., rib 6 (8). Rep. from * to end (last) st., rib 0 (inc. in last st.) 75 (85) sts.
Change to No. 5 needles and cont. in the foll. patt.:—
1st row—K1, P1 to last st., K1.
2nd row—P.
These 2 rows form the patt. Rep. them until work measures 13 (14½) ins. fin. after a 2nd patt. row.
Cast off 3 sts. at beg. of next 2 rows. Leave sts. on a spare needle.

THE POCKET LININGS
(2 required)

Using No. 5 needles cast on 22 (22) sts. and work in st.st. for 4 (3½) ins. fin. after a P. row. Leave for the present.

THE RIGHT FRONT
(Woman's Jacket)

Using No. 9 needles cast on 34 sts. and work thus:—
1st row—Front Edge—K2 (P1, K1) to end.
2nd row—(P1, K1) to last 2 sts., K2.
Rep. these 2 rows until welt measures 4 ins. fin. at front edge.
Next row—K2, rib 3, leave next 24 sts. on spare needle, then rib across pocket lining sts. thus: (rib 7, K. twice into next st.) twice, rib 6, then rib across rem. front sts.
Next row—Rib 2, * inc. in next st., rib 5. Rep. from * to last 2 sts., K2 (39 sts.).
Change to No. 5 needles and the foll. patt.:—
1st row—K2, P1, twist next 2 sts. thus: K. into second st. on left-hand needle, then into first st. and sl. both off needle together, P1, then K1, P1 to last st., K1.
2nd row—P. to last 6 sts., K1, P2, K3.
These 2 rows form the patt. Rep. them until work measures 13 ins. fin. after a 1st patt. row.
Cast off 3 sts. at beg. of next row and patt. to end. Leave sts. on spare needle.

THE RIGHT FRONT
(Man's Jacket)

Using No. 9 needles cast on 38 sts. and work thus:—
1st row—Front Edge—K2 (P1, K1) to end.

2nd row—P1, K1 to last 2 sts., K2.
Rep. these 2 rows until welt measures 3½ ins. fin. at side edge.
Next row—Rib 2, * inc. in next st., rib 8. Rep. from * to last 9 sts., inc. in next st., rib 5, inc. in next st., K2 (43 sts.).
Change to No. 5 needles and the foll. patt.:—
1st row—K2, P1, twist next 2 sts. thus: K. into second st. on left-hand needle, then into first st. and sl. both off needle together, P1, then K1, P1 to last st., K1.
2nd row—P. to last 6 sts., K1, P2, K3.
These 2 rows form the patt. Rep. them until work measures 7 ins. fin. after a 2nd patt. row.
Next row—Patt. 12, sl. next 22 sts. on to a spare needle and patt. across 22 sts. of one pocket lining, rib to end.
Cont. in patt. until work measures 14½ ins. fin. after a 1st patt. row.
Cast off 3 sts. at beg. of next row and patt. to end.
Leave sts. on spare needle.

THE LEFT FRONT
(Woman's Jacket)

Using No. 9 needles cast on 34 sts. and work thus:—
1st row—Side Edge—(K1, P1) rib to last 2 sts., K2.
2nd row—K2 (K1, P1) to end.
Rep. these 2 rows until work measures 4 ins. from beg. fin. after a 2nd patt. row.
Next row—Rib 5, leave next 24 sts. on spare needle, then rib across pocket lining sts. thus: (rib 7, K. twice into next st.) twice, rib 6, rib to last 2 sts., K2.
Next row—K2, * rib 5, inc. in next st. Rep. from * to last 2 sts., rib 2.
Change to No. 5 needles and work thus:—
1st row—(K1, P1) to last 7 sts., K1, P1, twist 2, P1, K2.
2nd row—K3, P2, K1, P. to end.
Cont. in patt. until work measures 13 ins. after a 2nd patt. row.
Next row—Cast off 3 sts., patt. to end.
Next row—In patt.
Leave sts. for the present.

THE LEFT FRONT
(Man's Jacket)

Using No. 9 needles cast on 38 sts. and work thus:—
1st row—Side Edge—(K1, P1) rib to last 2 sts., K2.

2nd row—K2 (K1, P1) to end.
Rep. these 2 rows until work measures 3½ ins. from beg. fin. after a 1st patt. row.
Next row—K2, inc. in next st., rib 5 * inc. in next st., rib 8. Rep. from * to last 3 sts. * inc. in next st. rib 2 (43 sts.).
Change to No. 5 needles and work thus:—
1st row—(K1, P1) to last 7 sts., K1, P1, twist 2, P1, K2.
2nd row—K3, P2, K1, P. to end.
Cont. in patt. until work measures 7 ins. fin. after a 2nd patt. row.
Next row—Patt. 9, then sl. next 22 sts. on to a spare needle, and patt. across 22 sts. of pocket lining, patt. to end.
Cont. in patt. until work measures 14½ ins. fin. after a 2nd patt. row.
Next row—Cast off 3 sts. patt. to end.
Next row—In patt.
Leave sts. for the present.

THE SLEEVES

Using No. 9 needles cast on 30 (34) sts. and work in K1, P1 rib for 3 ins.
Next row—* Inc. in next st., rib 2. Rep. from * to last 3 (1) sts. then inc. in next st., rib 1 inc. in next st. (rib 1). There are now 41 (45) sts.
Change to No. 5 needles and cont. in patt. for 4 rows, then inc. 1 st. each end of next and every 8th row until there are 57 (65) sts. Cont. straight until work measures 17 (20½) ins. fin. after a P. row.
Cast off 3 sts. at beg. of next 2 rows, and leave sts. on spare needle.

Assemble all sts. thus:—

Go back to Right Front sts., join on wool and using No. 5 needles work as follows:—
1st row—Patt. to last 4 sts., K2 tog., P1, then into the last st. of right front, and 1st st. on 1st sleeve work the " twist " 2, then across sleeve cont. with P1, sl.1, K1, p.s.s.o., patt. to last 4 sts., K2 tog., P1, then into the last st. of sleeve and 1st st. of back work the " twist " 2, then cont. across back, 2nd sleeve and Left Front to match, that is the twist 2 dividing each part and dec. each side of P1 at armhole edge.
2nd row—Keeping continuity of patt., work to end.

A Templeton Design

3rd and 4th rows—In patt. working the "twist" as on first row.

Rep. these 4 rows once more.

9th row—As 1st row.

10th row—As 2nd row.

Rep. these 2 rows until 123 (133) sts. rem., fin. after a wrong side row, then still dec. on alternate rows as for 1st row, cast off 2 sts. at beg. of next 2 rows, then dec. 1 st. at neck edge on each end of next row and every alternate row until 51 sts. rem.

Next row—K3 tog., patt. 4, K3 tog., patt. 4, sl.1, K1, p.s.s.o., patt. across back, sleeve and left front to match (41 sts.).

Next row—Patt. to end.

Next row—P3 tog., P3 tog., patt. 4, sl.1, K1, p.s.s.o., patt. across rem. sts. to match 1st half.

Next row—Woman's Jacket—Patt. to end.

Next row—K2 tog., patt. 4, sl.1, K1, p.s.s.o., patt. across back to last 8 sts., K2 tog., patt. 4, K2 tog.

Next row—Both designs. Cast off.

THE POCKET TOPS

Go back to sts. on spare needle. Rejoin wool and using No. 9 needles, work thus:—

Next row—For Man's Jacket only—K1, * inc. in next st., K2. Rep. from * to end.

For both Jackets, work in K1, P1 rib for 1 in. Cast off in the rib.

THE NECKBAND

Using No. 9 needles beg. at right front and pick up and K24 (25) sts. to back neck, 26 (28) sts. along back neck edge, and 24 (25) sts. to left front. Now work in K1, P1 rib for 1 in. Cast off in the rib.

TO MAKE UP

Press work with a hot iron over a damp cloth. Sew up sleeve and side seams. Sew pocket linings into position and sew down pocket edges. Sew in fastener. Press seams.

NORWEGIAN PULLOVER

Materials 20 ounces of Conella Double Knitting or ROBIN Double Knit Crepe in Main Shade. 10 ounces of the same wool in Contrast Shade
1 pair each 'Robinoid' Knitting Needles No.8 and No.10
1 set of 4 double-pointed needles No.10

Measurements To fit 38-40 inch chest. Length 25″
Length of sleeve seam 21″

Tension 6 stitches and 8 rows = 1 inch in stocking stitch on No.8 needles

Note It is important that the garment is worked at this tension in order to produce the same measurements. If this is not obtained on No.8 needles try a larger size if a tight knitter or a smaller size if slack knitter.

Abbreviations st. = stitch; st-st. = stocking-stitch; K. = knit; P. = purl; beg. = beginning; rep. = repeat; rem. = remain; inc. = increase; dec. = decrease; M. = main shade; C. = contrast shade.

THE BACK

Using M. and No.10 needles cast on 126 sts. and work 3½ inches in K.1, P.1 rib. Change to st-st. and No.8 needles and work for 1¾ inches ending with a P. row. Join in contrast shade and work from Chart A.

1st Row * K.3M, 1C, 2M, rep from * to end of row.

When the 17 rows of chart A have been completed proceed as follows: Break C. ** beginning with a P. row work 7 rows in st-st.

8th Row * K.5M, 1.C. Rep. from * to end of row.

Work 7 rows st-st. beginning with P. row.

16th Row * K.2M, 1C, 3M. Rep. from * to end of row. **

Rep. from ** to ** 5 times. Work 5 rows st-st. MS. Casting off 3 sts. at the beg. of the first 2 rows.

Now work from chart B as follows:
1st Row K.1C, 5M, 1C, 5M, rep. to end of row.
2nd Row P.1C, 3M, 1C, 1M, 1C, 3M, 1C, 1M.

When 51 rows of chart B have been worked cast off 40 sts. at the beg. of the 52nd and 53rd rows, leave remaining sts. on spare needle.

THE FRONT

Work as given for Back, until 46th row of chart B has been worked.

Shape Neck

47th Row Work in pattern from chart B for 48 sts. cast off the next 24 sts. work in pattern to end of row leaving sts. for left side on spare needle, work on rem. 48 sts. as follows:

48th Row Work in pattern from chart B. Dec. 1 st. at the end of the row. Turn.

49th Row Cast off 2 sts. at beg. of the row, work in pattern to the end of the row.

50th Row Work in pattern. Dec. 1 st. at the end of the row.

51st Row Cast off 2 sts. work in pattern to end of row.

52nd Row Work in pattern. Dec at the end of the row.

53rd Row K.2 tog., work in pattern to end of the row.

Cast off rem. sts. Rejoin wool at neck edge and work from chart B, reversing the shaping as follows:

48th Row Cast off 2 sts., work in pattern to end of row.

49th Row Work in pattern. Dec. at the end of the row.

50th Row Cast off 2 sts, work in pattern to end of the row.

51st Row Work in pattern. Dec. at end of the row.

52nd Row P.2 tog., work in pattern to end of row.

53rd Row Work in pattern. Dec. at the end of the row.

Cast off rem. sts.

THE SLEEVES

Using No.10 needles cast on 66 sts. with M. shade and work in K.1, P.1 rib for 3½ ins. Change to No.8 needles, join in C. and work the 17 rows from chart A.

Now work as for Back from ** to **, 4 times, at the same time inc. 1 st. at each end of the next and every following 4th row until there are 96 sts. on the needle, continue without further shaping until the 4th rep. is completed. Work 5 rows in st-st.

Now work the rows from chart B, when these are completed cast off.

NECK BAND

Join shoulder seams with right side of work facing, using the set of No.10 needles and M. only. K. across the sts. left on spare needle with second needle pick up and K. 14 sts. side of neck, 12 sts. to centre of neck. With 3rd needle pick up and K. 12 sts from front of neck, 14 from from side of neck, arrange the sts. evenly on the 3 needles and work in K.1, P.1 rib for 3 inches, cast off loosely in rib.

MAKE UP

Press the work lightly on wrong side, using a warm iron over a damp cloth. Join side and sleeve seams, darning in all ends. Set sleeves into armholes, sewing the 3 cast off sts. on either side of sleeves seam. Fold neck band in half and slip stitch into place on wrong side of work. Press all seams.

☐ = Main Shade

V = Contrast

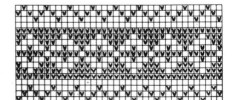

See colour plate on page 63

THE CONTINENTAL LOOK..

**the pattern
runs across
the back just
like the front**

Materials: Of Patons Moorland Double Knitting, 17 ozs. Black and 7 ozs. Light Natural 6502; or of Patons Double Quick Knitting, 18 ozs. Black and 7 ozs. Natural 212. A pair No. 11 "Queen Bee" needles. A set of four No. 8 "Queen Bee" needles, pointed both ends, 12 inch.

Measurements: To fit 38–41-inch chest; length from top of shoulders, 24 inches; sleeve seam, 19½ inches.

Tension: 5½ sts. and 7½ rows to an inch over stocking-stitch on No. 8 needles.

N.B.—When working Fair-Isle pattern strand wool not in use loosely across back of work. B.=Black; N.=Natural. Spots on chart are natural, blank squares are black.

BACK AND FRONT IN ONE

Begin at lower edge of back. With No. 11 needles and B. wool, cast on 115 sts. and work 4 inches k. 1, p. 1 rib, rows on right side having a k. 1 at each end.

Change to two No. 8 needles and stocking-stitch and work straight until back measures 7 inches. With right side facing, shape sides by increasing 1 stitch at each end of next and every following alternate row until there are 145 sts. Purl back. You will now need the other two needles to facilitate working.

Continue backwards and forwards in stocking-stitch and shape sleeves by casting on 7 sts. at beginning of next 24 rows: 313 sts. This completes sleeve shaping. Work 22 rows straight. Here introduce pattern from chart.

With right side facing, continue in stocking-stitch, working the 18 pattern rows from chart, reading knit rows from right to left and purl rows from left to right. Work the 14 pattern stitches 22 times, then last 5 sts. on knit rows and first 5 sts. on purl rows as indicated. When the 18 rows are done, break B. Work 10 rows straight in N.

Continue in N. only shaping for shoulders thus:—Knit to last 10 sts., turn; purl to last 10 sts., turn. Knit to last 20 sts., turn; purl to last 20 sts., turn. Knit to last 30 sts., turn; purl to last 30 sts., turn. Knit to last 40 sts., turn; purl to last 40 sts., turn.

Continue thus, working 10 sts. less each time until you have worked the rows knit to last 140 sts., turn; purl to last 140 sts., turn. NEXT ROW: Knit to end, picking up horizontal thread and knitting it together with next stitch through back of loops where work was turned to avoid a hole. NEXT ROW: Purl, picking up horizontal threads in the same way. Here divide for back of neck:—

Last 5 sts.   14 pattern sts.
k. row
First 5 sts. p. row

NEXT ROW: k. 140, turn and leave remaining stitches on a spare needle. Continue on first 140 sts. for right shoulder thus:—NEXT ROW: Purl. NEXT ROW: Knit. NEXT 2 ROWS: p. 10, turn; knit to end. NEXT 2 ROWS: p. 20, turn; knit to end. NEXT 2 ROWS: p. 30, turn; knit to end. NEXT 2 ROWS: p. 40, turn; knit to end. NEXT 2 ROWS: p. 50, turn; knit to end. NEXT 2 ROWS: p. 60, turn; knit to end. NEXT 2 ROWS: p. 70, turn; knit to last stitch, increase in last stitch. NEXT 2 ROWS: p. 81, turn; knit to last stitch, increase in last stitch. NEXT 2 ROWS: p. 92, turn; knit to last stitch, increase in last stitch. NEXT 2 ROWS: p. 103, turn; knit to last stitch, increase in last stitch. NEXT 2 ROWS: p. 114, turn; knit to last stitch, increase in last stitch (145 sts.). Leave these stitches for the time being.

With right side facing, return to 173 sts. of back and slip centre 33 on a spare needle for back of neck. With right side facing, rejoin wool to last 140 sts., knit to end, turn and purl back. Continue on these 140 sts. thus:—NEXT ROW: Knit. NEXT ROW: Purl. NEXT 2 ROWS: k. 10, turn; purl to end. NEXT 2 ROWS: k. 20, turn; purl to end. NEXT 2 ROWS: k. 30, turn; purl to end. NEXT 2 ROWS: k. 40, turn; purl to end. NEXT 2 ROWS: k. 50, turn; purl to end. NEXT 2 ROWS: k. 60, turn; purl to end. NEXT 2 ROWS: Increase in 1st stitch, k. 69, turn; purl to end. NEXT 2 ROWS: Increase in 1st stitch, k. 80, turn; purl to end. NEXT 2 ROWS: Increase in 1st stitch, k. 91, turn; purl to end. NEXT 2 ROWS: increase in 1st stitch, k. 102, turn; purl to end. NEXT ROW: Increase in 1st stitch, knit to end. NEXT ROW: Purl. At end of this row, cast on 23 sts. loosely for front of neck, then purl across 145 sts. of right shoulder (313 sts.). Work 10 rows straight in N. across all stitches.

With right side facing, change to pattern from chart but turn chart upside down and work the rows backwards, i.e., 18th row of chart will now be the 1st row and a knit row. When the 18 rows are done, change to B. over all stitches and work 22 rows straight.

Continue in stocking-stitch shaping sleeves by casting off 7 sts. at beginning of next 24 rows: 145 sts. Now shape sides by decreasing 1 stitch at each end of next and every following alternate row until 115 sts. remain. Work straight until side edge matches back.

Change to No. 11 needles and work 4 inches k. 1, p. 1 rib. Cast off in rib.

TO MAKE UP

Press parts carefully on wrong side under a damp cloth. With right side facing, B. wool and No. 11 needles, pick up and k. 104 sts. all round neck, including those on spare needles at back and front (you will need a spare double-pointed needle to facilitate working). Work backwards and forwards in k. 1, p. 1 rib for 2½ inches. Cast off loosely in rib.

In the same way, pick up and k. 52 sts. along each sleeve edge. Work 3½ inches k. 1, p. 1 rib; cast off in rib.

Join side and underarm seams. Join neck ribbing; turn under 1¼ inches to wrong side and slip hem loosely in position. Press all seams.

MAN'S SWEATER

The tension for this garment is :—7 sts. to one inch.

ABBREVIATIONS.

K-knit, p-purl, sts.-stitches, tog.-together, sl. 1-slip one stitch knitways, st. st.-stocking stitch (one row knit, one row purl), t.b.l.-through back of loops, D-dark, L-light.

After casting off stitches for shaping, one stitch will remain on the right hand needle which is not included in the instructions that follow.

MATERIALS.

12 ozs. Sirdar Majestic Wool, 4 ply, Dark (Long Sleeves and Polo Neck).

8 ozs. Sirdar Majestic Wool, 4-ply, Dark (Sleeveless and Round Neck).

1 oz. Sirdar Majestic Wool, 4 ply, Light.

1 pair Knitting Needles No. 8.

1 pair Knitting Needles No. 9.

1 pair Knitting Needles No. 11.

1 Zipp Fastener 4 inches in length for Polo Neck.

MEASUREMENTS.

Width all round at underarm, 38 inches.
Length from top of shoulder, 22 inches.
Length of sleeve seam, 20 inches.
N.B.—When working with two colours the colour not in use should be woven loosely across the back of the work to retain the elasticity of the fabric.

The Back.

Using the No. 11 needles and Dark Wool cast on 110 sts.
1st ROW. Sl 1, k1, * p1, k1, repeat from * to end of row.
Repeat the first row 37 times.

Change to No. 9 needles and proceed as follows :—

1st ROW. Sl 1, k1, * increase once in the next st., k7, repeat from * to the last 4 sts., increase once in the next st., k3, (124 sts.).

2nd ROW. Sl 1, purl to the last st., k1.

Continue in st. st. until the work measures 14 inches from the commencement, ending on the wrong side of the work.

Break off the wool.

The Armholes.

Slip the first 14 sts. on to a safety-pin.
With the right side of the work facing, rejoin the wool to the remaining 110 sts. and proceed as follows :—

1st ROW. Sl 1, knit to the last 14 sts., slip these 14 sts. on to a safety-pin (96 sts.).

Commencing with a purl row work 13 rows in st. st.

Break off the Dark wool, join in the Light.

Change to No. 8 needles and proceed as follows :—

1st ROW. Knit to end of row.

Break off the Light wool, join in the dark.

2nd ROW. K1, purl to the last st., k1.
Join in the Light Wool and working the 1st and 2nd rows as shown on the stitch diagram, proceed as follows :—

1st ROW. * K6D, 4L, 12D, 4L, 6D, repeat from * to end of row.

2nd ROW. * P5D, 6L, 10D, 6L, 5D, repeat from * to end of row.

Commencing with the 3rd row, proceed as shown on the stitch-diagram until the 24th row has been worked.

Break off the Light wool.**

Change to No. 9 needles and work 28 rows in st. st.

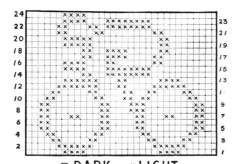

□ **DARK** ×**LIGHT**

One square equals one stitch.

The odd numbered rows, i.e., 1, 3, 5, etc., will be knit rows and are read from right to left.

The even numbered rows, i.e., 2, 4, 6, etc., will be purl rows and are read from left to right.

Shape the Shoulders.

Cast off 10 sts. at the beginning of each of the next 4 rows
Cast off 12 sts. at the beginning of each of the next 2 rows.
Break off the wool.
Leave the remaining 32 sts. on a stitch-holder.

The Front.

Using the No. 11 needles and Dark wool, cast on 110 sts.
Work exactly as given for the Back until ** is reached.
Change to No. 9 needles and work 8 rows in st. st.

Shape the Neck.

1st ROW. Sl 1, k37, k2 tog., turn.

Working on these 39 sts. only, proceed as follows :—
2nd ROW. K2 tog., purl to the last st., k1.

3rd ROW. Sl 1, knit to the last 2 sts., k2 tog.

Repeat the 2nd and 3rd rows twice, then the 2nd row once (32 sts.).

Work 12 rows in st. st. without shaping.

Shape the Shoulder.

1st ROW. Cast off 10 sts., knit to end of row.

2nd ROW. Sl 1, purl to end of row.

Repeat the 1st and 2nd rows once.

Cast off the remaining 12 sts.

Slip the next 16 sts. on to a safety-pin.

With the right side of the work facing, rejoin the Dark wool to the neck edge of the remaining 40 sts. and proceed as follows :—

1st ROW. K2 tog., knit to end of row.

2nd ROW. Sl 1, purl to the last 2 sts., k2 tog.

Repeat the 1st and 2nd rows 3 times (32 sts.).

Work 13 rows in st. st. without shaping.

Shape the Shoulder.

1st ROW. Cast off 10 sts., purl to the last st., k1.

2nd ROW. Sl 1, knit to end of row.

Repeat the 1st and 2nd rows once.

Cast off the remaining 12 sts.

Sew up the right shoulder seam.

The Polo Neck.

Using the No. 11 needles and Dark wool and with the right side of the work facing, pick up and knit 26 sts. evenly along the left side of the neck, working across the 16 sts. of the front left on a safety-pin (p1, k1) 8 times, pick up and knit 26 sts. evenly along the right side of the neck, working across the 32 sts. of the Back left on a stitch-holder (p1, k1) 16 times. (100 sts.).

1st ROW. Sl 1, k1, * p1, k1, repeat from * to end of row.
Repeat the 1st row 62 times.
Cast off loosely in rib.

The Round Neckband.

Using the No. 11 needles and Dark wool work exactly as given for the Polo Neck but repeat the 1st. row 8 times only.

Cast off loosely in rib.

If the garment worked is for a Polo Neck, proceed as follows :—

Commencing at the armhole edge sew up the left shoulder seam for 4½ inches.

If the garment worked is for a round neck, sew up the left shoulder seam.

The Armhole Bands for Sleeveless Model (both alike).

Using the No. 11 needles and Dark wool and with the

right side of the work facing knit the 14 sts. left on a safety-pin at the commencement of the armhole, pick up and knit 96 sts. evenly around the armhole, knit the 14 sts. left on the other safety-pin (124 sts.).

1st and every alternate ROW. Sl 1, k1, * p1, k1, repeat from * to end of row.

2nd ROW. Sl 1, (k1, p1) 6 times, k2 tog. t.b.l., p2 tog., * k1, p1, repeat from * to the last 17 sts., k2 tog. t.b.l., p2 tog., (k1, p1) 6 times, k1.

4th ROW. Sl 1, (k1, p1) 5 times, k1, p2 tog., k2 tog.,* p1, k1, repeat from * to the last 16 sts., p2 tog., k2 tog., (p1, k1) 6 times.

6th ROW. Sl 1, (k1, p1) 5 times, k2 tog. t.b.l., p2 tog.,* k1, p1, repeat from * to the last 15 sts., k2 tog. t.b.l., p2 tog., (k1, p1) 5 times, k1.

8th ROW. Sl 1, (k1, p1) 4 times, k1, p2 tog., k2 tog., * p1, k1, repeat from * to the last 14 sts., p2 tog., k2 tog., (p1, k1) 5 times.

9th ROW. Sl 1, k1, * p1, k1, repeat from * to end of row.
Cast off loosely in rib.

The Sleeves (both alike).

Using the No. 9 needles and Dark wool and with the right side of the work facing, knit the 14 sts. left on a safety-pin at the commencement of the armhole, pick up and knit 96 sts. evenly around the armhole, knit the 14 sts. left on the other safety-pin (124 sts.).

1st and every alternate ROW. Sl 1, purl to the last st., k1.

2nd ROW. Sl 1, k12, k2 tog., knit to the last 15 sts., k2 tog.t.b.l., k13.

4th ROW. Sl 1, k11, k2 tog., knit to the last 14 sts., k2 tog.t.b.l., k 12.

6th ROW. Sl 1, k10, k2 tog., knit to the last 13 sts., k2 tog.t.b.l., k11.

8th ROW. Sl 1, k9, k2 tog., knit to the last 12 sts., k2 tog.t.b.l., k10.

10th ROW. Sl 1, k8, k2 tog., knit to the last 11 sts., k2 tog.t.b.l., k9.

Continue decreasing in this manner until 98 sts. remain on the needle.

Commencing with a purl row continue in st. st. without shaping until the work measures 5½ inches from where the sts. were picked up round the armhole, ending on the wrong side of the work.

Continue in st. st. decreasing once at each end of the next and every following 6th row until 66 sts. remain.

Commencing with a purl row continue in st. st. without shaping until the work measures 19½ inches from where the sts. were picked up round the armhole, ending on the right side of the work.

NEXT ROW. Sl 1, p1, * p2 tog., p10, repeat from * to the last 4 sts., p2 tog., p1, k1 (60 sts.).

Change to No. 11 needles and proceed as follows :—

1st ROW. Sl 1, k1, * p1, k1, repeat from * to end of row.

Repeat the 1st row 29 times.

Cast off loosely in rib.

To Make Up the Sweater.

Press on the wrong side under a damp cloth with a hot iron. Sew up the side seams of the sleeveless model. Sew up the side and sleeve seams of the long-sleeved model. Turn down the ribbing at the neck to form a polo neck and stitch the Zipp-fastener in position, commencing at the top of the ribbing and ending on the shoulder, sewing through both edges of the turned down collar.

Press all seams.

Lumber Jackets

In Templeton's **Fisherknit** Wool

MATERIALS

Chunky yarn. *#Roy 1/2 oz*

32 ozs. of Templeton's Fisherknit Wool for Man's Jacket, or 27 ozs. for Woman's Jacket.

2 No. 3, 2 No. 5 and 2 No. 7 knitting needles. *Needles # 6, 4, 10*

6 buttons. 1 smaller button for adjustable neck fastening.

TENSION

$3\frac{1}{2}$ sts. and $5\frac{1}{2}$ rows to 1 inch in m.st. on No. 3 needles.

ABBREVIATIONS

K=knit; p=purl; sts.=stitches; m.st.=moss stitch; ins.=inches; beg.=beginning; inc.=increase; dec.=decrease; cont.=continue; tog.=together; sl.=slip; p.s.s.o.=pass slipped st. over; rem.=remain(ing); foll.=following; fin.=finishing; rep.=repeat.

MAN'S JACKET
MEASUREMENTS

Length—$25\frac{1}{2}$ ins.   To fit a 38-40 inch chest.

THE BACK

Using No. 5 needles cast on 74 sts. and work $3\frac{1}{2}$ ins. in K1, P1 rib, inc. 1 st. at end of last row (75 sts.) Cont. in m.st. until work measures $7\frac{1}{2}$ ins. from beg., then change to No. 3 needles and cont. in m.st. until work measures 15 ins. from beg.

Shape Armholes

1st row—K1, sl.1, K1, p.s.s.o., m.st. to last 3 sts., K2 tog., K1.

2nd row—P2, m.st. to last 2 sts., P2.
Rep. these 2 rows until 19 sts. remain. Cast off.

THE POCKET LININGS
(Both Alike)

Using No. 5 needles, cast on 19 sts. and work in m.st. for 4 ins. Leave on spare needle.

THE RIGHT FRONT

Using No. 5 needles cast on 51 sts. and work in K1, P1 rib for $3\frac{1}{2}$ ins.

Next row—Rib 20, m.st. 31.

Next row—M.st. 31, rib 20.

Cont. in m.st. over main sts. and rib over border sts. until work measures $/\frac{1}{2}$ ins. from beg., fin. at border edge.

Next row—Rib 20, change to No. 3 needles, m.st. 6, sl. next 19 sts. on st. holder, m.st. across 19 sts. of one pocket lining, m.st. 6.

Next row—M.st. 31, change to No. 5 needle, rib to end.

Cont. on these sts. with main sts. on No. 3 needles and border sts. on No. 5 needles until work measures 15 ins. from beg., fin. at front edge.

Shape Armholes

1st row—Rib 20, change needle, m.st. to last 3 sts., K2 tog., K1.

2nd row—P2, m.st. to last 20 sts., change needle, rib 20.

Cont. to dec. in this way until work measures 16 ins., fin. at front edge.

Shape for Collar

1st row—Rib to last border st., work twice into this st., change needle, m.st. to last 3 sts., work 2 tog., K1.

2nd row—P2, m.st. to last 21 sts., change needle, rib to end.

3rd row—Rib border sts., change needle, m.st. to last 3 sts., K2 tog., K1.

4th row—As 2nd row.

5th row—As 3rd row.

6th row—As 2nd row.

7th and 8th rows—Rib to 3 sts. from end of border, turn and rib back.

Cont. in this way, that is dec. at armhole edge on alternate rows, inc. at inside border edge on every 6th row of main work until 9 sts. have been added, and work 2 more extra rows on border after 6 rows on main work.

Cont. until 28 sts. have been dec. at armhole edge, fin. at front edge (inc. of 9 sts. at inside border edge now completed).

Next row—Using No. 5 needles, rib across all sts.

Cont. in rib, turning on every 7th and 8th row, but 6 sts. in from edge to allow for 3 extra m.st. sts. taken into rib.

When short edge of back collar measures $2\frac{1}{2}$ ins. Cast off in the rib.

THE LEFT FRONT

First place pins on right front border. 1st pin $\frac{1}{2}$ inch up from lower edge in centre of border, 2nd pin $15\frac{1}{2}$ ins. up from lower edge, and 4 pins at equal distances between.

See colour plate on page 61

38″/40″ and 34″/36″ FISHERKNIT WOOL

No. 1008
Price 6d

A *Templeton* Design

Using No. 5 needles, cast on 51 sts., and work in K1, P1 rib for ½ inch.

Next row—Rib 40, cast off 2, rib to end.

Next row—Rib 9, cast on 2, rib to end.

Cont. to match Right Front, working buttonholes as first buttonhole when pin positions are reached until work measures 7½ ins., fin. at side edge.

Next row—M.st. 6, sl. next 19 sts. on st. holder, m.st. across 19 pocket lining sts., m.st. 6, change needle, rib to end.

Cont. to match Right Front, but working button holes at indicated positions and working armhole dec. rows thus:—

1st row—(side edge) K1, sl. 1, K1, p.s.s.o., m.st. to last 20 sts., change needle, rib 20.

2nd row—Rib 20, change needle, m.st. to last 2 sts. P2.

THE SLEEVES

Using No. 7 needles, cast on 42 sts. and work in K1, P1 rib for 3½ ins., inc. at end of last row (43 sts.). Change to No. 3 needles and work in m.st. for 1 inch, then inc. 1 st. each end of next row and every foll. 10th row until there are 57 sts., then cont. straight until work measures 19½ ins.

Shape Top

Work the two rows of armhole shaping until 5 sts. rem., fin. after a wrong side row.

Next row—K1, K3 tog., K1.

Next row—P3 tog. Fasten off.

THE POCKET BORDER

Go back to sts. left on spare needle. Rejoin wool and using No. 5 needles, work thus:—

Next row—K1 (inc. in next st., P1, K1, P1, inc. in next st., K1, P1, K1) twice, inc. in next st., P1 (24 sts.).

Cont. in K1, P1 rib for 1 inch. Cast off.

TO MAKE UP

Press work lightly with a hot iron over a damp cloth. Sew sleeves into armholes, then sew up sleeve and side seams. Sew back neck edges together, and sew back of collar to neck edge.

Sew pocket linings in position and sew down small pocket edges.

Sew on buttons to correspond with buttonholes.

Press all seams, and turn back collar.

For adjustable neck fastening make a small button-hole stitched loop on the edge of the collar about 5 ins. above the top button and sew on the smaller button to correspond.

WOMAN'S JACKET MEASUREMENTS

Length—24 ins. To fit a 34-36 inch bust.

THE BACK

With No. 5 needles, cast on 66 sts. and work 3 ins. in K1, P1 rib, inc. 1 st. at end of last row (67 sts.).

Cont. in m.st. until work measures 7 ins. from beg. then change to No. 3 needles and cont. in m.st. until work measures 14 ins. from beg.

Shape Armholes

1st row—K1, sl. 1, K1, p.s.s.o., m.st. to last 3 sts., K2 tog., K1.

2nd row—P2, m.st. to last 2 sts., P2. Rep. these 2 rows until 17 sts. remain. Cast off.

THE POCKET LININGS
(Both Alike)

Using No. 5 needles, cast on 17 sts., and work in m.st. for 4 ins. Leave on spare needle.

THE LEFT FRONT

Using No. 5 needles, cast on 45 sts. and work in K1, P1 rib for 3 ins.

Next row—M.st. 27, rib 18.

Next row—Rib 18, m.st. 27.

Cont. in m.st. over main sts. and rib over border sts. until work measures 7 ins., fin. at border edge.

Next row—Rib 18, change to No. 3 needle, m.st. 5, sl. next 17 sts. on st. holder, m.st. across 17 sts. of one pocket lining, m.st. 5.

Next row—M.st. 27, change to No. 5 needle, rib to end.

Cont. on these sts. with m.st. on No. 3 needles and border sts. on No. 5 needles until work measures 14 ins. from beg., fin. at armhole edge.

Shape Armhole

1st row—K1, sl. 1, K1, p.s.s.o., m.st. to last 18 sts., change needle, rib 18.

2nd Row—Rib 18, change needle, m.st. to last 2 sts., P2.

Cont. to dec. in this way until work measures 15 ins. from beg., fin. at armhole edge.

Shape for Collar

Changing needles when required, work thus:—

1st row—K1, sl. 1, K1, p.s.s.o., m.st. to border sts., work twice into next st., rib to end.

2nd row—Rib 19, m.st. to last 2 sts., P.2.

3rd row—K1, sl. 1, K1, p.s.s.o., m.st. to border sts., rib 19.

4th row—Rib 19, m.st. to last 2 sts., P2.

5th row—As 3rd row.

6th and 7th rows—Rib 16, turn and rib back.

8th row—As 4th row.

9th row—As 3rd row.
10th row—As 4th row.

Cont. in this way, rep. 3rd-10th rows, that is, dec. at armhole edge on alternate rows, and working 2 more extra rows on border after 6 rows on main work.

Cont. until 25 sts. have been dec. at armhole edge, fin. at front edge.

Next row—Using No. 5 needles, rib across all sts. Cont. in rib turning as before, but 5 sts. in from

edge to allow for 2 extra m.st. taken into rib.

When short edge of back collar measures 2 ins., cast off in rib.

THE RIGHT FRONT

First place pins on left front border. 1st pin ½ inch up from lower edge, in centre of border, 2nd pin 14½ ins. up from lower edge, and 4 pins at equal distances between.

Using No. 5 needles, cast on 45 sts. and work in K1, P1 rib for ½ inch.

Next row—Rib 8, cast off 2, rib to end.

Next row—Rib 35, cast on 2, rib to end.

Cont. to match Left Front, working buttonholes as first buttonhole when pin positions are reached until work measures 7 ins., fin. at side edge.

Next row—M.st. 5, sl. next 17 sts. on st. holder, m.st. across 17 sts. of pocket lining, m.st. 5, change needle, rib to end.

Cont. to match Left Front, but working button-holes at indicated positions and working armhole dec. rows thus:—

1st row—(front edge) Rib 18, m.st. to last 3 sts. K2 tog., K1.

2nd row—P2, m.st. to border sts., rib to end.

THE SLEEVES

Using No. 7 needles cast on 36 sts. and work 3 ins. in K1, P1 rib.

Next row—* Rib 5, inc. in next st. Rep. from * 4 times, rib 6 (41 sts.).

Change to No. 3 needles and work in m.st. for 1 inch, then inc. 1 st. each end of next row and every foll. 8th row until there are 53 sts., then cont. straight until work measures 17 ins.

Shape Top

Work the two rows of armhole shaping until 5 sts. rem., fin. after a wrong side row.

Next row—K1, K3 tog., K1.

Next row—P3 tog. Fasten off.

THE POCKET BORDER

Go back to sts. left on st. holder. Rejoin wool and using No. 5 needles, work thus:—

Next row—K1 (inc. in next st., P1, K1, P1, inc. in next st., K1, P1, K1) twice (21 sts.).

Cont. in K1, P1 rib for 1 inch. Cast off.

TO MAKE UP

Press work lightly with a hot iron over a damp cloth. Sew sleeves into armholes, then sew up sleeve and side seams. Sew back neck edges together and sew back of collar to neck edge.

Sew pocket linings in position and sew down small pocket edges.

Sew on buttons to correspond with buttonholes.

Press all seams, and turn back collar.

For adjustable neck fastening, make a small button-hole stitched loop on the edge of the collar about 5 ins. above the top button and sew on the smaller button to correspond.

MAN'S RIB AND CABLE PULLOVER

A Chunky Jersey Quickly Knitted In Raglan Style

For the adventurous, canary yellow is the colour for him; but for a more conservative choice we suggest donkey brown, bottle green, maroon or grey.

MATERIALS

TWENTY-FIVE ounces of Bairns-Wear Femina Double Knitting Wool; a pair each of No. 10 and No. 7 knitting needles; a cable needle or short double-pointed needle for the cable stitches.

TENSION AND MEASUREMENTS

WORKED at such a tension that the cable panel (12 stitches) measures 1½ inches and 6 rib stitches measure 1 inch in width both worked with No. 7 needles, the measurements on the diagram below will be attained without pressing. The pullover will fit a chest measurement of up to 42 inches.

ABBREVIATIONS—
TO BE READ BEFORE WORKING

KNIT PLAIN; p., purl; st., stitch; tog., to-., gether; inc., increase (by working into the back and front of the same st.); dec., decrease (by

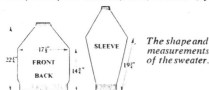

The shape and measurements of the sweater.

working 2 sts. tog.); to cable 12 F., to cable 12 front, slip the next 4 sts. on to the cable needle and leave at the front of the work, k. 4, then k. 4 sts. from cable needle, k. 4; to cable 12 B., to cable 12 back, k. 4, slip the next 4 sts. on to the cable needle and leave at the back of the work, k. 4, then k. 4 sts.

from cable needle; single rib is k. 1 and p. 1 alternately. Directions in brackets are worked the number of times stated after the last bracket.

TO WORK THE BACK OR FRONT (Both alike)

BEGIN at the lower edge by casting on 110 sts. with No. 10 needles and work 23 rows in single rib working into the backs of the sts. on the first row to give a neat edge.

INC. ROW: Rib 54, (inc.) twice, rib 54 (112 sts.).

Change to No. 7 needles and work in pattern as follows:

1st ROW: P. 2, (k. 1, p. 2) 16 times, k. 12, (p. 2, k. 1) 16 times, p. 2.

2nd ROW: K. 2, (p. 1, k. 2) 16 times, p. 12, (k. 2, p. 1) 16 times, k. 2.

3rd ROW: P. 2, (k. 1, p. 2) 16 times, cable 12 F., (p. 2, k. 1) 16 times, p. 2.

4th ROW: As 2nd.

5th ROW: As 1st.

6th ROW: As 2nd.

7th ROW: P. 2, (k. 1, p. 2) 16 times, cable 12 B., (p. 2, k. 1) 16 times, p. 2.

8th ROW: As 2nd.

These 8 rows form the pattern so repeat them 9 times more to bring the work to the armholes.

To Shape The Raglan Armholes: Continuing in pattern dec. 1 st. at both ends of the next 2 rows, then work 1 row straight.

Repeat the last 3 rows 17 times more and the first 2 rows again (36 sts.).

Change to No. 10 needles, and work as follows: (K. 1, p. 1) 8 times, k. 2 tog., p. 2 tog., (k. 1, p. 1) 8 times (34 sts.).

The Neckband: Work 10 rows in single rib.
Cast off in rib.

THE SLEEVES

USING No. 10 needles cast on 56 sts. and work 23 rows in single rib.

INC. ROW: Rib 3, inc., (rib 6, inc.) 7 times, rib 3 (64 sts.).

Change to No. 7 needles.

Now work the first 6 rows of pattern as set at the beginning of the back, but working the items in brackets 8 times instead of 16.

Continuing in pattern, inc. 1 st. at both ends of the next row and every following 6th row until the 15th inc. row has been worked, working the extra sts. in rib as set on each side of the cable panel, there will now be 41 sts. in rib on either side of the cable (94 sts.).

Work 21 rows straight, (this is for a 19¼-inch sleeve seam, more or less rows may be worked here for length required).

To Shape The Raglan Sleeve Top: Work as given for the raglan armhole shaping on the back, when there will be 18 sts. on the needle instead of 36.

Change to No. 10 needles and work as follows: K. 1, (p. 1, k. 1) 3 times, p. 2 tog., k. 2 tog., (p. 1, k. 1) 3 times, p. 1 (16 sts.).

The Neckband: Work 10 rows in single rib.
Cast off in rib.

Make another sleeve in the same way.

TO MAKE UP THE PULLOVER

DO not press. Set in raglan sleeves so that the cast-off edges form part of the neckband. Join sleeve and side seams in one line. Press all seams with the tip of the iron.

The patterns

For successful knitting of the classic patterns in this book, a few special instructions are required. These are contained chiefly in the Index (below) of every pattern reproduced in the book, suggesting for each the equivalent ply of modern yarn, a proprietary brand of yarn that will give the same appearance as the pattern-illustration, the modern needle/knitting pin equivalent and the correct tension/gauge.

British and American terms

BRITISH	AMERICAN
Balaclava	Cold weather hood
Cast off	Bind off
Double/treble crochet (DC, TR)	Single/double crochet
Double knitting (DK)	Sportsweight yarn
Garter stitch	Plain knitting/garter stitch
Hank	Skein
Jumper	Sweater
Knit up	Pick up and knit
Moss stitch	Seed stitch
Needle	Pin
Polo neck	Turtle neck
Stocking stitch/stocking-web stitch	Stockinette stitch
Tension	Gauge
Turtle neck	Mock turtle neck
Twinset	Sweater set
Waistcoat	Vest
Yarn round needle/forward	Yarn over

Sizes

The fashionable jerseys of the Thirties and Forties are generally short in the waist. They may be lengthened if desired by increasing the depth of the welt, or by repeating the main pattern once, twice, or more often, immediately above the welt or before the armhole is worked.

The patterns in the book include all sizes, from the very smallest—especially in the Twenties, Thirties and Forties, to the very largest—especially in the Fifties. It is possible to adjust the size of some garments by altering the tension. To vary the size, see the advice given in the Index.

Yarn Quantities

Modern yarns are heavier than the original yarns, and extra wool is often required today. For the patterns of the Twenties, Thirties and Forties it is advisable to increase the yarn recommended in the pattern by half as much again. For the patterns of the Fifties, the quantities stated in the patterns will suffice.

Different dye-batches vary in shade, consequently it is important to buy the full quantity of yarn at the outset. Falcon-by-Post will refund for yarn returned, and many stores and wool shops will be helpful in accepting returned yarn, or reserving yarn of the current dye-batch while the garment is being knitted.

The pattern-quantities are given in ounces and yarn is often sold in twenty-five, fifty or hundred gram balls. One ounce is the equivalent of 28.35 grams.

Needles

Knitters who have needles in the old British sizes, or who are buying equipment where this sizing continues, should consult the Index for the size recommended for the pattern, and then see the table of equivalents below.

Metric size mm	Equivalent American pin nos.	Original UK and Australian size. Canada, South Africa
2	00	14
2¼	0	13
2¾	1	12
3	2	11
3¼	3	10
3¾	4	9
4	5	8
4½	6	7
5	7	6
5½	8	5
6	9	4
6½	10	3
7	10½	2
7½	11	1
8	12	0
9	13	00
10	15	000

Tension

The tension of the knitting is all-important for success. Before starting to knit the pattern, test a sample of your knitting as follows:

1 Consult the Index for a suitable ply of yarn and needle size.
2 Knit a square approximately 5×5 in. (12.5×12.5 cm.) in stocking-stitch (or other stitch recommended by the Index).
3 Place the square on a flat surface without stretching, and using a metal tape or rigid rule, mark off with pins 4 in. (10 cm.), both across and down the fabric.
4 Count the number of stitches and rows between the pins and compare with the number specified in the Index.
5 If the number of stitches and rows is *greater* than specified, the knitting is too tight, and you should knit and measure a square on needles a size larger.
6 If the number of stitches and rows is *fewer* than specified, the knitting is too loose, and you should knit and measure a square on needles a size smaller.
7 If the number of stitches is correct but the number of rows is still incorrect, proceed with the pattern. Check the length as the fabric develops, and knit more or fewer rows in order to achieve the size required.

Index of modern yarns and needle sizes

10 'A three-colour pullover'. Any DK yarn such as Sirdar Majestic. FOR CHEST SIZE 36 in. (91 cm.): Needles 3 mm. (US 2) and 3¾ mm. (US 4); also a 3¾ mm. (US 4) circular needle. Tension on the 3¾ mm. needles over st. st., 24 sts and 32 rows to 4 in. (10 cm.). FOR CHEST SIZE 38–40 in. (97–102 cm.): Needles 3¼ mm. (US 3) and 4 mm. (US 5); also a 4 mm. (US 5) circular needle. Tension on the 4 mm. needles over st. st., 22 sts and 28 rows to 4 in. (10 cm.).

The colour plate on page 136 shows (right) the pullover knitted by the author for herself in Marriner's 5-ply worsted wool. For this small size, measuring 36 in. (91 cm.), length 24 in. (61 cm.), the yarn quantity required was four 100-gram balls (or, where yarn is bought in ounces, 11 oz.) of Breton Tan 1413 for the main colour, and two 100-gram balls (6 oz.) for each of the other colours, Fleet Blue and Natural. The needles were 4½ mm. (US 6) and a set of four 3¾ mm. (US 4) needles; also a 4½ mm. circular needle. Tension on 4½ mm. needles over pattern was 26 sts and 32 rows to 4 in. (10 cm.).

12 'For the country'. Any Shetland-type DK yarn such as Templeton's. FOR CHEST SIZE 36 in. (91 cm.): Needles 3 mm. (US 2) and 3¾ mm. (US 4); also a 3¾ mm. (US 4) circular needle. Tension on the 3¾ mm. needles over st. st., 24 sts and 32 rows to 4 in. (10 cm.). FOR CHEST SIZE 38 in. (97 cm.): Needles 3¼ mm. (US 3) and 4 mm. (US 5); also a 4 mm. (US 5) circular needle. Tension on the 4 mm. needles over st. st., 22 sts and 28 rows to 4 in. (10 cm.).

14 Cable-stitch sleeveless pullover. Any DK yarn such as Sunbeam Pure Wool DK. FOR CHEST SIZE 36 in. (91 cm.): Needles 3 mm. (US 2) and 3¾ mm. (US 4); also a set of four 3 mm. (US 2) needles. Tension on the 3¾ mm. needles over st. st., 24 sts and 32 rows to 4 in. (10 cm.). FOR CHEST SIZE 38 in. (97 cm.): Needles 3¼ mm. (US 3) and 4 mm. (US 5). Tension on the 3¾ mm. needles over st. st., 22 sts and 28 rows to 4 in. (10 cm.).

14 Bachelor's tea-cosy. Any DK yarn. Hook size 4.00 mm. (US H Bernat).

16 A knitted tie. Coats' South Maid cotton. Needles 2 mm. (US 00). Width 2 in. (5 cm.). Add two extra patterns to produce a tie of modern length: 50 in. (127 cm.). Yarn quantity: one 50-gram ball (2 oz.).

16 Golf stockings. Any Guernsey 5-ply yarn such as Poppleton's or Emu. FOR FOOT SIZE 10½ in. (27 cm.): Set of four 3 mm. (US 2) needles. Tension over st. st., 28 sts and 36 rows to 4 in. (10 cm.).

17 Motoring mittens. Any fine 4-ply yarn such as Pingouin Pingolaine. FOR GLOVE SIZE 6¾: Set of four 2½ mm. (US 0) needles. Tension over st. st., 36 sts and 44 rows to 4 in. (10 cm.).

18 'A new Fair Isle Pullover'. Any Shetland-type DK yarn such as Wendy Shetland. FOR CHEST SIZE 40–42 in. (102–107 cm.): Needles 3 mm. (US 2) and 3¾ mm. (US 4); also a 3¾ mm. (US 4) circular needle. Tension on the 3¾ mm. needles over st. st., 24 sts and 32 rows to 4 in. (10 cm.).

20 Sleeveless cardigan. Any 4-ply yarn such as Emu Superwash. FOR CHEST/BUST SIZE 36 in. (91 cm.): Needles 3 mm. (US 2) and 3¼ mm. (US 3); the 3¼ mm. needles to be long, otherwise use a circular needle to knit from edge to edge. Tension on the 3¼ mm. needles over st. st., 29 sts and 36 rows to 4 in. (10 cm.). FOR CHEST SIZE 39 in. (97 cm.): Needles 3¼ mm. (US 3) and 3¾ mm. (US 4); the 3¾ mm. needles to be long, otherwise use a circular needle. Tension on the 3¾ mm. needles over st. st., 26 sts and 34 rows to 4 in. (10 cm.).

22 'Patterned-all-over pullover'. Any DK yarn such as Patons' Clansman. FOR CHEST SIZE 40 in. (102 cm.): Needles 3 mm. (US 2) and 3¾ mm. (US 4). Tension on the 3¾ mm. needles over st. st., 24 sts and 32 rows to 4 in. (10 cm.). FOR CHEST SIZE 42 in. (107 cm.): Needles 3¼ mm. (US 3) and 4 mm. (US 5). Tension on the 4 mm. needles over st. st., 22 sts and 28 rows to 4 in. (10 cm.).

The colour plate on page 136 shows (left) the pullover knitted by the author for herself in Marriner's 5-ply worsted wool. In this small size, measuring 36 in. (91 cm.) round the chest and length 21 in. (53½ cm.), the yarn quantity required was three 100-gram balls (or, where yarn is bought in ounces, 11 oz.) of the main colour, Natural 1418, and one 100-gram ball (or 2 oz.) each of the other four colours, Peat Brown 1420, Amber Gold 1415, Breton Tan 1413 and Red 1421. Needles were 3¾ mm. (US 4) and 4½ mm. (US 6). Tension on the 4½ mm. needles over pattern was 26 sts and 36 rows to 4 in. (10 cm.).

24 Sweater, 'medium size'. Any Aran yarn such as Patons' Capstan. FOR CHEST SIZE 36 in. (91 cm.): Needles 3¼ mm. (US 3) and 4½ mm. (US 6). Tension on the 4½ mm. needles over st. st., 20 sts and 26 rows to 4 in. (10 cm.). FOR CHEST SIZE 38 in. (97 cm.): Needles 3¾ mm. (US 4) and 5 mm. (US 7). Tension on the 5 mm. needles over st. st., 18 sts and 24 rows to 4 in. (10 cm.).

24 A tie in open-work stitch. **The cover illustration** shows the tie knitted by the author to accompany Edward Fox's (see page 43), using Maxwell Cartlidge real silk (which knits as 4-ply) in shade S5H, 'Mink'. The yarn quantity was one 50-gram ball (or, where yarn is bought in ounces, 2 oz.). Knitting the tie on 2½ mm. (US 0) needles produced a rather nice cravat, measuring 4½ in. (11.5 cm.) at the widest part of the long end and 3½ in. (9 cm.) at the widest part of the short end, and with an overall length of 52½ in. (133.5 cm.).

24 Knee-caps. Any Guernsey 5-ply yarn such as Sunbeam or Marriner. Needles 3 mm. (US 2). Tension over st. st., 28 sts and 36 rows to 4 in. (10 cm.).

32 'A gift for a golfer'. Any Aran-type yarn such as Wendy or Sunbeam Aran. FOR CHEST SIZE 36 in. (91 cm.): Needles 3¾ mm. (US 4) and 5 mm. (US 7). Tension on the 5 mm. needles over st. st., 18 sts and 24 rows to 4 in. (10 cm.).

33 'The sort of cardigan Father likes'. Any 4-ply yarn such as Patons' Clansman. FOR CHEST SIZE 36 in. (91 cm.): Needles 2¾ mm. (US 1) and 3¼ mm. (US 3). Tension on the 3¼ mm. needles over st. st., 28 sts and 36 rows to 4 in. (10 cm.). FOR CHEST SIZE 38 in. (97 cm.): Needles 3 mm. (US 2) and 3¾ mm. (US 4). Tension on the 3¾ mm. needles over st. st., 24 sts and 32 rows to 4 in. (10 cm.).

34 'Jeffrey' design pullover. Any DK yarn such as Lister Motoravia. FOR CHEST SIZE 36 in. (91 cm.): Needles 3¾ mm. (US 4) and a set of four 3 mm. (US 2). Tension on the 3¾ mm. needles over st. st., 24 sts and 32 rows to 4 in. (10 cm.). FOR CHEST SIZE 38 in. (97 cm.): Needles 4 mm. (US 5) and set of four 3¼ mm. (US 3). Tension on the 4 mm. needles over st. st., 22 sts and 28 rows to 4 in. (10 cm.).

36 'Right with town or country clothes'. Any DK yarn such as Patons' Clansman. FOR CHEST SIZE 36 in. (91 cm.): Needles 3¼ mm. (US 3) and 4 mm. (US 5). Tension on the 4 mm. needles over st. st., 22 sts and 28 rows to 4 in. (10 cm.).

38 Two-way pullover. Any DK yarn such as Robin. FOR CHEST SIZE 40 in. (102 cm.): Needles 3 mm. (US 2) and 3¾ mm. (US 4); also a set of four 3 mm. (US 2) needles. Tension on the 3¾ mm. needles over st. st., 24 sts and 32 rows to 4 in. (10 cm.). FOR CHEST SIZE 42 in. (107 cm.): Needles 3¼ mm. (US 3) and 4 mm. (US 5); also a set of four 3¼ mm. (US 3) needles. Tension on the 4 mm. needles over st. st., 22 sts and 28 rows to 4 in. (10 cm.).

39 Scarf. Any DK yarn. Needles 3¾ mm. (US 4). Tension over st. st., 24 sts and 32 rows to 4 in. (10 cm.).

40 'An ingenious suit'. Any 4-ply yarn such as Lister Motoravia. FOR HIPS SIZE 38 in. (97 cm.): Needles 2¾ mm. (US 1) and 3¼ mm. (US 3). Tension on the 3¼ mm. needles over st. st., 28 sts and 36 rows to 4 in. (10 cm.).

41 Knitted sports shirt. Any 4-ply yarn such as Sirdar Majestic. FOR CHEST SIZE 38 in. (97 cm.): Needles 3 mm. (US 2). Tension over st. st., 30 sts and 40 rows to 4 in. (10 cm.). FOR CHEST SIZE 40 in. (102 cm.): Needles 3¼ mm. (US 3). Tension over st. st., 28 sts and 36 rows to 4 in. (10 cm.).

43 A Fair Isle pullover. Any DK yarn such as Patons' Clansman. FOR CHEST SIZE 36 in. (91 cm.): Needles 3¼ mm. (US 3) and 4 mm. (US 5). Tension on the 4 mm. needles over st. st., 22 sts and 28 rows to 4 in. (10 cm.).

The cover illustration shows the pullover knitted by the author for Edward Fox in the wool and colours of his choice: Falcon's Superwash Pure Wool 4-ply in Pepper (six 25-gram balls, or, where yarn is bought in ounces, 6 oz.), French Cream (five 25-gram balls, or 4 oz.), Wild Rose, Banana and Tobacco (three 25-gram balls, or 2 oz., each). For chest size 38 in. (97 cm.), length 24 in. (61 cm.), the needles were 4¼ mm. (US 6) and 3 mm. (US 2). Tension on 4¼ mm. needles over pattern was 32 sts and 28 rows to 4 in. (10 cm.).

The pullover has been knitted up most effectively on finer needles, using Robin 'Reward' 4-ply in shades Catkin (four 50-gram balls, or 7 oz.), Sable, Peppermint, Pompadour and Porcelain (two 50-gram balls, or 2 oz. each). For this loose knitter the chest size 38 in. (97 cm.) required 3¼ mm. (US 3) and 2¾ mm. (US 1) needles, with tension on 3¼ mm. needles over pattern, 28 sts and 30 rows to 4 in. (10 cm.). The length of this pullover was 23 in. (58.5 cm.).

44   Tennis pullover. Wendy Swiftknit. FOR CHEST 36–38 in. (91–97 cm.): Needles 4½ mm. (US 6) and 5 mm. (US 7). Tension on the 5 mm. needles over st. st., 17 sts 24 rows to 4 in. (10 cm.).

50   Jersey with cable yoke and aero cap. Jersey, Patons' DK. FOR CHEST SIZE 38–40 in. (97–102 cm.): Needles 3¼ mm. (US 3) and 4 mm. (US 5); also a set of four 4 mm. (US 5) needles. Tension on the 4 mm. needles over st. st., 22 sts and 28 rows to 4 in. (10 cm.).

52   Fatigue cap. Any 4-ply yarn. Needles 3¼ mm. (US 3). Tension over st. st., 28 sts and 36 rows to 4 in. (10 cm.).

53   Vest or pull-on garment. Any 4-ply yarn such as Patricia Roberts or Falcon Superwash. FOR CHEST SIZE 36 in. (91 cm.): Needles 3¼ mm. (US 3); also a crochet hook, 3.00 mm. (US F Bernat). Tension over st. st., 28 sts and 36 rows to 4 in. (10 cm.). Alternatively, for CHEST/BUST SIZE 38–40 in. (97–102 cm.), the vest-pattern adapts to make a shirt for men or women. Yarn quantity for this larger size is 350 grams (or, where yarn is bought in ounces, 13 oz.). It has been knitted up effectively in Jaeger Matchmaker, 'Storm' blue, on 3¼ mm. (US 3) needles. Tension over st. st. was 32 sts and 36 rows to 4 in. (10 cm.). *Alteration to pattern:* Cast on 146 sts decreasing at armhole-shaping as pattern until 134 sts remain. At the neck-edge, knit 45 sts, cast off 44 and continue on the last 45 sts, decreasing at the neck-edge as pattern until 37 sts remain. Sleeve: cast on 96 sts increasing as pattern until you have 130 sts; finally, shape the top by decreasing as pattern until 114 sts remain. Otherwise, as pattern.

53   A body belt. Any 4-ply yarn, especially a Thermal yarn for warmth, such as Lister's Thermoknit. Needles 3 mm. (US 2) and 4 mm. (US 5). Tension on the 4 mm. needles over the rib-pattern, approx, 24 sts and 30 rows to 4 in. (10 cm.).

54   Helmet with cape pieces (A). Patons' Capstan. Needles 4½ mm. (US 6). Tension over garter stitch, 20 sts and 38 rows to 4 in. (10 cm.).

54   Ribbed helmet (B) and 'Sleeping cap' (C). Patons' Capstan. Needles 4½ mm. (US 6). Tension over st. st., 20 sts and 26 rows to 4 in. (10 cm.).

54   Sports cap (D). Patons' DK. Needles 4 mm. (US 5). Tension over garter stitch, 22 sts and 36 rows to 4 in. (10 cm.).

The colour plate on page 99 shows the ribbed helmet (left) and 'sports cap' (right) knitted by Sarah Peart in Patons' Moorland DK 'Glengarry', for a looser, more textured effect. Yarn quantity for the ribbed helmet was 100 grams (or, where yarn is bought in ounces, 4 oz.). Needles were 5 mm. (US 7). Tension over the rib was 20 sts and 26 rows to 4 in. (10 cm.). The 'sports cap' required the same quantity of yarn. Needles were 4½ mm. (US 6). Tension over garter stitch was 18 sts and 22 rows to 4 in. (10 cm.).

55   A round-necked pullover. Any DK yarn such as Wendy. FOR CHEST SIZE 38 in. (97 cm.): Needles 3 mm. (US 2) and 3¾ mm. (US 4). Tension on the 3¾ mm. needles over st. st., 24 sts and 32 rows to 4 in. (10 cm.). FOR CHEST 40 in. (102 cm.): Needles 3¼ mm. (US 3) and 4 mm. (US 5). Tension on the 4 mm. needles over st. st., 22 sts and 28 rows to 4 in. (10 cm.).

56   Polo-neck jumper. Any DK yarn such as Sunbeam Pure Wool DK. FOR CHEST SIZE 36 in. (91 cm.): Needles 3 mm. (US 2) and 3¾ mm. (US 4); also a set of four 3¾ mm. (US 4) needles or a 3¾ mm. circular needle. Tension on the 3¾ mm. needles over st. st., 24 sts and 32 rows to 4 in. (10 cm.). FOR CHEST 40 in. (102 cm.): Needles 3¼ mm. (US 3) and 4 mm. (US 5); also a set of four 4 mm. (US 5) needles or a 4 mm. circular needle. Tension on the 4 mm. needles over st. st., 22 sts and 28 rows to 4 in. (10 cm.).

57   The 'Wonder-sock'. Any sock yarn such as Sunbeam, Patons', etc. FOR FOOT SIZE 10 in. (25.5 cm.): In 3-ply yarn, a set of four 2¼ mm. (US 0) needles. Tension over st. st., approx. 32 sts and 42 rows to 4 in. (10 cm.). In 4-ply yarn, a set of four 2¾ mm. (US 1) needles. Tension approx. 30 sts and 40 rows to 4 in. (10 cm.).

58   Pullover with or without sleeves. Wendy 4-ply. FOR CHEST SIZE 36 in. (91 cm.): Needles 2¾ mm. (US 1) and 3¼ mm. (US 3). Tension on 3¼ mm. needles over st. st., 28 sts and 36 rows to 4 in. (10 cm.).

65   Evening scarf. A real silk such as Dent 'Naturally Beautiful' (knits as 4-ply). Needles 3¾ mm. (US 4).

The colour plate on page 65 shows the scarf knitted in Dent silver silk (shade 701) by Francis Pigott. He used 2 hanks (or 200 grams) of silk for a scarf-length 54 in. (137 cm.) and width 10 in. (25.5 cm.). Do not press the silk.

66   Fair Isle pullover featuring a round neck. Any 4-ply yarn such as Lister Motoravia. For CHEST SIZE 38 in. (97 cm.): Needles 2¾ mm. (US 1) and 3¼ mm. (US 3). Tension on 3¼ mm. needles over st. st., 28 sts and 36 rows to 4 in. (10 cm.).

The colour plate on page 25 shows the Fair Isle pullover knitted in Patricia Roberts' Merino Extra Fine Lambswool, by Eileen Griffiths. The chest measurement is 38 in. (97 cm.), the length 21 in. (53.5 cm.). Yarn quantity was eleven 25-gram balls (or, where yarn is sold in ounces, 10 oz.) of the dark (shade 9), seven 25-gram balls (7 oz.) of the light (shade 2), and three 25-gram balls (2 oz.) of the medium (shade 7). If the length is to be increased by adding extra patterns, order extra wool. Needles 4 mm. (US 5) and 3 mm. (US 2). Tension on 4 mm. needles over pattern was 28 sts and 32 rows to 4 in. (10 cm.)

68   Pullover with or without sleeves. Any 4-ply such as Falcon's Superwash. FOR CHEST SIZE 36 in. (91 cm.): Needles 3 mm. (US 2) and 3¾ mm. (US 4). Tension on 3¾ mm. needles over st. st., 26 sts and 32 rows to 4 in. (10 in.).

70   Golf club covers. Any 4-ply yarn. Needles 3¼ mm. (US 3). Tension over st. st., 28 sts and 36 rows to 4 in. (10 cm.).

71   Diamond-stitch pullover. Any 4-ply yarn such as Patons' Clansman. FOR CHEST SIZE 40 in. (102 cm.): Needles 2¾ mm. (US 1) and 3¼ mm. (US 3). Tension on 3¼ mm. needles over st. st., 28 sts and 36 rows to 4 in. (10 cm.).

72   Knitted waistcoat. Any 3-ply yarn such as Jaeger or Sunbeam. FOR CHEST SIZE 38 in. (97 cm.): Needles 2¼ mm. (US 0) and 3 mm. (US 2). Tension on 3 mm. needles over st. st., 30 sts and 40 rows to 4 in. (10 cm.).

74   Long sleeved pullover in two-colour Fair Isle. Any 4-ply yarn such as Sirdar Majestic. FOR CHEST SIZE 38 in. (97 cm.): Needles 2¾ mm. (US 1) and 3¼ mm. (US 3); also a set of four 2¾ mm. (US 1) needles. Tension on 3¼ mm. needles over st. st., 28 sts and 36 rows to 4 in. (10 cm.).

76   Little boys' jerseys. Any 4-ply yarn such as Emu Superwash. FOR CHEST SIZE 22 in. (56 cm.): Needles 2¼ mm. (US 0) and 3 mm. (US 2). Tension on 3 mm. needles over st. st., 30 sts and 38 rows to 4 in. (10 cm.). FOR CHEST SIZE 24 in. (61 cm.): Needles 2¾ mm. (US 1) and 3¼ mm. (US 3). Tension 28 sts and 36 rows to 4 in. (10 cm.).

78   Muffler helmet. Any DK yarn such as Marriner, Robin, etc., used double. Needles 4 mm. (US 5) and 6 mm. (US 9). Tension on 6 mm. needles over st. st., about 16 sts and 22 rows to 4 in. (10 cm.). Alternatively, use a Double Double yarn such as Robin Landscape Chunky. Needles 4 mm. (US 5) and 5½ mm. (US 8), tension as above.

79   'A set in Fair Isle'. Patons' Clansman 4-ply. FOR CHEST SIZE 36–38 in. (91–97 cm.): Needles 2¼ mm. (US 0), 3 mm. (US 2) and 3¼ mm. (US 3). Tension on 3¼ mm. needles over st. st., 28 sts and 36 rows to 4 in. (10 cm.).

The colour plate on page 134 shows the set knitted by Brenda Ealey in Patons' Clansman 4-ply in Beryl and Black. It has been adapted for a 38 in. (97 cm) chest measurement, with length 24 in. (61 cm.). and under-arm length 16 in. (40.5 cm.). Needles were 3¾ mm. (US 4), tension over pattern was 28 sts and 30 rows to 4 in. (10 cm.). Yarn quantity for the jersey was five 50-gram balls (or, where wool is sold in ounces, 8 oz.), of the main colour and the same of contrast. The scarf required two 50-gram balls (or 3 oz.) each of main colour and contrast. The gloves required two 50-gram balls (3 oz.) of main colour and one 50-gram ball (1 oz.) of contrast. *Alteration to the jersey pattern:* At sleeve top, cast off 7 sts at beginning of next two rows, then decrease 1 st. at each end of every alternate row until 51 sts remain. Then decrease at each end of every row until 25 sts remain. Cast off. At neckband, sides 56 sts; back neck 37 sts.

80 Sports sweater. Any Dk yarn such as Emu Superwash. FOR CHEST SIZE 38 in. (97 cm): Needles 3 mm. (US 2) and 3¾ mm. (US 4). Tension on 3¾ mm. needles over st. st., 24 sts and 32 rows to 4 in. (10 cm.). FOR CHEST SIZE 40 in. (102 cm.): Needles 3¼ mm. (US 3), 4 mm. (US 5). Tension on 4 mm. needles over st. st., 22 sts and 28 rows to 4 in. (10 cm.).

The colour plate on page 64 shows the sweater knitted in grey M.P. Superspun 4-ply, from Needle Art House, by Mrs Maureen Gunn. The chest measurement is 36 in. (91 cm.), the length has been increased from the pattern to 24 in. (61 cm.). Yarn quantity, 400 grams (or, where yarn is bought in ounces, 13 oz.). Needles 3¼ mm. (US 3). Tension over pattern, 26 sts and 30 rows to 4 in. (10 cm.).

82 Bathing trunks. Any 4-ply yarn, such as Patons' Nylox. Needles 2¼ mm. (US 0). Tension over st. st., 36 sts and 44 rows to 4 in. (10 cm.).

84 Striped shirt. Pingouin Pingolaine for the wool and Fil d'Ecosse no. 5 for the cotton. FOR CHEST SIZE 38 in. (97 cm.): Needles 2¾ mm. (US 1) and 3¼ mm. (US 3) double pointed, or a circular needle. Tension on 3¼ mm. needles over st. st., 28 sts and 36 rows to 4 in. (10 cm.).

90 Adaptation from a Flamborough fisherman's jersey, modelled by the young Roger Moore. Any 4-ply yarn such as Sirdar's Majestic. FOR CHEST SIZE 40 in. (102 cm.): Needles 3¾ mm. (US 4) and 3 mm. (US 2). Tension on 3¾ mm. needles over st. st., 32 sts and 36 rows to 4 in. (10 cm.). For length 25 in. (63.5 cm.), knit to row 26, work 25 more rows. Cast off for armhole as pattern. Yarn quantity for jersey this length: 300 grams (or, where yarn is bought in ounces, 10 oz.).

93 Waistcoat. Any Aran-weight wool such as Templeton's. FOR CHEST SIZE 38–42 in. (97–107 cm.): Needles 3¾ mm. (US 4) and 4½ mm. (US 6). Tension on 4½ mm. needles over st. st., 20 sts and 26 rows to 4 in. (10 cm.).

94 'Father and son special'. Marriner's 4-ply. MAN'S CHEST SIZE 34–42 in. (86–102 cm.), BOY'S CHEST SIZE 24–32 in. (61–81 cm.): Needles 2¼ mm. (US 0) and 3¼ mm. (US 3). Tension on 3¼ mm. needles over st. st., 28 sts and 36 rows to 4 in. (10 cm.).

101 Sleeveless cable pullover. Any 4-ply yarn such as Templeton's H. & O. Shetland Fleece. FOR CHEST SIZE 36 in. (91 cm.): Needles 3¾ mm. (US 4), 3 mm. (US 2). Tension on 3¾ mm. needles over st. st., 22 sts and 32 rows to 4 in. (10 cm.).

The colour plate on page 100 shows the pullover knitted with H. & O. Shetland Fleece 4-ply in Cloverleaf Green (shade 29) by Betty Anderson. The chest size is 36 in. (91 cm.), the length 22 in. (56 cm.). Yarn quantity was ten 25-gram balls (or, where wool is bought in ounces, 8 oz.). Tension was 22 sts to 4 in. (10 cm.) over pattern. Knitting the straight-sided version, the knitter worked 8 sts, then increased in the next and every following 5th st. until 24 increases in all were made, making 156 sts on the needles (see end of pattern).

103 'Club Colours'. Patons' Moorland DK. FOR CHEST SIZE 38–40 in. (97–104 cm): Needles 3¼ mm. (US 3) and 4 mm. (US 5). Tension on 5½ mm. needles over st. st., 22 sts and 28 rows to 4 in. (10 cm.)

104 'For him and her'. Any 4-ply yarn such as Lister, Sunbeam, etc. FOR BUST/CHEST SIZE 32–36 in. (82–91 cm.): Needles 3 mm. (US 2) and 3¾ mm. (US 4). Tension on 3¾ mm. needles over st. st., 30 sts and 38 rows to 4 in. (10 cm.). FOR BUST/CHEST SIZE 34–40 in. (86–102 cm.): Needles 2¾ mm. (US 1) and 3¼ mm. (US 3). Tension on 3¼ mm. needles over st. st., 28 sts and 36 rows to 4 in. (10 cm.).

107 'Match mates'. Sirdar Majestic 4-ply. FOR CHEST SIZE 38 in. (97 cm.)/ BUST SIZE 34 in. (86 cm.): Needles 2¼ mm. (US 0) and 3 mm. (US 2); also a set of four 2¼ mm. needles. Tension on 3 mm. needles over st. st., 30 sts and 38 rows to 4 in. (10 cm.). FOR CHEST SIZE 40 in. (102 cm.)/BUST 36 in. (91 cm.): Needles 2¾ mm. (US 4) and 3¼ mm. (US 3); also a set of four 2¾ mm. needles. Tension on 3¼ mm. needles over st. st., 28 sts and 36 rows to 4 in. (10 cm.).

108 Matching set of Fair Isle socks, gloves and scarf. Patons' 4-ply. Scarf: Needles 3 mm. (US 2). Tension over Fair Isle pattern, 34 sts and 34 rows to 4 in. (10 cm.). Gloves: Needles 2¾ mm. (US 1). Tension over st. st., 32 sts and 40 rows to 4 in. (10 cm.). Socks: Needles 2¼ mm. (US 0), also a set of four 2 mm. (US 00) needles. Tension over st. st., 36 sts and 44 rows to 4 in. (10 cm.).

110 Wynnefield vest. Any 4-ply yarn such as Sunbeam or Patricia Roberts. FOR CHEST SIZE 36–38 in. (91–107 cm.): Needles 2¾ mm. (US 0) and 3¼ mm. (US 3). Tension on 3¼ mm. needles over st. st., 28 sts and 36 rows to 4 in. (10 cm.).

112 Slipover with Fair Isle borders. Any 4-ply yarn such as Sirdar Majestic. FOR CHEST SIZE 36 in. (91 cm.): Needles 2¾ mm. (US 1) and 3¼ mm. (US 3). Tension on 3¼ mm. needles over st. st., 28 sts and 36 rows to 4 in. (10 cm.).

115 Pullover with or without sleeves. Any 4-ply yarn such as Patons' Glansman. FOR CHEST SIZE 38–40 in. (97–102 cm.): Needles 2¼ mm. (US 0) and 3 mm. (US 2); also a cable needle. Tension over st. st., 30 sts and 38 rows to 4 in. (10 cm.).

The colour plate on page 133 shows the pattern knitted with a 3-ply yarn, Sunbeam's pure wool, in wine (shade 3906), by Mrs J. Knowles. In this ply, with needle size as above, tension over pattern was 32 sts and 40 rows to 4 in. (10 cm.). Chest size was 36–38 in. (91–97 cm.). The length was increased to 24 in. (61 cm.) by knitting an extra pattern before the armhole. Yarn quantity for this length: 350 grams (or, where yarn is bought in ounces, 12 oz.).

116 'Pullover to fit 37 in. chest'. Any 4-ply such as Patons' Clansman. FOR CHEST SIZE 38 in. (97 cm.): Needles 2¼ mm. (US 0) and 3 mm. (US 2). Tension on 3 mm. needles over st. st., 30 sts and 38 rows to 4 in. (10 cm.). FOR CHEST SIZE 40 in. (102 cm.): Needles 2¼ mm. (US 0) and 3¼ mm. (US 3). Tension on 3¼ mm. needles over st. st., 28 sts and 36 rows to 4 in. (10 cm.).

118 Pullover with and without sleeves. Any 4-ply yarn such as Lister Motoravia. FOR CHEST SIZE 38–40 in. (97–102 cm.): Needles 3 mm. (US 2) and 3¾ mm. (US 4). Tension on 3¾ mm. needles over st. st., 28 sts and 36 rows to 4 in. (10 cm.).

The colour plate on page 135 shows the slipover version knitted with Lister's Richmond 4-ply, in Fisherman, shade 3158, by Lister-Lee. Needles and tension as recommended above. Length 22 in. (56 cm.). Yarn quantity as pattern.

120 Fair Isle slipover. Any 4-ply yarn such as Lister Motoravia. FOR CHEST SIZE 38–40 in. (97–102 cm.): Needles 2¾ mm. (US 1) and 3¼ mm. (US 3). Tension on 3¼ mm. needles over st. st., 28 sts and 36 rows to 4 in. (10 cm.).

The colour plate on page 97 shows the slipover knitted by the author with Sirdar's Talisman 4-ply, using Dark Brown, shade 077 (four 50-gram balls, or, where yarn is bought in ounces, 5 oz.), and for the other colours, shades 059, 092, 132, 063, 090 and 091 (each one 50-gram ball, or 1 oz.). Needles were 2¾ mm. (US 1) and 3 mm. (US 2), tension on 3 mm. needles over pattern, 28 sts and 36 rows to 4 in. (10 cm.), to give a chest size 37 in. (94 cm.).

121 Slipover in Fair Isle patterning. Any Shetland yarn such as Templeton's Shetland Fleece. FOR CHEST SIZE 38–40 in. (97–102 cm.): Needles 2¾ mm. (US 1) and 3¼ mm. (US 3). Tension on 3¼ mm. needles over st.st., 28 sts and 36 rows to 4 in. (10 cm.).

123 Gloves with finger mitts. Any 4-ply yarn such as Emu Superwash. Needles 2¾ mm. (US 1). Tension over st. st., 36 sts and 44 rows to 4 in. (10 cm.).

124 Long-sleeved pullover. Any 4-ply yarn such as Wendy. FOR CHEST SIZE 36–38 in. (91–97 cm.): Needles 2¼ mm. (US 0) and 3 mm. (US 2), also a cable needle. Tension on 3¼ mm. needles over st. st., 30 sts and 38 rows to 4 in. (10 cm.). FOR CHEST SIZE 40 in. (102 cm.): Needles 2¾ mm. (US 1) and 3¼ mm. (US 3), also a cable needle. Tension on 3¼ mm. needles over st. st., 28 sts and 36 rows to 4 in. (10 cm.).

The colour plate on page 135 shows the pullover knitted by Penny Farthing with Wendy's Ascot 4-ply in Jersey Cream (shade 401), yarn quantity 400 grams (or, where yarn is bought in ounces, 15 oz.), and for the banding, Blue Lake, shade 418, and Bella Vista, shade 405 (each 50 grams, or 1 oz.). Needles and tension were as above for chest 38 in. (97 cm.). The length was 25 in. (63.5 cm.)

126 A very practical cardigan and simple sleeveless pullover. Templeton's 4-ply. CHEST SIZE 36 in. (91 cm.): Needles 2¾ mm. (US 1) and 3¼ mm. (US 3). Tension on 3¼ mm. needles over st. st., 28 sts and 36 rows to 4 in. (10 cm.).

128 Well-fitting golf hose. Templeton's 4-ply. SIZE ADJUSTABLE. Needles, a set of four 2¾ mm. (US 1). Tension over pattern, 36 sts and 36 rows to 4 in. (10 cm.). Work number of rows to give foot-length required.

129 'Sloppy Joe'. Any 4-ply yarn such as Sunbeam. FOR CHEST SIZE 38–42 in. (97–107 cm.): Needles 2¾ mm. (US 1) and 3¼ mm. (US 3). Tension on 3¼ mm. needles over st. st., 28 sts and 36 rows to 4 in. (10 cm.).

129 Raglan shirt. Any 4-ply yarn such as Patons'. FOR CHEST SIZE 38 in. (97 cm.): Needles 2¼ mm. (US 0) and 3 mm. (US 2). Tension on 3 mm. needles over st. st., 30 sts and 40 rows to 4 in. (10 cm.). FOR CHEST SIZE 40 in. (102 cm.): Needles 2¾ mm. (US 1) and 3¼ mm. (US 3). Tension on 3¼ mm. needles over st. st., 28 sts and 36 rows to 4 in. (10 cm.).

130 'Made for two'. Any DK yarn such as Sirdar Majestic. FOR CHEST SIZE 40–42 in. (102–107 cm.)/BUST SIZE 34–36 in. (86–91 cm.): Needles 3 mm. (US 2) and 3¾ mm. (US 4); also a set of four 3 mm. needles. Tension on 3¾ mm. needles over st. st., 24 sts and 32 rows to 4 in. (10 cm.); or, over pattern, 28 sts and 36 rows to 4 in. (10 cm.).

The colour plate on page 26 shows the sweater knitted by Esther Brundish with Sirdar Talisman DK in Brown (shade 031) in chest size 40 in. (102 cm.), with needles as above, tension 28 sts and 32 rows over pattern. The yarn quantity is fourteen 50-gram balls (or, where yarn is bought in ounces, 24 oz.).

131 Double knitting pullover. Patons' DK. FOR CHEST SIZE 38 in. (97 cm.): Needles 3¼ mm. (US 3) and 4 mm. (US 5). Tension on 4 mm. needles over st. st., 22 sts and 28 rows to 4 in. (10 cm.).

132 Gardening sweater. Any DK yarn such as Patons'. FOR CHEST SIZE 38–40 in. (97–102 cm.): Needles 3 mm. (US 2) and 3¾ mm. (US 4). Tension on 3¾ mm. needles over st. st., 24 sts and 32 rows to 4 in. (10 cm.).

137 Pullover in classic style. Any 3-ply yarn such as Sunbeam, Jaeger. FOR CHEST SIZE 42–46 in. (107–112 cm.): Needles 2¼ mm. (US 0) and 3 mm. (US 2). Tension on 3 mm. needles over st. st., 32 sts and 40 rows to 4 in. (10 cm.).

The colour plate on page 98 shows the pullover knitted with 4-ply yarn, Emu, in shade 469, by Jill Harding. The pattern was adapted to obtain a chest size 42 in. (107 cm.) with 2¼ mm. (US 0) and 2¾ mm. (US 1) needles, tension on 2¾ mm. needles over pattern, 28 sts and 36 rows to 4 in. (10 cm.). The back was worked as the pattern until, instead of increasing to 179 sts on the wider rib, the knitter increased to 169 sts (10 sts less), thus casting off 41 sts at the top instead of 51. For the front, she also worked 169 sts, so that when dividing for the neck, instead of turning to work on one side after 89 sts, she turned after 84. Therefore, 41 sts instead of 51 sts were picked up from the cast off edge for the neckband. The length of slipover is 21 in. (53.5 cm.). Yarn quantity is 300 grams (or, where yarn is bought in ounces, 10 oz.).

139 Sweater with crew neck. Any DK yarn such as Patons'. FOR CHEST SIZE 38–40 in. (97–102 cm.): Needles 3 mm. (US 2) and 3¾ mm. (US 4); also a cable needle. Tension on 3¾ mm. needles over st. st., 24 sts and 32 rows to 4 in. (10 cm.).

The colour plate on page 26 shows the sweater knitted with Patons' DK in Green Lovat, shade 6552, by Esther Brundish. Yarn quantity for chest size 38 in. (97 cm.), with needles and tension as above, is fourteen 50-gram balls (or, where yarn is bought in ounces, 24 oz.). The length is 25 in. (63.5 cm.).

140 Socks and slipover to match. Any 4-ply yarn such as Patons' Clansman. FOR SLIPOVER, CHEST SIZE 36–38 in. (91–97 cm.): Needles 2¾ mm. (US 1) and 3¼ mm. (US 3). Tension on 3¼ mm. needles over st. st., 28 sts and 36 rows to 4 in. (10 cm.). FOR SOCKS: Needles 3 mm. (US 2). Tension over st. st., 32 sts and 43 rows to 4 in. (10 cm.).

The colour plate on page 62 shows the socks and slipover knitted with Patons' Clansman 4-ply yarn in maroon and grey, by Theodore Every. Yarn quantities for the slipover: four 50-gram balls (or where yarn is bought in ounces, 6 oz.) of maroon, and two 50-gram balls (or 3 oz.) of grey. The needles for the main part of the work were 3¾ mm. (US 4), tension as above, size as above. The length of the slipover is 24 in. (61 cm.). Yarn quantity for the socks: two 50-gram balls (or 3 oz.) of maroon, and one 50-gram ball (or 1 oz.) of grey. Length of socks from tops to heel-base 21½ in. (32 cm.).

142 Lumber jacket (modelled by Roger Moore). Any DK yarn such as Wendy. FOR CHEST SIZE 38 in. (97 cm.): Needles 3 mm. (US 2) and 3¾ mm. (US 4). Tension on 3¾ mm. needles over st. st., 24 sts and 32 rows to 4 in. (10 cm.). FOR CHEST SIZE 40 in. (102 cm.): Needles 3 mm. (US 2) and 3¾ mm. (US 4). Tension on 3¾ mm. needles over st. st., 22 sts and 28 rows to 4 in. (10 cm.).

The colour plate on page 28 shows the jacket knitted in Wendy's Shetland DK 'Stronsey' (shade 83) by Elizabeth Briggs. Yarn quantity was ten 50-gram balls (or, where yarn is bought in ounces, 17 oz.) for chest size 38 in. (97 cm.) and length 22 in. (56 cm.). Needles were 4 mm. (US 5) and 3¾ mm. (US 4), and tension on 4 mm. needles over pattern was 22 sts and 32 rows to 4 in. (10 cm.).

144 Argyle slipover. Any 4-ply yarn such as Patons'. FOR CHEST SIZE 38–42 in. (97–107 cm.): Needles 2¾ mm. (US 1) and 3¼ mm. (US 3). Tension on 3¼ mm. needles over st. st., 28 sts and 36 rows to 4 in. (10 cm.).

146 Fisherman's sweater. Any 4-ply yarn such as Patons' Clansman. FOR CHEST SIZE 38 in. (97 cm.): Needles 2¼ mm. (US 0) and 3 mm. (US 2), also a set of four 2¼ mm. needles. Tension on 3 mm. needles over st. st., 30 sts and 40 rows to 4 in. (10 cm.). FOR CHEST SIZE 40 in. (102 cm.): Needles 2¼ mm. (US 0) and 3¼ mm. (US 3). Tension on 3¼ mm. needles over st. st., 28 sts and 36 rows to 4 in. (10 cm.).

147 'Figured in 4-ply'. Patons' 4-ply yarn. FOR CHEST SIZE 40 in. (102 cm.): Needles 2¾ mm. (US 1) and 3¼ mm. (US 3). Tension on 3¼ mm. needles over st. st., 28 sts and 36 rows to 4 in. (10 cm.).

148 Norwegian sweater. Any DK yarn such as Sirdar. FOR CHEST SIZE up to 36 in. (91 cm.): Needles 3 mm. (US 2) and 3¾ mm. (US 3). Tension on 3¾ mm. needles over st. st., 24 sts and 32 rows to 4 in. (10 cm.).

150 Cardigan. Any 4-ply yarn such as Robin. FOR CHEST SIZE 38–40 in. (91–102 cm.): Needles 2¾ mm. (US 1) and 3¼ mm. (US 3). Tension on 3¼ mm. needles over st. st., 28 sts and 36 rows to 4 in. (10 cm.).

The colour plate on page 27 shows the cardigan knitted with Robin 4-ply in Landscape Chunky (shade 6282) by Alma Adelaide Bruce. The chest size is 40 in. (102 cm.), the length of the cardigan 23 in. (58.5 cm.), with needles and tension as above. The yarn quantity required was 375 grams (or, where yarn is sold in ounces, 13½ oz.).

153 His-and-hers sweaters. Any Aran-type yarn such as Sunbeam, Marriner, etc. FOR CHEST SIZE 36–40 in. (91–102 cm.): Needles 3¾ mm. (US 4) and 5 mm. (US 7). Tension on 5 mm. needles over st. st., 18 sts and 26 rows to 4 in. (10 cm.).

154 The Continental Line. Patons' DK. FOR CHEST SIZE 36–40 in. (91–102 cm.): Needles 3¼ mm. (US 3) and 4½ mm. (US 7). Tension on 4½ mm. needles over st. st., 20 sts and 26 rows to 4 in. (10 cm.).

156 Lumber jackets 'for him and her'. Any Double Double yarn such as Robin Landscape Chunky. FOR CHEST/BUST SIZE 38–40 in. (97–102 cm.): Needles 4 mm. (US 5) and 5½ mm. (US 8). Tension on 5½ mm. needles over st. st., 16 sts and 22 rows to 4 in. (10 cm.).

158 Norwegian pullover. FOR CHEST SIZE 38–40 in. (97–102 cm.): Needles 3¼ mm. (US 3) and 4 mm. (US 5). Tension on 4 mm. needles over st. st., 22 sts and 28 rows to 4 in. (10 cm.).

The colour plate on page 63 shows the pullover knitted by Pauline Tabone with Robin's County DK, in shade 2075 for the main colour (eight 50-gram balls or, where yarn is bought in ounces, 14 oz.) and shade 2003 for the second colour (four 50-gram balls, or 7 oz.). Needles and tension were as above, and gave chest size 42–44 in. (107– cm.), length 28 in. (71 cm.).

160 The Continental Look. Patons' DK. FOR CHEST SIZE 40 in. (102 cm.): Needles 3¼ mm. (US 3) and 4 mm. (US 5), also a 4 mm. circular needle. Tension on 4 mm. needles over st. st., 22 sts and 30 rows to 4 in. (10 cm.).

162 Jersey with bicycle motif. Sirdar Majestic 4-ply: FOR CHEST SIZE 36–38 in. (91–97 cm.): Needles 2¾ mm. (US 1) and 3¼ mm. (US 3). Tension on 3¼ mm. needles over st. st., 28 sts and 36 rows to 4 in. (10 cm.).

164 Lumber jackets. Any Double Double yarn such as Pingouin Pingoland or Robin Landscape Chunky. FOR CHEST SIZE 38–42 in. (97–107 cm.)/BUST SIZE 36–38 in. (91–97 cm.): Needles 4½ mm. (US 6), 5½ mm. (US 4) and 6½ mm. (US 10). Tension on 6½ mm. needles over pattern, 14 sts and 22 rows to 4 in. (10 cm.).

The colour plate on page 61 shows the man's lumber jacket knitted with Pingouin Pingoland Chunky yarn in Dune (shade 952), by Mrs Margaret Kennedy. The chest size is 42 in. (107 cm.), needles were 5 mm. (US 7) to obtain tension as above. The yarn quantity is twenty-three 50-gram balls (or, where yarn is bought in ounces, 38 oz.). The length of the lumber jacket is 24 in. (61 cm.). The yarn quantity for the women's lumber jacket is twenty 50-gram balls (or 34 oz.). The length is 23 in. (58.5 cm.).

167 Rib and cable pullover. Any DK yarn such as Marriner's. FOR CHEST SIZE UP TO 42 in. (107 cm.): Needles 3¼ mm. (US 3) and 4 mm. (US 5). Tension on 4 mm. needles over st. st., 22 sts and 28 rows to 4 in. (10 cm.).

Instructions to Knitters

Some of the patterns will appeal to experienced knitters; others may equally be followed by the beginner. For beginners, and knitters who wish to be reminded of methods, a brief outline of techniques is given with the most commonly used abbreviations.

Yarn and needles

Before buying yarn and needles it is essential to read the special instructions for the patterns (pages 168–72). This information updates the instructions printed in the patterns themselves.

Yarn bought in skeins should be loosely wound into balls, ready for use. Needles should be long enough to hold the number of stitches needed for the pattern. A knitting counter is useful, and a non-stretch tape-measure is essential for accurate measurement of the tension, as well as for the garment itself as it grows. The first step is always to knit a tension square, see p. 168.

Casting on

Generally, the edges of a garment are knitted with finer needles than the body of the work, but the first row of loops is an exception. It is usual to make this row (cast on) with the larger size of needles to give elasticity.

There are many different methods of casting on, but one commonly used is the knitting method. For this, make a slip-loop on the left needle for the first stitch, and proceed as for knitting (see *Garter stitch* below) to give a loop on the right needle. The loop on the right needle is then slipped on to the left needle, by inserting the point of the left needle into the front of the loop, from left to right. Repeat to cast on the number of stitches required. To make a firm edge, the first row is knitted through the backs rather than the fronts of the loops (*Abbreviation*. t.b.l.).

The cable method gives a neat, firm edge without the need to knit into the backs of the loops. For this, after two stitches have been made as above, the third is made by inserting the right needle straight through the gap between the first and second stitch; then the yarn is taken round the right needle and drawn through, as for the first method.

Basic stitches

Garter stitch or *plain knitting* (*Abbreviation*: g. st.) makes a reversible fabric. For a knit stitch (*Abbreviation*: k) the yarn is held in the right hand, behind the right needle, while the needle containing the loops to be knitted is held in the left hand.

Insert the right needle into the front of the first loop, from right to left, passing below the left needle.

Carry the yarn under the point of the right needle, and over it to the back of the work. With the point of the right needle draw a loop of yarn through the old loop. There is now a stitch on the right needle. Slip the old loop (the worked stitch) off the left needle, and draw up the new loop on the right with the yarn in the right hand, firmly but not tightly, and with an even tension for every stitch. Repeat to the end of the row.

Stocking-stitch, stocking-web stitch, stockinette stitch (*Abbreviation*: st. st.) is made by knitting a row and purling a row alternately. A purl stitch (*Abbreviation*: p.) is made by bringing the yarn round under the right needle to the front of the work, before inserting the right needle into the front of the left stitch, in the direction right to left across the front of the left needle. Then, as for knitting, the yarn is carried round the point of the right needle, and drawn through the loop to make a new stitch, and the worked stitch is dropped.

Ribbing, or 'rib', is worked by alternating knit and purl stitches with an even number of stitches on the needle. For 'single' rib: *k.1, bring yarn to the front of the work, under the needle, p.1, take yarn back; rep. from * to end.

Moss or seed stitch (*Abbreviation*: m. st.) is made by knitting and purling alternately with an uneven number of stitches on the needle: *k.1, p.1, rep. from *, ending k.1. The pattern is formed by knitting stitches knitted on the previous row, and purling stitches previously purled.

Instructions in brackets

Instructions bracketed ( ) are to be worked the number of times stated after the closing bracket.

Picking up stitches

A neckline will be at its most elastic if, instead of being knitted separately, it is knitted with stitches picked up from the cast off edges. To pick up the number of stitches stated in the pattern, divide the length of the edges with pins into two, into two again, and so on, until you are able to judge how frequently you will need to pick up a stitch in order to achieve an even distribution around the neck. To 'pick up and knit' stitches (sometimes written 'k. up'), hold the work in the left hand with the right side facing, insert the needle into the cast off edge, carry the yarn round the point of the needle and draw a new loop through. Repeat for the number of stitches required.

Reading the stitch charts

Charts for multi-coloured patterns are to be read from the bottom upwards. In stocking-stitch, row 1, row 3, and all subsequent odd-numbered rows are knit rows, to be worked from right to left. All even-numbered rows are purl rows, and are worked from left to right.

Fair Isle knitting

When knitting a Fair Isle pattern, the yarn not in use must be carried along the back, at an easy tension. Place the reserved colour over the index finger of the left hand and hold it away from the knitting. If the yarn has to be carried over several stitches, it must be woven-in behind. To weave the yarn in at every alternate stitch, pass the point of the right needle through the stitch, then under the reserved colour, pass the right-hand yarn over the point of the right needle, and draw it through, allowing the reserved yarn to drop off. To bring the reserved colour into use, the point of the right needle is passed through the next stitch as for knitting, then over the reserved yarn and under it from right to left, pulling the yarn through.

Cables: see page 83

Joining the yarn

Yarn should always be joined by knotting at the ends of the rows, and later darning-in the cut ends. When knitting in rounds, the yarn may be spliced by fraying the two ends for a few inches, cutting each end into half-thickness, and twisting the two ends together.

Shaping by increasing

For simple increasing (*Abbreviation:* inc. 1 st.), knit (or purl) into the front of the stitch, then, instead of immediately dropping the stitch off the needle, knit (or purl) into the back of the same stitch, before dropping it off. This method of increasing produces an irregularity in the appearance of the fabric, and is mainly used at the edge of the work.

Less noticeable methods of increasing are:

a Knitting up a stitch (*Abbreviation:* k. up 1), when the next stitch *on the row below* is knitted before the next stitch on the left needle.

b Making a stitch (*Abbreviation:* m. 1) by picking up and knitting the thread lying between the needles. Pick up the thread with the left needle, from front to back, and knit into the back of the loop.

Methods of increasing which leave a small hole in the work are:

a Bringing the yarn forward (*Abbreviation:* w. fwd. or y. fwd., US: y.o.). On a knit row, bring the yarn forward as for a purl stitch, carry it over the needle and then knit the stitch in the usual way.

b Bringing the yarn round the needle (*Abbreviation:* w.r.n. or y.r.n., US: y.o.). On a purl row, carry the yarn over and round the right needle, then purl the next stitch in the usual way.

Finally, where a block of stitches is to be added, they are made by casting on, using the cable method described above.

Shaping by decreasing

Stitches are lost by two main methods which produce a 'slope' either to the right or to the left:

a Knitting (or purling) two stitches together as if they were one (*Abbreviation:* k. 2 tog., or p. 2 tog.). To decrease with the right side of the work facing, knit the two stitches together, through the *backs* of both loops at the start of the row, through the *fronts* of both loops at the end of the row. This variation, which may not always be mentioned in the pattern, ensures that the decreases, which slope respectively to left and right, will slope in the correct direction.

b Slipping a stitch from the left to the right needle without working it, knitting the next stitch, and then, with the tip of the left needle, passing the slipped stitch over the knitted stitch and dropping it off the needle. (*Abbreviation:* sl. 1, k. 1, p.s.s.o.). Here the decrease slopes to the left.

Finally, where a block a stitches is to be decreased, they are lost by casting off, either knitwise or purlwise, see below.

Casting off/binding off

Casting off should be no tighter than the tension of the rest of the knitting, and for the neck edge, which needs to be elastic, it is advisable to use a larger needle to cast off. For simple casting off, work two stitches, in knit or purl according to the pattern, then, with the left needle, pass the first stitch worked over the second stitch worked, dropping it off the needle. Work another stitch, and again pass the first stitch worked over the second, and drop it off the needle. Repeat to the end. Draw the end of yarn through the last stitch and pull it tight.

Crochet finish

Double crochet (UK)/single crochet (US) is applied to prevent the edges of the fabric from curling. A hook a size smaller than the needles makes a neat finish. Holding the work in the left hand with the right side facing, make a slip-loop and put it on the hook. *Pass the hook through the fabric, beneath the two sides of an edge-stitch. Draw the yarn through to give a second loop on the hook. Pass the hook under the yarn and draw it through both the loops on the hook. Repeat from * for each edge-stitch, to the end.

Grafting

Occasionally two sets of stitches of equal numbers are joined invisibly by grafting. Place the two sides together with the wrong sides of the work facing, needles pointing right, and the yarn attached at the right-hand end of the back knitting needle. Cut the yarn, leaving a length five times the length of the seam, and thread the yarn on to a wool needle. Pass the wool needle through the front knitting needle's first stitch, purlwise. Leave the stitch on the knitting needle. Pass the wool needle knitwise through the first stitch on the back knitting needle. Leave the stitch on the needle. *Pass the wool needle knitwise through the first stitch on the front needle, and slip the stitch off. Pass the wool needle purlwise through the second stitch on the front knitting needle, and leave it on. Now pass the wool needle purlwise through the first stitch on the back needle, taking it off, and then pass the wool needle knitwise through the second stitch on the back needle, leaving it on. Repeat from * until all the stitches are joined. Adjust the tension of the grafting yarn to that of the rest of the knitting. Fasten off by darning the yarn-end into the back of the fabric.

Swiss darning: see p. 77.

Making up

Pure wool may be pressed before the pieces are joined, but acrylic must never be pressed. Care instructions on the ball band should be followed. Pressing of wool is done under a damp cloth, on the wrong side, with the pieces pinned to a padded surface to maintain the shape. Raised patterns and rib are left unpressed.

Seams are sewn with a wool needle and the knitting yarn. First pin the edges of the pieces together, right sides facing, matching loop to loop on a straight edge. A *flat seam* is used principally for joining ribbing and inserting raglan sleeves. It is made by overstitching the edges, loop to loop, drawing up the thread loosely to allow some stretch. A *backstitched* seam is used for sides, shoulders, and arms, apart from the rib sections. It is a running stitch made just below the edges of the fabric, starting one knitted stitch long, with the needle returned to the start of the first stitch, and then passing to double the distance, before being returned to the end of the previous stitch again; and so on to the end.

At start and finish, the yarn is secured by several small running stitches, one above the other.

Care of the garment

The ball band will give instructions for hand or machine washing, or advice on dry cleaning. Hot water, rough wringing or high-speed spinning should be avoided. The garment should be dried flat, gently arranged into shape. Pure wool will wear for many years if it is well cared for. A few drops of olive oil added to the last rinse-water will help to keep it soft and springy.

Suppliers' addresses

While any good yarn of the correct ply will produce successful results, many knitters will prefer to knit up the classic designs in wool supplied by the publisher of the original pattern. Others will prefer the quality of pure wool, but find it difficult to obtain supplies locally. Addresses of stockists may be obtained from the agents listed below. Yarn is readily obtainable by mail order, by writing to the mail order address below requesting colour-swatch and price list.

COATS

Cotton only
UK
National Distribution Centre
39 Durham Street
GLASGOW G41 1BS

USA distributor
Coats & Clark Inc.
Coats & Clark's Sales Corporation
P.O. Box 1966
STAMFORD
Connecticut 06904

Canada distributor
J & P Coats (Canada) Inc.
421 Pie 1X Boulevard
MONTREAL
Quebec H1V 2B8

Australia distributor
Coats Patons (Australia) Ltd
P.O. Box 110
321–355 Ferntree Gully Road
MOUNT WAVERLEY
Victoria 3149

New Zealand distributor
Coats Patons (New Zealand) Ltd
P.O. Box 6149
Wellesley Street
AUCKLAND

EMU

Pure wool of all types except 3-ply
UK
Customer Service
Emu Wools
Leeds Road
Greengates
BRADFORD
W. Yorks

USA agent
Merino Wool Inc.
20th Floor
230 Fifth Avenue
NEW YORK
NY 10001

Canada agent
S. R. Kertzer Ltd
257 Adelaide Street West
TORONTO
Ontario M5H 1Y1

Australia agent and mail order
Mrs Rosemary Mallett
The Needlewoman
308 Centrepoint
Murray Street
HOBART
Tasmania 7000

S. Africa agent
E. Brasch & Son
57 La Rochelle Road
Trojan
JOHANNESBURG

FALCON-BY-POST

Pure wool of all types, including 3-ply, own brand and other brands such as Lister Motoravia DK
Mail order only
R. S. Duncan & Company
Falcon Mills, Bartle Lane
BRADFORD
W. Yorks BD7 4QL
UK

JAEGER see PATONS

LISTER-LEE

Pure wool of all types except 3-ply
UK
George Lee & Sons Ltd
Whiteoak Mills
P.O. Box 37
WAKEFIELD
W. Yorks WF2 9SF

USA agent information
Fransha Wools
P.O. Box 99
Parkside Mills
BRADFORD
W. Yorks
UK

Canada major stockist
Mrs Hurtig
Anita Hurtig Imports Ltd
P.O. Box 6124
Postal Station A
CALGARY
Alberta T2H 2L4

R. V. MARRINER

Pure wool 4-ply in 400-gram balls and 5-ply in 100-gram balls, also DK in 50-gram balls
Mail order only
E. H. Williamson
Knowle Mills
South Street
KEIGHLEY
W. Yorks BD21 1DW
UK

MAXWELL CARTLIDGE LTD

Silk only
Mail order only
10b Northgate Street
COLCHESTER
Essex
UK

MINERVA (COLUMBIA-MINERVA)

P.O. Box 300
Rochelle
ILLINOIS 61066
USA

NATURALLY BEAUTIFUL (DENT)

Both wools and silks
Mail order only
Main Street
DENT
Cumbria LA10 5QL
UK

NEEDLE ART HOUSE

Pure wool, 4-ply
Mail order only
Albion Mills
WAKEFIELD
W. Yorks WF2 9FG
UK

PATONS and JAEGER

Pure wool of all types including Jaeger 3-ply
UK
Patons & Baldwins Ltd *or*
Jaeger Handknitting
ALLOA
Clackmannanshire
Scotland

Mail orders
Woolfayre Ltd
120 High Street
NORTHALLERTON
W. Yorks
UK

USA
C. J. Bates & Son
Route 9a
P.O. Box E
CHESTER
Connecticut 06412

Canada agent
Patons & Baldwins Canada Inc.
1001 Roselawn Avenue
TORONTO
Ontario M6B 1B8

Australia
Coats Patons (Australia) Ltd
P.O. Box 110
321–355 Ferntree Gully Road
MOUNT WAVERLEY
Victoria 3149

New Zealand
Coats Patons (New Zealand) Ltd
Mohuia Crescent
P.O. Box 50–140
Elsdon
Porirua
WELLINGTON

S. Africa
Patons & Baldwins South Africa (Pty) Ltd
P.O. Box 33
RANDFONTEIN 1760
Transvaal

Hong Kong
Harry Wicking & Co. Ltd
Textiles Department
World Trade Centre
P.O. Box 30748
CAUSEWAY BAY

Japan
Jardine Matheson & Co. (Japan) Ltd
Daiwa Bank
Toranomon Building
6–21 Nishi Shinbashi, 1-chome
Minato-ku
TOKYO 105

PINGOUIN

Pure wool of all types except 3-ply
Head office and mail orders
Mr R. Mesdagh
BP 9110
59061 ROUBAIX
Cedex 1
FRANCE

UK
French Wools Ltd
7–11 Lexington Street
LONDON W1R 4BU

USA agent
Pingouin-Promafil Corp. (USA)
P.O. Box 100
Highway 45
JAMESTOWN
S. Carolina 29453

Canada agent
Promafil (Canada) Ltd
1500 rue Jules Poitras
379 ST LAURENT
Quebec H4N 1X7

Australia stockist
Mrs Rosemary Mallett
The Needlewoman
308 Centrepoint
Murray Street
HOBART
Tasmania 7000

S. Africa agent
Romatex/Yarns and Wools
P.O. Box 12
JACOBS 4026
Natal

PATRICA ROBERTS

Pure wool 4-ply and Chunky
Mail order
60 Kinnerton Street
LONDON SW1X 8ES
UK

ROBIN

Pure wool DK and Aran, 4-ply blends
UK
Robin Wools Ltd
Robin Mills
Idle
BRADFORD
W. Yorks BD10 9TE

USA and Canada agent
S.R. Kertzer Ltd
257 Adelaide Street West
TORONTO
Ontario M5H 1Y1
CANADA

Australia agent
Mrs Rosemary Mallett
The Needlewoman
308 Centrepoint
Murray Street
HOBART
Tasmania 7000

S. Africa agent
Intexma Cape (Pty) Ltd
P.O. Box 27
OBSERVATORY
Cape 7935

SIRDAR

Pure wool of all types except 3-ply
UK
Sirdar Ltd
Flanshaw Lane
Alverthorpe
WAKEFIELD
W. Yorks WF2 9ND

USA agent
Kendex Corp.
31332 Via Colinas
107 WESTLAKE VILLAGE
California 91362

Canada agent/distributor
Diamond Yarn (Canada) Corporation
153 Bridgeland Avenue
Unit 11
TORONTO M6A 2Y6

Australia agent
Coats Patons (Australia) Ltd
P.O. Box 110
321–355 Ferntree Gully Road
MOUNT WAVERLEY
Victoria 3149

SUNBEAM

All types of pure wool including 2-ply and 3-ply
UK
Sunbeam Wools (Richard Ingram & Co. Ltd)
Crawshaw Mills
PUDSEY
W. Yorks LS28 7BS

Mail order, all yarns
Woolfayre Ltd
120 High Street
NORTHALLERTON
W. Yorks
UK

USA stockists
Argyle Fashions Ltd
Fifth Floor
321 Fifth Avenue
NEW YORK
NY 10016

'Fibercraft'
11 West 37th Street
NEW YORK
NY 10018

Grandor Industries Ltd
4031 Knobhill Drive
SHERMAN OAKS
California 91403

Canada stockist
Estelle Designs & Sales Ltd
1135 Queen Street East
TORONTO
Ontario M4M 1K9

Swiss stockist
Herr Neuman
Herzentalstrasse 40
CH-4143 DORNACH

TEMPLETON

Pure wool 4-ply and DK
UK and mail order
James Templeton & Son Ltd
Mill Street
AYR
Scotland KA7 1TL

U S A stockists
The Little Mermaid
At the Castle
205 East Lawrence Street
APPLETON
Wisconsin 54911

The Wool Gatherer Inc.
1052 21st Street
WASHINGTON DC 20036

The Wool Shop
250 Birch Hill Road
LOCUST VALLEY
NY

Canada stockist
House of Heather
Lord Elgin Hotel
OTTAWA KIP 5K8

WENDY

Pure wool of all types except 3-ply
UK
Wendy International
P.O. Box 3
GUISELEY
W. Yorks

USA
United Notions
1314 Viceroy Drive
DALLAS
Texas

United Notions
P.O. Box 43145
5560 Fulton Industrial Blvd
ATLANTA
Georgia 30336

Wendy Yarns USA
P.O. Box 11672
MILWAUKEE
Wisconsin 53211

Canada agent
White Buffalo Mills Ltd
545 Assiniboine Avenue
BRANDON
Manitoba R7A OG3

Australia agent
The Craft Warehouse
30 Guess Avenue
ARNCLIFFE
N.S.W. 2205

S. Africa agent
Woolcraft Agencies
P.O. Box 17657
2038 Hillbrow
JOHANNESBURG

Hong Kong agent
Wing Tai Cheung Trading Co.
G/F 43A, Bonham Strand East
HONG KONG

Acknowledgments

The author is grateful for the invaluable help of Edward Fox, Jean Litchfield, David Hiscock, Michael Vaughan-Rees, David Griffin, Jan Truman, Mik Dunn, Richard Chopping, Penny Farthing and Esther Brundish.

Permission to reproduce is acknowledged to IPC for *Bestway Magazine*, *Bestway* series, *Farmer's Home*, *'Leachway'* series, *Weldons*, *Wife and Home*, *Woman and Home*, *Woman's Own*, *Woman's Weekly*; to Patons & Baldwins for *Beehive* series, *'Fashion Knits'*, *Greenock* leaflets, *Jaeger Hand-knit Series*, *Men's Book* series by *Stitchcraft*, *Stitchcraft* magazine; to Lutterworth Press for *Woman's Magazine*; to the Hamlyn Publishing Group for Odhams Press (for *Complete Family Knitting Illustrated*, *Knitting Illustrated*, *Gifts You Can Make Yourself Illustrated*, *Knitting For All – Illustrated*, *Modern Knitting Illustrated*. Leaflets reproduced include those of Bairnswear, J.D. Cole, Emu, Ladyship, Lister-Lee, Marriner, Columbia-Minerva, Robin, Secil, Sirdar, Templeton, Bernard Ullmann, Wendy.

For their assistance the author's thanks are due to Coats, Emu, Falcon-by-Post, R.V. Marriner, Maxwell Cartlidge, Minerva, Naturally Beautiful (Dent), Needle Art House, Patons & Baldwins, Pingouin, Patricia Roberts, Robin, Sirdar, Sunbeam, Templeton and Wendy.

The Prince of Wales' photograph is reproduced by courtesy of Radio Times Hulton Picture Library; the music cover was published by the Irwin Dash Music Co. Ltd; the photograph of Elvis Presley is by courtesy of MGM/UA Entertainments Company.